Internet Architectures

Internet Architectures

Daniel Minoli
Andrew Schmidt

Wiley Computer Publishing

John Wiley & Sons, Inc.

NEW YORK • CHICHESTER • WEINHEIM • BRISBANE • SINGAPORE • TORONTO

Publisher: Robert Ipsen

Editor: Marjorie Spencer

Assistant Editor: Margaret Hendrey

Managing Editor: Marnie Wielage

Text Design & Composition: North Market Street Graphics

Designations used by companies to distinguish their products are often claimed as trademarks. In all instances where John Wiley & Sons, Inc., is aware of a claim, the product names appear in initial cap or ALL CAPITAL LETTERS. Readers, however, should contact the appropriate companies for more complete information regarding trademarks and registration.

This book is printed on acid-free paper. ∞

This publication is designed to provide accurate and authoritative information in regard to the subject matter covered. It is sold with the understanding that the publisher is not engaged in professional services. If professional advice or other expert assistance is required, the services of a competent professional person should be sought.

Library of Congress Cataloging-in-Publication Data:

Minoli, Daniel, 1952–
    Internet architectures / Daniel Minoli, Andrew Schmidt.
       p.   cm.
    Includes index.
    ISBN 0-471-19081-0 (cloth : alk. paper)
    1. Internet (Computer network)   2. Computer network architectures.
  I. Schmidt, Andrew. II. Title.
  TK5105.875.I57M55723   1998
  004.67'8—dc21   98-41311
                                             CIP

Printed in the United States of America.

10 9 8 7 6 5 4 3 2 1

For Anna.
—Dan Minoli

For Clair and Catherine.
—Andy Schmidt

Contents

Acknowledgments

Dan Minoli would like to thank Pushpendra Mohta, AT&T's CERFnet Vice President, for his willingness to share his ideas and experience on this project. A veteran of the Internet industry, Pushpendra has been a key player in each evolutionary phase of the Internet, leading CERFnet through its rapid growth into a technically advanced and profitable Tier 1 ISP. He orchestrated CERFnet's merger with the Teleport Communications Group in 1997 and has taken a leadership role in integrating the IP Business since its 1998 merger with AT&T. In addition to guiding the technical expansion and rapid growth of CERFnet, Pushpendra has also helped establish other Internet organizations and enable their network infrastructures. He has trained and enabled new members of the Internet community in the United States, Canada, Mexico, Brazil, Venezuela, England, Germany, Japan, Korea, Fiji, Germany, India, Indonesia, and the United Arab Emirates.

Andrew Schmidt would like to thank Ms. Kimberly Price, Director Ameritech Data Services, and the staff of Ameritech Advanced Data Services for assistance provided.

Preface

The Internet is becoming the de facto way by which corporations extend their enterprise networks to reach branch locations, home offices, international locations, dispersed customers, collaborative partners, telecommuters, and mobile workers. This makes sense in an era when "the corporation is the network."

At the turn of the decade, as corporations embark on yet a new generation of enterprise network connectivity, there is a need to have more than a superficial understanding of how the Internet, the Public Switched Data Network par excellence, is constructed and works. This is particularly relevant in regards to new services such as virtual private networks (VPNs), quality-of-services/class-of-service differentiations, security (integrity and confidentiality), real-time multimedia support, and service-specific billing.

The purpose of this book is to aid the corporate planner in making appropriate decisions in selecting service providers by giving them the right questions to ask in reference to which architectures, technologies, protocols, design disciplines, and customer-service-support options these providers support, which may be important for the planner and his or her organization.

Part 1, "The Internet, Its Architecture, and the Stakeholders," addresses architecural and design issues. Chapter 1 looks at the history of the Internet and sets the stage for the discussion found in the book. Chapter 2 focuses on Internet service providers (ISPs), architectures, and services. Chapter 3 looks at Internet business relationships between ISPs and between the ISP and the user.

As we move forward into the new decade, a gamut of new applications are evolving and are needed. These applications are examined in Part 2, "Evolving Internet Requirements." Chapter 4 surveys evolving voice, video, and data requirements, while Chapter 5 sets the stage for the discussion on quality of service (QoS)–enabled communication.

QoS is becoming an important issue, particularly to support voice, video, and mission-critical VPNs at the IP layer. Part 3, "QoS Support in the Internet: Technologies and Protocols," focuses on this issue. QoS-enabled networks are needed not only for time-sensitive applications, such as voice and video, but also to support data applications, which, as networks become more congested and more integrated (both at the corporate and Internet levels), need to be guaranteed a certain level of performance. Chapter 6 examines the widely deployed frame relay service and the kind of QoS support that may be possible. Chapter 7 looks at ATM and addresses the possible benefits of this technology that the ISP may employ. However, ATM as a standalone technology is of limited use; hence, Chapter 8 provides an overview of IP, IPv6, Internet routing (inlcuding BGP), along with QoS capabilities and support (or lack thereof); QoS support is very challenging in interdomain environments, which is why BGP as a key architectural element needs to be considered. Continuing the implication of Chapter 8, Chapter 9 looks at the support of IP-over-ATM technologies, again addressing the QoS implications. Finally, Chapter 10 discusses RSVP and RTP, and what they have to offer in the QoS arena.

Access to the Internet backbone(s) is also becoming critical. This topic is covered in Part 4, "Evolving Access Technologies." The technology to eliminate the access bottlenecks exists in the form of fiber in the loop (FITL). However, macroeconomics work against such upgrades at this time, particularly on a broad scale. The family of Digital Subscriber Line (xDSL) capabilities is a near-term approach to providing increased access throughput in the access over existing copper-based loop-, distribution-, or dropwire-plant. Chapter 11 looks at evolving xDSL technologies. Chapter 12 examines ISDN and its evolution into ADSL. Chapter 13 provides more detailed protocol information on ADSL.

The Internet,
Its Architecture,
and the Stakeholders

CHAPTER 1

Introduction: From Concept to the De Facto Public-Switched Data Network

1.1 Internet-Based Enterprise Communication

That large collection of backbones, access subnetworks, server farms, and hypertext information known as the Internet is acquiring ever increasing importance, not only in the business community but also among the population at large. General access to information is proving increasingly valuable for education, collaborative work, scientific research, commerce, and entertainment. The advent of HTML-formatted, URL-addressable, and HTTP-obtainable information over the Internet—what is called, in short, the World Wide Web (the Web or W3)—has generated a lot of attention of late.

Beyond mere general interest, the Internet is fast becoming the wide area network (WAN) of choice for an increasing number of corporations. Not only it is easier to maintain a connection over the Internet (or over a "private" IP network offered by a provider to a limited group of commercial customers) as compared to owning one's own network, but the Internet also can provide more ubiquitous connectivity compared to a traditional enterprise network. The cost of ownership and the cost of connectivity (both for intra- and interenterprise applications) are almost invariably lower with Internet-based overlays to the basic corporate enterprise network, particularly for the support of branch office and international locations.

This book looks at aspects involved with the use of the Internet as an enterprise network overlay for intranet and extranet applications. Issues such as Internet service provider (ISP) selection; ISP technology; ISP network architecture; and services offered, including virtual private networks (VPNs), quality of service (QoS), overbooking ratios, support of voice and multimedia, and access options, are examined at length, as these issues ultimately determine the overall quality of the connectivity that is achieved via the overlay infrastructure.

1.2 Challenges Faced by Enterprise Users

Until very recently, the Internet was used mostly as an adjunct technology in corporate networking. Applications included:

- Casual e-mail, especially with outside parties, vendors, and colleagues
- Access to research/vendor/advertiser information
- E-commerce
- Help desk, call center, or data-entry functions from roving (sales) people
- Access to remote network devices, to download statistics and/or perform other network management tasks

Now corporations are looking to utilize the Internet in a more synergistic way, motivated by desires to reduce:

- Monthly recurring communication costs
- Costs for needed networking technologies
- Network management (including cost of ownership) costs, and utilize a single integrated service platform

Studies have shown that, in general, the recurring transmission costs equate to about 30 percent of the total yearly communications budget of an enterprise; the amortized cost of the equipment is 30 percent of the budget; and the network management costs are about 40 percent. It should be fairly obvious that since the following apply, savings should be achievable over a dedicated enterprise network of various technology vintages (especially if the networking technologies date from the mid- to late-1980s or early 1990s).

- The Internet is shared by a large number of users, particularly expensive long-haul and international links.
- Major technology elements are managed by the service providers.
- Otherwise inefficient connectivity to thin-route remote locations is supported in shared, rather than dedicated, mode, and the reach is near ubiquitous (at least in industrialized countries).
- There are a variety of access speeds and modes.
- There is implicit standardization, and hence, some simplicity in the supportive technology and systems.
- There is healthy competition in the market, leading to commoditization of the service.
- The relative newness of the service has led to low initial user service costs, to entice users away from other alternatives (although costs are expected to increase in the next few years).
- The service is best-effort (making it cheaper), but QoS support is expected to become available.

However, in order to make a sound decision in regard to Internet-based overlays to their corporate networks, planners need to consider a number of key factors, some of which were already identified: ISP selection; ISP technology; ISP network architecture; services offered, including VPNs, quality of service, overbooking disciplines, support of voice and multimedia, and access options.

1.3 Challenges Faced by Providers

Providers acknowledge that users need and demand reliable service with guaranteed levels of performance and security. This is even more true in the case of VPN services. Providers must meet these challenges even as traffic on their networks may be doubling every 6 to 12 months. In addition, it may be relatively difficult to secure transcontinental or intercontinental high-capacity transmission facilities, or to secure the links at modestly low costs, or as quickly as needed.

Providers also face limitations in the speed and throughput of routers. The pressing issue at this time is which evolving architecture should be used. Alternatives include traditional IP approaches, IP over Asynchronous Transfer Mode (ATM), IP over Synchronous Optical Network (SONET), IP over Wavelength Division Multiplexing (WDM), Layer 3 switching (using hybrid router/switches called Layer 3 switches), routing-at-the-edge-switching-at-the-core, and traditional architectures but with gigarouters, to list a few. Reliance on public versus private peering arrangements is constantly under consideration by the ISPs. The growing size of the network also is reflected in the number of IP routes that have to be maintained in real time throughout the network. Settlements among ISPs and billing mechanisms are key considerations. Users are also very interested in proactive customer network management. How to provide QoS, differentiated services, and multimedia over the Internet are also initiatives receiving much attention by leading providers. Finally, access technologies such as Integrated Services Digital Network (ISDN), Digital Subscriber Line (DSL), cable-modem access, access over direct broadcast satellites (DBS) and very small aperture terminals (VSATs), and dedicated access at DS3 and OC-3c speeds are also receiving a lot of attention from many ISPs, particularly the top 20 or so.

1.4 Scope of Analysis

By now, almost everyone has heard of or used the Web, whether for personal or corporate use; nevertheless, the Internet remains a mystical territory for many. It follows then that most people are either "passive navigators" of the Internet; establish a home page on some Internet-connected server; or provide content for the Internet. This book aims to explain what it takes to actively build the Internet. It addresses the access and internal architecture and the technologies to support it. Though most of the power and glamour of the Internet is in the backbone(s), that is also the least understood portion of the Internet.

To clarify the preceding paragraph, an analogy might be appropriate. Many people may go to an amusement park and navigate ("surf") the rides there. Other people may open up a shop ("home page") in the park and sell some goods. Still others may be in the business of bringing goods to all the stores ("content providers") in the park to stock them. But who builds the park to begin with? Who adds new rides? Who plans expansions? Who envisions the next great theme park from concept to inauguration? The answer is an amusement park architect, who is a developer, not just a user.

This book is for people who want to understand how the Internet is built, specifically to answer: What are the components? Who are the players? How can it be expanded, improved? How can a new company offer Internet services in the access or in the backbone? How can new services be developed? In answering these questions, this book can also help the more casual corporate planners gain a better understanding of how the Internet really works, thereby putting them in a position to make better use of it, particularly for overlay enterprise/VPN applications—although such planners may have no interest in building the Internet itself. In turn, the planner will be able to select the best provider for the corporation he or she works for, by being aware of the advanced technologies, services, and architecture that a sophisticated provider supports in the access, backbone, or peering segments of the network.

At first, the theme of this book might seem unusual, because this is the first book (we know of) that broaches this topic from this angle; also because the reader may not accept that the demystification of the Internet is either doable or desirable. That said, our angle on this topic is not necessarily as innovative at it appears prima facie. For argument sake, make the association between the Internet and the public switched telephone network (PSTN) we now have in the United States. The PSTN allows any properly equipped and connected user to reach any other person who is suitably connected and equipped with a handset in the United States or abroad. Similarly, the Internet allows any properly equipped and connected user to reach any server or host that is suitably connected and equipped with appropriate hardware and software, in the United States or abroad. Like the Internet, the PSTN is a collection of regional and backbone networks. It is an overlay of many regional and many backbone networks, and the user can pick a regional and a backbone network of choice. And as on the Internet, all these networks are interconnected so that any user can call any other user. And like the Internet, the PSTN comprises switching gear (belonging to a provider) and interconnecting links (owned or leased by the same provider).

To the surprise of some, the Internet is no different from any other network; it faces all the challenges faced by all these other networks. Given this demystification of the PSTN, someone should want—and be able—to plan, design, deploy, own, extend, and interconnect existing players with some or all portion(s) of the Internet, including local or backbone components. Once the corporate planner understands some of the internal architecture and technology of the Internet, he or she will be in a better position to ask pointed questions of the ISP(s), and to get better support and overall grade of service.

From a different perspective, in recent years it has been recognized that the "corporation is the network," meaning that a company's ability to compete effectively is increasingly based on its computing and communication infrastructure. The Internet will be playing an ever expanding role in this ubiquitous connectivity. During the 1990s, organizations of all sizes have introduced client/server and/or web-based systems to manage the corporate data store. At the network level, there has been the deployment of new LAN technologies, such as switched and/or 100Mbps Ethernet, and of new WAN technologies, such as frame relay services and, increasingly, ATM. TCP/IP has been the glue that has made end-to-end multi-subnetwork connectivity in a predictable and stable manner possible. Indeed, none of the gains in automation and productivity of the past decade would have been possible without the plethora of application software that has emerged. Baseline operating systems (such as Microsoft Windows), GUIs, and the well-known TCP/IP apparatus have made this software revolution possible.

Part 1, *The Internet, Its Architecture, and the Stakeholders,* addresses the architectural and design issues we have just alluded to. Note that, in the popular press, the term Internet refers to the entire system of user PCs, browsers, communication networks, information and ancillary servers (e.g., domain name servers, WAIS servers, etc.), and content attached to the Internet. Normally, when one thinks of the power of the public-switched network, one does not usually include the combined "brain trust" of all the people who can be reached by telephone and are part of or integral to it. Therefore, in this book, the term Internet tends to refer to what it really is: an interenterprise interconnection network. Chapter 1 reviews the history of the Internet, to set the stage for the discussion. Chapter 2 focuses on the ISPs, architectures, and services. Chapter 3 looks at Internet business relationships among ISPs and between the ISP and the user.

As we move forward into the new decade, a gamut of new applications are needed and are evolving. Multimedia, desktop videoconferencing, voice-over data networks, and computer telephony integration, to list a few, from both an intranet and Internet perspective, are expected to play increasingly important roles. These applications are required to reach the next plateau in business support tools and productivity gains. People want to use the Internet for the delivery of voice, video, and mission-critical data. Many of these applications need to be delivered over the Internet. These evolving applications are examined in Part 2, *Evolving Internet Requirements.* Chapter 4 surveys evolving voice, video, and data requirements, while Chapter 5 sets the stage for the discussion on QoS-enabled communication.

QoS, quality of service, is becoming an important issue, particularly to support voice, video, and mission-critical VPNs at the IP layer. Part 3, *QoS*

Support in the Internet: Technologies and Protocols, focuses on this issue. QoS-enabled networks are needed not only for time-sensitive applications, such as voice and video, but also to support data applications which, as networks become more congested and more integrated (both at the corporate and Internet levels), must have a guaranteed level of performance. Significant work is underway to address QoS in data networks. It includes ATM UNI 4.0, IPv6, Resource Reservation Protocol (RSVP), Resource Transfer Protocol (RTP), and network layer switching. At the same time, existing services such as frame relay may or may not be upgraded to support QoS. The key architectural questions at this point are: Which transport technology should be used by the ISP in the backbone? How should QoS be supported? As noted, currently, several options are available in principle, including ATM, RSVP, differentiated services (which makes use of the IP-level priority field and specific queue management disciplines), and even IPv6.

Chapter 6 examines the widely deployed frame relay service, and the QoS support that may be possible. Chapter 7 looks at ATM, the QoS-enabled service par excellence, and addresses which benefits are possible with this technology. ATM as a standalone technology is, however, of limited use; hence, Chapter 8 assesses IP and IPv6 technology, along with QoS capabilities and support (or lack thereof), Internet routing, and a discussion of the Border Gateway Protocol (BGP). Continuing the implication of Chapter 8, Chapter 9 looks at the support of IP over ATM technologies, again addressing the QoS implications. Finally, Chapter 10 discusses RSVP and RTP, and what they have to offer in the QoS arena.

Access to the Internet backbone(s) is also becoming critical. This topic is covered in Part 4, *Evolving Access Technologies.* As a backdrop to this discussion, we cite Moore's Law, which states that the power of PCs increases an order of magnitude every five years. Microprocessors operating at 50 MIPS (million instructions per second) are common today, and soon processors with capabilities of hundreds of MIPS will be a commodity item. According to Amdahl's Law, a megabit of input/output (I/O) capability is needed for every MIPS of processor performance. Some computing applications already require 1,000 MIPS. This implies that the I/O requirements are in the 6–125Mbps at this time, and will be higher by the end of the decade. With the trend toward network computing (NC), the requirements for I/O and for communication speed are converging. Even if one assumed that only one-eighth of the I/O requirement was needed for communication, one would have to have communication links in the range of 6–125Mbps for a PC. Analysis, however, shows that the user-accessible bandwidth at the wide area network only increases an order of magnitude every 20 years. This is a potentially severe bottleneck to the growth of multimedia communication, web- and electronic-based commerce, and broadband communications in general.

Movement of many kinds of entities is governed by the Law of Bottlenecks; that is, the maximum (instantaneous) throughput is limited by the link of smallest capacity along the designated end-to-end path. For communication links, these bottlenecks manifest themselves in the access component of the network. The technology to eliminate these bottlenecks exists in the form of *fiber in the loop* (FITL). However, macroeconomics work against such an upgrade at this time, particularly on a broad scale. The family of DSL capabilities (called xDSL to cover all members of the family) is a near-term approach to providing increased throughput in the access over existing copper-based loop-, distribution-, or dropwire-plant.

There are at least two technological aspects to xDSL-based technologies: the engineering of the loop-plant solution and the aggregation of the various xDSL loops onto a higher-layer service such as ATM or IP at the central office (CO). This section of the book provides a balanced view of this evolving technology, by looking both at the plant transmission issues (which are often covered in the trade press), and the ATM/IP aggregation issues (which to date have received much less attention). Aggregation is critical for end-to-end connectivity and services. Chapter 11 looks at evolving xDSL technologies. Chapter 12 examines ISDN and its evolution into ADSL. Chapter 13 provides more detailed protocol information on ADSL.

To put all of this in perspective, the corporate planner needs to know which pertinent questions to pose to the ISP, and which points to use to ferret out the best possible provider. Understanding the state-of-the-art technologies in Internet network design will guide these planners to focus on those pertinent factors that drive scalability, availability, QoS/class of service (CoS), and cost-effectiveness.

1.5   A Snapshot History of the Internet

For tutorial purposes, this section provides a background and chronology of the evolution of the Internet from its infancy to its current global reach and appeal. The appendix at the end of this chapter gives an abbreviated version of this 40-year history in the form of a time line. Planners not interested in the historical developments may go directly to Chapter 2. We want to emphasize again here that although some people would like the public to believe that the Internet is a unique network, it is in fact like any other network. It could be renamed the Public Switched Data Network (PSDN), in direct comparison with the PSTN. In fact, efforts have been made to establish a global packet-switched network, in the form, for example, of AT&T's Net1000 network of the late 1970s. Such networks were based on a Layer 3 networking protocol known as Packet Layer Protocol (PLP); the Internet uses a fairly similar Layer 3 networking protocol, the Internet Protocol (IP). There are two reasons why these early networks did not materialize on a large scale: First, PCs serving as intelligent user-friendly stations and as inexpensive servers were not yet a commodity; and, second, business-useful applications had not emerged (beyond basic transaction processing of the early 1980s).

During the evolution of the Internet, several major paradigm shifts took place in the way networks are built.

- Statically allocating bandwidth to a conversation is not necessary and not efficient. Data can be segmented into variable-length packages, called packets, which share network resources.

- The network can be constructed of relatively simple data-forwarding devices. Placing a great deal of intelligence in these devices is not necessary; more important is speed and reliability.

- The end users and application programmers understand best what types of services they want. They should, therefore, ultimately be responsible for choosing what types of error correction should be used; the network should not provide this function, to avoid redundancy.

The development of the Internet was made possible through the funding of the American public with taxes paid in the 1960s through the 1980s. Its researchers' goal was to examine the possibility of integrating communication media to produce a new infrastructure that would enable computer users to interact with one another. From the telegraph to digital technology to the computer, the stage had been set for a new comprehensive mode of communication. As a result, today there exists a complex global infrastructure that will continue to change as more people use this powerful tool. As noted already, this infrastructure is now in many ways similar to the global PSTN.

This section reviews the development of the Internet, covering its beginning from the early research in packet switching to the development of next-generation technology through the Internet2 [1] and the very high-speed Backbone Network Service (vBNS) [2].

NOTE To a certain degree, the information in this chapter was found on the World Wide Web. The authors' experience over the past 25 years also provided several of the details.

1.5.1 Packet Switching

Several major paradigm shifts are being driven by the Internet. To the end users, some of the most obvious are store-and-forward e-mail communication and extension of virtual presence via web-based technology. Other paradigm shifts are not so obvious from the perspective of a desktop PC. One of the most fundamental of these is a migration away from traditional telephony like multiplexing systems to a *packet*-based Internet. The advantages of packet technology were recognized in the late 1960s through the 1980s, though not exclusively in the context of the Internet (as projects such as AT&T's Net1000 and ITT's FAXPAK attest).

Traditional telephony systems allocated bandwidth in fixed increments, across the entire length of the network, for the duration of a conversion. The allocation is typically 64 kilobits per second (Kbps) in both directions whether it is necessary or not. For example, if a call is placed between Chicago and Tampa, the telephony carriers will create an end-to-end circuit of 64Kbps that will be dedicated to this single session. This type of communication is sometimes called time division multiplexing (TDM).

Packet switching, on the other hand, transmits data into the network only when there is actual data to communicate. Packet switching places the user data into variable-size packets that have a source and destination address. Because each packet is a standalone entity, like a piece of postal mail, it can share a common infrastructure without bandwidth being dedicated to any particular user-to-user communication session.

It is difficult to give one person sole credit for the idea of packet switching because several experts played key roles in its development. Some of the most important were Leonard Kleinrock at UCLA, Paul Baran of the Rand Corporation, and Donald Watts Davies of the National Physical Laboratory in the United Kingdom, each of whom independently conceived the principle of packet switching. In 1957, Kleinrock began researching data networks, and from this research, developed the underlying principles of packet switching. He published a paper on packet switching theory in 1961 and in 1964, the first book on this topic, *A Brief History of the Internet* (John Wiley & Sons). He demonstrated convincingly that packet switching was a more efficient method than the traditional circuit switching.

In 1959, when Paul Baran joined Rand, communication networks of the day were chained, point-to-point systems, with each segment on the network dependent on the link before it. Consequently, damage to one point affected the entire network. Baran began studying how to maintain functional communication networks when parts of the systems were damaged, and how to redesign communications infrastructures to ensure the remaining viable components continued to function as a cohesive entity when some of the parts were disabled. To this end, he used digital computer technology, allowing the message to be reproduced accurately and moved from switch to switch with less degradation than the existing method of analog transmission. He also proposed building the infrastructure using a distributed network instead of the existing centralized network that possessed vulnerable central switching points.

Baran proposed dividing messages into smaller parts, which he called "message blocks," that were each sent using a variety of potentially *different* routes and reassembled at the destination. The standard analogue of this method is shipping a house first by disassembling it into its component parts—message blocks—and placing each piece into a separate truck. Each truck needs to get to its destination taking the fastest possible route, which is determined by considering conditions such as traffic, weather, and road. All of these conditions could differ depending on when each truck left. Because assembly occurred only after all the pieces had arrived at the address (destination host), order of arrival would be unimportant. This is, anecdotally, how packet switching on the Internet works.

A lengthy message, for example a video clip, that must be moved across the network is subdivided into smaller pieces. Each piece is placed in a completely self-contained package and transmitted. Before transmitting, some error correction/detection information is inserted in the packet so that the receiver can be certain that the message arrived correctly. The video clip is segmented into some number of packets, each of which can take a different path across the network (unlikely but possible). Once the packets have arrived at the receiver, they can be reassembled into the original video clip. The receiver can optionally wait until the entire set of packets has arrived or start reassembly as soon as it has two concurrent packets.

At the time Paul Baran joined Rand, communications network lines were reserved for a single call and held open for the time period the line was being used, regardless of the number and duration of pauses in conversation. However, as mentioned, since data being transmitted over the line was released in short bursts followed by pauses, much of the bandwidth was wasted. Baran proposed allocating bandwidth to permit sharing it with different messages. Each message block would be dynamically routed in the network by switching *nodes* capable of directing the message block to the fastest route depending on the conditions of the nodes, the distances and delays. However, Baran stopped working on his project in 1965 without its ever being implemented [3].

Also during 1965, another researcher, Donald Watts Davies, formally proposed the idea of packet-switching. His theories of packet-switching and message blocks were similar to Baran's in that they used digital computer technology, switches, and identical packet size and data-transmission rate; but his theories differed fundamentally in motivation since packet-switching was not designed for redundancy and decentralization. In addition, Davies considered the problems of using disparate computer languages, hardware, and software, and began to consider the use of an intermediary device that could translate, assemble, and disassemble digital messages for other machines. In 1968, Davies' ideas were implemented when the first packet-switching network was set up at the National Physical Laboratory in Middlesex, England.

1.5.2 The Internet's Infancy: 1960s

Some have claimed ARPANET [4] was spawned from the military's need to ensure communication in the event of a Cold War crisis. In fact, its inception in the mid-1960s was benign. Through a project formulated at the Defense Advanced Research Projects Agency (DARPA), the ARPANET was intended to connect research facilities so scientists could share computer resources. Thus, it was intended to facilitate communication among these facilities.

DARPA (originally just called ARPA) had been formed as an outcome of the Sputnik 1 launch in 1957. President Eisenhower wanted a research and development agency, so ARPA was created. DARPA was designed to be a stopgap until the National Aeronautics and Space Administration (NASA), could be approved. After the creation of NASA in 1958, ARPA was left without a mission, so Roy Johnson, then its director, defined its mission to be as a research sponsor of basic research. It focused on military R&D until 1962, when the third director, Jack Ruina, hired Joseph C. R. Licklider to head the Command and Control Research division. Licklider began to seek contracts with academically based computer facilities and to undertake advanced research in time-sharing as a means of replacing batch processing. This new focus was reflected in the renaming of his division as the Information and Processing Techniques Office (IPTO).

IPTO evolved under the directorships of Licklider (1962–1965) and his successor Robert Taylor (1966–1969). In addition to supporting research in time-sharing technology, Licklider also pursued research in computer graphics and computer languages, and was the first person to envision a network of interconnecting computers, enabling people to access data from any other site. Taylor was responsible for implementing the idea of interconnecting computers to form the nascent Internet. Before this project, computers connected to a mainframe computer, and shared the memory and resources among the other attached computers. Because there was no way to interconnect the mainframes, people could not use resources other than those found on their mainframe. Taylor's contribution meant that resources could be shared among all attached mainframes.

While still at DARPA Taylor received approval to fund an experiment of interconnecting computers at separate locations, essentially to create interactive computer communication. Larry Roberts became the program's manager in 1966; he had, prior to joining DARPA, created the first wide area computer network with Thomas Merrill. He went to DARPA to develop his ideas of computer networks and the ARPANET. In 1967, he presented his ideas at the same conference at which Davies advanced his concept of packet switching.

In order for ARPANET, or any packet-switching network, to work, computers with different operating systems had to be able to understand each other. This required basic standardization of not only the packet format but also what the data inside the packet looked like. A standardized network had to be developed. In 1967, a meeting was held to discuss the notion of building a prototype of such a network, which would be composed of interface message processors (IMPs) conceived by Wes Clark, a researcher at DARPA. These IMPs, about the size of household refrigerators, provided the foundation for the world's first packet-switching *router.* The IMPs would be used to interconnect each of the host computers to the network. By having each IMP communicate with the other IMPs, this would standardized the network. However, additional protocols had to be developed so that communication could occur among the hosts.

In 1968, the contract for developing the IMPs was awarded to Bolt, Beranek and Newman (BBN), a then small company based in Cambridge, Massachusetts. It designed the IMPs and established the protocols allowing IMPs to communicate among each other. The protocols that permitted communication between an IMP and its host, the local area network, were left to each of the host site's computer scientists. Kleinrock and his colleagues at UCLA were responsible for the network measurement system; Roberts designed the network topology [3]. Figure 1.1 shows the distribution of IMPs in ARPANET.

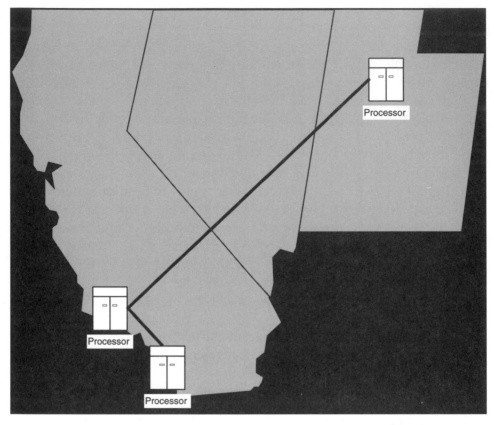

Figure 1.1 ARPANET's IMP distribution.

In 1969, the Network Working Group (NWG) was formed to ensure the stability of the communication protocols. This group was composed of graduate students from the first four host sites. Steve Crocker, a graduate student at UCLA, wrote the first minutes of the meetings, and distributed them, calling the document a *Request for Comments* (RFC). The intent was to solicit suggestions and comments from people who could contribute to the development and improvement of the workings of ARPANET. Today, RFCs are still one of the principal methods used to communicate within the computer networking community, and they are regularly produced by the Internet Engineering Task Force (IETF). Initially, the NWG functioned to create the host protocol designs, called *host-to-host protocols.* These allowed the host computer to communicate with another host computer, in addition to the host-to-IMP interface.

The first IMP was installed at Kleinrock's Network Measurement Center at UCLA in September 1969; and over the course of three months, the other three nodes were installed, with one going to SRI [5], UC Santa Barbara (UCSB), and the University of Utah. The last two nodes incorporated visualization projects: UCSB investigated methods for the display of mathematical functions using storage displays to deal with the problem of refresh over the network; and Robert Taylor and Ivan Sutherland at Utah investigated methods of 3D representations over the network. Once the four sites were interconnected, the IMPs could exchange packets; thus ARPANET was born, and researchers could access remote computers, share information by file transfer, and perform remote printing.

Getting ARPANET up and running with these first hosts was a significant accomplishment. The IMPs connected both host computers and other IMPs, and functioned to:

- Receive data.
- Check for errors.
- Retransmit if errors existed.
- Route the packets.
- Verify that packets terminated at the intended address.

The destination IMP used hop-by-hop acknowledgments and retransmission. These ensured that distinct messages were in order before being reassembled into the message. Since the host computers were different, software had to be designed to enable them to communicate. Called a *device driver* (see Figure 1.2), it is the application that acts as the interface between the host's operating system (central control software) and the networking hardware.

1.5.3 The Internet's Early Years: 1970s

In 1970, ARPANET hosts started to communicate using what was called the Network Control Protocol (NCP). This development was a key step in the history of the Internet because it helped formulate the idea of multiple interworking protocols cooperating to provide reliable, end-to-end communication. NCP (see Figure 1.3) is a protocol that describes host-to-host communication but goes beyond the packet format to also describe the format of data within the packet. Attachment of the first four hosts completed the initial phase of network project, and by the summer of 1970, the following nodes were added: BBN, MIT, Rand, System Development Corporation, and Harvard.

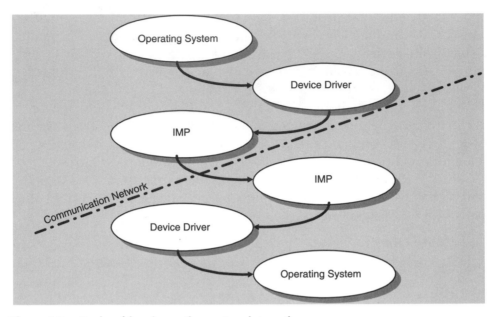

Figure 1.2 Device driver/operating system interaction.

The NCP protocol did have a fundamental flaw: It was able to transmit only a single packet at a time, then wait for an acknowledgment before sending another. In modern terminology, this would be called a *window of 1.* Waiting for an acknowledgment before sending more information can reduce performance. This problem was fixed as protocol research continued.

By 1971, there were 23 hosts and 15 IMP nodes established, including BBN, MIT, Rand, SDC, Harvard, Lincoln Lab, Stanford, University of Illinois, Case Western Reserve University (CWRU), Carnegie Mellon University (CMU), and NASA/Ames. Also during that year, AlohaNet [6] was created at the University of Hawaii. It used radio links to connect computers spread across four islands to broadcast data back and forth.

In 1972, the network had grown to 37 nodes. In addition, an exhibit called the International Conference on Computer Communications (ICCC) was held to demonstrate ARPANET to the public [3]. Also during this year, the Internetworking Working Group (INWG) was formed to establish protocols; the first chairman was Vinton Cerf at Stanford.

Shortly thereafter, Abhay Bhushan, a researcher at MIT, designed the first electronic mail, or e-mail, program capable of running on the network. (Though other programs did exist and could run between computers, they were not on the open network.) Additionally, Ray Tomlinson at

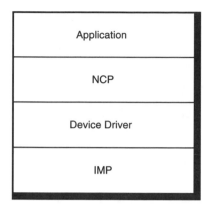

Figure 1.3   Protocol stack.

BBN wrote basic send-and-read software for e-mail messages. Roberts further developed Tomlinson's programs by giving them capabilities we take for granted today, such as to list, selectively read, file, forward, and respond to messages. As these programs' popularity increased, changes were implemented to improve compatibility among disparate e-mail programs.

When Robert Kahn, the president of the Corporation for National Research Initiatives, arrived at ARPA in 1972, he proposed the idea of an *open-architecture network.* Essentially, this meant setting standards so that each component was given a clearly defined role, and so that several different vendors' products could interwork seamlessly, allowing compatibility among the networks. Standardization meant that networks could communicate regardless of the type or manufacture of the host computer.

The next year, 1973, saw the first international connections to the ARPANET from the University College of London in England and the Royal Radar Establishment in Tromso, Norway. During this year, the first draft of Transmission Control Protocol (TCP) appeared. The TCP was intended to improve network reliability by placing the responsibility of reliability on the destination hosts. TCP specifies the format of data within a packet. It takes a lengthier message and segments it into smaller units that can be placed into packets. TCP also performs two critical functions:

Flow Control.   TCP provides what is called *positive acknowledgment,* which means that when a packet reaches the receiver, a message is sent back to the source signifying that the packet arrived successfully. If the source does not receive an acknowledgment, it assumes that the loss was due to network congestion. The source can then reduce its transmission rate and monitor for a series of successful acknowledgments. The source increases its transmission rate until it begins to see missing acknowledgments, at which point, the cycle of reduced transmission rate repeats.

Error Detection.   TCP has the capability to detect errors, because the protocol keeps track of sequence numbers of packets as they cross the network. If there is a gap in the sequence, then the missing data will not be acknowledged and will subsequently be retransmitted. In addition, TCP calculates a checksum over the packets, which means that if any of the bits within the packet were corrupted during transmission, the receiver will discard the packet; subsequently, the sender will not receive an acknowledgment and will retransmit the packet.

During the mid-1970s, the TCP specification continued to evolve, and the last iteration of the TCP suite came out in 1978. TCP ushered in a paradigm shift for the IMPs, because it migrated the responsibility of data formatting away from the network and toward the host transmitting the data. This was a fundamental change in which gateway computers communicated with other networks, and interpreted and routed packets by reading the address, thereby leaving the receiving hosts to read the contents of the packet, then assemble them.

Bob Metcalfe, a graduate student at Harvard, used queuing theory to address the problem of message failure while attempting to improve the performance of AlohaNet. By 1973, he had designed a simple network of computers that communicated in close proximity linked by cables. He achieved a significant reduction in message failure by utilizing a large portion of potential capacity. Metcalfe called this Local Area Network (LAN) technology *Ethernet*, which was essentially a network without switches or message processors. The Ethernet was a broadcast medium like air or a party line telephone whereby any time a computer transmitted a message, it could be heard by all of the other computers on that Ethernet. In 1974, the first Ethernet protocol was proposed. Today, this protocol interconnects the majority of LAN-attached computers in the world.

In July 1975, DARPA turned the ARPANET over to the Defense Communications Agency because of the growing military-related network traffic. This spawned the formation of other networks since ARPANET's guidelines restricted who could gain access to it. Because the overall vision of the Internet was to have many independent networks interconnected, researchers had also been developing other networks such as packet satellite and ground-based packet radio networks. Essentially, this approach would create an open architecture network in which each network could be designed differently, both architecturally and technologically, but could interface to all others. Prior to the split of the ARPANET, BBN launched Telenet, which was the first public packet data service.

In 1977, Internet communication was successfully demonstrated to the Defense Department. The display involved a simulation of communication during a mobile battlefield situation using a continental network. A continental network (mobile packet radio network and ARPANET) sent a message across an intercontinental satellite (SATNET) network to Europe, back to USC Information Sciences Institute in America (via SATNET and ARPANET).

Because of the open-architecture network environment, a new version of TCP had to be developed to allow distinct networks to communicate reliably. In 1978, Vinton Cerf, Jonathan Postel, and Danny Cohen at ISI proposed the idea of a separate Internet Protocol, or IP. Essentially, the IP datagrams would contain addressing and could be given to routers that would then forward them individually. This created yet another layer in the protocol stack; however, it provided critical segregation between data addressing and error/congestion detection. TCP guaranteed reliable delivery by segmenting and assembling datagrams, detecting errors or transmitting a datagram if it did not arrive at its destination. IP provided all the information needed by the interconnecting routers (the forwarding relays) to perform their basic packet-switch role. Consequently, today we have a very powerful protocol combination: TCP/IP; this protocol suite helped form the general infrastructure from which new applications and the network called the Internet could be created.

In 1979, USENET [7] was designed at Duke University and the University of North Carolina, by students Tom Truscott and Jim Ellis. It used the Unix operating system and a Unix-to-Unix Copy Protocol (UUCP). It consisted of a hierarchy of discussion groups that came to be known as USENET newsgroups, which received information from the ARPANET mailing lists. USENET and UUCP proved to be the network service and communications protocol that contributed significantly to the international growth of the internetworking principle. The newsgroups are still in existence today and have grown to include tens of thousands of topics.

1.5.4 The Internet's Growth Begins: 1980s

In the 1980s, the growth of networks occurred at multiple levels; and thanks to the TCP/IP protocol suite, these networks could communicate with one another. In 1981, 3COM released UNET, which was a Unix

TCP/IP product running on Ethernet. When the Unix operating system adopted TCP/IP, one of the most significant events to drive the Internet's growth and standardization was realized at the University of California Berkeley. Researchers there had been producing a public domain version of the Unix operating system distributed under the name Berkeley Software Distribution (BSD). This was critical because it moved the documented standard into functioning software that was freely distributed. Vendors like Sun Microsystems started using the software in their commercial workstation products, and the TCP/IP protocol reached a new level of general acceptance as the de facto standard for university data communications.

The early 1980s were also a time of regional growth, via the creation of networks, such as CSNET, that connected computer research facilities and computer science departments to allow non-ARPANET users to make dial-up connections to send and receive electronic mail. BITNET (Because It's Time Network), which connected IBM systems, also came into being as a cooperative effort to provide electronic mail and Listserv access. (A Listserv is a means for distributing information via electronic mail. A group of users who want to conduct a discussion can subscribe to a *list server* (Listserv). The Listserv has a special e-mail address for the group, and when it receives an e-mail message, it forwards a copy to the entire list.) These and other networks were collectively referred to as the Internet. (Internet with a capital *I* referred to the federally subsidized network, and internet with a lowercase *i* referred to any network using TCP/IP protocols.) LANs, of which Ethernet was the most widely used, became very popular on university campuses because they allowed communication within the network, as well as among other LANs connected to the Internet.

The substantial growth of e-mail forced a change in delivery; messages that originally rode on file transfer protocol (FTP) were sent by a separate mechanism. In 1982, Simple Mail Transfer Protocol (SMTP) and the e-mail format were created. On the Internet every computer needs a unique address, called its IP address. To direct packets toward the computer as they traverse the Internet, the routers use this address. When the network was small, computer scientists could remember all the IP addresses. As more computers were added, to make the associations easier, some computers were given names, and the IP address-to-name mappings were kept in a file, called the *host table*; for example, augustus.cs.uiuc.edu mapped to 128.174.240.10.

This system of placing a new entry in the host table when a university added a new computer was sufficient when the network was small, but it could not scale globally. To solve the problem, a protocol called the Domain Name System (DNS) was created. The DNS is a hierarchy of computers that maintain a database of host name-to-IP address mappings. The system can be queried to resolve—that is, to report—what the IP address is for a specified name. DNS rendered host tables obsolete. (Note: In 1986, the DNS was adopted for general use.)

In 1982, it was decided that all systems on the ARPANET would convert from NCP to TCP/IP, and by January 1, 1983, the conversion was complete, marking the official birth of the Internet. By standardizing on a single transport and address protocol suite, TCP/IP, the network could branch anywhere. However, sending multimedia such as audio and video over the network was problematic due to errors in the transmission of packets. As previously stated, TCP was designed to ensure reliability; but forcing retransmission of lost packets caused significant delays. TCP's processes of reassembling all packets as a collection required significant buffering, which caused difficulties in maintaining the flow of audio and video without a break. To correct this problem the User Datagram Protocol (UDP) was designed.

UDP provides some of the same functions of TCP, but it is left to the application to determine whether lost data should be retransmitted. In the case of streaming audio or video, the answer is definitely no, because once the data is gone, it no longer makes sense to play it at the receiver. UDP ignores the criterion of reliability, thus improving transmission of multimedia over the network.

Also in 1983, the Defense Communications Agency split the original ARPANET into two separate networks, the MILNET for sites that shared nonclassified military information and the ARPANET for the research community. MILNET would later be integrated with the Defense Data Network. During that year, the CSNET/ARPANET gateway was put into place. (A gateway is like a more sophisticated IP router in that it allows communication between two dissimilar networks or networking protocols.) Since networks were joining together, the nodes were being named in the DNS based on one of six *top-level domains* (TLDs): by location or by gov (government), mil (military), edu (education), com (commercial institutions), org (nonprofit organization), and net (gateways between networks).

The Internet Activities Board (IAB) also was formed in 1983, to guide the development of the TCP/IP Protocol Suite, provide advice and guidance on research in the Internet community, publish Internet-related documents, and "record various identifiers needed for protocol operation." The IETF was chartered with development of the TCP/IP Protocol Suite and to deploy protocols into Internet operation. The Internet Research

Task Force (IRTF) explored advanced concepts in networking. Also, the University of Wisconsin provided central control over the top level of the DNS, which allowed people to find other locations without knowing the exact addresses.

In 1984, moderated newsgroups were introduced on USENET (which subsequently changed in 1987). There was significant growth in Internet products in 1985 due to the emphasis on replacing time-sharing computers with LANs connected to the Internet. In addition, desktop workstations running the Unix operating system and networking software were being shipped in record numbers.

A year later, in 1986, the National Science Foundation (NSF) designated five supercomputing sites at Princeton University, University of Pittsburgh, University of California San Diego, the University of Illinois at Urbana-Champaign, and Cornell University. It funded a 56Kbps network that linked these supercomputer centers, thus creating a backbone network called NSFNET. Its initial purpose was to provide data communications supporting the IP protocol among the supercomputing centers. In addition, it allowed regional networks (CICnet, SURAnet, etc.) and nonsupercomputing center university computer centers to physically connect to the network, thereby gaining national interuniversity connectivity. The result was a large increase in the number of connections, especially from the universities. The NSFNET became the first multipurpose national IP backbone.

As part of NSFNET, which came online in 1986, eight regional networks also were formed. Each had proprietary control over its regional connections to the backbone and was responsible for building its regional distribution. The regional networks built starlike networks that first hubbed back to major universities; at the second level of aggregation, they hubbed back to the regional university with the NSFNET backbone link.

By 1988, the NSFNET backbone was completely filled, so the network was upgraded to T1, or 1.544Mbps. The T1 backbone served an additional 7 sites beyond the original five supercomputing sites, including the University of Michigan, National Center for Atmospheric Research, BARR-Net at Palo Alto, Wetsuit at Salt Lake City, North WestNet Seattle, Rice University at Houston, and Georgia Tech.

In 1988, an interesting trend had started when UUCP and USENET became commercially available through UUNET. (This trend peaked in 1994 when the network was completely privatized.) But disaster hit in 1988 with the invasion of the Internet *worm* virus, named for the way it snaked from computer to computer across the Internet. It is estimated that it infected from 6,000 to 60,000 hosts and wasted tens of thousands of labor hours to repair the damage.

The fallout from the worm was the creation of the Computer Emergency Response Team (CERT) which sends out bulletins whenever security compromises have been reported. CERT describes the compromised system and how to fix it. Another outcome was the severing of connectivity to sensitive governmental agencies, like the military. It could be said that the worm was actually beneficial because it focused attention on the increased potential of computer crime on the Internet.

In 1989, Reseaux IP Européens (RIPE) formed to permit the operation of the Pan-European IP Network. RIPE played an important role in coordinating plans for government-sponsored research networking in Europe, and implemented a system for IP address allocation. The year also saw more movement toward commercial use of the Internet. The first relays between a commercial electronic mail carrier and the Internet were created by MCI Mail through the Corporation of the National Research Initiative (CNRI), and CompuServe through Ohio State University. CSNET and BITNET merged to form the Corporation for Research and Education Networking (CREN). Finally, the Internet Engineering Task Force (IETF) and Internet Research Task Force (IRTF) came into formal existence under the Internet Activities Board (IAB).

The growth explosion from 1983 from some 200 computers on the network to 1.3 million in 1993 was only the beginning of this phenomenon. Whereas in 1983 there were a handful of networks, there are now more than 20,000. In the 1990s, commercial Internet service providers formally emerged from intermediate-level networks sponsored by the NSF. Prior to 1994, NSFNET was the major backbone network interconnecting IP regional networks. Though this arrangement was helpful in fostering growth and providing stability, because the network was government funded, its use was limited. For example, intercompany communication was prohibited because the NSF was not in the business of subsidizing U.S. industry. The NSF's policy was referred to as the Acceptable User Policy (AUP).

Since 1988, the number of host computers with direct connection to TCP/IP has doubled every year. Also during that year, Archie, one of the first mainstream Internet tools that allowed users to scan lists of information with only a single query, was written by Peter Deutsch, Alan Emtage, and Bill Heelan at McGill University. From Archie came Campus Wide Information System (CWIS), HYTELNET, WAIS, and others. In 1991, Mark McCahill and others from the University of Minnesota developed Gopher, a CWIS that organized data on the Internet into hierarchical menus that users could then scroll through. This gave a method of pointing to information, and dramatically increased the ability of Internet users to search through the growing number of online archives.

1.5.5 Internet Privatization: 1990s

In 1990, ARPANET ceased to exist, and commercial and nonprofit information service providers started to link their networks to get around the NSFNET AUP. Perhaps as important as the march toward a commercial Internet was the maturation of Internet information storage and retrieval applications. Before the 1990s, there was no consistent way to retrieve material until the inception of the Web. Originally a notebook program called Enquirer-within-upon-Everything, the program that would become the Web was written by a CERN physicist, Tim Berners-Lee, in 1980. In 1992, Berners-Lee formally created the World Wide Web. It was initially intended to facilitate communication among researchers working in high-energy particle physics.

The Web is a way to organize Internet-based information and resources using *hypertext*, first conceived of in the 1960s. Hypertext allows document owners to insert names and pointers to their items on the Internet. In addition to inventing the Web, Berners-Lee also wrote the first web server and browser. And he further outlined the HyperText Transmission Protocol (HTTP), which enabled PC users to move web pages written in the HyperText Markup Language (HTML) between the client and server. The Web became available within CERN in 1990 and to the rest of the world in 1991.

In 1991, the NSFNET backbone was upgraded to DS3 speed of 44.73Mbps and the first high-speed Internet was created. Along with learning to run and provide high-speed links, the industry learned how to build IP routers that could maintain those speeds.

In 1993, President Clinton received e-mail at president@whitehouse .gov. During that year too, the first commercial exclusion was lifted, so commercial sites were then allowed to use the Internet. In addition, the National Center for Supercomputer Applications (NCSA), at the University of Illinois, Urbana-Champaign, developed a graphical HTTP browser and the first real web browser called Mosaic.

The development of Mosaic was critical because it put an easy-to-use graphical interface on the tools, such as file transfer, computer scientists had been using for years. In essence, Mosaic put these tools in the hands of anyone who could click a mouse. Mosaic's point-and-click graphical user interface enabled people to navigate the Web by selecting links using their mouse. More important, the browser was extensible, meaning users could add software modules for sound, to view GIF images, or to view any file type as it was received from the Internet.

Around 1993, a group of Mosaic programmers left the NCSA to form Netscape Communications Corporation. They created the popular Internet browser called Netscape, an advanced Mosaic browser that provides FTP capabilities, TELNET, e-mail, and USENET newsgroups.

Also during the 1990s, other commercial services became widely available; commercial and nonprofit information service providers were linked. This brought the Dow Jones, Telebase, Dialog, CARL, the National Library of Medicine, and RLIN to the public. In 1994, an online company made its first business order, and shopping "malls" arrived on the Internet.

The NSF has had a mission to "foster and support the development and use of computer and other scientific methods and technologies, primarily for research and education in the sciences." In 1986, NSF created the Division of Networking and Communications Research and Infrastructure (NCRI), whose responsibility was to assist with this goal. The NCRI conceived a three-tiered model of internetworked infrastructure consisting of an NSFNET national backbone, midlevel networks that connected the institutions to the backbone, and connections to universities, colleges, and research companies.

Along with Internet growth came concerns about pricing, privatization, security, and network addressing. In the early 1990s, the NSF decided that the Internet experiment was a success and that it was time for the network to be privatized. In order to gracefully maneuver this shift yet ensure that the Internet would continue to be fully interconnected, the NSF created a five-year plan of controlled migration. And to remove itself from the business of running production networks, which by the early 1990s, the Internet had become, the organization devised a plan to create four interconnection points called network access points (NAPs). NAPs (see Figure 1.4) are much like major airport hubs that serve several airlines. And, like an airport, service providers can come to the facility knowing that other major carriers will be there, and passengers—or in this case IP packets—can be exchanged.

The NSF's plan was to require that any ISP receiving government contracts or receiving money from public universities must connect to all of the NAPs. This was an excellent strategy because, at the time this plan went into action, regional networks, which relied on government support, still heavily populated the Internet. With the NAPs awarded and functional, portions of the NSFNET began to be decommissioned in April 1994. The NSF backbone ceased operation in late 1994 and was replaced

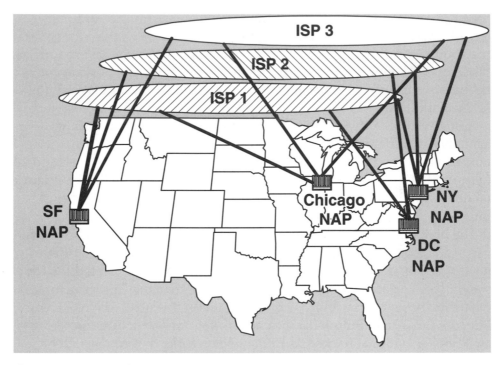

Figure 1.4 NAPs and ISP interconnections.

by the four NAPs operated by Ameritech in Chicago, Pacific Bell in San Francisco, Sprint in New York, and Metropolitan Fiber Systems (MFS) in Washington, DC.

But in the interest of staying involved in high-performance network research and keeping the supercomputer center interconnected, one of the original intents of the Internet, the NSF created two research programs. In 1995, the NSF authorized the creation of a very high-speed Backbone Network Service (vBNS) to provide high-bandwidth connectivity among the NSF's Supercomputer Centers (SCCs). This network provided high-speed (155 to 622Mbps) connectivity between the Cornell Theory Center, National Center for Atmospheric Research, National Center for Super-computer Applications, Pittsburgh Supercomputer Center, San Diego Supercomputer Center, and the NSF NAPs. This system revitalized the initial role of the Internet, and provided a means for universities or end users to access the SCCs via the NAPs.

The second major initiative from the NSF was to keep to the innovations of the Internet alive and thriving via the creation of a high-performance computation fund and what is called Internet2. The first program's goal was to provide funding for universities to gain access to the vBNS, typically via major entrance aggregation sites called GigaPOPs (for gigabit points of presence). This funding has been allocated to more than 100 top universities, and has played a key role in ensuring that major research and education facilities have access to SCCs. The second project, Internet2, is not entirely sponsored by the NSF; however, they play a critical guidance role. The Internet2 is a hybrid network whose members are major universities and research organizations. The intent of Internet2 is to keep the Internet moving forward by subdividing its research topics into major categories and then organizing the efforts to solve these problems. One of the reasons for the creation of Internet2 was to ease the congestion on the commodity backbones. Other Internet2 goals include quality of service support, multimedia integration, high-performance applications, virtual reality, and next-generation architectures.

At the time of this writing, the Internet industry is making additional transitions. There is a continued migration toward aggregation of businesses to larger entities. Many, if not all, midsized Internet service providers have been acquired by major telecommunication providers. The next significant evolution was the increase in access speed technology. Low-speed residential Internet users access their providers on 56Kbps modems. Slightly higher-end users utilize ISDN for 64–128Kbps access, and sophisticated residential customers can gain Internet access at 1.5Mbps or above, using cable modems or xDSL.

Finally, research and educational institutions continue their quest for higher speeds and improved quality of service not only by embracing the vBNS but also by enlisting the support of corporate America's high-speed commercial service. This can be seen in the Abilene [2] network that is expected to be launched in early 1999. This network provides universities with a minimum of 622Mbps connections, and formed the foundation for QoS research.

1.6 Conclusion

In 1998, an estimated 50 million computers were connected to the Internet, an astounding number considering the total was almost zero only 10 years earlier. What is even more impressive is that the number continues to double every year. Clearly, the experiment is a success. The fundamental principles have been developed and deployed on a massive scale. In addition, the idea of packet-switching datagrams across a simple network of IP routers has proven to provide an excellent communication medium.

The future of the Internet entails further development and the resolution of several key problems:

- A domain system to support global scale and international policy
- IP address space allocation to keep routing manageable and to avoid address starvation
- A means for coping with ever-changing regulations

The 1960s through 1980s can be described as decades of consolidation of information technology and implementation of Internet protocols. The 1990s have been a decade of mainstreaming the technology and the dramatic rise of both business and residential Internet use. The Internet has been affected by many forces, including the United States government advancing the idea of the so-called information superhighway; the business opportunities; new markets as seen by the telecommunication industries; the deregulation of global markets; and the rich variety of Internet uses.

Now the Internet is coming of age. It started out as a research network, with its own jargon, idiosyncrasies, and providers. As the Internet becomes part of the fabric of life, it is clear that to continue to describe it in unique terms is to do a disservice to the user community. The Internet is, simply, a public-switched data network, which allows interenterprise and intraenterprise connectivity when a protocol-standardized end device (a standardized browser and/or server) is used. The network is composed of "switching nodes" (pure routers or hybrid switches-routers), interconnected by high-speed transmission links. Protocols exist for understanding information outside one's administrative domain; and the common staple of transmission is an IP datagram (just as in the global PSTN, the common staple is a pulse code modulation [PCM] sample). To scale, the same network design principles used for other networks will have to be employed. Availability, reliability, and monitorability will be achieved by similar, but data-network-specific, methods.

References

1. www.internet2.edu
2. www.vbns.net
3. Katie Hafner and Matthew Lyon. *Where Wizards Stay Up Late.* (NY: Simon & Schuster), 1996.
4. info.isoc.org/guest/zakon/Internet/History
5. www.sri.com

6. www.alohanet.com
7. Douglas Comer. *Internetworking with TCP/IP.* (Upper Saddle River, NJ: Prentice-Hall), 1995.

Appendix: Internet Time Line

1957

- Sputnik is launched. DARPA is created.
- Leonard Kleinrock at UCLA develops underlying principles of packet switching.

1958

- NASA is formed.

1959

- Paul Baran joins Rand Corporation.

1962

- The Rand Corporation begins research into robust, distributed communication networks for military command and control.
- Joseph C. R. Licklider named as head of the Command and Control Research at DARPA. Division renamed as Information and Processing Techniques Office (IPTO).

1965

- DARPA sponsors research into "cooperative network of time-sharing computers."
- Paul Baran ceases work on network project.
- Donald Watts Davies formally proposes idea of packet switching.

1967

- Delegates at a symposium for the Association of Computing Machinery in Gatlinberg, TN discuss the first plans for the ARPANET.

1966

- Larry Roberts becomes the program manager of DARPA.

1967

- The first meeting held to discuss building a network composed of interface message processors (IMPs).

1968

- BBN awarded contract for developing IMPs.
- Donald Watts Davies' ideas implemented at the National Physical Laboratory in Middlesex, England.

1969

- NWG is formed.
- Researchers at four U.S. campuses create the first hosts of the ARPANET, connecting Stanford Research Institute, UCLA, University of California Santa Barbara, and University of Utah.
- The first IMP is installed at UCLA.

1970

- ARPANET commences using NCP.
- Initial phase of network project is completed, including BBN, MIT, Rand, System Development Corporation, and Harvard.

1971

- The Internetworking Working Group (INWG) is established.
- ARPANET grows to 23 hosts connecting universities and government research centers around the country.

1972

- The INWG becomes the first of several standards-setting entities to govern the growing network. Vinton Cerf is elected the first chairman of the INWG, and later becomes known as the "father of the Internet."
- The International Conference on Computer Communications is held.
- Abhay Bhushan designs the first electronic mail program capable of running on the open network.
- AlohaNet, developed at the University of Hawaii, joins ARPANET.
- Robert Kahn proposes idea of open-architecture network.

1973

- The ARPANET goes international with connections to the University College in London, England, and the Royal Radar Establishment in Tromso, Norway.
- The first draft of TCP is released from Cerf's lab.
- Bob Metcalfe designs Ethernet, which soon becomes the LAN technology of choice.

1974

- Bolt, Beranek and Newman opens Telenet, the first commercial version of the ARPANET.

1975

- DARPA turns ARPANET over to the Defense Communications Agency.

1977

- Triple network Internet communication is demonstrated to the Defense Department.

1978

- The last iteration of TCP is produced; a separate Internet Protocol (IP) emerges.

1979

- USENET newsgroups are developed. Users from all over the world join these discussion groups to talk about the Net, politics, religion, and thousands of other subjects.

1980

- Tim Berners-Lee writes a notebook program called Enquirer-within-upon-Everything, the precursor to the World Wide Web.

1981

- ARPANET has 213 hosts. A new host is added approximately every 20 days.
- 3COM releases UNET.

1982

- The Simple Mail Transfer Protocol (SMPT) and the e-mail format are created.
- The decision is made to convert all systems on the ARPANET from NCP to TCP/IP.
- The User Datagram Protocol is designed.

1983

- DCA splits ARPANET into two separate networks, MILNET and the Internet.
- Some 200 computers are now on the network.
- The Internet Activities Board (IAB) is formed.

1984

- Moderated newsgroups are introduced on USENET.

1985

- Time-sharing computers are replaced by LANs; desktop worksta-tions arrive with Unix and networking software.

1986

- NSF creates Division of Networking and Communications Research and Infrastructure (NCRI).

- The Domain Name System (DNS) addressing scheme is adopted for e-mail.

- Five supercomputing sites are designated, one each at Princeton University, University of Pittsburgh, University of California San Diego, University of Illinois Urbana-Champaign, and Cornell, forming the backbone network called NSFNET.

- Eight regional networks are formed.

1987

- UUCP and USENET become available commercially.

- Number of hosts exceeds 10,000.

1988

- The "worm" virus infects thousands of hosts.

- The Computer Emergency Response Team, CERT, is formed to address security concerns raised by the worm virus.

- T1 backbone arrives, adding 7 sites.

1989

- Number of hosts exceeds 100,000.

- RIPE is formed.

- First relays are set up between a commercial e-mail carrier and the Internet.

- CSNET and BITNET merge to form CREN.

- IETF and IRTF come into existence under IAB.

1990

- ARPANET is decommissioned, leaving only the vast network-of-networks called the Internet.

- Number of hosts exceeds 300,000.

- Corporations wishing to use the Internet face a serious problem: Commercial network traffic is banned from the National Science Foundation's NSFNET, the backbone of the then-Internet.

- The Web becomes available within CERN.

- Archie, CWIS, HYTELNET, WAIS, and other navigation applications become available.

1991

- The NSFNET backbone is upgraded to T3 speed of 44.73Mbps.

- The NSF lifts the restriction on commercial use, clearing the way for the age of electronic commerce.

- The World Wide Web goes public.

- Gopher is developed at the University of Michigan.

1992

- More than 1,000,000 hosts are part of the Internet.

- Mosaic, a GUI interface to the Web, becomes available.

- Traffic on the Internet expands at a 350 percent annual growth rate; an estimated 1.3 million computers are on the system.

- More than 10,000 networks are in existence.

- The ATM Forum is formed.

- RSVP work started.

1993

- PPP standardized—key protocol for dialup.

- Dynamic Host Configuration Protocol (DHCP) is released—protocol used to allocate IP addresses efficiently.

- Multipurpose Internet Mail Extensions (MIME) is specified.

- Classless Interdomain Routing (CIDR) is specified.

1994

- The Internet is completely privatized.

- Portions of NSFNET are decommissioned, replaced by NAPs.

1995

- The NSF backbone is totally phased out and replaced by four Network Access Points.

- NSF authorizes the creation of a very high-speed Backbone Network Service (vBNS).
- The ADSL standard is published by ANSI.

1996

- Private Internet service providers (ISPs) gain market share.
- Network backbone speeds reach 155Mbps.
- IPv6 is published.
- Internet2/NGI is announced.

1997

- Exponential growth in the number of Internet hosts continues.
- Network backbone speeds reach 622Mbps.
- More versions of Resource Reservation Protocol (RSVP) are published.

1998

- The public begins to realize that the Internet is like any other network; it becomes the Public-Switched Data Network par excellence.

1999

- Quality of Service and service-level agreements will become available, thus advancing business-class Internet usage.

Internet Service Provider Architectures and Services

Internet-based services are becoming building blocks for the extended enterprise networks now being put in place in many corporations. Understanding ISP architectures and services enables corporate planners to get the most out of the public shared network that is the Internet, particularly in reference to throughput (which relates to the ISP's network capacity and overbooking) and performance (which relates to the ISP's approach to QoS, overbooking, network element power, and architecture).

The previous chapter outlined the Internet's history from its inception as the ARPANET, through its formative years of protocol design and network deployment, culminating in privatization, with the creation of NAPs and the vBNS (more baseline information on this is contained in Appendix A at the end of Chapter 3). Over the past 20 years, the network and its protocols have been improved to the point where they are now poised to provide the infrastructure for the public-switched data network for global communications. Indeed, only hardware robustness and ISP experience seem to stand in the way of packet-switched networks being as reliable as the public voice networks. This chapter describes how ISP networks are built and the issues facing providers regarding their architecture and their services. This chapter also defines the components of an

ISP, starting with telecommunications building blocks, followed by a discussion of common ISP hardware. Basic services that are supported by most ISPs, including customer access, backbone transport, and managed services, are also addressed in the second half of the chapter.

Following the definition of the components, we explore how national ISPs join their regional networks into a fault-tolerant interconnection. Emphasis is placed on network architectures that support redundancy, high performance, and quality of service. This material is important because it lays the foundation for understanding how ISP networks are built. The material leads into Chapter 3's description of inter-ISP relationships. It also helps to explain how ISP business models change as they migrate from metropolitan, or regional providers, to the scale of a national Internet service provider. Furthermore, this material allows planners to understand how their Internet service is delivered, and how they can participate in building ISP networks, or ask for specific capabilities from the ISPs they have selected.

2.1 ISP Services and Architectures

An ISP is an organization that connects businesses or residential customers to the Internet (backbone). ISPs can be differentiated from other types of online information services, such as CompuServe or America Online, because typically they do not provide content, but focus only on providing Internet connectivity. An ISP's emphasis is on Internet tools such as USENET News and Web connectivity, and on the supporting infrastructure that allows its customers to get connected. ISPs can also be differentiated from bulletin board systems (BBSs), which normally do not have direct access to the Internet.

Currently, the scope of the ISP business can be subdivided into three major areas (see Figure 2.1). The first category comprises ISPs that provide access services, such as dial-up or digital subscriber-line type services. Second are ISPs that provide transit (described later) or backbone type connectivity. And third are ISPs that provide value-added services such as managed web servers and/or firewalls.

There are a variety of different transport services provided by ISPs, and the types of services greatly influence their network architecture. Typically, the services provided by an ISP change according to the portion of the market being addressed. For example, a smaller ISP will focus only on providing dial-up services, while larger, national ISPs will offer dial-up plus web hosting and caching services.

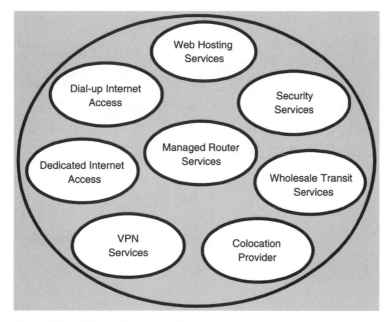

Figure 2.1   ISP service categories.

Regardless of the size of the ISP's network, however, the basic components are the same. IP networks are constructed of access devices, data-forwarding network elements called routers, and information servers, as shown in Figure 2.2.

2.1.1 Dial-Up Access Network Architectures

By far the most common type of network connections today, due to the total number of Internet subscribers, is in the access category, used in the mass market. Examples of this connectivity are dial-up services, such as 28.8Kbps modems, 56Kbps modems, Integrated Services Digital Network, cable modems, and digital subscriber line (see Figure 2.3).

Dial-up access connectivity elements are used by ISPs to connect users to the ISP's backbone. If an ISP is small, it can maintain modem pools that contain only 24 modems connected to a *local exchange carrier* (LEC, also known as Incumbent LEC, or ILEC) or *competitive LEC* (CLEC) via a T1 facility. The connection from the modem pool, or *access concentrator,* is usually a T1-based or a *primary rate* ISDN-based link. Both of these lines are very similar: They terminate on the carrier voice grade switch and provide 24 64Kbps channels. As the number of subscribers grows, the ISP

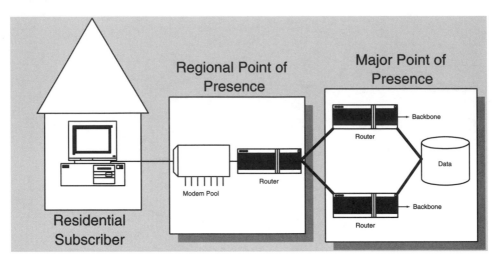

Figure 2.2   Internet components.

can either add more points of presence (POP) or increase the density of its major POP(s). An ISP POP is a location where the service provider is allowed to install equipment. In some cases, the physical location is owned by a different company and shared by many ISPs. This is called *colocation.* Figure 2.4 depicts an example of a dial-up access POP.

Expansion decisions with regards to POPs are often driven by telecommunication costs. For example, if the local toll charges are low, then single large POPs serving large areas are best. If local toll charges are high, then the distributed small POP architecture may be best.

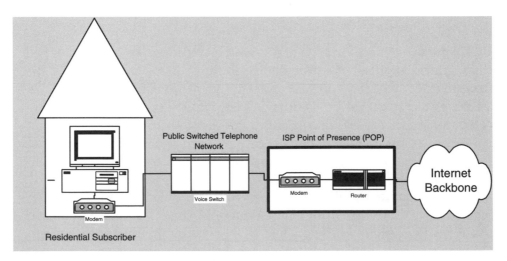

Figure 2.3   Dial-up access connectivity.

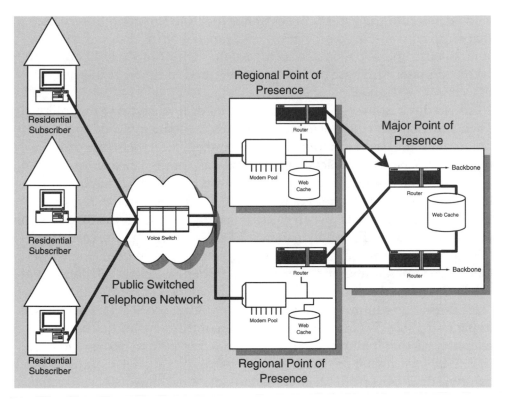

Figure 2.4   Dial-up access POP.

For the most part, ISP dial-up POPs are similar. They contain the access concentrator, a device that concentrates several modems into a single chassis. The access concentrator is connected to a colocated router across a LAN within the POP, usually an Ethernet hub. The router is then connected back through the telecommunication carrier to the ISP's IP transit provider or to an *upstream* POP.

2.1.2 Integrated Services Digital Network

A regional POP can grow by adding additional T1/PRI interfaces to the access concentrator, thus increasing the number of inbound calls that can be terminated by multiples of 24. The POP can also serve as a termination point for *dedicated* Internet access, where either the entire T1/PRI or a subsection is permanently allocated to a single customer. (This is described further in the subsection on dedicated access.)

In addition to the access concentrator, the POP can contain servers that support web-based services. These range from web servers that contain customers' pages to web caches that temporarily hold currently accessed material. These services are described in detail at the end of this chapter.

Access devices are used to connect a LAN or household to the Internet. Their function is to interface with the physical media attached to the computer; or, in the case of modems, to interconnect directly on the computer's internal communication bus. Modems are responsible for converting the digital signals from the computer into a format that can be transmitted over analog telecommunications facilities. In the case of ISDN, the conversion is just an electrical change to match the carrier's line voltages, and a modification to match ISDN's framing. In the case of analog modems, the digital signal is converted from pulses to analog waves that can be transmitted on the traditional Public Switched Telephony Network. DSL services also require modems.

ISDN is a telecommunications system of digital connections developed in the mid-1980s. What makes ISDN different from traditional analog telephony is that it allows information to be transmitted end to end digitally. ISDN uses what are called *bearer channels* (B channels), occupying a bandwidth of 64Kbps to carry voice and data simultaneously across the same physical wire. The signaling, used to pass dial string information, occurs over a *data channel* (D channel) at 16Kbps on low-speed ISDN or at 64Kbps on the faster T1 service.

ISDN service comes in two varieties: *Basic Rate Interface* (BRI) and *Primary Rate Interface* (PRI). BRI service was designed to support small business and residential applications, and is popular for lower-speed Internet accesses. The fundamental difference between the two services is the number of B channels and D channels delivered from the telecommunications carrier to the customer. A BRI consists of two 64Kbps B channels and one 16Kbps D channel, for a total of 144Kbps. This channel allocation allows higher data transfer rates than analog lines. In addition, ISDN equipment, using a channel aggregation protocol such as *B channel bonding* or *Multilink-PPP* (Point-to-Point Protocol), has the ability to aggregate the channels into a single logical high-speed connection. For example, with Multilink-PPP, a data transfer rate of 128Kbps can be achieved by combining the two B channels of a BRI.

PRI differs from a BRI in the amount of data that can be transmitted simultaneously. A PRI contains 23 B channels, plus one 64Kbps D channel, for a total of 1,536Kbps. In Europe, a PRI consists of 30 B channels, plus one 64Kbps D channel, for a total of 1,984Kbps. Because of its larger capacity, a PRI is typically used for business Internet connectivity, or as described later, to aggregate large amounts of traffic at Internet service provider offices.

PPP and its predecessor SLIP (Serial Line Internet Protocol) are schemes that make it possible for IP to be used over dial-up lines, rather than over traditional dedicated lines. With SLIP or PPP, it is possible to undertake TCP/IP communications as if directly attached to the Internet. In order to use the options, one would load SLIP or PPP drivers that work with TCP/IP software installed on one's computer. The software allows the calling computer to be assigned a temporary IP address, which lasts the duration of the telephone connection. (In some cases, the service provider may offer a permanent IP address that will always be used when the user dials in to a dedicated port.) There is some overhead to setting up such configurations, but the payoff is that one can run the same client software at home or on the road as one could over a corporate or campus network directly attached to the Internet.

PPP is the newer of the two schemes; it is more sophisticated and feature-enriched. It can monitor the stream of data moving over the telephone line. (It also can be used for protocols other than IP.) PPP also can automatically have packets retransmitted if they get garbled, a not uncommon occurrence on some dial-up telephone lines. SLIP, in contrast, does not check the packets being sent, and so is faster than PPP, but not as reliable. SLIP, as the older of the two, is currently more widely available, although PPP is considered to be its eventual replacement.

ISDN services may be priced differently from analog, although in some areas the service is priced like telephony, and customers only need to specify that they need a digital ISDN line. Due to signal strength limitations, however, ISDN subscribers must be within 18,000 feet of their carrier's *central office* (CO); beyond that, *repeaters* are required devices placed between the CO and the customer that regenerate the ISDN signal. Unfortunately, repeaters increase the cost of the service. At the customer premise, the connection to the ISDN services is made with a device called a *terminal adapter* (TA). The TA converts the carrier's signaling and line voltages into a format that is more acceptable to computers, like a serial or Ethernet.

NOTE Currently, only about 1 percent of the total U.S. loops (about 1 million) are actually utilizing ISDN. Deployment continues to be slow, and the service may soon be considered too slow as higher-speed technologies like cable modems and DSL are deployed. ISDN is covered in more detail in Chapter 12.

2.1.3 Customer's Access Router

Another component required for Internet connectivity is the customer-end router. Routers operate at Layer 3 of the Open System Interconnection Reference Model (OSIRM). Layer 3 is called the network, or IP layer. The principal function of a router is to manage data flows and ensure that individual datagrams are forwarded correctly as they pass between LANs and WANs. Routers utilize the IP address of a packet, which is globally unique, to determine the appropriate path for the packet. In the case of a customer router, the path is generally just the single physical connection to the network; however, for backbone cases there may be numerous paths to choose from. In order to understand which IP networks are reachable, routers participate in the exchange of routing information with adjacent routers.

2.1.4 Digital Subscriber Access Architectures

Digital subscriber line (DSL) technologies come in many flavors (asymmetric, symmetric, very high speed, and so on, which is why people refer to them as xDSL; the x is a place holder). However, the most commonly deployed technology is asymmetric digital subscriber line (ADSL). Various types of DSLs are interesting technologies because they allow the copper component interconnecting a customer to the CLEC/ILEC central office to be used to carry data rates much higher than ISDN. For example, ADSL deployments are usually provisioned with 1.5Mbps from the ISP to the customer with a back channel of 128Kbps. However, today the majority of lines are implemented via a multiplexed fiber link (over what is called the feeder plant), which terminates in a *digital line carrier* (DLC) system. DLC-based xDSL is just now beginning to appear. Overall deployment of xDSL technologies may well track the ISDN penetration. (In principle, since no switch is required, deployment could be somewhat faster. On the retarding side, one can list LEC's unfamiliarity with IP, new network elements being required, and no operation systems support in the LEC's network.)

From a high level of abstraction, DSL network deployments are similar to dial-up connectivity. The connectivity in the home or business is accomplished with a modem or PC *network interface cards* (NIC). The major difference from dial-up services is that the digital signal is terminated at the CO on a device called a *digital subscriber line access multiplexer* (DSLAM). If DSL modems are used in the home, the interface from the PC to the modem is Ethernet, and the PC can transmit IP datagrams as if it were on a LAN. The modem may use ATM to segment the IP datagram and forward it to the CO.

The DSLAM (see Figure 2.5) is responsible for terminating the DSL signal from potentially hundreds of customers and multiplexing their IP data onto a single ATM connection. This is a fairly basic job in that only OSIRM Layer 2 functionality is involved; the DSLAM does not need to route IP packets because all the data that arrives from customers via ATM cells is reassembled and forwarded to the ISP connected to the DSLAM.

From the CO-based DSLAM, the connection to the router (which for regulatory reasons may or may not be colocated in the CO) is made via an ATM connection. CLECs may support both DSL and Internet access technology, in which case the router may be colocated or included with the DSLAM. Several DSLAMs can be aggregated across an ATM switched network so that a single router can service several COs. When the ATM connection from the DSLAM has been made to the router, ATM is no longer necessary, and the datagram can be routed based solely on its IP addresses. ADSL is discussed more in Part 4 of this book.

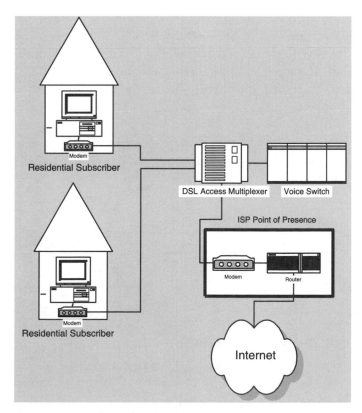

Figure 2.5   Digital subscriber line access multiplexer.

2.1.5 Dedicated Access Technologies

The second category of Internet connectivity is designed for small- to medium-sized businesses or corporations that have fairly consistent Internet connectivity requirements; that is, their connectivity is usually required 24 hours per day with heavy loading. Therefore, this type of Internet connection does not use dial-up modems or ISDN (although there are cases where dedicated access can be provided via cable modems or DSL; we address those separately from more traditional dedicated technologies).

There are two categories of dedicated Internet access: leased lines and switched data services (see Figure 2.6). The first category, leased lines, allows the customer Internet connectivity at speeds ranging from 56Kbps up to 155Mbps. Leased lines dedicate the complete capacity of the telecommunications circuit to a single customer. There is no multiplexing of other customers' traffic on the leased lines between the Internet service provider's router and the customer's premise. This is both good and bad: The customers can feel confident that their circuit to the ISP will never be congested and should provide predictable performance; however, because the circuit it dedicated to one customer, the ISP cannot realize any statistical gains, and therefore will face higher operational costs (naturally there will be overbooking at the router level).

In a network constructed with dedicated access, the ISP runs the circuits back to a router in its POP. In most cases, the physical connection on the ISP's router will terminate the complete circuit; that is, the physical port

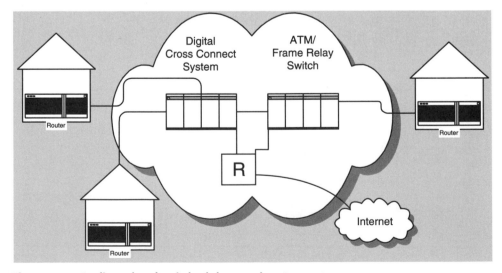

Figure 2.6   Dedicated and switched data services Internet access.

will be 56Kbps, 1.5Mbps, 2Mbps, or up to 155Mbps, or whichever services the carrier can supply. That said, note that modern routers support the ability to accept a *channelized* interface. This means that a single port on a router can terminate a carrier facility containing several subcarriers. For example, a channelized T3 port on a router understands that the physical interface is actually 24 T1s or 672 DS0s (64Kbps) circuits. In many instances, the circuit will be terminated on a digital cross-connect system, especially if the serving central office and the ISP router are not colocated.

2.1.6 Packet over SONET

Another option for ISPs to build backbone or high-speed dedicated access technology is Packet over SONET (POS). SONET [1] is a physical media standard designed to carry high-speed digital communications in a fault-tolerant, scalable manner. The redundancy is realized in SONET by building rings, much like FDDI [2], that allow communication to continue even after a fiber cut.

If a facility failure causes a link to become damaged on a SONET ring, the ring can "protection-switch" onto the fiber transmitting the signal in the opposite direction. The time allowed for the cutover to the working fiber is on the order of 50 microseconds. Because the cutover is so fast, the IP routers may not notice that a facility failure occurred. This can be very desirable because the routers do not need to recompute topological reachability.

High speeds are realized with SONET because the actual speed of the data traversing the ring continues to grow as optical technology improves. See Figure 2.7. Furthermore, SONET interworks well with tra-

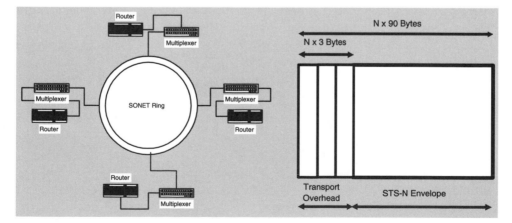

Figure 2.7   SONET ring and framing.

ditional telephony systems; in fact, SONET multiplexers were designed with telephony in mind and have the capability to deliver high-speed circuits to customers, which would be used for their local voice switch. This means that a single SONET multiplexer at the customer premise can be used to interconnect outbound service for voice and data. These days, many of the dedicated access circuits (discussed in the previous section) are delivered via SONET. But POS is more than just the use of SONET.

Before POS was available, ISPs requiring higher speeds than DS3 could only use ATM at OC-3c or OC-12c speeds. While effective for segregating traffic and policing flows, ATM introduces overhead because of the cell header. POS does away with this overhead by allowing individual IP packets to be directly mapped into the SONET payload. Although the POP interfaces are still considered point-to-point by the IP routers, they can be protected by SONET's redundancy (see Figure 2.8).

2.1.7 Frame Relay Service

Another type of dedicated Internet access that has become popular due to its low cost and wide availability is called *frame relay*. Frame Relay connections are physically similar to the dedicated services just described; however, on a frame relay connection, the link between the customer and the ISP's router can be shared by other customer applications. If the customer and the ISP POP are quite far, then there may be an entire intervening frame relay network rather than just an access line. This sharing is done via the carrier's frame relay service, a data product allowing for

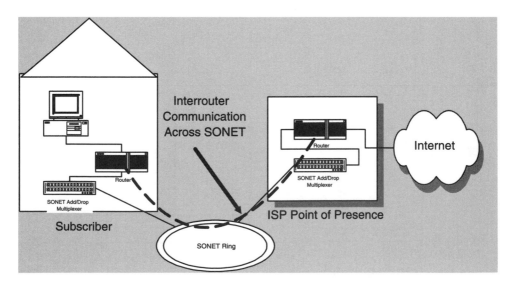

Figure 2.8 Dedicated access with POS interfaces.

many-to-one connectivity over a single physical connection (see Figure 2.9). Frame relay has become popular because it enables ISPs cost-effective expansion of their network.

In frame relay networks, the service provider has a network of switches that share the total amount of bandwidth available. This is because bandwidth utilization is primarily a function of the network architecture and instantaneous load. If the carrier has overengineered the network, all traffic will be delivered without packet loss due to congestion. If, however, the network is overloaded, there may be packet loss in the carrier's network of frame relay switches.

When frame relay is used to carry Internet traffic, the network is typically a *star* architecture, with one leg of the star connected to the ISP and the other legs connected to customers. If traffic in the network gets heavy, the provider can either add bandwidth to the links by increasing physical line speeds (from 56Kbps to 1.5Mbps) or by limiting the logical amount of data that can be transmitted on each link. Limiting the amount of traffic a frame relay network can carry is called *policing*, a technique that uses peak and average volume values.

The average amount of data that the frame relay network can carry, as specified in the contract with the frame relay service provider, is called the *committed information rate* (CIR). The CIR represents a minimum amount that the network should be able to carry. For example, assuming that the frame relay carrier has not oversubscribed its network, the customer should be able to purchase 25Kbps CIR on a 56Kbps physical circuit, and be able to depend on 25Kbps, and occasionally be able to burst to 56Kbps.

Frame relay service is attractive, because if a customer feels that he or she may someday have the potential to generate or receive a lot of Internet traffic, he or she can subscribe to the physical circuit without incurring high initial service costs. As customers' traffic grows they can

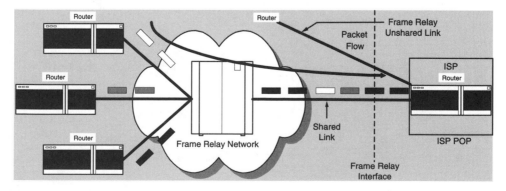

Figure 2.9   Frame relay.

increase their CIR by paying more to the carrier, and consequently get a higher-speed connection to their ISP. (This same principle applies to Asynchronous Transfer Mode, ATM; however, it has not been widely deployed as an access technology.)

As shown in the Figure 2.9, the connection to the frame relay network is done via a router that has a built-in frame relay interface or to a router via a V.35 [2] interface and an external CSU/DSU. Frame relay is covered in more detail in Chapter 6.

2.1.8 ISP Points of Presence Architecture

With the preceding discussion of components and carrier services in mind, we can begin to describe the content of an ISP's POP. Often, because the diversity of architecture and customer demands, the devices in the POP need to support POS, ATM, channelized interfaces, dedicated customers, and dial-up interfaces; therefore POPs can become fairly complicated. Whether the POP is in the ISP's switch site or in a colocation space, the contents will always contain "access" equipment and an IP router (see Figure 2.10).

At the core of the POP is a router labeled "core0" that acts as the central hub for routing within the POP and is also used to terminate high-

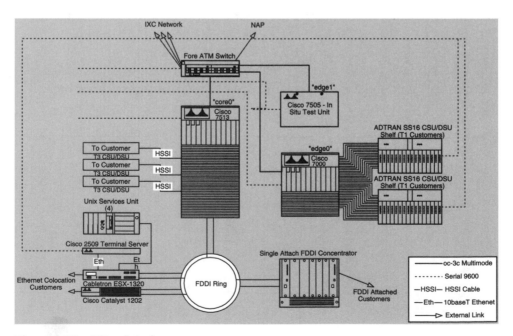

Figure 2.10   ISP point of presence.

capacity connections. The router is shown terminating four network connections and one management connection. Three *high-speed serial interfaces* (HSSI) [2] that are capable of running at 52Mbps are terminated on the left side of the router. Each of these interfaces occupies one slot of the router's chassis. At the top of the router, an ATM interface is connected to a LAN ATM switch manufactured by Fore Systems [3]. Each of these high-speed interfaces, HSSI and ATM, can support a large amount of traffic; consequently, the total number of these interfaces must be limited on older hardware.

To the right of the core router is a low-speed access router labeled "edge0." This router is used to terminate T1 (1.5Mbps) customers. In this POP, each customer is connected first to the Adtran Channel Service Unit/Data Service Unit (CSU/DSU) rack, which converts line voltages and then passes the signal to a serial port on the edge0 router. The port on the router is a V.35 interface [2]. The access router can also be used to terminate frame relay service.

The Adtran CSU/DSU rack can directly terminate T1s from the carrier; or, the ISPs sometimes install M13 multiplexers [2]. As described, the multiplexer would allow the carrier to supply a channelized DS3 to the ISP and the 24 individual T1 channels could be separated and connected to a CSU/DSU. Buying higher-capacity channelized facilities usually translates into lower per-channel costs.

The bottom of Figure 2.10 shows LANs and an FDDI ring that is deployed in the POP to form a high-speed interconnection path. Until recently, FDDI has been a common interconnection medium on a single attached concentrator used to interconnect routers, web servers, web caches, and bridges. (Switched 100Mbps Ethernet is now also being used. Gigabit Ethernet may also be used.) Due to the high price of FDDI interfaces, some devices, like web servers, may be connected to their router only via Ethernet. To the left of the FDDI ring are two Ethernet/FDDI bridges that serve this purpose by forming the link to the colocated web servers. These bridges have one connection to the FDDI ring and multiple switched Ethernet ports. One switched port is allocated to each colocated web server.

The ATM switch pictured at the top of Figure 2.10 plays several key roles in the POP. First, the ATM switch can be used as a replacement for the FDDI ring because it can provide faster access than FDDI (OC-3c at 155Mbps) and its interfaces are less expensive. In addition, the ATM switch is used as an aggregator of access lines coming into the POP for customers or communication with other ISPs. Because ATM has the capability to subdivide one physical connection into a number of different bandwidth logical connections, it makes an excellent *feeder* technology;

that is, a single ATM connection into a carrier or switch can be subsequently used to *aggregate* dozens of customers' traffic onto a single router interface.

On the bottom right of Figure 2.10 is a remote access device, the Cisco 5200. This device is used to terminate Plain Old Telephone Service (POTS) and ISDN services. In addition to the telephony termination ports, this device must have some type of interface that can be used to interconnect to the POP's routers. In the figure, this is shown as an ATM interface that connects to the LAN ATM switch. The access device usually terminates channelized T1s, PRIs, or channelized DS3s. In addition to Cisco's device, it is common to find this access concentrator as being manufactured by Ascend (e.g., TNT), or 3COM (e.g., Total Control).

In this POP, the "out of band access" management connection is illustrated as a dotted line originating from the Cisco 2509. The 2509 is a terminal server that contains multiple serial ports and a single Ethernet port. The serial ports can be individually accessed from the Ethernet so that if the POP's LAN hub were to fail, the network manager could dial in to the 2509 via a POTS or ISDN connection and establish a console session with any of the devices in the POP.

Not shown, but critical for ISP POP operation, are uninterruptible power supplies (UPS). Most ISP POPs require an industrial-grade UPS that operates on either diesel fuel or natural gas. They are usually installed to automatically activate when the power fails. Commercial grade units cost a minimum of $10,000.

The POP usually also has a backbone router that provides the connectivity between the access subnetwork and the Internet backbone. The power of this router is based on the function it supports. The router may be used to connect the aggregated traffic to the peering point (typically for smaller ISPs), or to the ISP's own national backbone. Typically, these are high-end Cisco routers, such as the 7200 series. Because of the increasing demands on the interconnected Internet backbones (both in terms of raw traffic and number of dispersed ancillary networks that have to be interconnected), providers are investigating the use of next-generation routers, typically called *gigarouters*. Again, key vendors include Cisco and Ascend. Other vendors include NetStar GigaRouter. Table 2.1 lists some of the typical forwarding rates targeted by gigarouters.

A number of projects to provide high-speed routing are underway, for which information is available: the Multigigabit Router [4], IP/ATM [5], the Cell Switch Router (CSR) [6], and IP switching [7]. Note that the NetStar GigaRouter is an early commercial implementation of a gigabit router [8]. In general, all of the designs use the same functional compo-

Table 2.1 Gigarouter Forwarding Rates

INTERFACE	PPS PER-CARD RANGE
HSSI	70K
10/100Base-T	120K
FDDI	125K
HPPI	10K
ATM OC-3c	60K
ATM OC-12c	600K
POS OC-3	150K
POS OC-12	600K

nents. The line card contains the physical layer components necessary to interface the external data link to the switch fabric. The switch fabric is used to interconnect the various components of the gigabit router [9].

The gigarouter forwarding engine inspects packet headers, determines to which outgoing line card they should be sent, and rewrites the header. The network processor runs the routing protocols and computes the routing tables that are copied into each of the forwarding engines. The gigarouter processor handles network management and housekeeping functions, and may also process unusual packets that require special handling. A switch fabric is used for interconnection, as it offers a much higher aggregate capacity than is available from the more conventional backplane bus. The NetStar Multigigabit Router will use a 15-port crossbar switch with each port operating at 3.3Gbps. The NetStar GigaRouter also uses a crossbar switch fabric, with 16 ports each operating at 1Gbps. The IP/ATM, CSR, and IP switch solutions use ATM for the switch fabric. In the case of the IP switch, a complete ATM switch, not just a fabric, may be used. This allows use of more highly integrated switch solutions that, for example, integrate line card and switch fabric functionality [9].

The advantage of an ATM switch is that the hardware is standardized and available in many different sizes from different vendors with different cost/functionality trade-offs. Additionally, advanced features such as hardware quality of service support and hardware multicast are typically available in ATM switches. The disadvantage of an ATM switch is that it is cell-, not packet-, based and is connection-oriented, unlike the connectionless network protocols that are the subject of high-speed routing. The forwarding engine may be a physically separate component or may be integrated with either the line card or the network processor [9]. If the forwarding engine is a separate component, the packet forwarding rate may be set independently from the aggregate capacity by adjusting the ratio of forwarding engines to line cards. This is the approach taken in the Multigigabit Router, and is an option in the IP/ATM solution. However, separating the line card and the forwarding engine creates additional overhead across the switch fabric. The NetStar GigaRouter integrates a forwarding engine with each line card. In the current realization of an IP switch, the forwarding engine is combined with the network processor, although combination with the line card or a separate implementation is not prohibited by the architecture [9].

A key difference between the router approach and the IP switching architecture is that IP switching allows most data between ATM ports to traverse the switch without being handled at all by a forwarding engine, whereas a router approach always requires use of at least one forwarding engine. Measurements from the Internet indicate that the average packet size is now about 2000 bits [7]. This has increased from an average of 1000 bits just five years ago because of the increase in large transfers due to Web usage, which now represents almost 50 percent of Internet traffic. Thus, at present, we need a forwarding rate of about 500Kpps (kilo packets per second) for each 1Gbps of traffic, though this may change as the traffic profile changes. Two approaches have been proposed to achieve packet forwarding rates of this magnitude: the silicon forwarding engine and a high-speed general-purpose processor with destination address caching using an on-chip cache [9].

While this technology continues to evolve, ISPs will begin gigarouter deployment in their networks. A question a corporate planner should ask his or her provider is whether the provider has started such deployment in its network.

IP switching is an alternative to the gigarouter [9]. An IP switch maps the forwarding functions onto a hardware switch such as an ATM switch. A similar idea evolved independently at about the same time to three groups. The devices based upon this idea are called: IP/ATM [5], the IP switch [7], and the Cell Switch Router (CSR) [6, 10]. Another mechanism for binding forwarding functions to an ATM VCI is also discussed in Yukinori Goto's paper "Session Identity Notification Protocol" [11]. In addition, the Cisco Tag Switching proposal is similar to these earlier works [12]. IP switching may be used with any higher-level IP functionality; it is not restricted to particular IP routing protocols or routing domains, and thus may be used, for example, between an ISP and its customers or between ISPs.

Each approach uses the concept of a *flow.* A flow is defined as a sequence of packets that are treated identically by the possibly complex routing function. An example of a flow is a sequence of packets sent from a particular source to a particular destination (unicast or multicast) and forwarded through particular ports with a particular QoS. The forwarding and handling of each flow is determined by the first packet in the flow. Once the flow is classified, these decisions may be cached, and further packets in the flow may be processed according to the cache entry, without requiring the full flow classification.

Each of the previous three solutions uses an ATM switch as the switch fabric for a high-speed router. Incoming flows are mapped onto ATM virtual channels (VCs) established across the ATM switch [9]. Only one or a few packets from each flow need to be inspected to perform the mapping and establish an ATM virtual channel. Once the virtual channel is established for a flow, all further traffic on that flow can be switched directly through the ATM switch, greatly reducing the load on the forwarding engine(s). The IP/ATM solution uses a pool of preestablished permanent virtual channels (PVCs), which are taken by active incoming flows. Packets on a new flow are not forwarded until a PVC has been activated. The IP switch uses a protocol, IFMP (RFC1953), to propagate the mapping between flow and VCI upstream, and forwards packets using the forwarding engine until the cut-through connection is established across the ATM switch. The Cell Switch Router attempts to be more general than the IP switch in that it will permit entire Classical IP over ATM (RFC1577) subnets between CSRs; it proposes using the RSVP protocol to propagate the mapping between flows and VCIs [9]. New approaches may evolve in the next couple of years. These topics are treated in more detail in Chapter 9.

2.2 Putting It All Together: National Services and Networks

Services provided by ISPs that are large enough to operate national networks are sometimes referred to as *network service providers*, or NSPs. NSPs are in the wholesale network services business; today, many are national in scope and several have global reach. In many cases, they are affiliated with major facilities-based carriers, because access to fiber optic systems is critical when building large high-speed networks. This section describes a number of NSP backbone technology alternatives that have recently been announced or made available and that could help solve the problems of increasing traffic load and routing scalability. Backbone architecture and equipment is described, along with upgrade strategies. The chapters that follow provide more details.

Large NSPs face a variety of challenges in maintaining stability and acceptable service performance in their backbones. Traffic levels continue to rise rapidly; consequently, underpowered backbone routers and switches may reach their forwarding capacity shortly after installation, due to the growing number of ISPs mandating interconnections to many other ISPs at NAPs, or privately, and several interconnections to the same provider, all of which create very large routing tables. The combination of traffic and routing load has reached a level where the traditional backbone architecture, consisting of routers and point-to-point circuits, is no longer satisfactory for large ISPs. Techniques such as "route at the edge and switch at the core" are being considered. The concepts described earlier of IP switching in the generic sense (including Cisco's Tag Switching, Ipsilon's IP Switching, and the IETF MPLS) are all directed at addressing the issue of more efficient movement of information, while minimizing the number of times that and manner by which the data itself is touched in the network.

2.2.1 National Architectures

This subsection describes network architectures used by national ISPs to interconnect their regional POPs. Figure 2.11 lists some of the issues being considered by ISPs. Figure 2.12 depicts service provider criteria.

In order to provide national services, ISPs have built sophisticated networks that are distributed across the country. These *backbone* networks are used to interconnect the ISP's regional POPs and to establish connections to customers. An ISP's backbone usually consists of interconnected routers and in some cases, frame relay or ATM switches. As shown in the ISP POP diagram in Figure 2.10, one router is required at each POP to provide backbone routing and forwarding decisions for traffic crossing POPs on the backbone. Interconnecting the POPs are backbone routers, which may be connected to one or more ATM switches when ATM is used as the backbone core, as is common among most nonfacilities-based North American ISPs. In order to determine where data should be sent, the routers support an Interior Gateway Protocol (IGP) such as Open Shortest Path First (OSPF) [13]. These issues are covered in more detail in Chapter 8.

There are currently about 20 ISPs in the United States with national networks, and this number is growing every year. Because there are so many providers, one of the challenges faced by ISPs is getting connected to all of the other providers. Interconnection to other ISPs is done at designated

- Internet/Web explosion
  - ⇨ High-speed access required by many corporations (DS1, DS3, OC3c, and higher)
  - ⇨ Integrated access
  - ⇨ Web-hosting services
  - ⇨ VPNs
- Desire for "IP Dialtone"
  - ⇨ IP as de facto data networking standard
  - ⇨ Infrastructure and optimization required at lower layers
- Drive to
  - ⇨ Reduce costs
  - ⇨ Improve profits
  - ⇨ Support QoS

Figure 2.11   ISP drivers.

POPs that support the specialized functions of *peering* and other interconnection agreements. Physical connectivity is implemented via dedicated point-to-point circuits, Packet over SONET, a LAN, or a switched data link service such as ATM. The network access points (NAPs) are public exchange points used as well-known locations for meeting ISPs. See Figure 2.13 for an ISP example. Figures 2.14 and 2.15 depict the arrangements pictorially.

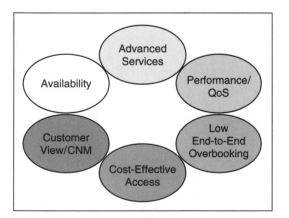

Figure 2.12   Service provider criteria.

- Peer with All Tier I Internet Service Providers
    - ⇨ Tier 1 ISPs:
        - 24 × 7 Customer Care
        - Presence at four NAPs
        - National backbone network
    - ⇨ Eastern United States
        - Sprint or New York NSF NAP
        - MAE-East (Washington, DC)
        - Ameritech or Chicago NSF NAP
    - ⇨ Western United States
        - MAE-West (San Jose)
        - MAE-West (Moffet Field)
        - Commercial Internet Exchange (CIX)
        - DEC Palo Alto Internet Exchange (PAIX)
- Several Dozen Agreements Signed with Tier 2 ISPs
- Sell Transit Service
- Private Peering Agreements
    - ⇨ Connection between two ISPs is dedicated to traffic flowing between those ISPs only.

Figure 2.13   Peering arrangements.

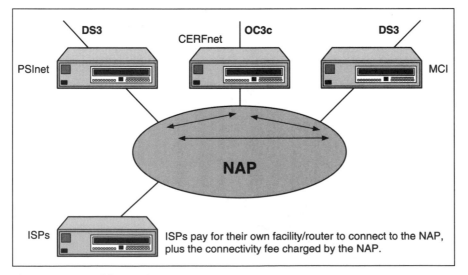

Figure 2.14   Public peering.

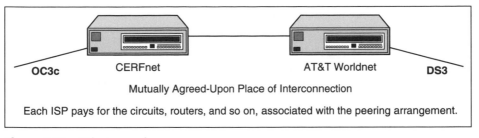

Figure 2.15   Private peering.

NAPs typically consist of switched LAN (FDDI) or switched ATM connections; in addition, some interconnection facilities (e.g., Digital Internet Exchange/PAIX) provide private interconnects using local fiber cross-connects within the colocation facility. Fundamentally, all the exchange point is providing is a means to move IP packets from one ISP to another. Hence, at the distant end, the facilities supporting the switched or dedicated-line services are connected to the ISP's POP router. No matter which type of physical interconnection is used, the interconnection between ISPs is always implemented between IP routers. These inter-ISP routers use the Border Gateway Protocol (BGP), a sophisticated interprovider protocol, to support the exchange and selection of routing information between providers. BGP is covered in Chapter 8.

2.2.2 Design Criteria

Several nationwide ISPs are currently utilizing router-based backbones with DS3, OC-3c, or OC-12c connectivity. This high-speed packet-switching technology was proven in the early 1990s, and is commonly available in routers that can carry traffic at line rates. When bandwidth requirements increase beyond this speed, there are a limited number of choices for backbone connectivity. The first is to migrate toward ATM at OC-3c speed; this approach was announced in 1995 by MCI. At that time it migrated its backbone to an ATM switching network using Fore System's products. The interswitch links in this network were OC-3c; in 1996, those began to be upgraded to OC-12c (622Mbps).

ATM in the ISP backbone has received some attention. ATM is the only broadband switched WAN service available today. That said, overhead is introduced when data is carried across an ATM network, because each IP packet needs to be segmented into ATM cells that are only 48 bytes long. Because of this segmentation process, additional overhead of 5 bytes is required for each 48 bytes of payload as addressing information. The overhead can be significant, up to 25 percent of data, and this is the best case overhead for ATM; in the worst case, where the IP packet size occupies 49 bytes, or two ATM cells, the overhead can be very high indeed.

An additional complexity of ATM is that it has its own bandwidth control and provisioning mechanisms that do not necessary interwork with IP's best-effort paradigm. Bandwidth must be managed carefully by the ISP so that the routers do not produce more data than can be transmitted by the ATM network, according to the established traffic contract. This problem is addressed by configuring the routers to use *rate shaping,* a configurable feature on routers with ATM interface processors. Rate shaping is always on and can cause reduced throughput because the routers are also running in an artificially slow mode in order to abide with the traffic contract. This typically occurs when an ISP uses a low *sustainable cell rate* (SCR), which is comparable to the CIR concept mentioned earlier in reference to frame relay. If the ISP utilizes SCR values close to the line rate, traffic shaping becomes less of a network policing control (NPC) function and more of a maximum line rate function (whose consequences would have to be faced by any protocol engine, not just ATM). In addition, congestion handling by ATM switches may result in degraded performance at the network and transport layers because the ATM switches may drop cells from several different packets during overload. This tends to occur in networks that are poorly engineered; proper traffic engineering is a must on all networks. It is impossible to put a ton of x into a one-pound bag, no matter what x is. ATM does, however, offer ISPs some clear advantages over traditional media; most notably, the capability to implement permanent virtual circuits with assigned bandwidth values has shown to be a very flexible feature for bandwidth sharing and segregation. ATM is treated in more detail in Chapter 7.

As an alternative to ATM, some ISPs and national research networks (e.g., NORDUnet) began early trials of Packet over SONET interfaces in 1996. This technology supports OC-3c interfaces on a point-to-point basis between routers, and has been used to directly connect backbone routers in different POPs or across a single POP when FDDI was deemed too slow. This type of interconnection is not yet used at public exchange points because there is no way to share the interface; that is, there is no analogy to a Layer 2 switch from POS vendors. The current phase of the POS evolution is toward higher speeds. It is now common to find OC-12c interfaces being deployed, and some OC-48c (2.4Gbps) are also beginning to see implementation.

Several criteria drive the decisions as to how and where a backbone network should be built.

Fault tolerance.   Most national providers have built their networks to support fault tolerance using three techniques: redundant paths between POPs, SONET interconnecting the POPs, and hardware redundancy in the POP.

Meets at NAPs.   Backbone architectures are often very similar because, for the most part, all ISPs use the public exchange points (NAPs) to exchange data. Because the NAPs are located in five well-known locations, it is very common to find all major ISP backbones in the NAP cities.

Access to high concentrations of customers.   Clearly, one of the motivating factors for backbone design is access to customers. This almost always means heavy deployment in California and the Eastern seaboard.

Access to colocation space.   Because creating a new facility, which includes finding and renting a building, can be difficult, most ISPs attempt to share colocation space. This space usually belongs to interexchange providers or major ISPs with a presence in the region.

Access to domestic/international facilities.   As the Internet grows, the capacity of telecommunication circuits, both active and planned, cannot keep up with demand. Nowhere is this more evident than in long-distance high-capacity connectivity. For this reason, when facilities do become available, ISPs will often share the capacity. This leads to service providers partnering on their networking infrastructure, but it also means that many ISPs end up with similar networks.

Scalability.   Being able to increase individual link capacities, the total number of customers serviced from a single device, and the amount of data that can be forwarded are all critical for large ISP network designers.

Due to these design criteria, it is common for major ISPs to have similar network architectures. Figure 2.16 shows the AGIS Network; this backbone contains several common traits of major ISPs and is helpful in illustrating these design decisions. The AGIS network is built to survive a major failure of a POP or a long-haul facility. In order to accomplish this, the network has taken on a characteristic figure 8 shape, which allows the network to survive an outage either by relying on the IP routers to modify traffic flows or by allowing any underlying ATM/SONET infrastructure to reroute traffic. It is also clear in the figure that AGIS has a presence in all of the major public Internet exchange points. This allows it to pass traffic off the network quickly if it is des-

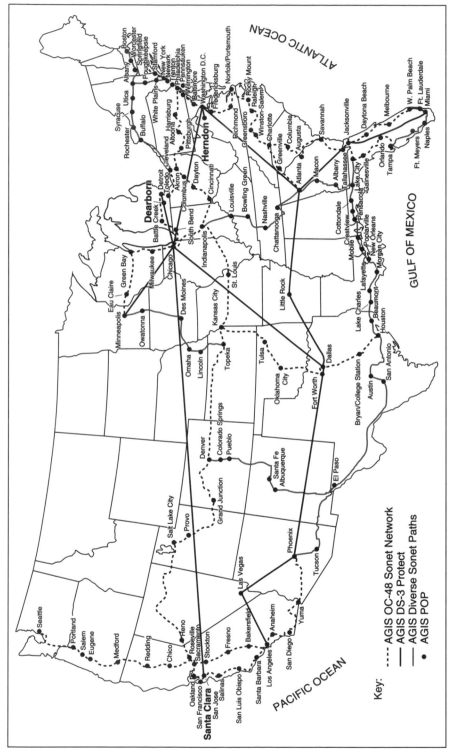

Figure 2.16 AGIS network architecture.

tined for another provider's customer, and it allows it to directly sell Internet services in those major markets.

Several goals propel the layout of an ISP's backbone, and it is not coincidental that several major ISPs have constructed networks that look very similar. Figure 2.17 depicts TCG CERFnet's network. Figures 2.18 and 2.19 show a more general view of the backbone, while Figures 2.20 and 2.21 depict the nodal architecture.

2.2.3 Transit: A First Look

A national ISP may participate in the sale of access services such as dial-up and frame relay; however, they typically focus their efforts on dedicated service to business customers, or they sell to regional ISPs what is called *transit connectivity*. Transit service, when sold to regional ISPs, is the equivalent of long-distance IP service.

The responsibility of Internet service providers selling transit services is to be able to accept packets from their customers, either end users or smaller ISPs, and deliver those packets to their ultimate destination. ISP connectivity to a transit provider is typically done via a private peering point; that is, the circuit to the ISP and transit provider is completely dedicated, like a T1 into the POP. In some cases, however, ISPs purchase their connectivity to a transit provider across a national exchange point.

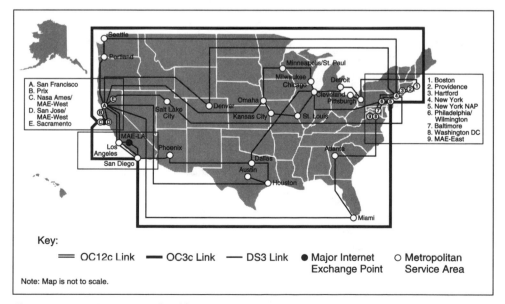

Figure 2.17 TCG CERFnet backbone.

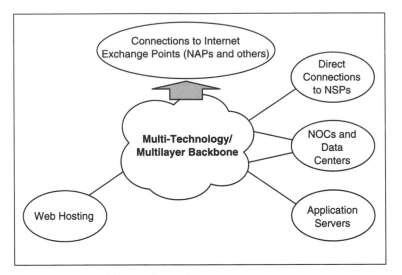

Figure 2.18 Architectural overview.

The benefits of acquiring transit at a NAP are many. First, because national exchange points contain dozens of service providers, ISPs buying their transit service there can pit several ISPs against each other to *yield* lower pricing. The second major benefit is that regional ISPs will often peer with each other at exchange points for free (see Figure 2.22). These types of arrangements are called *multilateral peering agreements* (MLPAs)

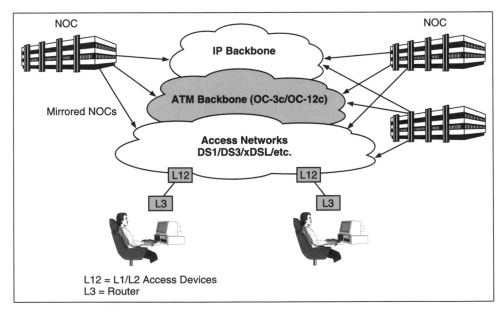

Figure 2.19 Backbone components.

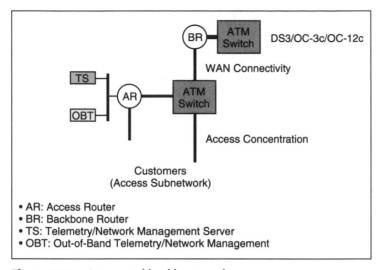

Figure 2.20   Access and backbone nodes.

and have become very popular, because any traffic that can pass between two regional providers should take that shortest path and not be forced to traverse the NSP's network. These types of arrangements are also becoming more attractive as national providers migrate toward usage billing. These concepts are described in more detail Chapter 3, and Appendix B at the end of Chapter 3 depicts one example of an MPLA.

The MPLA benefits the customer because ISPs at the NAP can peer with dozens of other ISPs, thereby providing their customers with faster, more direct routes to the destination. The idea of customers connecting to a central facility, much like an Internet mall, is one of the themes of Internet2 work, where this model is called a *GigaPOP*, and the customer can

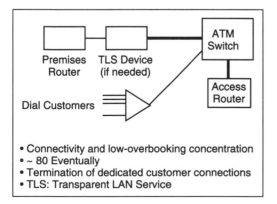

Figure 2.21   Concentrator node.

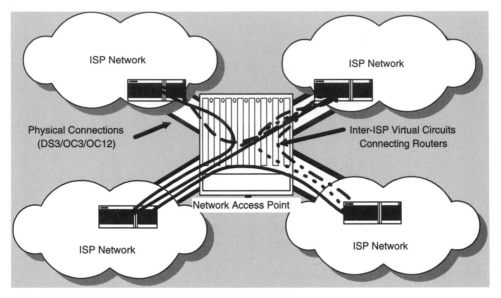

Figure 2.22   Inter-ISP connectivity at a NAP.

gain IP transit services along with access to other such Web service as audio/video servers or IP telephony.

2.2.4 Value-Added Services

In addition to selling IP colocation and hosting services, typically, major Internet service providers are in the business of selling colocation, web caching, web hosting, and VPNs. Colocation is typically used to host the physical presence of an ISP's equipment in space owned by the different ISP. Colocation space is usually sold based on denominations of one-half of a *cabinet.* When an ISP requires more space than two or three cabinets, then that ISP is sometimes given the option of renting a small self-contained caged area. Colocation facilities provide heat, air conditioning, electrical power, 24-hour access, and security. Within the colocation space, ISPs are generally allowed to place any type of equipment they desire [5]. In the case of a NAP, ISPs typically colocate a router that is used to connect to the NAP and a web cache that is used to reduce backbone loading. Finally, the colocation facility should provide good connectivity to the CLECs, ILECs, and several long-distance transit providers. (This is often not the case in carrier-based colocation spaces where only transmission equipment is allowed.)

Additional services often provided by major ISP transit providers are web caching and web hosting, which allow corporations or other ISPs to outsource the operation of what can sometimes be a sophisticated activity. Web caches are devices that act as proxies between a web request originated by a browser and the ultimate web server that contains the desired information. When an end user is accessing information on the Internet via his or her browser, the web cache is initially queried for the page and can either request the information immediately on behalf of the end user from the original web server and reply; or, if the cache already has the page, it can reply to the web browser with the requested page (see Figure 2.23).

While the browser is accessing the original for the document, the cache can simultaneously request the page. Web caches are capable of supporting a variety of *population algorithms;* however, they typically wait until they have received several requests for the same information before storing the document on a regional web server. Once they have requested the document from the web server, they process a copy locally; thus, subsequent requests for that document can be satisfied without traversing an ISP backbone.

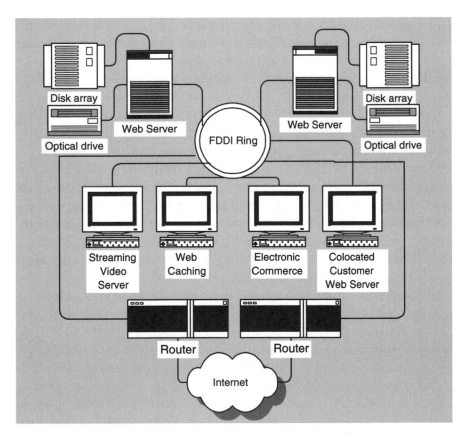

Figure 2.23   Web caching/server farm (courtesy TCG CERFnet).

The desired effect of a well-implemented web cache is a local server that contains up-to-date copies of most commonly accessed web pages. Therefore, when the ISP's customers access sites like Microsoft or Netscape, they only have to wait for the local copy to be transmitted to their computer; a page fetch that crosses the ISP's backbone is not required. The commonly accessed pages (e.g., cnn.com) will typically be refreshed on the cache several times each hour. Very high-cache hit rates have been reported for larger ISPs, and there seems to be a direct correlation between the number of users and the quality of the cache.

Some major ISPs offer web hosting services in which the operation of the computer that acts as a web server is outsourced to the ISP. The benefits of this type of service are that the page or pages of information can be duplicated at several concurrent locations. For example, a major Internet service provider will have a mirroring facility on the East and West coasts of the United States, along with facilities in London and Tokyo.

Another example of an ISP value-added service can been seen in the newer VPN services that are now emerging. VPNs allow corporations to derive the equivalent of an intranet over the Internet (or a private ISP's IP network). Even though the open Internet is increasingly important to companies, it represents only one mode of communication. Companies also need private data communications both inside the enterprise and with external business partners. Increasingly, this data also utilizes standard Internet protocols. High-end service providers such as TCG CERFnet offering IP-based VPN services give business customers a secure, reliable, and cost-effective alternative to expensive wide area leased-line connections. For example, TCG CERFnet's Enterprise Quality-VPN (EQ-VPN) service provides both remote access and site-to-site VPNs. It also offers the scalability and flexibility required to integrate applications among main and remote offices, with mobile employees, or among suppliers in a secure fashion over the TCG CERFnet private IP backbone. TCG CERFnet can also provide businesses with a fully managed, dedicated VPN by combining their wide area ATM and frame relay services.

Security is a key concern of business executives who are considering the migration to an IP-based VPN. To that end, high-end ISPs such as TCG CERFnet utilize IPSec-compliant encryption units for the EQ-VPN service. Transport mode encryption services and the IPSec tunneling mode protocol are both supported. These ISPs provide security services through hardware devices designed to minimize the delay associated with the computationally intense encryption algorithms. Companies can save substantially over private leased-line networks, while focusing on core competencies, by cosourcing wide area connectivity. When properly designed, VPN supports a 99.8 percent availability guarantee. Monthly online utilization reports and performance statistics are included.

2.3 ISP Creation Costs

This chapter concludes with an economic analysis of the costs incurred in setting up an ISP. While every ISP is different, and this analysis could never be exact due to the constant changes in the industry, our intent is to provide enough material to enable the reader to understand the magnitude of the costs. In turn, this can assist corporate planners understand some of the factors that impact not only their own costs, but also the quality of the service (e.g., where the ISP may choose to "cut a corner").

As described, there are several components required to construct an ISP network. ISP costs can be subdivided into:

Customer Access Equipment. Used to provide connectivity from the customers' computers to the ISP network. This can be as simple as a modem or as complex as a managed campus network with egress routers.

Carrier Facilities and Services. These services are used to provide connectivity between the customer and the ISP's POP, or between ISP POPs. Related to this fee is the IP transit or long-distance IP charge.

Network Routing Hardware. This equipment terminates customer connections and routes data. In most cases, it is restricted to modem pools and routers; however, more sophisticated ISPs will often run their own frame relay or ATM overlay networks.

Network Services Hardware. This equipment makes up the category of web servers, caches, streaming content servers, and so on.

2.3.1 Customer Access Equipment

The first category of required equipment connects the customer premise to the ISP. For low-speed connections, this has traditionally been a modem or ISDN terminal adapter. For faster connections, the device at the egress of the customer premise will be a router with 56Kbps or greater outbound connectivity. Some ISPs require that customers purchase the required equipment for both ends of the connection; that is, modem, router, and CSU/DSU (see Table 2.2).

Table 2.2   Customer Premise Equipment Costs

EQUIPMENT	PURCHASE PRICE	INSTALLATION COST
28.8Kbps modem	$200	N/A
56Kbps CSU/DSU	$250	See Section 2.3.2
T1 CSU/DSU	$1,000	See Section 2.3.2
Low-end IP router	$2,500	$1,000 with DSU

The decision as to who owns this hardware can be based on two factors: cost and complexity. As either increase, the component is more likely to be owned and operated by the ISP. If the equipment is low-cost (modem, smaller router, etc.), it can generally be purchased at retail computer stores and support standard configurations. Therefore, the total cost of ownership (TCO) is relatively low from the customer's perspective, and the service is not contracted. If, on the other hand, the device is relatively expensive, like a high-performance IP router, then it is likely that the ISP will bundle the router in with the basic service price. Unfortunately, due to customer price sensitivity, the latter type of connection is sometimes fairly expensive; nevertheless, the industry trend is to develop products based around outsourcing.

ISP revenue sources from equipment can be found in initial sale and installation of switches and routers. In addition, ongoing monitoring and maintenance should be considered as ways to increase business revenue.

A second factor affecting ownership of equipment is complexity. As already noted, as equipment becomes more complex, the likelihood of customer ownership decreases. Whereas modems are very simple to operate and require little to no configuration, routers can be complex and far beyond the ability of a typical customer to operate. Therefore, generally ISPs assume router operations but skip modems. Finally, there is an element of risk assumed when IP routers are connected to an ISP because the router may propagate or inject corrupt routing information into the ISPs database and pollute routing tables. This can be mitigated with routing filters, but unfortunately not all ISPs are diligent in maintaining current best practices.

2.3.2 Carrier Facilities and IP Transit Services

Telecommunication carrier rates vary almost as much as the range of possible services. As outlined, the majority of residential Internet users connect via dial-up modems on POTS lines. The next major category is ISDN, followed by frame relay; finally, a small percentage of links are high-speed SONET or ATM. On the low end, carrier rates for 28.8Kbps SLIP on conventional residential lines cost around $20 per month. Fees for dedicated services for a 56Kbps connection range from about $100 to $200 per month. Prices for T1 service (dedicated or for frame relay) range from $400 to $1,000 a month, depending on the committed information rate (for frame relay) and the distance between the subscribers and the ISP. In addition to the carrier access fees, there is also a long distance IP (LDIP) charge, or transit, as described in Table 2.3.

2.3.3 Network Services Hardware

Table 2.4 lists the approximate costs for ISP equipment. The type of device is shown in the first column, followed by the cost for the device. The last column, Number of Shared Users, gives an approximate number of subscribers that an ISP can allocate per device; it is defined as the number of Internet subscribers that can concurrently share the circuit coming into the ISP's POP. For example, if an ISP only had one 28.8Kbps modem, and was selling service to typical dial-up users, it should be able to support three customers. As shown in the table, higher-capacity lines and routers are attractive because they occupy small amounts of space and can support very high numbers of typical Internet subscribers; however, initial capital expenditure can be high. These economies of scale can make the Internet business less attractive for smaller providers.

In addition to routers and interconnecting frame relay switches, ISPs in the business of hosting content will incur costs in building the computing infrastructure. Most of the high-end ISPs base web hosting and network

Table 2.3 Fees Associated with Long-Distance IP

TRANSIT SERVICE COST	APPROXIMATE MONTHLY TRANSIT COST	APPROXIMATE CONNECTION FEE	APPROXIMATE COST PER Mbps
28.8Kbps	$20	$20	$1,500
56Kbps	$350	$100	$7,000
1.5Mbps	$3,000	$600	$2,200
10Mbps	$6,000	$4,000	$1,000
34Mbps	$15,000	$4,000	$600

Table 2.4   ISP POP Equipment Costs

EQUIPMENT	APPROXIMATE COST	NUMBER OF SHARED USERS
28.8Kbps modem	$200	3
56Kbps router with CSU/DSU	$2,750	8
1.5Mbps router with CSU/DSU	$3,500	200
Backbone router	$100,000	30,000
Backbone frame relay switch	$100,000	30,000

news distribution on Unix machines. This type of equipment, such as Sun and Silicon Graphics workstations, can easily cost $5,000 to $10,000 each. For a major ISP POP, there may be two Unix machines, for redundancy and load sharing, coupled to large hard-disk arrays. The total cost of these high-performance server systems is $75,000 or more. These numbers, combined with the cost of Internet routing and switching hardware, can drive the cost of a medium-size ISP POP upward of $300,000.

2.3.4 Personnel Costs

Finally, one of highest costs and one of the most difficult to quantify is personnel. Engineers experienced in router management, configuration, and operation are in great demand. Advanced network engineers capable of routing design and analysis and network planning are in even greater demand. The late 1990s saw the lowest unemployment rates in this field since 1970. Turnover of networking staff is an ongoing problem, with the typical tenure being 1.5 to 2 years, thanks to the wealth of opportunities. For example, a BITS-clock expert (a kind of clocking used by large ILECs) or a SONET ring expert may have half a dozen jobs to choose from in a single geographic area. But an IP expert may have thousands of opportunities in a metropolitan area, from a medium-size commercial establishment with an intranet network to a commercial web site.

Unfortunately, human resource VPs, especially in telecommunication carrier groups, are often out of touch with reality, and think they can offer salaries of $30,000 to $45,000 per year, based on downsized voice personnel from the telcos, to build advanced, experience-proven IP, VPN, multicast, push, web-shadowing, and multimedia packet networks. It is necessary to make room for viable contemporary ideas, so that stakeholders can be effective in their pursuits of new networking products, thereby helping the carrier's stock sustain market growth and retire anachronisms. The following are some observations from experience in running ISPs:

- A rule of thumb for head count is to plan on one network engineer per router in the ISP network.

- Network operations centers (NOCs) represent a large expense due to high turnover of skilled personnel and the high cost of maintaining 24-hour per-day operations. One difficulty in designing NOCs for ISPs is that they operate across several different problem domains: telecommunications, data processing, LAN, WAN, and so on.

- An often overlooked component of large ISPs' customer care service is the help desk. As network offerings become more diverse and ISPs begin to move down market, the cost of operating a help desk can be very high.

- One of the most likely places for the network to fail is at the telecommunication facility. Progressive ISPs should invest in engineering staff with telecommunications experience and in telecommunications test equipment.

Table 2.5   ISP Staff Costs

TITLE	EDUCATION	SALARY	ISP COMMENT	EXPERIENCE
Junior Engineer	Undergraduate or student	$15–25/ hour	Usually well motivated	Little to none.
Network Engineer	Bachelors degree Engineering degree	$40–60K/yr.	Computer scientist	May have used Unix or worked as a system administrator.
Senior Engineer	Masters Computer Science or Electrical Engineering	$60–110K/yr.	Advanced programmer, 5+ years experience	Has used Unix or worked as a system administrator.
Backbone Design Engineer	Masters in Computer Science	$120K+	10 years experience, probably at NSF regional network	Has participated in the design of major national ISP(s).

One of the difficulties facing ISPs is the lack of staff training, so it is common for junior engineers to gain experience on the job. Courses, such as the Cisco Certified Internet Engineer (CCIE), are very useful and are beginning to be considered as a metric of basic competence. Training costs around $500 per day (also consider time off from work); between 10 and 20 days per year, per person is typical.

There are several categories of router engineers. The salary figures listed in Table 2.5 are estimates based on our hiring experience in the industry (amounts are in U.S. dollars). Categories are based on educational and work experience.

Currently, there is a great deal of turnover in the ISP industry as employees move from one company to another, usually due to better offers or staff modifications after an acquisition. Engineers can be recruited using headhunters or employment search firms that specialize in the network industry. However, word of mouth is the most likely method for finding good staff.

References

1. D. Minoli. *Enterprise Networking: Fractional T1 to SONET, Frame Relay to BISDN.* (Norwood, MA: Artech House), 1993.
2. D. Minoli, A. Schmidt. *Network Layer Switched Services.* (New York: John Wiley & Sons, Inc.), 1998.
3. Fore Systems, www.fore.com, 1998.
4. C. Partridge, "A 50-gigabit-per-second IP router." Paper in preparation.
5. G. Parulkar, D. C. Schmidt, J. S. Turner. "IP/ATM: A Strategy for Integrating IP with ATM," in *SIGCOMM Symposium on Communication Architectures and Protocols,* Cambridge, MA, September 1995, pg. 9.
6. H. Esaki, and K. I. Nagami, M. Ohta. "High-Speed Datagram Delivery over Internet Using ATM Technology." Networld+Interop, Las Vegas, March 1995, E12–1.
7. P. Newman, T. Lyon, G. Minshall, "Flow Labelled IP: A Connectionless Approach to ATM." Proc. IEEE Infocom, San Francisco, March 1996, 1251–1260.
8. D. Kachelmeyer, "A New Router Architecture for Tomorrow's Internet," NetStar, Inc. Alameda, CA, 1997.

9. Peter Newman, Greg Minshall, Tom Lyon, and Larry Huston. Ipsilon Networks Inc, IP Switching and Gigabit Routers, http://www.ipsilon .com/about/technology/papers/ieee_comm96.htm.

10. Y. Katsube, K.-I. Nagami, and H. Esaki, "Router Architecture Extensions for ATM: Overview." IETF Internet Draft, draft-katsube-router-atm-overview-02.txt, March 1996.

11. Y. Goto, "Session Identity Notification Protocol (SINP)," IETF Internet Draft, draft-goto-sinp-02.txt, January 1996.

12. Y. Rekhter, B. Davie, G. Swallow, "Tag-Switching Architecture Overview." IETF Internet Draft, draft-rfced-info-rekhter-00.txt, September 1996.

13. Bassam Halabi, *Internet Routing Architectures.* (Indianapolis, IN: Cisco Press), 1997.

CHAPTER 3

ISP Business Relationships

The issue of relationships between ISPs, which ultimately relates to network interconnectivity, is a poorly understood and poorly documented aspect of the Internet. This is partially due to changes that occur so rapidly in the industry and the fact that there are still relatively few people involved in establishing ISP policy. This chapter attempts to address this shortcoming by describing inter-ISP business relationships; how money changes hands between ISPs; how current and future national traffic exchange points are built; and different ISP billing models. For completeness, some information about Internet2 is also presented. Understanding these issues can help communication planners appreciate pricing, QoS, and interconnection capabilities supported by providers.

3.1 Peering Arrangements

The Internet, with its multibackbone architecture, requires support of peering (the free exchange of routing information and traffic between networks) and transit (the transport of a provider's packets to a third party for monetary compensation) capabilities. What is required of a regional ISP to be able to get a peering agreement with the bigger ISPs? The answer is to become big enough to make the agreement equally beneficial for the bigger ISP. If you are a regional ISP, you cannot get peering with most of the NSPs without having a national network, and even that may not be enough. An ISP that wants to peer with the big providers will probably need to have a presence at multiple Internet exchange points.

Currently, there are five criteria that NSPs have decided upon to determine the "tier" of their NSP business partners. The requirements are:

1. The NSP must have at least DS3 (45Mbps) speed on their national backbone.

2. The NSP must appear at a minimum of three national public exchanges (NAPs).

3. The NSP must have connectivity on both the East and West Coasts of the United States.

4. The NSP must maintain a staff network operations center that never closes.

5. The NSP must peer with other tier 1 providers and have the technically competent staff to support those peering sessions.

The different tiers in this model correspond to different levels of connectivity. The large, well-staffed NSPs are considered tier 1; for example, tier 1 service providers have either a national or international presence. Tier 2 providers may cover only a region or group of major metropolitan areas. Tier 3 providers typically service only one city. By developing the tiered model, NSPs have been able to document policy that can determine whether another ISP must pay for their connectivity or can exchange traffic without monetary compensation.

Since the establishment of MAE-East in 1992, continuing through the deployment of the three NSF NAPs in 1994, ISPs were willing to offer free *peering* (an agreement to exchange traffic) to each other at exchange points, as covered in Chapter 2. For all of the large ISPs, peering sessions are handled on an equitable basis without fees or settlements. A number of settlement models have been proposed, but so far, no single settlements model predominates for peering today.

The type of inter-ISP relationship where one provider sells wholesale access is referred to as a *peering agreement*. If the lower-level ISP—that is, smaller in number of customers or regional scope—is buying transit service from a single IP provider, then the smaller ISP can configure its routers and retransmit all traffic not directly connected to its network via the transit provider's router. This type of connectivity, referred to as *static* or *default routing*, is described in greater detail in Chapter 8.

From a business perspective, there are two types of peering arrangements whether they occur at public or private Internet exchange points:

Multilateral Peering Agreements (MLPA).   A by-product of the creation of public exchange points. A multilateral peering agreement[1] is designed to facilitate peering at the exchange point in that the agreement specifies that any ISP executing the MLPA will settlement-free peer (without charge) with any other MLPA number. An MLPA at a major exchange looks like a cooperative agreement where the participating ISPs agree that each is comparable in size and therefore charging each other is unnecessary. This type of arrangement is typically implemented between regional ISPs.

Bilateral peering agreements.   A bilateral agreement is constructed between two ISPs, either when one ISP is purchasing the transit services of the other (that is, a peering with a settlement agreement) or as an arrangement such as a traffic exchange between two providers. In the latter case, there is seldom an exchange of money associated with the peering session. It is a business and technical arrangement designed to facilitate traffic flow and management of data traversing the Internet.

Why do NSPs make it difficult for the smaller ISPs to peer with them? There are a number of technical and business reasons for these policies. First, ISPs spend approximately the same amount of time bringing up a peering session for the smaller ISPs' routers as they do to bring up a peering session for the larger ISPs' routers. So why not peer with someone who is going to enhance your service as much as you enhance his or hers? In addition, the larger NSPs must be concerned with the smaller ISPs' capability to properly administer a safe Border Gateway Protocol (BGP) peering connection (BGP is covered in Chapter 8). Another NSP concern is whether the smaller ISP has the necessary technical staff. If the session is incorrectly configured, serious network outages in the larger provider's network can result.

Another reality is that, in many cases, the ISPs know that *not* peering with the smaller ISPs is not going to make a difference to their customer base. If smaller ISPs cannot get traffic to the larger NSPs, they will be providing poor service, thus requiring the smaller ISP to buy transit (probably from one of the NSPs). The NSPs do not want the administrative burden of keeping another peer active (which means more people to contact if they change router configurations, etc.) when they get little perceived benefit from the peering session.

3.1.1 Peering Requirements

With the rise in the number of ISPs entering the market in the late 1990s, many of which cover a single metropolitan area or one or more states, large ISPs have expressed a strong reluctance to offer settlement-free peering at exchange points. Some large ISPs have completely cut off peering as a new service or have placed a moratorium on new peering agreements, and in some cases have disabled existing peer sessions with local/regional providers.

For example, MCI, Sprint, and AGIS publicly announced limitations in their peering policies. AGIS made its policy public in October 1996 at a North American Network Operators Group (NANOG) [1] meeting, with the following points:

- Peers must have a DS3 backbone.
- Peers must be connecting their routers at:

  MAE-West

  MAE-East

  Pacific Bell NAP

  Ameritech Chicago NAP

  Sprint NAP
- Peers must not be AGIS customers.
- Peers must also be peering with Sprint, MCI, UUNET, BBN, PSI, ANS, and Netcom.
- Peers must have a 24 × 7 network operations center.
- Peers must be advertising routes consistently now and have been doing so in the past.

These policies support the position that ISPs with less infrastructure should not be allowed to obtain peering that forces larger ISPs to carry traffic to customers without reimbursement. The issue is protection from competitors who have substantially smaller investments in their infrastructure. From the large ISPs' point of view, free peering enables competitors to draw away business by reselling to customers at lower rates. In addition, a strong network operations center and routing consistency requirement minimize the operational costs for the large ISP. MCI has complained that peering has placed excessively high costs on its operations center in managing the instability in the peer networks.

UUnet went as far as to announce that it will withdraw existing peering sessions and strengthen requirements for adding new peer sessions. UUNET issued a press release responding to pressure from new types of peers, notably web-hosting services (or "web farms"), in which essentially the same peering rules as the AGIS (and MCI, and Sprint) are being enforced. There is no evidence, however, that UUNET is reducing its willingness to peer with providers with sufficient national infrastructure, as some have feared.

Finally, all of the large ISPs see local and regional ISPs as a target market for sales of Internet connections. Most of the large ISPs have aggressively marketed this type of connection. Such a direct connection, where the large ISP provides dedicated transit to the small ISP, precludes the problem of peering and simplifies engineering for the small ISP. The large ISPs have made a strong statement that dedicated transit is a stable method of entering the market and continuing during growth phases. Only when the new ISP establishes a large infrastructure will it be considered a peer with full privileges.

3.1.2 ISP Tiering

In order for an ISP to be capable of selling transit[2] service, it can either position itself as a wholesaler and resell connectivity of a larger ISP, or it can establish its own national presence similar to the largest ISPs'. Most Internet service providers experiencing substantial growth are striving to become national providers. The relative magnitude of an Internet service provider is translated into tiers, as covered earlier.

The significance of the tier levels is important from the standpoint that they are often used to determine the flow of money in the Internet and are sometimes referred to in ISP marketing literature (see Figure 3.1). Internet service providers in the tier 2 or tier 3 bands must purchase transit services from a higher-tier ISP. What the tier 2 and tier 3 providers are purchasing is a guarantee that data delivered to larger ISP will be carried across the Internet. The ISP that accepts the packets must transmit to the ultimate destination or pass across an Internet exchange (NAP) and deliver them to the ISP that claims the ultimate destination as a customer. When an ISP has reached the level of a tier 1 provider, it typically does not pay for Internet connectivity to other tier 1 providers—that is, any further settlement is unnecessary.

It should be obvious that most ISPs would strive to reach tier 1 level because at that level revenue potential comes from selling directly to end

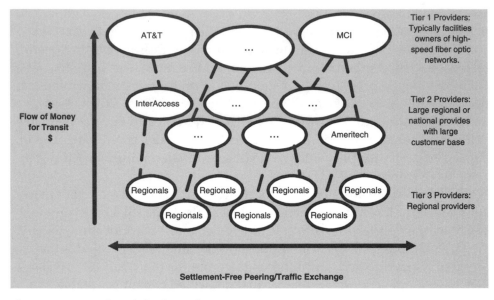

Figure 3.1   Transit and the flow of money.

users and selling wholesale Internet connectivity to tier 2 or tier 3 providers. However, attaining the level of a tier 1 ISP is not a trivial task. With the cost of backbone connectivity at $600/Mbps/month, two cross-country OC-3cs and two coastal OC-3cs would cost an ISP around $5M per year. There are several criteria that can be cited today to designate tier 1 status, and the bar is always rising.

Tier 1 ISPs typically need to maintain connectivity at all of the major network access points as a basic requirement. This criterion can cost several hundred thousand dollars per month in telecommunications expenses. The tier 1 Internet service provider will have to maintain a backbone network with a minimum of DS3 capacity. The transit provider must also maintain the network operations staff and Internet engineering staff 24 hours per day, 365 days a year. Clearly, these requirements are significant and are constantly evolving to be more difficult. For example, it is not uncommon for the qualifications of a new provider to be measured as a minimum of an OC-12c backbone with pockets of OC-48c links interconnecting all of the major U.S. NAPs, plus connectivity to NAPs in Asia and Europe.

3.2 NAPs and Traffic Exchange

As the Internet grows in size, number of users, and usage, ISPs continue to exchange increasing amounts of data traffic. A basic underpinning of the Internet are the points at which inter-ISP traffic can be exchanged. To help cope with the ever-increasing amount of Internet traffic, many new exchange points (EPs) have been deployed, and growth in use of existing EPs has increased (see Figure 3.2). This trend is expected to continue, as it seems to directly support the growth of the local and regional ISP industry, allowing local traffic exchange and reduced dependency on the large, established ISPs.

The basic premise of an exchange point is that ISPs can purchase a connection to this location and gain the capability to exchange traffic with other ISPs at the exchange point. An analogy to this model would be a major hub airport in which several different airlines are served. At that airport, the airlines can exchange passengers between their flights in much the same way that ISPs can exchange IP packets across the EP.

3.2.1 NAP Case Study

To illustrate the design and operation of a NAP, let's take a closer look at the Chicago NAP, which is the largest ATM-based Internet exchange in the world. It makes an interesting study because it is heavily used by ISPs but also serves as an Internet2 GigaPOP, as defined later in the chapter. This NAP is constructed around a cluster of ATM switches that route traffic to a very large central switch that supports speeds ranging from DS3 to OC-12c (see Figure 3.3).

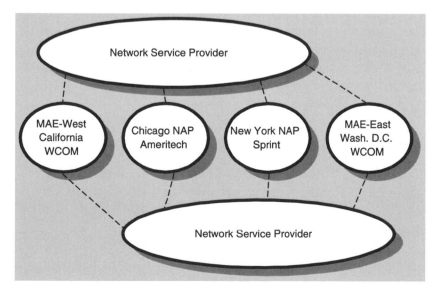

Figure 3.2   Exchange point distribution.

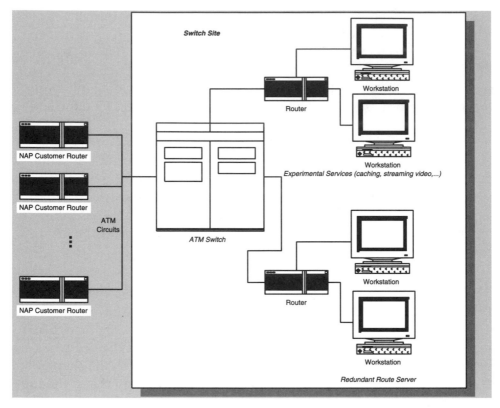

Figure 3.3   Chicago NAP architecture.

It is interesting to note the total amount of traffic that flows through a major Internet exchange like the Chicago NAP [2]. If one considers that a typical written page contains approximately 30,000 bits of information, then the Chicago NAP carries the equivalent of an average of 30,000 full pages of text every *second* (see Figure 3.4).

Following, courtesy of Ameritech, is the product description of the Chicago NAP.

Chicago NAP Description

The Ameritech Advanced Data Service (AADS) Network Access Point (NAP) is an Internet exchange point where Internet service providers (ISPs) can meet to exchange traffic with other attached ISPs. The NAP is a Layer 2 switched service that is not directly involved with routing IP datagrams, but only with forwarding Asynchronous Transfer Mode (ATM) cells between ISPs. The NAP is a Layer 2 service only because it will not restrict internetworking protocol or routing policy selection.

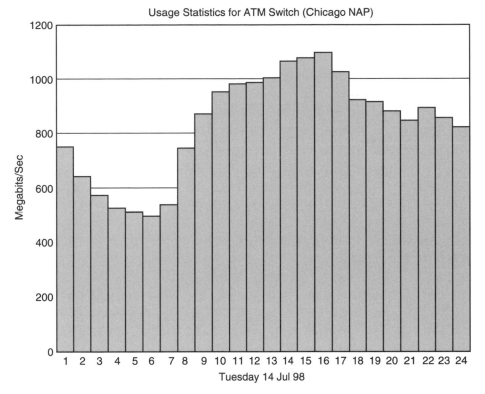

Figure 3.4   Chicago NAP traffic.

The fabric of the Chicago NAP is an ATM switch that provides both high speeds and a high degree of scalability. Interface speeds currently supported include:

- DS-3 (45Mbps) HSSI with ADSU
- DS-3 Native ATM
- OC-3c (155Mbps) SONET

VPI/VCI Assignment

Customers of the NAP service use ATM *permanent virtual circuits* (PVCs) to exchange traffic between routers. A full mesh PVC configuration among NAP customers is included in the NAP access fee. By default, the NAP operator will create a full mesh of PVCs between connecting ISPs. At any time, ISPs may request that any of the PVCs be deleted to prohibit communication to other selected ISPs.

Each PVC endpoint has an associated unique virtual path identifier and virtual circuit identifier (VPI/VCI) pair. All NAP customers are assigned a VPI/VCI pair that is unique to their ATM port. When PVCs are built interconnecting two ISPs, the VPI/VCI used at each endpoint is associated with the customer on the opposite end of that PVC. AADS project managers provide their customers with the VPI/VCI assignments.

IP Address Assignment

The AADS NAP address space (198.32.130/24) administration is handled as part of the Routing Arbiter project by ISI. To obtain an IP address, use the form included at the web site info.ra.net/div7/ra/ipadd-req.html. To see a list of current IP address assignments, check the NAP home page; or, ISPs can pull the IN-ADDR.ARPA zone file for the AADS NAP space from ns.isi.edu.

Peering: Multilateral Peering Agreement and Bilateral Agreements

Attaching customers should plan to make bilateral or multilateral agreements with other NAP-attached networks and to participate on the Chicago NAP mailing list. A physical connection to a NAP should not be considered as an "Internet connection," and peering arrangements between ISPs should be made before connecting.

There are two ways to arrange peering:

1. Join the Multilateral Peering Agreement (MLPA).

2. Form bilateral agreements.

Many NAP customers participate in a Multi-Lateral Peering Agreement, which facilitates peering for exchange of traffic. The text MLPA can be found at nap.aads.net/MLPA.html. A link on that page also contains a list of current MLPA members.

The MLPA is a document developed to facilitate peering among customers connected to an Internet exchange point. When ISPs agree to the terms of the MLPA, they are agreeing to form and support peering agreements with all other MLPA participants at the NAP. They should also peer with the router server.

When an organization has joined the MLPA group, AADS will build PVCs to interconnect all existing and future MLPA members and provide a list of VPI/VCI assignments. ISP contact information is added to the MLPA contact web page.

Not all NAP customers are MLPA members so sometimes it is necessary or preferable to form bilateral peering agreements. Once the agreement has been made and both parties have notified AADS, AADS will build the appropriate PVC. E-mail should be addressed to pvc-request@nap.aads.net.

AADS will disconnect any customer who is disrupting, maliciously or accidentally, the reliable operation of the NAP and will attempt to contact the network(s) involved.

Route Servers

Route servers are workstations running routing software developed by the RA project that performs the routing exchange and processing function described in detail later. The route server (RS) facilitates routing exchange among the NAP-attached ISPs by gathering routing information from participating ISP routers on the NAP, processing the information based on the ISP's routing policy, and passing the processed routing information to each ISP router. The RS uses BGP-4 as the interdomain routing protocol to exchange routing information with NAP-attached ISP routers.

The route server does not forward packets among the NAP-attached ISPs. Instead, it uses BGP's third-party routing information capabilities to pass routing information from one ISP to another, with the next hop pointing to the ISP router that advertises the route to the RS. Traffic is, therefore, exchanged directly among the ISP routers on the NAP, even though the route server provides the routing information.

One key use of the route server is to reduce the number of Border Gateway Protocol peering sessions router(s) will need to maintain at the NAP. As an MLPA member, it may become beneficial to make extensive use of the route servers located at the NAP. Additional information about this option can be found at www.ra.net/route.server.html.

Example Router Configuration

The two most common routers used for NAP connections are those made by Cisco Systems and Bay Networks. This section covers sample configurations for the former because Bay routers use a GUI for configurations.

Using a Cisco router, the possible interfaces for NAP connections are:

- HSSI (with an ATM DSU)
- AIP for DS-3
- AIP for OC-3c

When configuring the router, it is important to take note of the type of AAL5 encapsulation, as it must match your peers in order to communicate with them. The two types of encapsulation are NLPID (RFC 1490) and LLC/SNAP (RFC 1483). NLPID is compatible with frame relay and is more prevalent.

The following code examples show how to configure an ATM interface (DS-3 or OC-3) and a HSSI interface for use with an ATM DSU.

Sample ATM interface configuration:

```
interface ATM3/0
ip address 192.168.1.1 255.255.255.0
atm pvc 1 0 50 aal5nlpid
atm pvc 2 0 51 aal5nlpid
atm pvc 3 0 52 aal5snap
map-group aads_nap
!
!
map-list aads_nap
ip 192.168.1.2 atm-vc 1
ip 192.168.1.3 atm-vc 2
ip 192.168.1.4 atm-vc 3
```

The corresponding HSSI interface configuration:

```
interface Hssi1/0
ip address 192.168.1.1 255.255.255.0
encapsulation atm-dxi
dxi pvc 0 50 nlpid
dxi pvc 0 51 nlpid
dxi pvc 0 52 snap
dxi map ip 192.168.1.2 0 50
dxi map ip 192.168.1.3 0 51
dxi map ip 192.168.1.4 0 52
```

Testing IP Connectivity

After your NAP circuit has been tested and turned over to you, you should immediately begin testing for connectivity with your peers. The three main problems encountered with new turn-ups are as follows:

1. **Problem:** VPI/VCI to IP mapping incorrect or nonexistent at one side.

   Solution: Do not assume your peer has you configured on his or her router. Get explicit confirmation that this work has been done and that it has been rechecked from a technical contact on that side. Do the same for your router.

2. **Problem:** Mismatched AAL5 encapsulation.

   Solution: Find out what your peer is using, as your encapsulation type should match it exactly. If he or she is using frame relay behind an ATM DSU, you should be using AAL5-NLPID.

3. **Problem:** PVC provisioned incorrectly by AADS.

    Solution: If problems 1 and 2 have been checked and a problem still exists, contact AADS Operations and have the switch checked for provisioning errors.

3.2.2 Route Servers

Route servers at NAPs act as central repositories or databases for Internet routing information. The route servers (RS) [3] are Unix workstations attached to the exchange point that runs routing software developed by the Routing Arbiter [3] project. These computers perform routing exchange and processing functions for ISP-attached routers and, potentially, eliminate corrupt inter-ISP routing information. The RS is typically funded by the NAP owner but operated by the Routing Arbiter project, a joint undertaking of Merit Network, Inc., and the University of Southern California Information Sciences Institute (ISI).

The route server facilitates routing exchange among the NAP-attached ISPs by gathering routing information from participating ISPs' routers on the NAP, processing the information based on the ISP's routing policy requirements and policies and then passing the routing information to each ISP router. The RS uses BGP-4 as the interdomain routing protocol to exchange routing information with NAP-attached ISP routers. The route server does not forward packets among the NAP-attached ISPs; all inter-ISP traffic is passed across the actual NAP. Instead, it uses BGP's third-party routing information capabilities to pass routing information from one ISP to another, with the next hop pointing to the ISP router that advertises the route to the RS. Traffic is, therefore, exchanged directly among the ISP routers on the NAP, even though the route server provides the routing information.

One key use of the route servers is to reduce the number of BGP peering sessions that ISP routers will need to maintain when peering across the NAP. The reduction in load occurs because each ISP at the exchange point maintains a peering session with the RS rather than at multiple individual peering sessions. At the larger NAPs, this service is critical because the number of individual BGP peering sessions supported by today's routers typically is no greater than 60.

An additional use of the RS is to "sanitize" the routing information being exchanged by ISPs. Because the RS provides a very sophisticated tool set for managing the inter-ISP routing updates, the data can be filtered for invalid conditions, or a routing policy can be applied by the RS on behalf of the ISP's preestablished criteria.

3.2.3 Direct Interconnections

Beginning with the NSFNET transition in 1994, the major U.S. ISPs (ANS, MCI, PSI, Sprint, UUNET, and others) established peering via the original NSF NAPs (Sprint/New York, MFS/Washington, DC, Ameritech/Chicago, and PacBell/San Francisco). As the number of connected ISPs and aggregate traffic grew at exponential rates during 1994 to 1997, the Metropolitan Area Exchanges (MAEs) became congested. Further, traffic carried on each ISP backbone, and traffic exchanged between the major ISPs, grew exponentially. This led to the need for large ISPs to make use of all available bandwidth for transmitting traffic to other ISPs. NAP circuit utilization grew to near 100 percent, to the point where the shift of traffic caused by a failure of one NAP or corresponding hardware would cause a corresponding congestion collapse of another part of an ISP backbone.

To address these problems, large ISPs began establishing private interconnect circuits. The earliest report of a major private interconnect was by ANS and Sprint in early 1995 [4]. In June 1995, ANS, Sprint, and MCI reported adding private interconnects [5]. There is evidence that all of the larger providers established interconnects about this same time, though the ISPs typically consider this information proprietary.

It is estimated that large ISPs typically maintain approximately 50 direct peering arrangements. Often, these connections are made at public exchange points by running dedicated fiber between the two ISPs. In the case of non-NAP direct connections, where facilities costs are involved, the price of the connection is shared between the two ISPs, or the ISPs will take turns purchasing connectivity into each other's networks. The ISP that purchases the connection is responsible for trouble isolation during an outage.

3.3 Billing Models: Usage, Session Accounting, and Quality-Based

As the Internet has evolved from a research network to a mainstream communication medium, the billing models, for both end users and content providers, have changed. When the network was in its infancy, as the NSFNET, the billing model was very simple. Networks attached to the Internet were responsible for covering the costs required to reach the closest NSFNET backbone sites. At its peak, there were a total of 13 sites, which usually meant that a university would purchase a DS1 connection spanning hundreds of miles. In addition, the university was required to purchase the router at both ends of the connection.

One of the principal reasons for the creation of regional networks was the high cost incurred in connecting to the NSFNET backbone sites. As the regional networks began to mature, the state of network designs was heavily influenced by the cost of the long haul (i.e., DS1) circuits, which could easily cost several thousand dollars each month. While this pricing was high, it is very similar to current Internet pricing models. Today the prices are lower primarily due to the reduced back-haul costs of reaching the ISP's point of presence.

The billing models used widely today can be subdivided into three main categories with an optional fourth:

Flat Rate. The provider charges one fee regardless of connection time or volume of data transmitted.

Usage-Based. Some metric is used to measure a traffic quality or usage time.

Quality-Based. Various grades of pricing are available depending upon the type of traffic carried. This requires the customers to be able to be segregated into their various categories.

Hybrid (optional). Any combination of a flat rate for "commodity" traffic, coupled with quality-based for mission-critical applications.

The first category is clearly the easiest to support and thus will continue to be commonly used in the near future. The second category will become more commonly used as billing systems become more sophisticated and networking equipment becomes better capable of measuring user traffic. As will be described shortly, the quality-based systems will be some of the most interesting developed. When implemented, they will allow the Internet to provide a rich set of varying services. Finally, the hybrid billing model will be offered by advanced ISPs, and will most likely be the desired approach for ISPs.

3.3.1 Flat Rate

Flat-rate billing traditionally has been the only billing model supported on the Internet for ISPs; and in some cases, it also applies to end users. When the flat-rate model is used, the price of the connection is based on the connection speed (e.g., 28.8 Kbps, DS1, DS3, etc.); and where a special high-speed telecommunication circuit is required, a mileage component is added to the price of the connection.

For a residential Internet connection, the mileage charge may come in the form of an intra-LATA toll charge. The mileage component price, if the circuit covers a large geographic distance, is the same problem that universities faced when they connected to the original NSFNET sites.

To circumvent the high circuit charges, major ISPs often establish several POPs across a geographic region. Establishing several POPs allows the ISP's customers, both end users and businesses, to reduce, or possibly eliminate, the facilities charges for connecting to the ISP. For example, in Chicago, an ISP may have as many as 20 POPs. Unlimited Internet service for a fixed cost per month is a very pleasing and easy-to-understand billing method for the average user. There are no surprising balances at end of the billing period that cause budgets to explode. Whether attached for an hour per day or 10 hours per day, users always know they will never pay more than the flat rate.[3]

One interesting change taking place on the Internet is the assignment of a flat rate model based on whether the customer is an end user or a business. During the last few years, the market has seen steadily decreasing prices for the end user or consumer market. The downward pricing has been especially accelerated by AT&T Worldnet and other carriers as they continue to introduce flat-rate pricing below that of their competition. In contrast, the rates businesses and smaller ISPs pay for their Internet connections has been steadily increasing. Thus, shrinking the margins realized at the low end of the market is putting the future of end-user connection into the realm of only the largest ISPs.

Due to pressures from changing prices and increasing consumer traffic loads, the flat-rate model will likely see continued change. As the ISP market becomes more competitive and as the price of access equipment continues to fall, the cost of providing service to the end user service will be very low; however, most of the margin realized in providing that service will be consumed by the "upstream" ISP's fee. As the prices for upstream service continue to rise, the market may even reach a point at which commodity end-user Internet service is provided free from banks, credit card companies, or other traditional service providers in an attempt to retain customer relationships.

3.3.2 Usage-Based

According to most estimates, Internet traffic during 1998 increased by at least 200 percent. As more end users sign up and a greater number of bandwidth-hungry applications are developed, the future promises continued explosive growth. Furthermore, with the advent of new audio and video applications, which enable the Internet to be used for radio or television distribution or for placing telephones calls, there will be an even greater increase in bandwidth consumption. In addition, corporations are realizing that they can tie their intranets to the Internet more cost-effectively than by using their own private networks. When a corporation is planning their Internet service connection, some of the most difficult questions are: What will basic service cost? How can the connection be engineered to support growth, yet remain economically viable?

These new applications, which mix the mainstream Internet with corporation intranet communications, are exerting a great deal of pressure on the major ISPs to develop a new billing model to provide a corporate customer with flexibility. Driving this change is the fact that, in order to continue to supply services at flat-rate pricing, an ISP must be able to predict usage, which may be impossible. Logically, then, if ISPs cannot predict statistical usage, they cannot maintain a flat-rate pricing structure, and therefore, must adopt a pricing structure sensitive to the consumption of the supplied capacity—that is, to bill for measured usage.

Usage-Measured Billing

How does one measure usage? One approach is to sample use on the line and calculate an average percent of total bandwidth being consumed for a specified period of time. This data is readily available from the routers or from other networking hardware, as in the case of a switch data service, like frame relay. In most cases a report generation program that can graphically depict the network's usage over a period of time collects the data. The collection process is accomplished with the Simple Network Management Protocol (SNMP) [6], and many large ISPs use software from report-generating applications, like that of Concord Inc. [7] to create end-user reports. The average traffic flow can then be calculated to classify the user by intensity so that a billing system can be applied to the resulting data.

Another approach to usage billing is to count the actual number of packets sent and received. Again, the process of collecting the data would be done with SNMP; however, this method could present significant problems. For example, a customer would have to be isolated to a single switch or router interface to realize accurate measurements. Isolating customers is not always possible on sophisticated networks.

Another, and more probable problem would be meeting the challenge of measuring the usage of a large corporate customer or an ISP connected to a larger upstream ISP backbone. Though the upstream ISP would be able to generate the report showing how much data passed the interface and then generate a bill on that information, the individual use of the departments within the corporation or the customers of the smaller ISP would be lost.

Unfortunately, the Internet is not a connection-oriented network, like telephony, that allows for keeping track of every single user's call. Consequently, the usage-based billing will raise challenges. But because it is the next logical step from flat rate, most major ISPs have begun to adopt it. The key benefit of a usage-based model is that it allows the corporation to purchase a connection to the ISP and pay only for what they actually use. This means a business can buy a physical connection that is far greater in potential capacity than is currently needed, but be charged only for the portion used. As the corporation begins to use new multimedia applications, its Internet usage will grow and so will its ISP bill, in the same way that a phone bill increases with more use.

3.3.3 Quality-Based

How fast can a packet of data be delivered between point A and point B? If you are reading your e-mail, you probably do not really care; but, if you are part of a videoconference session, real-time performance is essential. Thus, there is a need to categorize data into different service classes and assign each a different priority as they traverse the intranet/Internet; and, more important, an ISP can capitalize on the service classes by offering different prices depending on the packet type. A major portion of this book is dedicated to this topic.

Most ISPs still sell a single product that provides only a best-effort service delivery. In other words, packets of data are sent and received during a time frame that varies by how congested the network is. The number of times packets need to be retransmitted before they arrive at their destination is also dependent upon load, because the packets are discarded when interconnecting routers become overloaded.[4] If a corporation is interconnecting its intranet across an ISP's backbone or is running voice communications to one of its customers, it is very likely that it needs a delivery service that is better than the best-effort delivery service. For ISPs to meet the demands for the same quality of service that private networks provide, the development of an appropriate class of service is needed, along with a means for segregating data into that special higher class.

With the increased adoption of Internet and IP technology by business customers, ISPs are increasingly being asked to offer variable QoS for different customer profiles. Some methods for implementing variable grades of service are becoming available, and new technologies are expected to improve this situation. This topic is treated at length in Part 2. Existing technologies include configuration of:

- ATM virtual circuit bandwidth
- Implementations of the Resource Reservation Protocol
- Proprietary features from router vendors

ATM virtual circuits can be configured to support selectable bandwidth limits subject to the capacity of the circuits provided. Using ATM, traffic can be engineered such that certain customers receive a fixed amount of bandwidth to predefined destinations. Commodity IP traffic, statistically multiplexed within available circuits, is thus confined to a smaller bandwidth than it otherwise would have received. Unfortunately, in most ISP networks, bandwidth configuration is a manual process and cannot be adjusted easily or allocated on a real-time basis.

Resource Reservation Protocol (RSVP) and other queuing priority and precedence-ordering methods, such as weighted fair queuing, random early detection, and others, are available from router vendors [8]. These protocols allow queue scheduling in the router to be modified to incorporate selectable priorities, including source/destination prefixes, IP precedence setting, and customizable flow priorities.

Many ISPs are looking at scalable technology to implement selectable quality of service. ATM is scalable, can support QoS, and can carry IP. But router vendors continue to bad-mouth ATM, as it threatens revenue streams for their tested or untested solutions, for example, e.g., Multi-Protocol Label Switching (MPLS).

MPLS features the principle of *label switching*, a forwarding enhancement that can be used in both routers and switches. In MPLS, a label distribution protocol is used to reserve tags and distribute knowledge of them to active network components. Often, labels are associated with routes or differentiated quality of service. Edge routers identify traffic flows by examining the labels and placing the appropriate new labels on each packet. Backbone routers and switches also identify labels and can apply customized priority, precedence, or any queuing behavior to the flow.

MPLS has yet to see any commercial implementations, but proponents advance it as a very attractive option from the ISP's perspective because it operates at the level of aggregation of a route, which can be associated with a single corporation. At the application level, in order to provide a means for applications to differentiate the QoS that they receive from the network, they can use a technical method of signaling for reserved bandwidth by using the RSVP (RSVP is covered in greater detail in Chapter 10). Application reservation is a model whereby the user application software (e.g., videoconferencing) places a request to reserve a certain amount of bandwidth for a specified time between it and the destination user's computer. RSVP is a methodology for requesting a better delivery service by issuing special messages from the clients to the routers. If the network of interconnecting routers can honor the request based on specific resources, you would inhibit use of those resources by other best-effort packets during the time of your reservation.

Payment for this reservation must be more than the best-effort delivery, and some of the greatest challenges faced by ISPs attempting deployment of an RSVP system are:

- How to collect the billing information from the routers. If each RSVP session (videoconference) generates a unique bill record, then the amount of billing data can become very large.

- How to establish policy and security so that unauthorized use of the reserved bandwidth is not possible.

- How to deal with the problem of handing off the high-quality packets to another ISP whose routers do not understand RSVP.

The current thinking is that RSVP will be used at the edges of the network and MPLS in the core of the network. To implement this model across multiple IP domains, however, will turn out to be very challenging.

3.4 Exchange Point Roles in the Future: Internet2 and GigaPOPs

3.4.1 What Is Internet2?

Internet2 (I2) is a cooperative project involving more than 120 top U.S. universities, along with invited high-technology corporations. One of the primary goals of Internet2 is to develop the next generation of computer network applications and the underlying broadband infrastructure to facilitate the research and education missions of universities. To yield the best results, Internet2 work is shared among several groups. Universities are driving the project because they have the unique ability to both demand cutting-edge applications and be able to help develop the working implementations. Each university is responsible for contributing resources geared toward developing applications that use broadband networks (e.g., ATM Signaling, RSVP) [9].

At regular intervals, researchers from the involved universities and the invited corporations coordinate their efforts. Internet2 universities are working with federal agencies, private corporations, and nonprofit organizations with specialized networking experience and knowledge in developing computer networks. These groups provide Internet2 members with resources and expertise that may not be available on their campuses.

The current list of invited corporations includes ANS, Cisco, Fore, IBM, Ameritech, Digital, MCI, Sprint, and Sun Microsystems.

The future of exchange points, beyond just the services of the NAPs, is in the introduction of enhanced services. This is being realized at Internet2 GigaPOPs, gigabit points of presence, high-capacity, state-of-the-art exchange points at which Internet2 participants share advanced services traffic with other I2 participants. GigaPOPs serve to interconnect institutions, advanced R&D networks, and commercial Internet service providers.

What are some differences between a GigaPOP and a NAP?

- A NAP is a neutral, Layer 2 meet point for ISPs to exchange routes and traffic.
- A GigaPOP is a value-added, Layer 2/3 meet point where sites meet other sites and service providers.

From the experience gained on the NSFNET and the Internet, leading universities now see advanced networking as a core technology necessary for their teaching and research missions. To keep the flow of innovative technology moving, Internet2 is based on developing leading-edge applications such as teleimmersion, digital libraries, and virtual laboratories. The project will simultaneously push the leading edge of multimedia broadband networking and help meet the growing production requirements of member universities. Initially, the research conducted by Internet2 members is focused on broadband network design, network management, and QoS applications. Network engineering will be developed as needed to enable these applications. The primary goal of phase one for network engineering is designing high-performance GigaPOPs.

The basic I2 GigaPOP provides a peering point among high-technology networks, and serves as the regional aggregation point for many advanced Internet services and capabilities (see Figure 3.5). What differentiates the GigaPOP from traditional NAPs is that these next-generation peering points will offer the connecting sites a variety of services from one central location. The Internet2 serves two general functions related to GigaPOP architecture and interconnection: first, the consolidation of traffic from campus networks into a regional meet point(s), similar to a NAP but more feature-rich; second, the physical interconnection among other regional GigaPOPs so that high-speed, QoS-aware, inter-GigaPOP communications can take place. In practice, GigaPOPs will be organized into two broad categories:

Type I. Relatively simple, serving only I2 members, routing their I2 traffic through one or two connections to other GigaPOPs, therefore having little need for complex internal routing and firewalling.

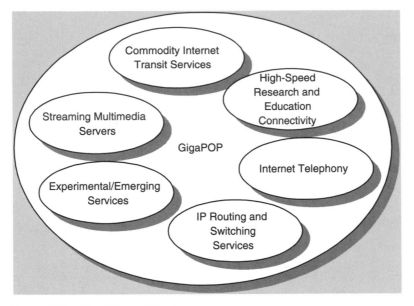

Figure 3.5   GigaPOP architecture.

Type II.   Relatively complex, serving both I2 members and other networks to which I2 members need access, having a rich set of connections to other GigaPOPs, and therefore needs to provide mechanisms to route traffic correctly and prevent unauthorized or improper use of I2 connectivity.

A key point to consider is that by providing several services from one location, the task of procuring networking features/functionality is facilitated. Some of the proposed services are:

Commodity Internet service.   Traditional Internet connectivity; however, typically the connecting university is offered access at speeds of up to 155Mbps.

Research network services.   High-end value services such as ATM Switched Virtual Circuits, IPv6 routing, PPP over SONET, and Multicast IP routing.

Special information services.   Such as access to terabyte disk arrays for temporary data storage, web cache servers, and stratum 1 network clocks.

Corporations or research institutes connected to a GigaPOP are able to pick and choose from the menu of available services. Institutions are attracted to the prospect of being able to obtain various types of services from one physical connection that is effectively lower in cost compared to procuring similar individual circuits and services. By connecting to a GigaPOP, the institution can aggregate research and commodity traffic onto a single high-bandwidth link.

This consolidation of traffic enables the institution to save money on local loops, back-haul, equipment, and support costs, thus allowing the institution to step up to a higher aggregate level of service (i.e., higher-speed access) than would be possible otherwise. This philosophy also has the potential to create economies of scale for commodity Internet services because the EP can be used as a wholesale distribution point serving a large number of customers.

3.4.2 GigaPOP Services

There is still a great deal of debate over which services are considered requirements of the GigaPOP service provider. Currently, it is believed that a GigaPOP must offer:

Bandwidth access ranging from DS3 to OC-12c.   This access can be provided over a circuit-switched technology like ATM or over a clear channel technology like Packet over SONET. The most common GigaPOP connections will be made on ATM; however, some researchers will demand PPP over SONET.

Switched Layer 2 and 3 connectivity options.   Both ATM switching and IP routing will be required at the GigaPOP.

Connectivity to research partners and other organizations.   To be used when I2 members wish to communicate. In the short term, this connectivity will be provided via the Internet or the vBNS.

Connectivity to other high-performance wide area networks.   For example, those that government agencies (e.g., DOE, NASA, ARPA) may implement for their own missions and research. In the short term, this connectivity will be provided via the Internet or the vBNS.

Connectivity to other metropolitan area or community networks.   For example, to provide distance education.

Other network services.   For example, commodity Internet service providers. This connectivity will be easy to achieve for existing NAPs that want to augment their product to encompass a GigaPOP role.

3.4.3 GigaPOP Operations

As opposed to the NAPs and MAEs that are primarily operated by telecommunications carriers, operational management of the GigaPOP is a joint effort involving the I2 institutions and network operators. Operations work includes collecting network utilization and performance data; making the necessary data available to schedule, monitor, and troubleshoot; and accounting for I2 network service in a manner befitting the connected campus-network managers. Operational support will be provided by a small number of I2 network operations centers. These centers will offer high-level coordination and troubleshooting among I2 entities. No end-user support services will be available; therefore, the GigaPOP operator is expected to cooperate on end-user support with the bulk being offered at the institutional level.

3.4.4 GigaPOP Quality of Service

GigaPOPs must supply the aggregate bandwidth demands of participants while serving a number of customers with special QoS requirements. Based on discussions thus far, it is expected that I2 will strive to support at least five dimensions of quality of service requests among I2 entities; however, these criteria are likely to change as concrete applications are developed. The work in specifying QoS will utilize RSVP, coupled with focused research on mapping RSVP to ATM signaling.

The following list of parameters illustrates some of the values that need to be determined and communicated by the application to the network.

Transmission speed.   The minimum available effective data rate and a sustainable maximum limit. For example, a user might request a connection whose sustainable data rate never falls below 10Mbps, but would agree not to expect transmission faster than 20Mbps. On the other hand, the application may request an average data rate, along with the minimum acceptable rate that can be tolerated.

Bounded delay and delay variance.   These parameters specify the maximum effective lag and/or delay variability allowed specially for video and other signals that carry real-time information. For example, users may specify, via an ATM signaling message, that the delay between packets should not be long enough to interrupt or freeze live video.

Throughput.   The amount of data transmitted in a designated time period. For example, a user may notify that a gigabit of data is to be moved between two hosts in no more than one minute.

Schedule.   The start and end times for the requested service. For example, a user may want the requested connectivity to be available at some exact time in the future for some specified length of time.

Loss rate.   The maximum acceptable bit error rate over a specified time interval that results in corrupted data that must be discarded by the destination.

References

1. www.nanog.org
2. Statistics reports for NAPs can be found at: MAE-East, www.mfst .com/MAE/east.stats.html; MAE-West, www.mfst.com/MAE/west .stats.html; Chicago NAP, nap.aads.net/~nap-stat
3. www.ra.org
4. www.ans.net/WhatsNew/PressReleases/Press/Sprint-ANS-AOL .html
5. www.ans.net/WhatsNew/PressReleases/Press/ANS-MCI-Sprint .html
6. www.ietf.org
7. www.concord.co
8. www.cisco.com/warp/public/732/General/cos_wp.htm
9. A. Schmidt and D. Minoli. *Multiprotocol Over ATM: Building State of the Art ATM Networks.* (Upper Saddle River, NJ: Prentice-Hall), 1998.

Notes

[1] An example of the Chicago NAP's MLPA is included for reference in Appendix B in Chapter 3.

[2] That is, accepting packets where the destination is not a part of either ISP's network. Therefore, the packet crosses the transit provider's network and exits at another ISP, which is closer to the real destination.

[3] This billing model has, however, caused substantial problem for the telecommunications providers of residential services because their networks were not engineered for long hold times that are typical when end users connect to their ISP. In addition, since the ISP constructs several POPs, the carrier does not realize any additional revenue because the connection to the ISP is not a toll call.

[4] One of the major reasons the TCP/IP protocol is so successful on the Internet is because it performs two critical roles. First, it notices when packets have been lost and automatically requests a retransmission. Second, when data is lost due to congestion, it automatically reduces its transmission rate to try to help alleviate the congestion.

Appendix A

NETWORK ACCESS POINT MANAGER, ROUTING ARBITER, REGIONAL NETWORK PROVIDERS, AND VERY HIGH-SPEED BACKBONE NETWORK SERVICES PROVIDER FOR NSFNET AND THE NREN PROGRAM

National Science Foundation

I. Purpose of This Solicitation

NSFNET has supported the data networking needs of the research and education community since 1986. It has become an essential infrastructure for that community, and is used daily to facilitate communication among researchers, educators, and students, and to provide them with remote access to information and computing resources. The number of users, the number of connected networks, and the amount of network traffic continue to grow rapidly.

NSFNET also supports the goals of the High Performance Computing and Communications (HPCC) Program, which was delineated in the President's Fiscal 1992 and 1993 budgets and which became law with the passage of The High Performance Computing Act of 1991 (Public Law 102-194). The National Research and Education Network[1] Program, one of the four components of the HPCC Program, calls for gigabit-per-second networking for research and education by the mid-1990s. As steps towards achieving the goals of the NREN Program, "The National Science Foundation shall upgrade the National Science Foundation–funded network, assist regional networks to upgrade their capabilities, and provide other Federal departments and agencies the opportunity to connect to the National Science Foundation funded network."[2] This program solicitation relates directly to these activities.

Since the creation of the NSFNET in 1986, the data networking industry has evolved considerably. New companies have been created, and a number of existing companies have shown increasing interest in data networking. These and other evolutionary changes have prompted the need for a new architecture for NSFNET. The expiration of the current Cooperative Agreement for NSFNET Backbone Network Services has prompted the need for a new solicitation for NSFNET services.

To provide for the continued development and growth of NSFNET and to support the goals of the NREN Program, a new architecture has been formulated and is specified here. The implementation of the architecture includes four separate projects for which proposals are herein invited: one or more Network Access Point (NAP) Managers; a Routing Arbiter (RA) organization; a provider organization for very high-speed Backbone Network Services (vBNS); and a set of Regional Networks, which connect client/member institutions and which provide for interregional connectivity by connecting to NAPs and/or to Network Service Providers (NSPs), which are connected to NAPs. No solicitation is presented here for NSPs, as it is anticipated that costs of operation of the NSPs will be recovered from users of the services that they provide.

The solicitation invites proposals for one or more NAP Manager organizations to arrange for and oversee NAPs (as specified below) where the vBNS, NSPs, and other appropriate networks may interconnect. This component of the architecture will provide access for other networks to the U.S. research and education community, and will provide for the interconnection of networks in a NAP environment.

The solicitation also invites proposals for an RA organization to establish and maintain databases and routing services, which may be used by attached networks to obtain routing information (such as network topology, policy, and interconnection information) with which to construct routing tables. This component of the architecture will provide for an unbiased routing scheme, which will be available (but not mandatory) for all attached networks. The RA will also promote routing stability and manageability and advanced routing technology.

The solicitation also invites proposals for a vBNS Provider to establish and maintain a vBNS that will support applications that require high network bandwidth. In the tradition of NSFNET and as discussed below, the vBNS Provider will demonstrate leadership in the development and deployment of high-performance data communications networks. This component of the architecture will: provide for the interconnection of NSF Supercomputing Centers (Cornell Theory Center, National Center for Atmospheric Research, National Center for Supercomputing Applications, Pittsburgh Supercomputing Center, and San Diego Supercomputing Center); connect to all NSF-designated NAPs; provide for the interconnection of other locations, which may be subsequently specified by NSF; support the development of a national high-performance computing environment (the MetaCenter[3]); support other high-bandwidth applications, such as distributed high-performance computing and isochronous visualization; and promote the development and deployment of advanced routing technologies. Traffic on the vBNS must be in support of research and education.

Regional networks have been a part of NSFNET since NSFNET's inception, and have been a major force in the drive towards ubiquitous network connectivity for the research and education community. The important role that regional networks have played and will continue to play is recognized in this solicitation. Existing and/or realigned regional networks may seek support to provide for interregional connectivity by connecting to NSPs that are connected to NAPs, or by connecting directly to NAPs. Regional Network Providers are also anticipated to: connect regional network client/member organizations; support the general networking needs of clients/members; and provide for the special networking needs of clients/members who have applications that justify high bandwidth. These later functions of regional networks are among the evaluation criteria for Regional Network Provider proposals, but only the interregional connectivity function will be supported under this solicitation.

It is anticipated that this solicitation will result in two or more separate five-year cooperative agreements between NSF and the organizations and/or consortia of organizations chosen as NAP Manager(s), RA, and vBNS Provider. It is also anticipated that this solicitation will result in a number of four-year cooperative agreements with organizations chosen as Regional Network Providers. Combinations of solicited services (such as NAP Manager and vBNS Provider) may be proposed with the exception that the same organization and/or consortium cannot propose to be both the vBNS Provider and the RA. If the same organization or consortium wishes to propose for both the Regional Network Provider Project and for one or more of the other projects, the Regional Network proposal must be submitted separately. Total NSF funding for all awards resulting from this solicitation is expected to be approximately $18,000,000 per year.

This solicitation is issued pursuant to the National Science Foundation Act of 1950, as amended (42 U.S.C. 1861 et seq) and the Federal Cooperative Agreement Act (31 U.S.C. 6305) and is not subject to the Federal Acquisition Regulations.

II. Background

The network of networks known as the Internet includes more than 10,000 IP (Internet Protocol) networks. These networks interconnect more than 1 million computers and millions of users throughout the world. The domestic portion of the Internet contains a number of NSF-supported networks. These include: campus network connections at educational institutions, regional networks, and the NSFNET Backbone Network Services.

Broadly speaking, NSFNET consists of all of these networks, together with a number of other networks at locations such as government laboratories and private corporations, which are connected to regional networks.

The Internet also includes other federally sponsored networks such as the NASA Science Internet (NSI), the DOE ESnet, and the DARPA DARTnet and TWBnet. The multiagency NREN Program includes these networks in addition to the NSFNET. These sponsoring agencies have provided for the interconnection and interoperability of their networks at Federal Information eXchange (FIX) access points.

It is anticipated that networks such as NSI and ESnet will continue to have acceptable use policies, which restrict traffic to that which is in support of the missions of their funding agencies. On the other hand, any traffic that is in support of research and education will be permitted on the VBNS.

Because of the breadth of the charter of the NSFNET, and because of its wide use by the research and education community, it is projected that the NSFNET user base will continue to grow and that its users will continue to require new levels of connectivity and network services. In addition to the anticipated growth in aggregated traffic, new applications such as distributed high-performance computing and isochronous visualization make the provision of increasingly high network performance necessary for the continued success of NSFNET and to achieve the goals of the NREN and the HPCC Programs.

After consulting with many segments of the Internet community, issuing a draft solicitation, and receiving and considering comments on that draft, the National Science Foundation has developed this solicitation for one or more NAP Managers, an RA organization, a vBNS Provider, and Regional Network Providers. In the manner specified below, it is anticipated that NSFNET will: develop increasingly high-performance network services; accommodate the anticipated growth in numbers of users and networks and in network traffic; and transition to a networking infrastructure that is increasingly provided by interconnected network service providers operating in a competitive environment.

III. Network Architecture and Project Requirements

NSF intends to establish a new network architecture for NSFNET in the following manner. A number of NAPs, as specified below, will be established where a vBNS and other appropriate networks will be interconnected. One or more NAP Manager organizations will arrange for and oversee the NAPs. An RA organization will provide routing services such as route servers and route databases for attached networks, and will provide and make available certain routing services in support of the Internet community. Finally, regional networks will continue to provide various services for their client/member organizations and to provide for interregional connectivity through NAPs and/or NSPs that are connected to the NAPs. This section gives more details on this architecture and gives specific project requirements.

A. Network Access Points

Network Access Points (NAPs) are to be proposed, subject to the locations and characteristics described below, by organizations responding to the NAP Manager(s) Project. NAPs are described separately in this section because of their relevance to all projects described in this solicitation.

An Internet NAP is defined as a high-speed network or switch to which a number of networks can be connected via routers for the purpose of traffic exchange and interoperation.[4] A NAP should have capacity adequate to keep up with the switching requirements of the attached networks. The attached networks are presumed to be part of the connected Internet, but the NAP itself may be of a lower protocol level; for example, it may be a level two network or switch.

The NAP will be a conceptual evolution of the FIX and the Commercial Information eXchange (CIX). The FIX is currently built around a level two network, a 100Mbps FDDI ring, with attached Internet networks operating at speeds of up to 45Mbps. Neither the FIXes nor the CIX currently have dedicated route servers with route databases.

Examples of NAP implementation include but are not limited to: a LAN (like the FIXes); a MAN (Metropolitan Area Network) using a service such as Switched Multimegabit Data Service (SMDS); and a high-speed switch such as an ATM switch.

Traffic on NAPs awarded under this solicitation will not be restricted to that which is in support of research and education. This will, for example, permit two attached networks to exchange traffic without violating the use policies of any other networks interconnected at the NAPs. NSF will utilize announcements in the Federal Register and public discussion with the U.S. research and education community and other interested parties to develop policies on traffic and usage at NSF-supported NAPs.

Priority and desirable NAP locations are specified below. NAPs will be established at the priority locations if at all possible. NAPs will be established at one or more of the desirable locations if finances and other circumstances permit. Only general geographic locations are given. Specific locations should be proposed, and NAP attachment policies should promote fair and equitable pricing for and access to NAP attachment.

Priority NAP locations

- California
- Chicago
- New York City

Desirable NAP locations

- Atlanta
- Boston
- Denver
- Texas
- Washington, DC

B. NAP Manager(s) Project

One or more NAP Manager organizations will be selected to arrange for and manage NAPs, which they have proposed. Prospective NAP Managers may utilize different subawardees for different NAPs where appropriate.

The specific anticipated duties of the NAP Manager organization(s) are as follows:

- Establish, operate, and maintain, possibly with subawardees, all or a subset of the specified NAPs for the purpose of interconnecting the vBNS and other appropriate networks. Traffic on NAPs will not be restricted to that which is in support of research and education.

NAPs can be proposed to be implemented as LANs or MANs or other innovative approaches. NAPs must operate at speeds commensurate with the speeds of attached networks and must be upgradable as required by demand, usage, and Program goals. NAPs must support the switching of IP (Internet Protocol) and CLNP (Connectionless Networking Protocol) packets.

- Develop and establish attachment policies (including attachment fee schedules), which would apply to networks that are connected to NAPs.

- Propose NAP locations subject to the given general geographic locations. Propose fair and equitable pricing for NAP attachment as discussed above.

- Propose and establish procedures to work with personnel from other NAP Managers (if any), the RA, the vBNS Provider, and regional and other attached networks to resolve problems and to support end-to-end connectivity and quality of service for network users.

- Specify reliability and security standards for the NAPs and procedures to ensure that these standards are met.

- Specify and provide appropriate NAP accounting and statistics gathering and reporting capabilities.

- Specify appropriate procedures for access to the NAP premises (if any) for authorized personnel of connecting networks and ensure that these procedures are carried out.

C. Routing Arbiter Project

Under the current cooperative agreement, the same consortium that provides the NSFNET Backbone Network Service also acts as routing arbiter. Under the new cooperative agreements described here, the routing arbiter function will be distinct from the vBNS. That is, the same organization and/or consortium cannot propose to be both the vBNS Provider and the RA. The RA will provide for equitable treatment of the various network service providers with regard to routing administration and will provide for a common database of route information to promote stability and manageability of the network.

The RA will provide database management for information such as network topology, policy (routing path preferences), and interconnection information, which can be used by attached networks to build routing table configurations. The RA will make this data publicly accessible, but will not mandate its use by attached networks. In addition, this information will be used to configure attached route servers in support of NSPs and other attached networks. Route servers are to support stable routing of the Internet and to provide for simplified routing information to NSPs and other attached networks. It is expected that route servers will use standard routing protocols, such as BGP (Border Gateway Protocol, RFC 1267) and ISO IDRP (Interdomain Routing Protocol, ISO 10747).

The RA organization will also provide certain other services that will facilitate the logical interconnection of the attached networks. For example, it will assist in the development of new routing technologies and the deployment of simplified routing strategies for attached networks. It will also assist in the development of tools that can be used to configure, manage, and operate network routing systems.

The specific anticipated duties of the RA organization are as follows:

- Promote Internet routing stability and manageability.

- Establish and maintain network topology and policy databases, possibly at each NAP, by means such as exchanging routing information with and dynamically updating routing information from the attached Autonomous Systems using standard interdomain routing protocols such as BGP and IDRP. RA activities must support the network service providers that switch IP (Internet Protocol) and CLNP (Connectionless Networking Protocol) packets.

- Propose and establish procedures to work with personnel from the NAP Manager(s), the vBNS Provider, and regional and other attached networks to resolve problems and to support end-to-end connectivity and quality of service for network users

- Develop advanced routing technologies (such as type of service and precedence routing, multicasting, bandwidth on demand, and bandwidth allocation services) in cooperation with the global Internet community.

- Provide for simplified routing strategies, such as default routing, for attached networks.

- Promote distributed operation and management of the Internet.

D. Very High-Speed Backbone Network Services Provider Project

Since its inception, the NSFNET has been a leader in providing for high-speed networking services for the research and education community. The vBNS will continue this tradition and will provide for: high-speed interconnection of NSF Supercomputing Centers (SCCs); the development of a national high-performance computing environment (the Meta-Center); applications involving distributed high-performance computing and isochronous visualization; and connection to the NSF-specified NAPs. The vBNS connections to the NAPs will, for example, facilitate connecting the SCCs to research institutions that have meritorious high-bandwidth network applications.

The vBNS must be able to switch both IP and CLNP packets, and it must operate initially (at least between SCCs) at speeds of 155Mbps or

higher. Speeds should be achieved directly, not by the provision of multiples of slower-speed services. Speeds higher than 155Mbps are desirable
and may be preferred if finances and other circumstances permit. Additionally, the vBNS Provider must participate in the development and
deployment of advanced Internet routing technologies such as type of
service and precedence routing, multicasting, bandwidth on demand, and
bandwidth allocation services.

The vBNS may have connections and customers beyond those specified
by NSF, provided that the quality and quantity of required services for
NSF-specified customers are not affected. In this regard, the vBNS
Provider must be able to distinguish between NSF customer traffic and
that of other customers, and to gather and report traffic statistics (such as
throughput and delay) based on these categories. It must also be able to
assure proposed service levels for NSF-specified customers.

The specific anticipated duties of the vBNS Provider are as follows:

- Establish and maintain a 155Mbps or higher transit network service,
  which switches IP and CLNP packets and which interconnects NSF
  SCCs (Cornell Theory Center, National Center for Atmospheric
  Research, National Center for Supercomputing Applications, Pittsburgh Supercomputing Center, and San Diego Supercomputing
  Center) and the NSF-specified NAPs (and possibly other specified
  locations in the future).

- Propose and establish a set of quality of service (QoS) metrics which
  will be used to characterize the proposed network services and to
  ascertain and publicize network performance on an ongoing basis.

- Propose and establish a schedule to enhance the speed at which the
  network operates, quality of service measures, and type of service
  offerings in line with NSF's broad program goals and consistent
  with anticipated NSF customer requirements and available funding.

- Propose and establish procedures to work with personnel from the
  NAP Manager(s), the RA, and regional and other attached networks
  to resolve problems and to support end-to-end connectivity and
  quality of service for network users.

- Participate in the development of advanced routing technologies
  (such as type of service and precedence routing, multicasting, bandwidth on demand, and bandwidth allocation services) in cooperation with the RA and with the global Internet community.

- Subscribe to the policies of the NAP Manager(s) and the RA; implement procedures based on standard interdomain routing protocols,

such as BGP and IDRP, to assist in establishing and maintaining the network topology and policy databases.

E. *Regional Networks Project*

Regional networks have been a part of NSFNET since its inception and have been a major force in the drive towards ubiquitous network connectivity for the research and education community. Regional Network Providers connect an increasingly broad base of client/member organizations, provide for interregional connectivity, and provide other networking services for their clients/members. One such networking service may be the provision of special connections for their client/member institutions that have meritorious high-bandwidth network applications.

It is anticipated that regional networks will continue to play these important roles. Existing and/or realigned regional networks are invited to propose how they will meet the interregional connectivity needs of their client/member organizations. Under awards resulting from this solicitation, NSF will support regional networks for the provision of interregional connectivity. They may connect to NSPs, which connect to NAPs, or they may connect to NAPs directly. (If they connect to NAPs directly, they may require additional arrangements with one or more NSPs to provide them with inter-NAP connectivity.)

Under awards resulting from unsolicited proposals and/or from proposals submitted in response to existing and anticipated solicitations and program announcements, NSF may support regional networks for activities such as: providing special connections for client/member institutions that have meritorious high-bandwidth network applications; providing innovative information services to client/member organizations; and providing connection assistance to new client/member institutions of higher learning.

Regional networks may attach to one (or more) NSPs that are connected to NAPs to obtain interregional connectivity. Regional networks may also attach directly to one (or more) NAPs. Under this second approach, some further arrangement (such as procuring inter-NAP connectivity services from an NSP) would be required to obtain full interregional connectivity.

Under this solicitation, regional networks may propose to NSF for support of the fee for either attachment to and use of one NSP or attachment to and use of one NAP. The amount of available funds may limit the number and size of awards that can be made. The amount of each award will in general be related to the number of proposed clients/members that are institutions of higher learning and to the aggregate bandwidth requirements of those clients/members. In each year after the first, NSF support for the NSP fee and/or the NAP fee will decrease and will cease at the end of the regional network cooperative agreement (which shall be no more than four years).

The specific anticipated duties of the Regional Network Providers are listed below. Only the first-listed duty will be supported under awards resulting from proposals submitted in response to this solicitation.

- Provide for interregional connectivity by means such as connecting to NSPs that are connected to NAPs and/or by connecting to NAPs directly and making inter-NAP connectivity arrangements with one or more NSPs.

- Provide for innovative network information services for client/member organizations (in cooperation with the InterNIC, the NSFNET Network Information Services Manager).

- Propose and establish procedures to work with personnel from the NAP Manager(s), the RA, the vBNS Provider, and other regional and other attached networks to resolve problems and to support end-to-end connectivity and quality of service for network users.

- Provide services that promote broadening the base of network users within the research and education communities.

- Provide for, possibly in cooperation with an NSP, high-bandwidth connections for client/member institutions that have meritorious high-bandwidth network applications.

- Provide for network connections to client/member organizations.

F. Other Architectural and Policy Considerations

It is possible that other NAPs beyond those specified by NSF may be established by members of the networking community. The various network service providers called for in this solicitation may at their own discretion and expense utilize the services provided by such NAPs provided that the quality and quantity of required services for NSF-specified customers are not affected. These providers will be neither required by nor supported by NSF to include such NAPs in their interconnectivity tasks unless specifically designated and/or approved by NSF in advance.

It is anticipated that networks other than the vBNS will connect to the NSF-specified NAPs. Examples of such networks include: NSPs, other federally sponsored networks, other network service providers (beyond those connecting regional networks), and international networks.

To qualify for NSF support for NSP attachment and/or for the provision of interNAP connectivity, a regional network must attach to an NSP that connects all NSF-specified priority NAPs. Such NSPs must also be able to assist such attachment-supported regional networks to provide special connections to a NAP for client/member institutions that have meritorious high-bandwidth network applications. Other qualifying networks can connect to one or more NAPs as requirements dictate.

Attachment to one or more NAPs will require the payment of both an initial and an annual fee (which will depend on parameters such as number of NAP connections and bandwidth of each connection). Fees will be proposed by the NAP Manager(s) and approved by NSF.

To attach to a NAP, a network must implement BGP- and IDRP-based procedures to assist in establishing and maintaining the network topology and policy databases maintained by the RA. Networks attaching to NAPs must operate at speeds of 1.5Mbps or greater, and must be able to switch both IP and CLNP packets. The requirements to switch CLNP packets and to implement IDRP-based procedures may, however, be waived by NSF based on the overall level of service to the R&E community, stimulus to the growth of the network and economies of scale, the government's desire to foster the use of ISO OSI protocols and other considerations of the public interest.

Footnotes to Appendix A

[1] NREN is a service mark of the United States government, administered by the National Science Foundation. Organizations receiving awards as a result of this solicitation may be asked to enter into trademark licenses in connection with the use of the NREN service mark.

[2] Public Law 102-194—Dec. 9, 1991. 15 USC 5521 (Section 201).

[3] MetaCenter Networking: A white paper, Lambert et al, 1992.

[4] The interconnection of networks produced by a NAP should be viewed more as an FIX interconnection than as a CNSS (Core Nodal Switching Subsystem) or ENSS (External Nodal Switching Subsystem) interconnection, both of which are components of the current NSFNET Backbone Network Service.

[*] The NSF Grant Policy Manual (NSF 88-47, July 1989) is for sale through the Superintendent of Documents, Government Printing Office, Washington, DC 20402; telephone (202) 783-3288.

Appendix B: Chicago NAP Multilateral Peering Agreement*

Version 3.2
May 1, 1995

I. The Multilateral Peering Agreement

In order to improve the efficiency of routing in the Midwest region of the United States, and improve the general connectivity of the Internet, the following is agreed to:

1. Peering for route exchange at the NAP between all NAP participants. Peering for the purposes of this agreement will be defined as the advertising of routes via BGP4 for customers of the NAP participants. The transit of packets from the Chicago NAP to other meet points is not covered under this agreement. That means:

    A Multilateral Peering Agreement Participating ISP is:

    a) Obligated to advertise all its (participating) customers' routes to all the other MLPA (Multilateral Peering Agreement) participating ISPs and accept routes from the customers' routes advertised by the ISPs;

    b) Obligated to exchange traffic among the customers of all the MLPA participating ISPs;

    c) Entitled to select routing paths among the MLPA participating ISPs; and

    d) Entitled to make Bilateral Peering Agreements with non-MLPA participating ISPs.

    A Multilateral Peering Agreement Participating ISP is NOT:

    a) Obligated to provide transit to other MLPA Participating ISPs; or

    b) Obligated to announce the routes obtained from its Bilateral Peering Agreement partners to the MLPA participating ISPs.

    Participating ISPs agree that route prefixes advertised to each other under this agreement will be of maximum prefix length of 24 bits. Aggregation of routing information will be done where possible and technically feasible.

* This appendix is reprinted with permission of Ameritech.

2. Exchange of routes will be performed using BGP4. Routing policy will conform with RIPE 181 and/or future recommendations of the IETF.

3. All participants agree to use the Routing Registry provided by the Routing Arbiter (RA) via the Routing Arbiter Data Base (RADB).

4. All the participants agree to peer with the RS provided by the RA.

II. Implementation of This Agreement

The Multilateral Peering Agreement could be executed by utilizing the Routing Arbiter provided services: RS (Route Server) at NAPs and Routing Registry.

1. Initial Establishment of Multilateral Peering Agreement

    a. An ISP gains connectivity to the NAP.

    b. The ISP signs this Multilateral Peering Agreement.

    c. The ISP sends a confirmation of consent with the Multilateral Peering Agreement to the NAP provider.

    d. The ISP sends a copy of this Multilateral Peering Agreement along with contact information (administrative and technical contacts) to the RA. A description of the RA services can be found in Attachment 1 to this agreement.

2. Maintenance of the Multilateral Peering Agreement.

    When an ISP withdraws from the Multilateral Peering Agreement, the ISP will need to:

    a. Notify the RA about the changes.

    b. Update the policy in the RADB accordingly so the RA can change the RS configuration to reflect the policy change.

III. The Management of This Agreement

Ameritech Advanced Data Services (AADS) will appoint a NAP coordinator as a common point of contact for all NAP participants. AADS as a subsidiary of Ameritech acts in a nondiscriminatory manner with respect to the NAP customers.

IV. Regulation of This Agreement

1. For the purpose of regulating this agreement, AADS will maintain a list of authorized representatives (both a primary and an alternate) from each NAP participant. The authorized representative will represent the policies of the participating organization at the Chicago NAP meetings.

2. An annual meeting of NAP participants will be held to discuss NAP policies and exchange technical information.

3. Special meetings may be held at any time upon request by a majority of NAP participants' authorized representatives. All requests for special meetings will be arbitrated via e-mail exchange with the AADS NAP coordinator.

4. Changes in this agreement shall be made through a majority vote of the NAP participants at annual or special meetings.

5. No monetary settlements are required by this agreement.

6. Participation in this agreement is voluntary. This agreement is non-binding, and is implemented by each party on a best-effort basis.

7. Any party has the right to withdraw at any time. Thirty days notice of such withdrawal shall be given, in writing, to the NAP Coordinator.

8. This agreement does not obligate the RA to perform the services mentioned in Attachment 1.

V. Commitment to Free Exchange of Information

The NAP shall be treated as a common carrier point. All traffic passing across the NAP between peers shall not be filtered or tampered with, nor shall it be examined for content.

Attachment 1: Routing Arbiter Services

Upon receiving a signed MLPA agreement and contact information, the RA will do the following:

- Contact the ISP to help them register necessary information, such as customer routes, routing policy, and router information in the RA-provided Routing Registry.

- Notify current MLPA members of the new member.
- Update participating MLPA members policies as registered in the RADB to allow them to automatically receive routes from the new ISP.

(An ISP is given the option of having RA perform default MLPA policy update in RADB or managing its own policy update in RADB. The choice should be made known to the RA when entering the MLPA.)

- Configure the RS to pass routing information between the newly joined ISP and other MLPA participating ISPs based on the updated policy registered in the Routing Registry to enable traffic exchange.

Evolving Internet Requirements

CHAPTER 4

The Need for QoS-Based Communications

This chapter describes the general need for QoS-based communications, with an emphasis on multimedia. The discussion is general and has an enterprise-network point of reference, but because many corporate networks use the Internet in some fashion, this translates ultimately into a requirement on the Internet itself. Chapter 5 examines the Internet more specifically, in terms of QoS-enabled data communication requirements. The services and protocols capabilities to deliver QoS in one fashion or another are described in Part 3 of this book. Networking planners need to be aware of the available tools, and inquire whether their ISP supports these advanced technologies.

4.1 Background

Significant gains in automation and productivity have been seen in North America in the past decade. These gains have been made possible by the plethora of application software that has emerged. The near-ubiquitous penetration of "standardized" PC operating systems, such as Microsoft Windows on the client side and Windows NT and Unix on the server side, friendly graphical user interfaces (GUIs), along with Network GUIs (specifically, web browsers), and the Transmission Control Protocol/ Internet Protocol (TCP/IP) apparatus, have made this software and productivity revolution possible.

The 1990s saw widespread introduction of client/server and web-based systems in the corporate environment. In the enterprise network supporting these informatics applications, there has been the deployment of new LAN technologies, such as switched and/or 100Mbps Ethernet, and of new WAN technologies, such as frame relay services and, increasingly, ATM. The TCP/IP suite of protocols has been the glue that has made end-to-end multinetwork connectivity possible.

As we move forward, a gamut of new applications are evolving, which also need to be deployed in order to reach the next plateau in business support tools and ensuing productivity gains. Multimedia, desktop videoconferencing, voice-over-data networks, and computer telephony integration, to list a few, from both an intranet and Internet perspective, are expected to play an increasingly important role in the corporate landscape during the next 10 years.

These applications, as well as more traditional but mission-critical applications, require networks that support quality of service (QoS). QoS includes guaranteed bandwidth on demand (minimum, average, and peak), as well as predictable (small) end-to-end delay, delay variation, and unit (block, cell, frame) loss. QoS-enabled networks are needed not only for time-sensitive applications, such as voice and video, but also to support data applications which, as networks become more congested and more integrated (both at the corporate and Internet levels), must receive a guaranteed level of performance.

Significant work is underway to address QoS in data networks. These include Asynchronous Transfer Mode (ATM) User-to Network Interface (UNI) 4.0, IPv6, Resource Reservation Protocol (RSVP), Integrated Services Architecture (ISA), Real-time Transport Protocol (RTP), and network layer switching. At the same time, existing services such as frame relay may or may not be upgraded to support QoS, which could turn out to be a problem.

Currently, router vendors such as Cisco Systems are starting to build products to support QoS, to do integrated voice/data/video networking at the branch level, as well as over the intranet and Internet. Leading-edge vendors are including RSVP capabilities in their routers. They are also modifying their routers to accommodate better buffer management to deliver predictable QoS in a standard IP environment. Of course, ATM's claim to fame is QoS support—but is that the wave of the future?

The topic of QoS-enabled communication is beginning to receive attention in the industry at large. QoS in the Internet is a very timely topic.

Consultants are now covering this topic at conferences on next-generation networks and in the press.

4.2 Evolving Time-Sensitive Applications

The need for QoS is driven by three factors, at this time:

1. Support of voice-over-*packet-networks* (intranets and Internet) with ensuing statistical gains and lower cost. There has been an interest going back at least to the mid-1970s (if not earlier) to utilize integrated networks that support all of the organization's media, because of the efficiencies in transport and management that would result [1–4].

2. Support of desktop video over the enterprise network and the Internet. Newly developed standards such as ITU-T H.263/H.323 are expected to see penetration in corporate LANs in the next couple of years.

3. Support of priority-based data applications over the intranet and Internet.

At the technology level, networks have shifted in two directions, in comparison with, for example, a decade ago (late 1980s):

- There is a movement away from time division multiplexing (TDM) transmission facilities of fixed bandwidth, particularly when focusing at the whole (nationwide) network (rather than just the access tail, which continues to be based on traditional telephony facilities, such as DS1 or DS3 lines).

- There is a movement away from dedicated point-to-point lines, which become impractical as the number of interconnected sites increases, and toward the use of packet technology (whether at the network layer in the form of IP-routed systems or at the data link layer, such as frame relay and ATM).

These two trends have both benefits and drawbacks. In general, the benefits have weighted on the side of economics and scalability; the drawbacks have weighted on the side of performance and QoS.

As just implied, many Fortune 500 companies now use packet network services (e.g., frame relay, ATM, IP) for corporate data, intranet, and electronic commerce applications. Hence, there is interest in addressing the question of services and media integration. Integration has found reasonable effectiveness in the frame relay context for the support of small office/home office (SOHO) locations. In the end, an integrated network has a great deal of appeal for transmission efficiencies and technology/ network management reasons (e.g., see Figure 4.1). The goal is, therefore, to achieve integration and at the same time to support QoS.

There have been successful as well as unsuccessful attempts to address the integration/QoS issue over the years (see Table 4.1). Efforts in the Integrated Services Digital Network (ISDN) and ATM have also been aimed at voice support in general and multimedia in particular. Efforts on the data side have included support of voice in local area networks (such as IEEE 802.9 and FDDI II, and now 802.1p and 802.1q), enhancements to routers, IP (e.g., IPv6 and RSVP), and network-layer handling of packets such as MultiProtocol Label switching (MPLS), Multiprotocols over ATM (MPOA), and Tag Switching/NetFlows.

The QoS issue has to be addressed both at an end-to-end level—that is, on a LAN-WAN (Internet)-LAN basis—as well as at multiple layers of the communication protocol suite (specifically, data-link layer and network layer). Under the end-to-end view, one has to look at the various LAN technologies and understand their QoS support; then, one has to do the same for the WAN technologies. On the protocol layer view, one could look at the problem as being addressed end to end, regardless of the underlying subnetworks, *if* the QoS reservation protocol is end to end (endsystem-to-endsystem) and if every element at the layer under discussion (e.g., routers, if one is looking at the IP/RSVP level) supports the QoS fulfillment mechanism. When considering the discrete subnetworks, LAN technologies tend to have the issue of QoS driven by protocol considerations (e.g., contention) rather than by bandwidth (and hence, cost) issues. For WANs, this is exactly the opposite: The QoS support in protocols may exist, but the bandwidth is expensive, so the QoS fulfillment has to be done in a cost-effective manner. For this reason, this book looks at the problem from a WAN technology point of view and makes the assumption that the higher-layer protocol can handle the end-to-end delivery of QoS.

ATM is mentioned throughout this book because it is a QoS-based technology in its own right at the LAN—and even more so at the WAN—level; it can be used to support frame relay services; it can be used to support classical IP applications; it can be used to support RSVP; it can be used to support newer Layer 3 services, such as Tag Switching and IP switching; and it can be used intrinsically to the network (invisible to the end user, just to secure statistical gains). Hence, it will play an important role in the coming years. However, its mention should not be construed as an endorsement or preference as the technology of choice. This book aims to take as "clinical" a stance toward the various technologies, stand-alone or in combination, as possible.

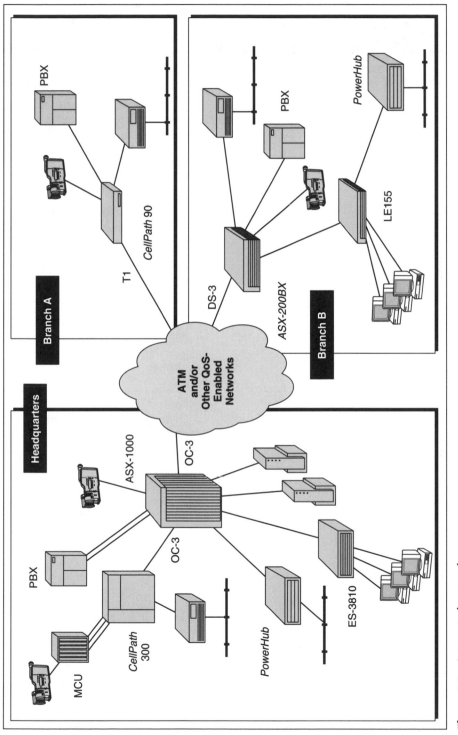

Figure 4.1 Integrated network.

Table 4.1   Support of QoS on Existing, Evolving, or Obsolete Technologies

TECHNOLOGY	TYPE	INTEGRATION SUPPORT	QoS SUPPORT	SUCCESS
Packet	STDM, WAN	Yes	Unlikely; depends on packet switch	Limited deployment now
ISDN Packet on B	TDM/STDM, WAN	Yes	Unlikely; depends on packet switch	No deployment
ISDN Packet on D	TDM/STDM, WAN	Yes	Unlikely; depends on packet switch	No deployment
ISDN 2B+D/ 23B+D/H0/H11	TDM, WAN	Yes	Yes, but fixed bandwidth	Limited deployment for integration purposes; mostly for Internet access
Frame relay on ISDN	STDM, WAN	Possible	Limited: via engineering; no intrinsic support	No deployment
Frame relay	STDM, WAN	Possible	Limited: via engineering; no intrinsic support (FRF.13 provides SLA definition)	Wide-scale deployment
ATM WAN	STDM, WAN	Yes	Yes	Medium deployment
ATM LAN	STDM, LAN	Yes	Yes	Very limited deployment
IEEE 802.9	TDM-like in circuit channel; LAN	Yes	Yes, but fixed 64Kbps channels	No deployment
FDDI II	TDM-like in circuit channel; LAN	Yes	Yes, but fixed channels	No deployment
IEEE 802.1p and 802.1q	STDM, LAN	Yes	Yes	No deployment at this time

Table 4.1 *(Continued)*

TECHNOLOGY	TYPE	INTEGRATION SUPPORT	QoS SUPPORT	SUCCESS
Ethernet (shared)	STDM, LAN	Yes with some effort	Minimal	Ubiquitous
Ethernet (switched)	STDM, LAN	Yes	Some, based on reduced congestion	Ubiquitous
100Mbps Ethernet (shared/ switched)	STDM, LAN	Yes	Some, based on reduced congestion	Prevalent
IP	STDM, LAN/WAN	Yes	Limited; perhaps "gigarouters" have more punch and can lower delay and delay variation compared to existing routers	Ubiquitous
IPv6	STDM, LAN/WAN	Yes	Possible to some degree if vendors implement feature	Not yet deployed
RSVP with IP	STDM, LAN/WAN	Yes	Yes, but it is only a reservation mechanism; IP and (perhaps) ATM needed	Only now being deployed
RTP	STDM, LAN/WAN	Yes	Yes	Limited deployment
Network Layer Switching (flavors)	STDM, LAN/WAN	Yes	Some, based on the fact that a more efficient treatment of IP is possible	Limited deployment

4.2.1 **Voice-over-Data Networks**

In recent years, voice-over-packet-network applications, including over the Internet, have continued to see penetration. Equipment supporting voice, specifically voice-enabled frame relay access devices (FRADs), is now available from dozens of vendors; and voice-over-frame-relay technology is seeing commercial introduction. The Frame Relay Forum (FRF) recently approved a specification to enable multivendor interoperability for on-net voice support; connectivity to the public switched telephone network (PSTN), however, remains a future goal, at least at the practical service level. Still, effective support of quality voice depends on network-level QoS. The new FRF.13 specifies the language for at least describing, if not delivering, Service Level Agreements (SLAs).

Similarly, the ATM Forum has approved a set of specifications for Voice Telephony over ATM (VTOA); again there is the technical possibility for interconnection with the PSTN, but in general it also remains a future service. ATM supports QoS, but compared to voice-over-frame-relay, the economics of voice-over ATM are not yet as favorable—unless an organization already has an ATM-based enterprise network that uses ATM via edge multiplexers, and is interested only in on-net voice. Off-net voice connectivity over an ATM network is just now being made available as individual case basis (ICB) applications by some forward-looking carriers. In ATM, ATM adaptation layers (AALs) provide both legacy support and various services to the applications riding above. Well-known AALs include AAL 1, AAL 5, and a newly developed AAL 2. Voice-over-ATM can be accomplished using AAL 1, using constant bit rate (CBR)/circuit emulation service (CES) or AAL 2, using variable bit rate (VBR) services; some use of AAL 5 was also made in the past.

The ATM Forum started work on voice transport in the early 1990s, and it was not until the mid-1990s that the VTOA working group published its first document, which contained the unstructured CES and structured CES specs. Unstructured circuit emulation maps an entire T1 (1.544Mbps) circuit to a single ATM virtual circuit, thus limiting it to point-to-point applications. Structured circuit emulation allows switches to map individual 64Kbps circuits in a T1 line to ATM VCs, and it can be used for point-to-multipoint connections. Each requires voice to be treated as CBR traffic. A problem is that CBR traffic forces customers to reserve bandwidth for voice even when they are not actually sending it.

Sending voice as VBR traffic is the obvious alternative. Silence suppression and voice compression will be a part of a new specification that would provide greater use of bandwidth. AAL 2 is a proposal in ITU-T Study Group 13; although AAL 2 defines VBR service for low bit rate voice traffic between a wireless base station and mobile switch center, it could be parlayed into a new voice standard. VTOA work is focused in two areas: VTOA trunking for narrowband services, targeted primarily at applications in private voice networks, and VTOA legacy voice services at a native ATM terminal, targeted at applications in private and public networks, where interworking and interoperation of ATM and non-ATM networks and services for voice is necessary (see the following sidebar). In either case, the use of ATM QoS features is paramount.

Indeed, with the recent adoption of the Frame Relay Forum FRF.11 and the ATM Forum VTOA standards for voice-over-frame-relay and ATM, respectively, it is likely that increased deployment of voice-over data-link-layer protocols will take place in enterprise networks, including WAN extensions. QoS questions have to be addressed. By contrast, some see voice-over-the-Internet as being nearly free, and would like to take advantage of this apparent bonanza without having to worry about owning their own WANs. Another advantage would be the ability to support off-net voice applications. However, the cost of the Internet, particularly for guaranteed QoS, is going to continue to increase, so that the economics will be changing in the next two to three years. Also, the ultimate benefits may be more due to voice compression at the source than from the transport vehicle itself (namely, the Internet).

QoS plays a crucial role in support of voice-over-data-networks. Table 4.2 depicts some of the key requirements for the support of voice, which any new alternative architecture is expected to accommodate. On frame relay and/or IP networks, capabilities are needed to transform best-effort communications into functionality that can support both streaming voice as well as bursty data traffic. QoS-enabled communication is being addressed through a number of technologies, such as RSVP, Tag Switching, and MPLS. Efforts aimed at deciding which ATM QoS class is better for voice are underway, as noted. Originally, ATM was designed to support CBR and VBR traffic types, with user-to-network traffic contracts. More recently, the computer industry has requested that best-effort services, such as Available Bit Rate (ABR) and Unspecified Bit Rate (UBR) be added (currently only a few switches/carriers support ABR).

Note that the applications, standards, maturity, and economics for voice-over-ATM, voice-over-frame-relay, and voice-over-IP are all differ-

RECENT WORK IN VOICE-OVER ATM WITH QoS SUPPORT

- **Circuit Emulation Service (CES) Interoperability Specification. This service has a CES and a Dynamic Bandwidth CES version. Features are as follows:**

CES

Constant bit rate (64Kbps) service.

Structured service for fractional applications (FT1/FE1).

Unstructured service for DS1/E1/DS3.

Options for carrying channel associated signaling (CAS).

Configured bandwidth used whether there is traffic or not.

ATM overhead makes this more costly than TDM solutions.

Dynamic Bandwidth CES

CES Structured Service models FT1/FE1.

Bandwidth allocated dynamically based on active channel indication.

Uses CAS or common channel signaling (e.g., ISDN's D channel).

Requires the user to allocate bandwidth for the maximum number of channels.

- **Trunking for Narrowband Services. This specification is based on the use of an interworking function (IWF) between the ATM network and each interconnected narrowband network. This includes a Land Line I, a Land Line II, and a Mobile Trunking specification.**

Land Line I

Targets ISDN trunking over an ATM network.

Call-by-call routing to make effective use of bandwidth.

---

ent. Developers hope that voice-over-enterprise-networks (IP/RSVP-based) will be possible. Routers are also being redesigned to support QoS-based policies; specifically, disciplined queue control (e.g., Cisco's Weighted Fair Queuing).

As a bottom line, for this technology to be successful and for voice applications to experience widespread deployment in corporate enterprise environments, QoS-enabled networks will have to be deployed.

The reader may refer to Dan Minoli's book set: *Delivering Voice over IP Networks* and *Delivering Voice over Frame Relay and ATM* (John Wiley & Sons, Inc., 1998), for more extensive treatment of the voice-over-data-networks topic.

Dynamic bandwidth, by allowing VCC setup in response to call 64Kbps channels.

No silence suppression.

Land Line II

Targets access and private trunking applications.

Call-by-call routing to make effective use of bandwidth.

Uses new AAL 2 to multiplex multiple channels in a cell.

Supports compressed voice and silence suppression.

Supports switched calls to outgoing trunks.

Supports fax.

Mobile Trunking

Targets cellular networks.

Supports transport between the base station and the mobile service central office.

Efficiently transports voice that is already compressed by mobile handset.

Uses AAL 2 to multiplex multiple channels into a cell.

- Voice and Telephony over ATM to the Desktop Specification. This document specifies the functions required to provide voice and telephony services over ATM to the desktop. It describes the functions of the interworking function (IWF) and a native ATM terminal. This version covers only the transport of a single 64Kbps A-law or mu-law encoded voiceband signal.

4.2.2 Video and Multimedia Applications

Observers[1] make the claim that new software and hardware are changing the way people work in the corporation. At the basis of this claim is the introduction of video technology in a variety of enterprise settings. Video takes the form of PC-based conferencing, multimedia, video-server-based computer-based training, reception of digitized broadcast video on a PC window, and imaging-based document management/workflow systems. The field of desktop video communications (DVC) is emerging. Indeed, there are indications that corporate America is going to capitalize on the

Table 4.2 Basic Voice Feature Requirements for Voice-over Data Applications

FEATURE	DESCRIPTION	REQUIREMENT IN ATM	REQUIREMENT IN IP NET	REQUIREMENT IN FRAME RELAY
Compression	Sub-PCM compression significantly reduces the amount of bandwidth used by a voice conversation, while maintaining high quality.	Nice to have	Must have	Must have
Silence suppression	The ability to recover bandwidth during periods of silence in a conversation makes that bandwidth available for other users of the network.	Nice to have	Must have	Must have
QoS	Assuring priority for voice transmission is critical. This keeps delay, delay variation, and loss to a tolerable minimum.	Must have. ATM has been developed with significant QoS/traffic management support.	Must have. Very little current support (Type Of Service/TOS not generally implemented in routers). There is a hope that the Resource Reservation Protocol (RSVP), which reserves resources across the network, will help. However, RSVP is only a protocol; intrinsic network bandwidth must be provided before a reservation can be made.	Must have. Frame relay does not explicitly support priority-based QoS. Recent development is attempting to address this limitation.

FEATURE	DESCRIPTION	REQUIREMENT IN ATM	REQUIREMENT IN IP NET	REQUIREMENT IN FRAME RELAY
Signaling for voice traffic	Support of traditional PBXs and the associated signaling is critical.	Must have for real applications.	Must have for real applications.	Must have for real applications.
Echo Control	Echo is annoying and disruptive; control is key.	Must have for real applications.	Must have for real applications.	Must have for real applications.
Voice switching	Data network equipment can generally support on-net applications. Off-net is also critical. At the very least, the adjunct equipment must decide whether to route a call over the internal data network, or to route it to the Public Switched Telephone Network.	Ability to route off-net is a must for real applications.	Ability to route off-net is a must for real applications.	Ability to route off-net is a must for real applications.

video-bred culture of its workforce to assault global competition. One of the by-products of the implementation of the General Agreements on Tariffs and Trade (GATT) will be a more aggressive use of advanced technologies in the office and on the manufacturing floor within a span of a few years. Again, QoS will play a crucial role in making multimedia technology ubiquitous.

Corporate video includes disciplines such as videoconferencing, video telephony, simulations, information access, instruction, synthetic video, two- and three-dimensional CAD/CAM, visualization, video windowing, and video editing, among others. Vendors such as First Virtual Corporation, Lucent, PictureTel, Bay Networks, and Microsoft had products at the time of this writing, with many other companies getting into the field (see Table 4.3). Figure 4.2 shows a recent survey depicting features being considered for DVC systems [5].

Table 4.3   Examples of DVC Products and Players

COMPANY	TYPE	NAME	TYPE OF CONNECTION
8×8, Inc.	Codec chip Camera	VCP ImpressionCam	10 Mbps Ethernet 10 Mbps Ethernet
Accord Video Telecommn's	Video terminal MCU		10 Mbps Ethernet 10 Mbps Ethernet
Connectix	Camera	Quickcam	10 Mbps Ethernet
Digital Semicon	Video Terminal Video Terminal		10 Mbps Ethernet 25 Mbps ATM
First Virtual Corp.	Video terminal	PictureTel PCS 50	25 Mbps ATM/ISDN
Kenwood USA	PCMCIA Card	Conference Card	10 Mbps Ethernet
Lucent Tech.	Gateway	RADVision L2W-323	10 Mbps Ethernet
Microsoft	Conferencing software	NetMeeting	Internet
PictureTel	Video terminal Gateway	LiveLAN PicTel Live Gateway	10 Mbps Ethernet 10 Mbps Ethernet
RADVision, Inc.	Gateway		10 Mbps Ethernet
VCON, Inc.	Video terminal	Armada Cruiser	10 Mbps Ethernet
VDOnet Corp.			10 Mbps Ethernet
RVideoserver	MCU Gateway	H.323 H.323	10 Mbps Ethernet 10 Mbps Ethernet/ISDN
Vista Imaging	Digital Camera	ViCam	10 Mbps Ethernet
Zydacron, Inc.	Video terminal	Z250	10 Mbps Ethernet/ISDN

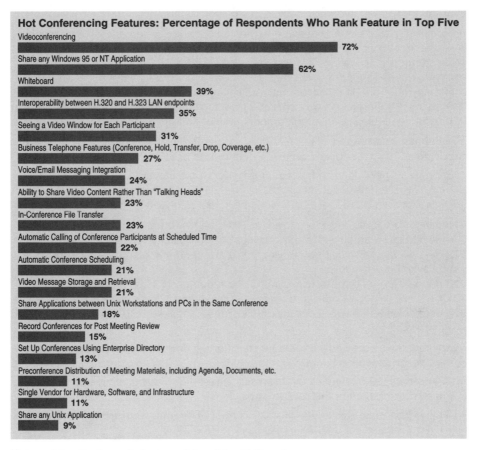

Figure 4.2 Features being considered for DVC systems.

Appropriate local area, campus, wide area, and international communication infrastructures will be needed to support this move to digital video and other broadband applications, including QoS support. Video streams have markedly different requirements compared with traditional data flows, which supported applications such as e-mail, word processing, and financial analysis.

During the late 1990s, a battery of new standards were approved by the ITU-T for LAN-, intranet-, and Internet-based multimedia, which promise to enable interworking among products and lower prices. The key new umbrella standard is H.323. See Table 4.4 [6] and Figure 4.3. Once standards are widely supported, a technology may see rapid introduction. Industry forecasts predict more than 6 million DVC shipments worldwide by 2001 in the business market and 14 million shipments in the residential market (see Figure 4.4 [7]).

Table 4.4   Evolving LAN-Based Interoperability Standards for Multimedia

H.323 is an umbrella standard that provides the framework for voice, video and data transport over non-guaranteed quality of service packet switched networks, including the Internet. It can provide the means to do the following:
- Interoperate with systems supporting H.320, via a gateway.
- Operate over many different bit rates and network configurations.
- Control the amount of traffic present on a LAN and provide address translations, via a gatekeeper.
- Provide multipoint conferencing via a multipoint controller and processor.

Video ■ H.261 defines the transport of voice and video over P×64 kbps channels. QCIF defines a picture size of 176 × 144 pixels while CIF defines one of 352 × 288.

■ H.263 defines a new video codec (coder-decoder) for use over POTS by the H.324 standard. This is a new codec that is based on H.261 but includes many new features not available when H.261 was first developed. It can also work at higher bit rates.

Audio ■ G.711 defines an audio codec occupying a 3-kHz bandwidth requiring bit rates of 48, 56, or 64 kbps to reproduce. This is equivalent to "toll quality" audio.

■ G.722 defines an audio codec occupying 7 kHz and requiring 48, 56, or 64 kbps to reproduce "toll quality" voice.

■ G.728 defines an audio codec occupying 3 kHz requiring 16 kbps to reproduce.

■ G.723.1 defines an audio codec occupying 3 kHz requiring 5.3 and 6.3 kbps to reproduce.

■ G.729 defines an audio codec occupying 3 kHz requiring 8 kbps to reproduce "near-toll quality" voice.

Data T.120 is the universally accepted standard for transporting data. It, too, is an umbrella standard encompassing many other standards.

Multiplex and Signaling H.225.0 defines the messages needed for call signaling and packetization and synchronization of the data streams.

Control H.245 defines the messages needed for the control of opening and closing the channels and other control requests and commands.

	H.320	H.324	H.323
Network	N-ISDN	PSTN	Packet-Switched
Video	H.261 QCIF (M) H.261 CIF	H.261 QCIF (M) H.263 (M)	H.261 QCIF (M) H.261 CIF H.263
Audio	G.711 (M) G.722 G.728	G.723.1 (M) G.729	G.711 (M) G.722 G.728 G.723.1 G.729
Data	T.120	T.120	T.120
Multiplex	H.221 (M)	H.223 (M)	H.225.0 (M)
Control	H.242 (M)	H.245 (M)	H.245 (M)
Signaling	Q.931		H.225.0 (Q.931)

N-ISDN = Narrowband ISDN.
PSTN = Public Switched Telephone Network (POTS).
M = Mandatory.

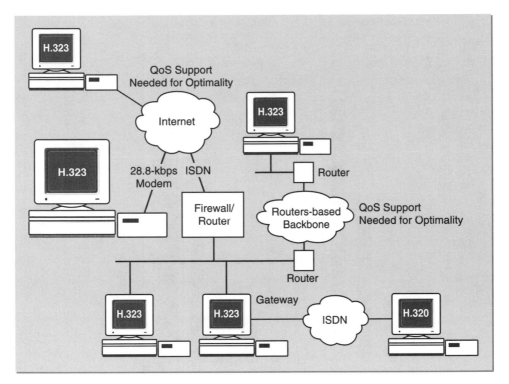

Figure 4.3 Key new umbrella standard, H.323.

Video has two important characteristics that impact the type of transmission technology that can be employed for its delivery [8–22]:

- Packetized video must be delivered with low and predictable end-to-end delay. Additionally, the delay variation must be small. Usually, one cannot use store-and-forward methods except for nonreal-time video, unless the network is well tuned, the data rate is very small (e.g., 2 × 64Kbps in H.261), or the network supports QoS. Traditional protocols, not to say routers, do not have the ultimate performance capabilities for supporting hundreds of simultaneous corporate users using the enterprise backbone or LAN.

- Simple digitization of a video signal can yield from 140Mbps for traditional full-motion NTSC (National Television Standards Committee) video, to 1Gbps for HDTV. Newly developed digital compression algorithms and supporting hardware reduce these values by about 100-fold or better.

Compression is an economical method for storage and transmission of video in limited-bandwidth environments, including an organization's

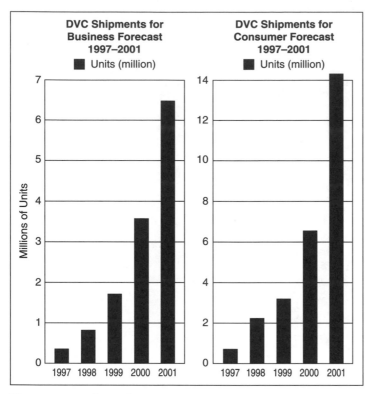

Figure 4.4   Industry forecasts.

enterprise network. Compression methods include Motion Joint Photographic Expert Group (JPEG), Motion Picture Experts Group (MPEG) schemes (Versions 1, 2, and 4), Digital Video Interactive (DVI), and wavelets, to list just a few [8]. However, the data rate is still fairly high, as follows:

- Desktop videoconferencing applications using H.320/H.261/H.263 ITU-T standards produce from 128Kbps to 768Kbps per user.

- Multimedia applications, using, for example, Intel's Indeo methods, produce about 1.5Mbps per user.

- Entertainment video and distance learning applications using MPEG-1/MPEG-2 standards produce 1.5Mbps or 6Mbps, respectively, per user.

Although it must be noted that the H.320/H.323 standards make video on LANs possible at the technology and interoperability levels, as soon as more than a few users fire up conferences (particularly multipoint conferences/multicasts), the network and the quality of the conference may be severely impacted. QoS-enabled networks at the LAN/WAN level will be necessary, from a jitter/delay point of view; from a capacity point of view, broadband in the corporate internet will be needed. After all, if the H.261 stream is 128Kbps (the low end), then only a handful of users can be supported over a T1-based router-to-router link.

This brief discussion should make it clear that traditional *shared* Ethernet operating at 10Mbps and over a traditional router-based network of low bandwidth is marginally adequate for the support of video in the corporation. Studies indicate that unless the video quality on PCs approaches the quality to which users are accustomed on their TV sets or VCRs, the deployment of video in the organization will be negatively impacted. This baseline requirement leads to the realization that one needs signal bandwidth of 1.5 to 6Mbps *per user* for some business applications (lower resolution will be acceptable for other applications). A traditional Ethernet would then be able to support only one to four users per segment. An increasing number of vendors and users have taken the approach of microsegmenting existing Ethernets to support a single user per segment, and then using Ethernet switches to achieve the desired connectivity. Although these switches are fairly inexpensive (e.g., $500 per port or less) and are readily available from dozens of vendors, an enterprisewide video architecture based on such approach can be somewhat limiting. Another approach developers are taking to address the problem is 100Mbps Ethernet: 100Mbps could support from 15 to 60 video users at 6Mbps or 1.5Mbps, respectively, unless one used switched Ethernet. A high-speed switch would still be required to support segment-to-segment or segment-to-server connectivity. By contrast, ATM *dedicates* appropriate bandwidth resources to *each* user as a matter of course, up to the maximum allowed by the switch's backplane (or line card bus). These observations relate to the campus/building network. This is not to imply that ATM to the desktop is superior to other technologies, such as 100Mbps Ethernet, only that bandwidth and QoS (e.g., frame delay, frame delay variation, frame loss) must be accounted for.

The issue is more obvious in the WAN: A 100Mbps Ethernet infrastructure in two buildings with an interbuilding router backbone operating at T1 rates will be completely limited by the bottleneck in bandwidth.

Packetized digital and video is entering not only the corporate world, but the entire broadcasting business, both over the air and over cable [8]. These advances have been called "broadcasting's third revolution; the first were radio, then television" [23]. Realizing the impact that the first two events had, one can appreciate the implied impact of the third. Today, advanced TV (ATV) units not only can carry a mix of video, audio, and data services, but they also provide the mechanism for adding new services in the future without obsoleting receivers already in the field. For example, during a commercial, a browseable brochure can also be downloaded in the "data channel," which can be consulted via a PC to obtain information such as product specifications, available options, dealers, and more.

The broadcast industry is seeing the decline of the analog videotape as the medium for storing video. Videographic designers have been using disks for some time as their primary medium, with videotape reserved for output and occasional input; the trend is now expected to permeate the industry. Vendors of video servers are now highlighting the advantages of tapeless production and tapeless distribution, including "digital ad insertion." Disk-based storage of video is convenient not only because it is digital and random-accessible, but because the information can be transmitted over an (internal) backbone data network for workflow purposes. Digital technology is making it possible to include more functions into video-editing systems now reaching the market; these very new systems are available at prices that were unthought of five years ago [24].

Uncompressed digital editing has been used during the past few years; but with the introduction of compressed video, the need has arisen to also deal with these newer formats. The 6Mbps data rate makes it easier to store, download, process, distribute, and archive this material. Video compression is entering the teleproduction industry very rapidly. Soon, similar teleproduction techniques will enter the mainstream corporation, whether in the public relations department, the training department, or the library, or on the production floor or the departmentalized server. Applications include disk-based nonlinear editors, video file servers, and on-air automated playback systems. Improvements in compression technology create a dynamic environment of innovation as to how a company does business. MPEG encoders can now be found for desktop applications, ranging from as little as $700 to $150,000 (high-end real-time systems); many were around $5,000 at the time of this writing. We are in a transition era during which disk-based compression systems are replacing videotape; the use of nonlinear editors to produce video products continues to increase [25]. The data rates for these applications range from 50Mbps to 3Mbps, which relate to compression rates ranging from 4.5:1 to 72:1 (note that a two-hour feature film requires about 5GB).

In this context it is also worth mentioning Digital Video Disc (DVD) technology, which is now entering the market. DVDs may be used in servers or jukeboxes, and may serve corporate video applications such as training; probably these servers will be networked.

DVD is the next generation of optical disc storage technology. It is essentially a bigger, faster CD that can hold video as well as audio and computer data. DVD aims to encompass home entertainment, computers, and business information with a single digital format, eventually replacing audio CD, videotape, laserdisc, CD-ROM, and perhaps even video game cartridges. DVD has widespread support from all major electronics companies, all major computer hardware companies, and most major movie and music studios, which is unprecedented and says much for its chances of success [26].

It is important to understand the difference between DVD-video and DVD-ROM. DVD-video (also often simply called DVD) holds video programs and is played in a DVD player hooked up to a TV. DVD-ROM holds computer data and is read by a DVD-ROM drive hooked up to a computer. The difference is similar to that between audio CD and CD-ROM. DVD-ROM also includes future variations that are recordable one time (DVD-R) or many times (DVD-RAM). Most people expect DVD-ROM to initially be much more successful than DVD-video. DVD-video features are described in the following sidebar.

DVD FEATURES

- More than two hours of high-quality digital video.
- Support for wide-screen movies and regular or wide-screen TVs (16:9 and 4:3 aspect ratios).
- Up to eight tracks of digital audio (for multiple languages), each with up to eight surround channels.
- Up to 32 subtitle/karaoke tracks.
- Automatic "seamless" branching of video (for multiple story lines or ratings on one disc).
- Up to nine camera angles (different viewpoints can be selected during playback).
- Menus and simple interactive features (for games, quizzes, etc.).
- "Instant" rewind and fast forward, including search to title, chapter, or track.
- Durability (no wear from playing, only from physical damage).
- Not susceptible to magnetic fields. Resistant to heat.
- Compact size (easy to handle and store; players can be portable).

DVD has the capability to produce near-studio-quality video and better-than-CD-quality audio. DVD is vastly superior to videotape, and can be better than laserdisc. However, quality depends on many production factors. Until compression knowledge and technology improve, we may often see DVDs that are inferior to laserdiscs. Also, since large amounts of video have already been encoded for VideoCD using MPEG-1, some early DVDs will use that format (which is no better than VHS) instead of higher-quality MPEG-2. DVD video is compressed from studio ITU-R 601 format to MPEG-2 format. This is a "lossy" compression, which removes redundant information (such as sections of the picture that do not change) and information that is not readily perceptible by the human eye. The resulting video, especially when it is complex or changes quickly, may sometimes contain "artifacts" such as blockiness or fuzziness. It depends entirely on the quality of compression and how heavily the video is compressed. At average rates of 3.5Mbps, artifacts may be occasionally noticeable. Higher data rates result in higher quality, with almost no perceptible difference from the original master at rates above 6Mbps. As MPEG compression technology improves, better quality will be achieved at lower rates [26].

Capacities of DVD-ROM and DVD-video are as follows (for reference, a CD-ROM holds about 0.64GB; in the following list, SS/DS means single-/double-sided, and SL/DL means single-/dual-layer):

- DVD-5 (12cm, SS/SL): 4.38GB (4.7G) of data, over 2 hours of video
- DVD-9 (12cm, SS/DL): 7.95GB (8.5G), about 4 hours
- DVD-10 (12cm, DS/SL): 8.75GB (9.4G), about 4.5 hours
- DVD-18 (12cm, DS/DL): 15.90GB (17G), over 8 hours
- DVD-1? (8cm, SS/SL): 1.36GB (1.4G), about half an hour
- DVD-2? (8cm, SS/DL): 2.48GB (2.7G), about 1.3 hours
- DVD-3? (8cm, DS/SL): 2.72GB (2.9G), about 1.4 hours
- DVD-4? (8cm, DS/DL): 4.95GB (5.3G), about 2.5 hours

DVD is primarily the work of Toshiba, Philips, and Sony. There were originally two next-generation standards for DVD. One format was backed by Sony, Philips, and others. The competing SD format was backed by Toshiba, Time Warner, and others. A group of computer companies led by IBM insisted that the DVD proponents agree on a single standard. The combined DVD standard was announced in September 1995, thus preventing a confusing and costly repeat of the VHS versus Betamax videotape battle. No single company "owns" DVD. The DVD

Licensor Consortium now comprises Hitachi, JVC, Matsushita, Mitsubishi, Philips, Pioneer, Sony, Thomson, Time Warner, and Toshiba.

As this technology enters the corporate landscape, the need for networking services will increase as soon as there is a desire to store the material at a central server.

Multimedia

Multimedia as a general field is a technology based on the multisensory nature of people and the capability of computers to store, manipulate, and display information such as video, graphics, audio, and text. Multimedia has been enabled by the synergistic confluence of the PC, the television, and the optical file server. Broadband communication networks are another key technical driver. There are now many practical multimedia business applications, including presentation development, kiosks, computer-based training, preparation of business presentations, online magazines, and desktop videoconferencing [22].

The multimedia market has been estimated by some to become a $25 billion market by 2000. Industry observers agree that multimedia is one of the key technologies influencing how people will use computers over the next few years. The majority of new PCs now support multimedia. Corporations are examining the possibility of putting multimedia to work for them, to support their transition to a competitive business posture in the context of the global economy of the 1990s. Multimedia is not a single technology, but a class of technologies and applications that span two (voice and data) or more (voice, data, video, and graphics) media. Multimedia can operate by delivering from as little as 56Kbps of information to a user to as much as 20Mbps (for new HDTV applications), and even higher. The 1.5 to 6.0Mbps data rate per user is a basic range being designed to by multimedia technology developers, for example for instructional purposes. MPEG-1 products operating at the 1Mbps rate have seen good penetration. Table 4.5 summarizes some important multimedia milestones achieved during the past decade.

Initial multimedia applications, however, have been confined to the desktop, where all required information resides in a PC-attached CD-ROM videodisc. Recent enterprise networking history has shown that *standalone islands* are untenable over time, even in the case of traditional business applications. Companywide connectivity is expected in the next few years in regard to multimedia and digital video. Desktop videoconferencing, access to remote libraries of video or multimedia material, access to archived multimedia corporate records, and downloading of server-based

Table 4.5 Multimedia Milestones

1982	Introduction of compact disc—consumer audio
1984	Introduction of CD-ROMs; Macintosh GUIs
1986	Initial CD-I (compact disc interactive) specification; Microsoft Windows
1987	Announcement of DVI (digital video interactive) technology
1988	Erasable optical disks; initial ATM standards
1990	MPC (Multimedia PC) standard; IMA (Interactive Multimedia Association) Compatibility Project; commercial multimedia applications
1992	ATM-based LAN development (155Mbps to the desktop); FDDI 100Mbps connections possible for less than $1,000
1994	Wide-area ATM networks; networked multimedia systems and applications
1995	Development of new low-speed voice compression standards (e.g., G.729, G.723.1, G.729A) and other interoperability standards for desktop multimedia; launch of DVD
1998	Increased penetration of multimedia in corporate America for mission-critical applications

multimedia instruction are just some examples of desirable networked multimedia applications, requiring both local and wide area connectivity. Beyond the desktop-based platforms, multimedia requires high-capacity digital networks to provide real-time services such as retrieval, messaging, conversation, and distribution. QoS-enabled networks are needed: What has held back broadband applications in general, and multimedia in particular, has been the lack of adequate bandwidth and QoS, not only at the WAN level, but also at the local level. ATM is the underpinning technology for high-end networked multimedia applications, while services such as ISDN and other "fast packet" services can support midrange applications. That said, one may not want to run ATM natively because of the changes required, and because these changes would be required throughout many elements of the corporate network. Preferably, one wants to be able to run IP over ATM, and so only change a few backbone routers to ATM. For this reason, the support of embedded protocols is important while searching for QoS-based solutions.

Communication technology that has adequate capacity, quality of service, and flexibility is a critical enabling technology that will be required to enable multimedia to migrate from dedicated desktop systems to more efficient distributed systems, making more, preferably most, employees of a corporation actual users of multimedia applications. As noted, the 1990s are burgeoning with new high-quality high-speed wide area digital services at the local and wide area levels. However, QoS-enhancing technologies will be needed, particularly in the WAN where bandwidth restrictions may exist and where the organization and/or the carrier may overbook (oversubscribe) bandwidth.

Videoconferencing

In addition to networked multimedia per se, a variety of vendors and suppliers are pursuing the objective of bringing real-time two-way video to the corporate desktop, as seen earlier. For example, multimedia conferencing enables designers in remote locations to review and/or work cooperatively on the same project using PCs that incorporate text, graphics, audio, visual, and tactile (touch-screen) capabilities. An increasing number of companies are now utilizing videoconferencing as part of their normal business practices even though most of the applications are still in the conference room-to-conference room arrangement, rather than being desktop-based. Such desktop conferencing systems, however, are now beginning to appear. The most basic form of desktop videoconferencing is achieved using simple "video telephones." More sophisticated systems utilize PCs and high-end workstations that employ ISDN and/or ATM services. Proponents argue that videoconferencing on the desktop is only a matter of time. They quote well-known "benefits" that are direct carryovers from traditional videoconferencing: reduced travel expenses; more effective use of time; and the ability to connect dispersed workgroups. Conference room applications cost from $15,000 to $50,000, while desktop systems can be as inexpensive as $200 (see Table 4.6 [27]).

From the perspective of videoconferencing service supported by current user equipment, the following elements impact on network connection options:

- Point-to-point connection
- Bridging (i.e., point-to-multipoint, multipoint-to-multipoint)
- Inverse Muxing (i.e., one video channel obtained via multiple network connections)

In the existing network, the provisioning of point-to-point connections is the network's responsibility; bridging and inverse muxing are roles of the user's equipment with current videoconferencing services. New services, particularly ATM (cell relay service) can be utilized to place some of this functionality in the network. The LAN (of adequate bandwidth) will

Table 4.6   Camera Market Price Segments

<$200	This is the mainstream of the desktop market and includes both analog and digital cameras
$200–500	This is the high end of the desktop cameras and generally provides higher-quality video. Enhancements include glass optics instead of plastic, automatic gain control, iris control, white balance, etc. Some of these cameras may also provide more than 330 lines of resolution.
$500–1200	This is the bulk of the small-group-systems camera market. Added features include pan/tilt/zoom control, better microphones. For the desktop, these cameras often suit dual purposes, such as document imaging and still photography.
$1200–5000	Higher-end group system cameras include autotracking systems, remote camera control and other functions to make group meetings as natural as possible.
>$5000	This range today extends all the way to $30,000, including cameras used in distance education and broadcast TV. These use the highest quality optics, and a full range of pan/tilt/zoom/focus automation.

become a major enabling technology for desktop videoconferencing. A growing number of products are being developed for the LAN. However, the issue of network capacity and QoS on a legacy LAN remains; in addition, concerns about the ability of routers are real [28].

Videoconferencing can be viewed in the context of supporting collaborative work. Low-cost desktop videoconferencing equipment and data collaboration technology will impact corporations both in the conference room and at the desktop. Some see data collaboration as being even more important than just the "blurry" picture on the screen. Most desktop videoconferencing systems have document conferencing packages (sometimes also called audiographics software) that include whiteboard and file-sharing programs for joint viewing and annotating documents. An increasing number of these include full-fledged document collaboration features that let users run applications remotely. Videoconferencing that supports quality video requires higher bandwidth than is achievable over a modem or a shared LAN, as discussed previously.

Codecs receive considerable attention, because they are the basis for the entire application. Codecs must be compatible (that is, conform to industry standards, e.g., ITU-T H.320), be relatively inexpensive (e.g., a $250 chipset), and support reasonable quality. ITU-T H.320 is a key group of standards developed for traditional videoconferencing applications. H.320 utilizes the H.261 video-encoding specification, which in turn uses the px64 codec. Adoption of standards ensures compatibility; still, some vendors have introduced proprietary systems that claim to be better, but in fact are not a significant improvement. The H.320 operates up to 1.544Mbps (for U.S. implementations) per user. (For comparison, Motion JPEG can go as high as 20 to 45Mbps per user, and offers significant quality improvements.) Introduction of H.320, however, has been slower than initially expected. Industry groups such as Personal Conferencing Workgroup (PCWG) and International Multimedia Teleconferencing Consortium (IMTC) are now advancing the interworking details of H.320 and T.120 (whiteboards). A specification for LAN video application interworking with H.320, specifically H.323, has emerged, addressing the interoperability question.

Web Access, Including Hypermedia

Many kinds of information are now available on World Wide Web servers. The Web offers hypertext technology that links a "web" of documents so that these can be navigated in any number of ways, as well as while using a more sophisticated GUI, such as Netscape, Explorer, and so on. (Hypertext is any document that contains links to other documents; selecting a link automatically displays the second document.) Some of the information on the Web consists of hypermedia (hypertext whose content includes some or all of the following: text, graphics, video, voice, and music). Corporate users may elect either to access the Internet over a dial-up line, or better yet, through the corporate LAN. Web home pages and hyperlinked screens can be data-intensive. QoS-enabled communication will be needed, as more employees in the corporation work at their desks by accessing some remote web site and as hypermedia on the Web becomes even more prevalent.

More specifically, the Web is a set of public specifications and a library of code for building information servers and clients. It is ideal for supporting cooperative work in complex research fields. The Web uses Internet-based architectures employing public and open specifications, along with free sample implementations on the client and server ends, so that anyone can build a client or a server. The three key components of the Web are the URL (uniform resource locator), HTTP (HyperText Transfer Protocol), and HTML (HyperText Markup Language). A URL is the address of the document that is to be retrieved from a network server; it contains the identification of the protocol, the server, and the filename of the document. When the user clicks on a link in a document, the link icon in the document contains the URL, which the client employs to initiate the session with the intended server. HTTP is the protocol used in support of the information transfer; it is a fixed set of messages and replies that both the server and the client understand. The document itself, which is returned using HTTP upon the issuance of a URL, is coded in HTML; the browser interprets the HTML to identify the various elements of the document and to render it on the client screen.

Observers see the web market as still in its infancy. Issues center on networking, performance (that is, QoS), security, and presentation richness. There already are extensions underway to the basic web browsers. Today's web browsers are limited to HTML specifications, which are reasonable for two-dimensional page layout, but not necessarily for truly interactive browsing. Newly emerging languages such as the Virtual Reality Markup Language (VRML) and Java are designed to enhance the browsing experience [29]. Sun's VRML offers a method of describing three-dimensional space so that users can navigate in 3D. Java is an object-oriented language that adds animation and real-time interaction through inline applications. Both are processing-intensive (e.g., they work well on a SPARCstation 20) and can be communication-intensive, depending on the application. Priority-based QoS communications will be of value in VRML- and Java-based applications.

The emergence of new features or de facto industry extensions (e.g., Netscape's extensions) will introduce some lack of interoperability in the short term, but users are now looking for more "flashy, colorful, and attractive places to hang out" [30]. The user and corporate requirement is in the direction of increased sophistication, complexity, speed, and bandwidth. Activities on the Web that are CPU- and communications-intensive include applications generating real-time graphics using charts and colors to show trends in the stock market, voter returns, geographic information systems (GISs), weather maps, database statistics, and analysis related to economic commerce.

Many magazines, reports, and other content now are available *only* on web servers, having migrated there from a previous paper format. Likewise, advertisements and technical information are now being delivered via web servers, raising the concern about the ability to access the volumes of information over the corporate enterprise network. Perhaps in the not-too-distant future, many magazine, specs, documents, and so on of business interest will be available on these servers, generating considerable corporate traffic as knowledge workers access them via the enterprise network.

Web server software now allows the delivery of live, real-time audio and video over the Web. Some of this software is based on the concept of streaming media, which delivers audio- and video-on-demand, rather than requiring a user to download a file off the Web and play it back off the local server or hard drive. Using this technology, some say that more than 100 stations could soon be broadcasting live, FM-quality or better programming on the Internet; TV broadcasting is also anticipated. Again, QoS-enabled communications will be required, if not immediately, in the near future [31].

The bottom line is that more bandwidth and QoS-based services (from the intranet and/or from the public network/Internet) will be required to support the basic as well as the hypermedia-based applications found on the Web. ATM will likely be part of that vehicle, whether in the corporate campus, in the Internet access WAN subnetwork, or within the Internet itself.

4.3 QoS-Enabled Communication Is Coming—Read On

A revolution in QoS-based communication is on the horizon. By the year 2000, it will be clearly visible. Network planners should start to address the impact of users' requirements for QoS now, given that a full network transition could take a number of years to complete. Since many enterprise networks now utilize the Internet in some fashion, a discussion of QoS requirements in that space is warranted.

References

1. D. Minoli, "Packetized Speech Networks, Part 1: Overview." *Australian Electronics Engineer*, April 1979, pp. 38–52.
2. D. Minoli, "Packetized Speech Networks, Part 2: Queuing Model." *Australian Electronics Engineer*, July 1979, pp. 68–76.
3. D. Minoli, "Packetized Speech Networks, Part 3: Delay Behavior and Performance Characteristics." *Australian Electronics Engineer*, August 1979, pp. 59–68.
4. D. Minoli, E. Minoli. *Delivering Voice over IP Networks*. (New York: John Wiley & Sons, Inc.), 1998.
5. *Desktop Video Communications*. July/August 1997, p. 45.

6. M. Pihlman, "H.323 Videoconferencing over Packet Networks." *Desktop Video Communications*, March/April 1997, pp. 13 ff.
7. S. Borthic, "Turning Up the Heat at DVC West." *Desktop Video Communications*, July/August 1997, pp. 7 ff.
8. D. Minoli, *Video Dialtone Technology, Approaches, and Services: Digital Video over ADSL, HFC, FTTC, and ATM* (New York: McGraw-Hill), 1995.
9. D. Minoli, "Digital Video Compression: Getting Images Across a Net." *Network Computing*, July 1993, pp. 146 ff.
10. D. Minoli, "Distributed Multimedia: Bringing the Infrastructure Up to the Challenge." *WAN Connections/Communications Week*, August 1993, pp. 60 ff.
11. D. Minoli, "Multimedia: Opportunities for Carriers and Service Providers." *Market Report*, Probe Research Corporation, June 1993.
12. D. Minoli, "Distance Learning Applications." *Broadband Networking*, DataPro Report 1015BBN, November 1993.
13. D. Minoli, "Concocting a Recipe for the Right Multimedia Mix." *Network World*, September 12, 1994, p. L10.
14. D. Minoli, "Imaging Communications." *Broadband Networking*, DataPro Report, June 1994.
15. D. Minoli, "Videoconferencing." *Broadband Networking*, DataPro Report, April 1994.
16. D. Minoli, "Designing Scalable Networks." *Network World Collaboration*, January 10, 1994, pp. 17 ff.
17. D. Minoli, "Communications-based Imaging." *Market Report*, Probe Research Corporation, September 1994.
18. D. Minoli, "An Assessment of Digital Video and Video Dialtone Technology, Regulation, Services, and Competitive Markets." DataPro Market Report on Convergence Strategies & Technologies, April 1995.
19. D. Minoli, "1995: The Year of Video in Enterprise Nets." *Network World*, December 5, 1994, p. 21.
20. D. Minoli, "Video Dialtone (VDT): Overview." DataPro Report 1090CNS, May 1995.
21. D. Minoli, "Video Compression Schemes." DataPro Market Report on Convergence Strategies & Technologies, May 1995.
22. D. Minoli, B. Keinath. *Distributed Multimedia through Broadband Communication Services* (Artech House), 1994.
23. G. Pensinger, "Sarnoff Assumes Role in Broadcasting's 'Third Revolution.' " *TV Broadcast*, June 1995, pp. 19 ff.
24. R. Eggers, "On-line, Off-line Editing Systems Converging." *TV Broadcast*, June 1995, pp. 19 ff.

25. J. Van Pelt, "Objective Testing for Video Compression." *TV Broadcast,* June 1995, p. 86.
26. FAQ for the alt.video.dvd Usenet newsgroup, www.videodiscovery .com/vdyweb/dvd/dvdfaq.html.
27. A. Davis, "Cameras for Desktop Videoconferencing." *Desktop Video Communications,* March/April 1997, pp. 18 ff.
28. P. Jerram, "Videoconferencing Gets in Sync." *Newmedia,* July 1995, pp. 48 ff.
29. R. Kohlhepp, "Next-Generation Web Browsing." *Network Computing,* August 1, 1995, pp. 48 ff.
30. R. Karpinski, "Fracturing the Web: A Design Dilemma." *Interactive Age,* July 31, 1995, pp. 8 ff.
31. D. Minoli. *Internet and Intranet Engineering.* (New York: McGraw-Hill), 1997.

Notes

[1] Portions based on the article by the author, "Supporting Multimedia and Other Evolving Applications Using Broadband," in the book *Annual Review of Communications,* International Engineering Consortium, Volume 50, 1997, pages 729 ff, Chicago, IL.

Contemporary Example of QoS Requirements in the Internet: A Case Study with Wider Implications

In the previous chapter we looked at evolving QoS requirements for general enterprise network applications now being deployed by progressive companies, particularly in support of multimedia needs. As noted throughout this book, enterprise networks utilize the Internet in a variety of ways (e.g., VPNs, extranets, etc.). Hence, these QoS requirements translate into Internet requirements. Other companies are interested in QoS support in the Internet mainly for data applications and for company-to-world communication; again, this imposes a set of requirements on the Internet.

Corporate network planners in the near future will be evaluating ISPs and NSPs by their support mechanisms related to, and their capabilities in the area of, QoS. To demonstrate this, this chapter presents a case study, the Automotive Network Exchange, and the kind of requirements it is imposing on ISPs. These specifics may become the baseline set of normative requirements that other companies will seek in the future. This chapter also looks at QoS from a business perspective, to answer what are the goals and how can providers be measured. The chapters that follow discuss the various technologies and protocols that the providers utilize to support these kinds of requirements in various segments of their networks.

Specifically, this chapter describes the work underway to advance the state of the art in building reliable IP networking [1]. The goal is to educate corporate enterprise network planners via the description of an industry-focused effort (in the automative area) related to QoS, so that they can understand the project enough to be able to use this type of service-level agreements (SLA) network services as they would any utility, and be confident in migrating their mission-critical networks to public services. The architectures and protocols described here have evolved during the late 1990s under the guidance of major automotive manufactures and leading ISPs. We present high-level views of certain material because the details are still proprietary; as time progresses, more details will be made public.

5.1 Overview

Throughout the Internet's history, due to the Internet's inability to provide SLAs and QoS, the majority of its precommercialization use has been focused on academia or business applications that were not mission-critical. These limits were imposed by protocol deficiency, inadequate network capacity, or poor network architectures. During the early days of the Internet, improvements in quality came only when the backbone link speeds were upgraded [2]. ARPANET's migration to the NSFNET illustrate this point. The network started with 56Kbps links that were upgraded to T1 and then again to T3. Each time the network was upgraded, the end users experienced a higher perceived interuniversity communication quality because congestion was reduced. Better service was, unfortunately, short-lived, because the load eventually grew to once again congest the network.

We are now in a phase of the Internet's evolution during which the underlying protocols have been generally accepted as the de facto standards for inter-intracorporate communication, and major industries are migrating their entire network infrastructures to the Transmission Control Protocol/Internet Protocol (TCP/IP) [1] suite. (This topic is covered in more detail in Chapter 8.) Nevertheless, there has been some reluctance on the part of major corporations to move to Internet technologies provided by ISPs because of concerns over security, network reliability, trouble resolution, and performance measurement.

A second major trend is the desire to outsource corporate communications. This trend is particularly evident in industries where data communication networks have grown very large and span administrative domains. In these cases, running the network is complicated and requires a large staff. Running a global IP network is not the core competency of most manufacturing vertical industries; therefore, a reliable means of outsourcing is desirable.

These two trends are key motivators behind a project called the Automotive Network eXchange (ANX).[1] This project is unique in that it is the first time a major industry, automotive manufacturing, has clearly stated it would completely outsource its network operations and has documented the network's requirements. The combination of a clear understanding of the technical merits of the desired network architectures and acceptance that operating sophisticated networks is not a core capability of the automotive industry has driven the business decisions for the project. The fundamental goal of the network is to provide high-quality IP services between the major automotive manufactures and their part/service suppliers by, for the first time, clearly documenting what is expected from ISPs and NSPs.

The ANX also demonstrates a fundamental paradigm shift, regarding QoS, away from the Internet's model of best-effort service, which implies a general lack of any QoS: The network essentially tries to deliver packets to their destinations, but if for any reason they are discarded, the originating host is responsible for retransmitting these packets until they eventually arrive successfully. The are no guarantees that the packets will reach their destination, and higher-level protocols, like TCP, must ensure end-to-end reliability. For the most part, this is the way the commodity Internet works today, and severe packet loss dramatically reduces the perceived QoS. In addition, the traditional Internet architecture does not have the capability to offer any guarantees at the protocol level. In contrast, baseline network performance metrics have been established in the ANX, thereby breaking away from best-effort and seeking to provide SLAs.

The work on this project is being conducted under the guidance of the Automotive Industry Action Group (AIAG), which has subcontracted the day-to-day management to SIAC (Bellcore) [3], [4]. Bellcore is, therefore, responsible for updating which network performance values are measured and for determining which values are acceptable for involved ISPs. Bellcore is also responsible for keeping the metric document up to date. Finally, Bellcore, as the ANX Overseer (ANXO) is responsible for certifying which ISPs meet the metrics, thus also acting as the chief mediator during services outages and increasing the metrics over time.

5.1.1 Business Drivers

Before the establishment of ANX, the automotive industry communication infrastructure was made up of several overlapping networks interconnecting suppliers with major manufacturing sites. In the best case, a supplier might have only a single network connection between itself and one major manufacturer. In the worst case, a supplier might have multiple connections that would link itself to several manufacturing sites and several other partner supplier sites. Clearly, this redundancy led to unnecessary cost and complexity.

The ANX has the potential to result in significant cost reductions by organizing infrastructure requirements in support of growth in networked applications. Some of the chief goals are to:

- Offer the industry significant savings by improving the ability to conduct more business electronically, consequently, shortening production cycles and reducing operational costs.

- Reduce multiple redundant network connections between corporations.

- Provide a seamless and ubiquitous infrastructure for legacy, current, and future TCP/IP-based applications.

- Provide an infrastructure to enable companies to establish VPNs that enable secure, encrypted communication.

- Improve business cycles.

To achieve SLAs as strict as those specified in the ANX, a central management organization, ANXO, has been created. The ANXO acts as the central authority that monitors the ongoing quality of every aspect of the network; it is capable of performing spot checks on QoS. In addition, the ANXO is responsible for certifying ISPs that want to provide IP services to the automotive industry. The ANXO is then responsible for checking candidate ISP networks for ANX conformance and for certifying that ISPs can meet the strict quality control standards. The overseer is also responsible for providing some IP route servers (RS) and Domain Name Services (DNS) [1] [6].

The ANX differs from the traditional Internet in the following ways:

- ANX is a managed collection of interconnected certified service provider networks.

- ANX is designed to meet its subscribers' business communication requirements.

- ANX provides centralized network administration and management services.

- ANX includes infrastructure, services, and a common set of business practices, including business-oriented "acceptable use" policies.

- ANX provides common security methods.

The ANX network is divided between two categories of ISP (see Figure 5.1). The actual ISP type services (i.e., running routers and connecting end users) is done by organizations called certified service providers (CSP). The interconnection between the CSPs is provided at an exchange point (EP) that is constructed from ATM equipment [1]. The customers on the ANX network are referred to as *trading partners.*

The network is subdivided into these parts so that each provider's role is clearly differentiated. For example, in the ANX, CSPs can build their IP

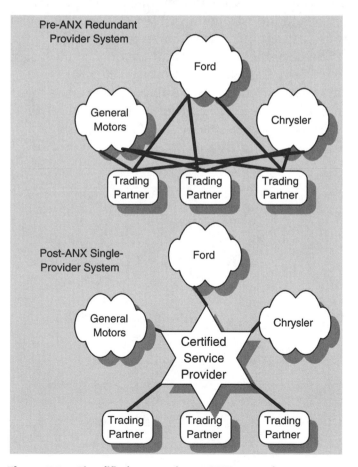

Figure 5.1   Simplified pre- and post-ANX network.

networks in any manner they choose; however, their interconnection must occur at the certified exchange point. This reduces latency, simplifies network architectures, and reduces routing complexities (see Figure 5.2).

In specifying, documenting, and monitoring the quality of service metrics, the overseer has created a group of eight categories that, for the first time, allow ISPs to gauge their service. More important, the metrics represent clear signals from the customer about which quality-of-service variables are critical. The overseer determines when CSPs are compliant and can sell services in the ANX, and which CSPs are no longer compliant and are to be removed from the network.

A key point to consider is that the performance metrics specified by the ANX overseer are very difficult to achieve; therefore, CSPs and the exchange point operator (EPO) have expended considerable effort to improve infrastructure to increase reliability. Thus the services provided by the certified carriers will be very unique in their quality, and the ISPs that possess the knowledge and infrastructure will have an advantage as business-class internets expand to other virtual markets.

The intent of the first release of the ANX is to address only connectivity in North America (United States, Canada, and Mexico). The majority of the network is located in southeast Michigan, because of that state's high concentration of automotive suppliers. The metric values come directly from trading partner assessments, where the initial ANX designers looked at specific application requirements, such as TELNET response

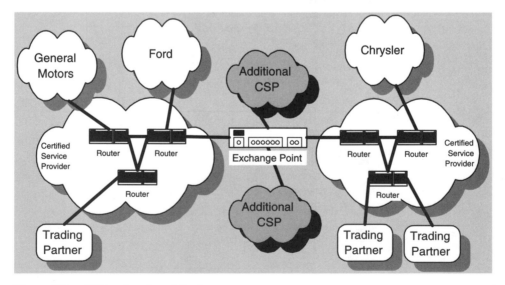

Figure 5.2 ANX network architecture.

times. The metric designers anticipate that ANX will grow globally, and when it does there will be a need to define some subset of criteria in a way that is specific to the given geography outside of North America. For example, metrics specifying total end-to-end latency will have to be relaxed.

The ANX managers are contemplating releasing new metrics approximately every year. Subsequent releases will build on the knowledge gained from CSPs in the program, and they will also be changed to keep pace with technological improvements. Release 2 will expand ANX outside of the borders of North America to parts of the world where there has been considerable interest in being able to obtain the benefits offered by ANX. A very likely follow-on phase of this work will be expansion of the ANX outside of the automotive industry. The same requirements for high-quality, outsourced networking exist in health care, education, insurance, and other industries.

5.1.2 History

In 1994, the AIAG suppliers and key manufacturing members published a document titled "Trading Partner Data Telecommunications Protocol Position." This publication was critical within the industry because it recommended the data network protocol TCP/IP be used as the standard for transport of automotive trading partner electronic information. In 1995, Chrysler, Ford, and GM endorsed TCP/IP as the standard protocol suite for interenterprise data communications among automotive trading partners.

Since then, many trading partners have successfully developed internal TCP/IP networks, but have met with limited success in extending these networks to include external trading partners. They have not always been able to successfully maintain high-quality communication across the traditional Internet because the quality has been unpredictable.

To realize the desire for standards-based networking that met trading partner business requirements of open systems and high reliability, the AIAG's Implementation Task Force (ITF)[2] developed the concept of a TCP/IP network for all automotive trading partners called the Automotive Network eXchange. The goal for the ANX was to provide automotive trading partners and suppliers with a single secure network for electronic commerce and data transfer. This new open system is intended to replace complex, redundant, proprietary, and costly connections that existed between industry members.

To implement the ANX network, the AIAG realized early on that monitoring and central management would be critical. In 1995, the AIAG issued a request for proposals (RFP) that explained how the overseer role would be defined and implemented. The winning RFP was awarded to Bellcore. Its proposal was a four-phased program whereby it would do the definitional work of the certification criteria first, followed by an implementation of the required function; the third phase would be a pilot, and the fourth phase would be the operation of the overseer function.

The first step became the contract because it described in detail what had to be done and how. The conditions were straightforward because Bellcore deferred detailed contract definitions to the subsequent phases and continued to discuss them with AIAG even while they were doing the definitional work. Bellcore approached the contract for phase 2 with the view that it was the contractor that could best serve the interests of the AIAG. The definitional contract began in January 1997, and phase 2 in May 1997.

The ANX pilot, the phase the project was in at the time of this writing, was to run about four months. At the end of that period, the network was slated to go into ANX release 1, the initial operational phase where the overseer would be certifying service providers. At that point the metrics should be well understood and any unattainable values will be modified. Once the pilot is complete, any ISP will be able to participate in the ANX network and will have the ability to purchase the metrics document.

5.2 ANX Certification Metrics

ANX certification involves evaluating an ISP's ability to supply high-quality connectivity. Because quality of service has traditionally been a subjective measure, ANX has made an attempt to concretely document certain values that can be used to measure the performance of a network. ANX certification metrics are organized into eight categories, and each is an aspect of service quality that is to be measured either during the certification process or at a later time during random spot checks.

The exact values of the metrics came from the trading partner business process, in which application requirements were key drivers. The overseer then used experience in engineering large telecommunications and data networks to augment the set. In addition, the feasibility of service providers being able to meet these criteria in the required time frames was determined. It was important to add "reality checks," because these attended to the service provider's perspective and ensured that the stringency of the requirements was within reason.

The various service metrics are quantitative criteria that must be met by every service provider. In addition to the performance measurements, there are also requirements addressing frequency and content of reports for areas in which the service provider is required to submit measurements to the overseer. The eight major categories of metrics are:

1. Core Network Services. Describes the types of technology used to access the network and the types of services that can be purchased from providers:

   ■ Link Utilization Reports. Analyzes trends.

   ■ Optional Services. Supplies a variety of access technologies.

   ■ Web Managed Services. Optional Web services.

2. Interoperability. Specifies network architecture.

3. Performance. Quantifies desired network quality.

4. Reliability. Used to document resiliency.

5. Business Continuity and Disaster Recovery. Specifies network hardening.

6. Security. Documents security measures for authentication and encryption.

7. Customer Care. Used to quantify sales, ordering, and provision metrics.

8. Trouble Handling. Specifies how to resolve trouble in a timely manner.

The AIAG delineated the eight areas based on automotive suppliers' operational requirements and state-of-the-art ISP capability to support them. The business processes and applications drove the selection of specific metrics and specific criteria metrics. For example, the measurement of latency across the network, the time required as a packet travels from a supplier to a manufacturer, is capped to the maximum time that would support a domestic U.S. TELNET application. Some of the other metrics, such as maximum packet loss, were developed to help quantify the end-to-end quality of the Internet service providers. Summing all eight categories, there are approximately 100 different measurements that a CSP must meet.

5.2.1 Network Core Services

The first class of metrics is composed of core services (i.e., access technology and speeds) required by certified service providers. This class addresses basic connectivity issues of network architecture and assures that any trading partner will be able to use the ANX to reach any other trading partner. There is an additional set of optional services that a certified service provider may offer, if it chooses to do so, but these offerings must be compliant with all the other service-quality requirements. This optional list of services includes all the acceptable access speeds and technologies. The particular type of access used to connect a trading partner to the ANX is subject to the agreement of the access provider and trading partner. In addition, service providers do not have to offer all speeds and all technologies; in most cases, certified providers will focus only on a few key access technologies like DS1 frame relay or 28.8Kbps dial-up service.

Reporting. The next subclass of the core requirements comprises link utilization reports. These reports are composed of monthly trending analyses of access circuit utilization statistics that must be given to ANX trading partners. The intent of these reports is to help the trading partners size their access link(s) correctly. Without an appropriately utilized link, which is not overly saturated, the other benefits of the ANX will not be easy to obtain. All trading partners are also required to purchase these basic service components.

Required Value-Add Services. The third subclass of core services are those that are required to be offered by the certified service providers but in many cases may be declined by the trading partner. These services provide a class of features that are not critical for business-class IP services, but greatly enhance their ease of use. Such a service would be to lease or purchase a router for the trading partner's premises. Another example is World Wide Web-based access to trouble-ticketing software. This type of service is very useful for changing the communication between the trading partner and the customer to a completely electronic state. This service could also be used for electronic bonding between the service provider trouble-ticket system and the trading partner trouble-ticket system.

Optional Value-Add Services. A fourth subclass of core services that certified service providers might offer, Managed Service, is today outside the scope of the certification program. Typical examples of this type of service are SMTP mail servers, Web caching/mirroring servers, and Web hosting. In addition, commodity Internet service falls into this category because it is not considered a core requirement. The ANX network is built with IP technology, but worldwide Internet access is not mandatory.

The reasons for excluding Internet access from the required set of features are based on the premise that Internet service does not necessarily need to be a core product of a certified provider. And, in some cases, regulatory restrictions may prevent some certified providers from offering long-distance Internet services. The ANX is a virtual private network, or *extranet*, and the IP service providers may or may not have public Internet access as a current network product. Other services will be added to this core category and will have clear quantitative values as the industry gains experience.

5.2.2 Interoperability

The next major category of metrics is based on measurements of interoperability. These measurements concern network architectural design decisions that dictate interprovider connectivity requirements. In this class of metrics, the total end-to-end latency of the network is quantified by dictating the ways that certified providers interconnect.

As shown previously, between any two trading partners there can be at most two certified service providers. Given that constraint, the ANX overseers have engineered some of the quantitative numbers for performance and reliability criteria, such that, given only two certified providers between trading partners, one can relate the certification requirements for each individual service provider to the trading-partner-to-trading-partner service quality. In addition, limiting interprovider connection complexity is one of the reasons the network should be easier to troubleshoot.

The interoperability requirements can further be specified as:

- Provide adequate capacity on backbone and interconnection circuits to service demand provided by trading partners.
- Use of only DS3 or OC-3c ATM at the exchange point.
- Use of only ANXO-defined route between trading partners.
- At most two CSPs between any two trading partners.
- Trading partners can be multihomed to multiple CSPs.
- Trading partners cannot pass data to the ANX via uncertified ISPs.

5.2.3 Performance Metrics

The collection of performance metrics is the third major category. It addresses the quality perceived instantaneously by ANX users; for example, within the performance metrics category fall the file transfer delay measurements. Here the overseer will take active measurements to ascertain whether a file of a certain size gets across the network of a service provider within a specified period of time. Installing test equipment at trading partner sites and then moving bulk data across the network is how the test is performed. This is an example where the criterion was driven by the need to exchange CAD files over the ANX.

In addition, there are requirements governing packet latency and packet loss that drive network architecture decisions for the previous category. For example, 125 milliseconds is the maximum allowable packet latency. Metrics related to routing requirements specify values for the maintenance of routing stability and dictate the use of the route server. A broad range of performance metrics and conformance to these values dictate simplified network designs.

Performance metric examples include:

- Packet latency
- File transfer delay
- Throughput
- Packet loss

5.2.4 Reliability

The fourth category, reliability, is the next major group for measured performance. The availability of the service provider network is divided into three components.

- Topological, with a local access provider part
- Certified service provider backbone part
- Exchange points

Each of these groups has its own unique set of rules, and the ANX has a set of criteria for a certified exchange point operator. Multiple certified service providers, through a peering arrangement, share the exchanges, because the quality of private interconnections between a pair of providers would fall under the service quality measurements of those providers. As an example of measurements in this category, in the ANX, a certified ISP's network will be available for use 99.97 percent of the time, or all but 2.63 hours per year (this does not include the local loop, which is covered by reliability).

There are metrics on the access network, which consists of the premises router and the local loop. These values cover the link between the premise router and the ANX CSP. These numbers are separate from those for the service provider because the local loop may or may not be under the direct control service provider. For example, the trading partner itself could furnish the local loop, or it could be under the control of a competitive access provider. Either way, the access network shall have 99.8 percent availability.

Reliability metric examples include:

- Availability
- Service restoration time
- Total network unavailability
- Connectivity upon failure

5.2.5 Business Continuity and Disaster Recovery

The fifth category is business continuity and disaster recovery. It is used to demonstrate the fault tolerance of the ANX, and the focus is on the service providers to show they have a robust plan for avoiding disasters; or, in the event of a disaster, that they can ensure trading partners with continuity of service.

To provide high degrees of fault tolerance, the network designs of the certified service providers and the exchange point must be well documented; contain highly robust underpinnings; and be shared with the ANXO. The techniques used to construct a highly resilient IP network can be subdivided into the major categories of facility survivability and equipment survivability. In the ANX, some of the applications of these categories can be seen in the following examples:

Diverse Local Loops. When entering a major certified service provider's equipment building, access to the telecommunications carrier(s) should be redundant and be at opposite ends of the structure.

Dual Homing Option. Even though the quality of the service is expected to be exceptional compared to today's Internet, survivability can be improved by connecting trading partners twice to the ANX, each connection being provided by a different CSP.

Redundant Exchange Points. To assure that the connectivity between CSPs almost never becomes a point of failure, not only is the exchange point an extremely fault-tolerant device, but it is also duplicated. Interconnection between the CSPs is therefore possible over an identical, redundant, exchange point. For reasons of resilience, the secondary exchange point is geographically distant from the primary.

SONET Entrance into Exchange Points. Connections from Interexchange carriers or regional carriers into the exchange point are made over SONET [7] technology. This provides for an extremely fault tolerant local loop.

Fault-Tolerant Backbone Designs. The architectures used by CSPs have to be crafted so that little if any single points of failure exist. For example, the single path from a trading partner to the CSP should be the weakest link in the network, by design. Once those links reach the CSP point of presence, they need to be carried over a network with multiple path and reserved standby bandwidth.

Fault-Tolerant Equipment. To reduce the potential of a network outage, most CSPs will employ fault-tolerant equipment whenever possible. This means that routers with redundant power supplies, network ATM switches with 1 + 1 port protection, and any device making switching or routing decisions should have redundant controllers.

The overseer will have the ultimate responsibility for reviewing CSP and EPO business continuity disaster-recovery plans, by making site visits, reviewing design documents, and reviewing disaster recovery plans.

5.2.6 Security Metrics

The sixth category comprises security metrics and concerns values that apply to service providers ability to build networks that prohibit unauthorized access and eavesdropping. This work is subdivided into several subsections.

IETF-Developed Protocols. These support encrypted communication between endpoints; that is, the IP Security Working Group (IPsec) [8] shall be used for both intertrading partner communication and during exchange of network management information.

Certificates of Authenticity (CA). Used to uniquely identify communicating endpoints.

Traffic Spoofing. A source modifies a packet's source address. This infraction must be detected in order to reduce the probability of denial-of-service (DoS) attacks.

Given that trading partners will be using IPsec-encrypted data, the focus of the security metrics will be on DoS attacks. The service provider must be able to recognize then discard spoofed packets. This type of attack has become very common on the Internet, and could be extremely damaging if allowed to disrupt intertrading partner communication for long periods. The use of a spoofed source address is particularly attractive for attackers because it is difficult to locate the source of the malicious activity.

The typical procedure for preventing this type of attack is for ISPs to configure their routers to check packets entering the network from their customers and ensure that they have the correct IP subnetwork addresses. Such a source address filter is typically placed on the border router, and currently is very taxing on the router, but nevertheless mandatory. The overseer will do active testing to be sure that this capability is in place.

The trading partner's security will be supported by the public key infrastructure of the service providers, the overseer, and the trading partners. Eventually, the infrastructure will support a federated architecture of certificate authorities with the overseer as the sole source of the cross-certification of certificate authorities operated by CSPs. The trading partners can also own certificate authorities that can be cross-certified by the certified service providers. A certificate infrastructure will be created to support the IPsec exchanges between partners. The overseer will impose requirements as to how the service providers operate their certificate authorities.

Finally, there are general security requirements that govern general behavior of network engineers and network operations personnel. For example, spot checks may be performed to assure that router passwords are not weakly administered. In addition, all network operations communication between devices must be encrypted to assure that eavesdropping will not uncover customer data or router passwords. To confirm certified service provider compliance, the overseer will actively test the network, that is, check password and IPsec deployment, to determine compliance.

Security metric examples include:

- Satisfactory security policy
- Monitoring and implementation of fixes from security bulletins
- Password complexity and lifetime
- Third-party auditor scan for weak passwords
- Detection of intrusion activity
- Blocking of spoofed and source-routed packets
- Integrity of machine configuration

5.2.7 Customer Care

The seventh category is the customer care metrics group. For example, the performance of the help desk is measured to determine whether they can quickly and correctly respond to customer questions or problems. Unique to the ANX are metrics for a variety of human interfaces between the service provider and the trading partner. For example, inquires can arrive via telephone, e-mail, or the Web to the certified provider. For each of these interfaces there is an associated metric for which the CSP must show responsiveness.

Beyond the service provider's ability to respond to inquires by telephone or e-mail, ANX metrics go on to document values for initial contact with the service provider; for example, how quickly the service provider activates services in relationship to its commitment time is bounded. To determine ongoing satisfaction, a survey process performed by the overseer will gauge CSPs over time.

Customer care examples include:

- Customer satisfaction ratio
- Customer care help desk availability (99 percent)
- Service activation delay

5.2.8 Trouble Handling

The eighth, and final, category comprises trouble-handling metrics. CSPs will be required to classify network trouble reporting in ways that the overseer can quickly process—which in turn will make it easier when trouble/outages escalate, because all involved will be speaking a common interprovider language. Certified service provider troubleshooting begins when a trading partner has a network problem and has determined the trouble is not in their own network or end to end at the application level.

At this point, the trading partner notifies the service provider either electronically via the Web or calls the certified service provider. The service provider that receives the trouble report is required to respond in a bounded timely manner and then to work with all the others in the chain to solve the problem within a set time. If the customer and service provider are unable to resolve the trouble, the problem is referred to the overseer who then considers the gravity of the situation. If the problem is not resolved in a timely manner, the overseer may consider decertifying the Internet service provider.

Reducing the number of service providers limits the complexities of trying to resolve trouble tickets among multiple parties. In practice, trouble isolation, even in a network as robust as the ANX, can be difficult, and usually requires concurrent close cooperation between the source and destination trading partners and among all of the certified service providers in between.

Trouble-handling metrics include:

- Trouble-handling and escalation policy
- Trouble response time
- Dispatch delay to customer premises

5.2.9 Certification Procedures

In the previous discussion it was noted that there are approximately 100 different metrics that fall into the eight required categories for CSPs. Certification takes place when the ISP supplies information to the ANXO; the ANXO takes active measurements; and the ANXO performs audits. The certification process begins when an ISP makes a formal request to the overseer and purchases the complete set of metrics from the overseer. The overseer collects a certification application fee and then begins the process of monitoring the metrics to ascertain whether the ISP is eligible to begin the process of certification.

The steps for certification are:

1. Application. The ISP requests up-to-date metrics and notifies the overseer of intent to participate.
2. Verification. The Overseer makes the initial measurement.
3. Certification. The overseer makes the final verification.

Initially, interested ISPs will enter a stage called certification application during which the ISP purchases the necessary metrics documentation, notifies the overseer of intent to participate, begins acquiring knowledge on how to satisfy the metrics, and pays the initial certification fee to the overseer. Then the ISP will enter the certification assessment phase that involves initial assessment by the overseer to determine basic metric compliance. Once past this stage, which includes the first measurements of the ISP's network performance, the service provider can enter into certification verification.

When an ISP is formally in the certification verification stage, the ISP can operate as an ANX certified service provider though there will be ongoing measurement by the overseer to determine compliance with the metrics. When the service provider is 100 percent compliant with the certification assessment criteria, it can enter into final certification when it undergoes a process to meet what is, in effect, a second and final set of criteria. At the time of this writing, the details of the final stages have not been set; the pilot is being used to determine the requisite time line for certification assessment.

In addition to the certification application process just described, there is a certification "watchdog" process that involves both trading partners and service providers. It is important to note that use of the ANX network is considered mandatory by the AIAG for suppliers to the automotive industry. A trading partner begins its use of the network by registering with the overseer prior to subscribing to an ANX service from an ANX certified provider. The trading partner will be given a list of CSPs from which to choose a service provider. To ensure use of the network, the ANXO has created some general rules governing ANX members.

- An ANX certified provider must ensure that all its trading partner customers have registered prior to delivering ANX service to them, and a trading partner may not subscribe to an ANX service before registering.

- Only certified service providers can take a trading partner's application for ANX service to route packets to other automotive trading partners.

- ANX is the service provided to this registered set of trading partners by their certified service providers over the network connecting the trading partners.

- Routing information and domain registry are to be taken off the overseer's route server and DNS.

5.3 Conclusion

This chapter has provided an overview of the network called the ANX that has been created to provide high-quality IP services to its users. The underlying goals of the project are to create well-documented data communications SLAs so that all involved understand the customers' expectations. Because the SLAs are documented, the corporate buyer can begin to feel comfortable with outsourcing key data communication networking infrastructure components of their business. The project also serves as a critical milestone in the evolution of the Internet in that, for the first time, groups of networking experts have documented quantitatively what values customers can expect from leading-edge ISPs.

It should be clear to most ISPs that best-effort service is just one of many products that they will need to offer in the future and that the ANX model is an excellent attempt at advancing the state of the art in networking. In response to high-grade service and guaranteed QoS type requests, most ISPs today are struggling with service definitions and network architectures. The work of the ANX helps this process by providing clearly documented metrics that have been specified by major communications buyers as having been achieved on major ISP networks. The metrics have been communicated and are currently being implemented by major ISPs. In addition, it is firmly believed that the project will be very successful not only within the automotive industry but across a number of other vertical industries. Other business communities of interest will have similar needs to the ANX. The ISPs who realizes this need and can upgrade their networks to meet this customer demand will ultimately realize the most success in the business market.

The chapters that follow discuss the technologies and protocols that the ISPs will have to use to support these QoS requirements and to give planners a basic understanding of the technologies and methods, to enable them to ask the right architectural questions of their ISP when the subject of QoS is covered.

References

1. D. Minoli and A. Schmidt. *Switched Network Services.* (New York: John Wiley & Sons, Inc.), 1998.
2. K. Hafner and M. Lyon. *Where Wizards Stay Up Late.* (New York: Simon & Schuster), 1996.
3. www.aiag.org
4. www.bellcore.com
5. www.ra.org
6. A. Schmidt and D. Minoli. *Multiprotocol over ATM:* Building State-of-the-Art ATM Networks. (Upper Saddle River, NJ: Prentice-Hall), 1998.
7. D. Minoli. *Enterprise Networking.* (Norwood, Mass: Artech House), 1992.
8. S. Kent, R. Atkinson. "Security Architecture for the Internet Protocol," www.ietf.org, draft-ietf-ipsec-arch-sec-01.txt.

Notes

[1] ANX and Automotive Network eXchange are registered in the U.S. Patent and Trademark Office as service marks by the Automotive Industry Action Group (AiAG), Southfield, Michigan.

[2] The Implementation Task Force is a committee chartered with overseeing the metrics used in the network, managing the ultimate control of the certifications, and seeing that the implementation from the pilot flows smoothly.

QoS Support in the Internet: Technologies and Protocols

CHAPTER 6

Frame Relay Technology for ISP Support and QoS Questions

The previous chapters explained the evolving need for QoS-supported communications over the Internet. The chapters in this part describe the various technologies and protocols that ISPs can utilize to support the kinds of requirements that have been identified for intranet, extranet, and VPN applications. This information may be useful to the corporate planner in posing inquiries to prospective ISPs as to the QoS capabilities that are available.

An Internet-based connection is composed of various network components, where different technologies are applicable. Hence, contrary to the provincial view of some techno-religionists, all technologies eventually find a place in the Internet, from connectors to fiber channel standard links, from T1 to SONET, from frame relay to ATM, from IP over ATM to MPLS, from Ethernets to token rings, from FDDI to microwave, from satellites to cable modems, from dial-up to fax-over-IP, and on and on.

In general, one can identify three major elements in an Internet connection:

The Access Subnetwork (ASN). Set of facilities that enable a user to reach the aggregation equipment of an ISP. This includes the local loop to the CLEC/ILEC switch, the link to the ISP, and the ISP's concentration access system. High-speed dedicated lines, cable-modem technology, ISDN, xDSL, direct broadcast satellite, are some of the elements of the access subnetwork.

ISP Aggregation Subnetwork (IASN).   Set of equipment that supports aggregation of user streams into concentrated routable traffic. This includes DSLAMs, routers and ATM switches, which provide a high-speed interface into the NSP backbone.

NSP Backbone Network (NBN).   National/international backbone, including the high-capacity ATM switches or POS routers, the long-haul facilities, and the public and private peering points.

Each of these elements can make use of a number of distinct technologies. In the chapters that follow, QoS support in the various technologies supporting these three elements is addressed. We start here with Layer 2 technologies and later move up to Layer 3.

Readers interested in basic frame relay features should go through Sections 6.1 and 6.2. Readers interested in a more complete description of frame relay services, perhaps as part of a major frame relay versus Internet VPN services analysis may find the entire chapter of interest. For direct ISP applications the salient points are:

- Frame relay is generally available to 1.544Mbps DS1/T1 rates (although when aggregated/handed off by a router via high-speed serial interface (HSSI) for aggregation subnetwork applications, it also supports 45Mbps DS3 rates). Its major application is in the access side of the network.

- Frame relay currently has very limited QoS support. When QoS is important, other Layer 2 or Layer 3 services are better suited. The new FRF.13 specification defines SLA terminology but provides no QoS (or throughput, for that matter) guarantees.

6.1 Motivation for Frame Relay

Frame relay services typically find application in private enterprise networks. However, ISPs can make use of this technology in the access subnetwork as well as, in some cases, the output protocol from a DSLAM in the aggregation subnetwork (although ATM is more prevalent in this application).

This section looks at frame relay from a somewhat general perspective, and at the same time addresses QoS support for both ISP and voice/ video-over frame relay network applications.

With the increased interest in full-featured, companywide connectivity for enterprise networks and intranets, access technology for SOHO support is playing an ever more important role in the total communication solution that corporate planners are seeking to deploy at this time. Specifically, there is interest in integrated multimedia access technology: Planners look for equipment that supports data, LAN, voice (compressed), videoconferencing, and fax applications over public or private frame relay networks, utilizing a single communication access facility (see Figure 6.1). Remote branch offices are prime candidates for such "entry-level," yet significantly important connectivity equipment. Given the fact that there may be many remote locations, cost-effectiveness of the equipment and bandwidth efficiency are critical. At the same time, carriers, especially CLECs, prefer to deliver only a single facility to a location and service all of the customer's needs in that manner, including Internet access.

Currently, many of these SOHO requirements are being met with frame relay-based enterprise networks; in the future, many of these requirements may be met with Internet services, which in turn may use frame relay in the access subnetwork. Note that in the former case, the planner needs a companywide frame relay infrastructure; in the later case, frame relay is used only in the access subnetwork, and end-to-end connectivity is supported by the Internet.

Frame relay has become a major networking technology of the 1990s. It is a statistics-supported, frame-based, connection-oriented "data" service that provides transparent transfer of information across a public or private network on a best-effort basis, which implies there is no guarantee of delivery or delivery within a stipulated time window; the network can discard frames in congestion situations or when the user exceeds the "traffic contract" established with the carrier. The protocol provides a minimal set of switching functions to forward variable-sized data payloads through a network. It is a Layer 2 service (hence, it is connection-oriented at Layer 2); IP, in contrast, is a Layer 3 protocol, and the so-called IP-dialtone is a Layer 3 (best-effort) service.

A 1996 report commissioned by the Frame Relay Forum (FRF) confirms that frame relay has become the predominant method for the wide area interconnection of corporate enterprise networks. The growth rate in the number of worldwide users has been 300 percent a year for the 1994–1996

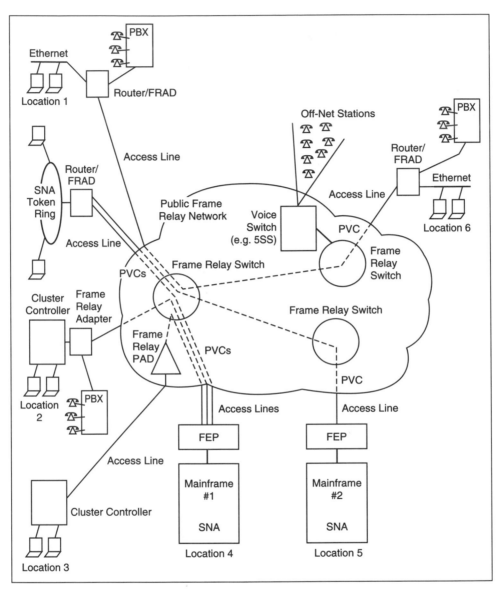

Figure 6.1 Frame relay-based enterprise network (traditional environment).

period; the number of organizations using it grew from 1,500 in 1994 to 15,000 in 1996. Growth rates are now smaller, but still positive: the same study found that the most common port speed is still 56/64Kbps. Overall, the market is expected to grow at about 25 percent a year for the rest of the decade. Hence, the support of voice-over frame relay is a relevant design question. Frame relay has evolved from a solution for transmitting legacy and LAN data to handling more delay-sensitive protocols (System Network Architecture, SNA) to the current challenge of delivering voice and fax across WANs. Besides traditional telephony, currently, voice-over-frame-relay seems to have the best chance of all the voice-over-packet alternatives to be used for commercial applications during the next couple of years. Unfortunately, there is relatively little support for QoS in frame relay; nevertheless, given its relative ubiquity there is a need to understand this technology. Work has just been completed in the FRF to define service levels, but this is only a first step in providing QoS.

Initially, voice-over frame relay makes sense over enterprise networks (even if implemented with public carrier frame relay services), rather than for generic off-net applications. Furthermore, it makes the most economic sense for calls between a company's domestic and international sites. However, as time goes by, there is the real possibility of central office (CO) interworking, allowing global access; the carrier in question, however, must deploy interworking equipment to achieve this.

The key specifications for the service are ANSI's T1.617 and T1.618. The FRF also has developed a set of critical implementation agreements (IA). This successful industry consortium continues in its efforts to promote use of frame relay products and services around the world, riding on the success of frame relay in North America and the growing markets in Europe and Asia. Key FRF specifications are FRF1.1, FRF.4, and FRF.8.

Initially, these standards did not include intrinsic voice support; now voice can be accommodated once a compression scheme is identified (so as to achieve greater packing density), and appropriate quality of service parameters for the frame relay service are established. Since 1997, a voice-over frame relay standard has become available. Voice carriage over frame relay does not generally rely on pulse code modulation (PCM) techniques used to digitize voice since the early 1960s. PCM uses a constant stream of bits in a TDM channel. Such techniques require 64Kbps, based on Nyquist's theorem and dynamic range/quantization considerations. The DS0/DS1/DS2/DS3 digital hierarchy still used in North America is based on this technology. Frame relay, on the other hand, is a form of statistical frame-based multiplexing with the associated possibility for frame-to-frame delay variation, frame loss, and jitter. To be able to support voice-over a *shared* 64Kbps access/backbone link, the industry has therefore moved to compressed voice. Video has used compression for many years; voice is now following suit.

Many companies rely on public frame relay services from carriers such as AT&T, Sprint, and MCI/Worldcom. New pricing trends are also giving impetus to the voice-support question: In the recent past, frame relay service charges have decreased, after several years of stability. For example, in 1996, some carriers decreased costs by up to 10 percent. In addition, AT&T now includes frame relay in its Tariff 12. This is important because companies have been swapping out private line services in favor of frame relay; however, because of the more favorable economics of frame relay, and because frame relay revenue was not counted toward the company's revenue commitment, this in effect worked "against" Tariff No. 12. Port-speed tariff prices for long-haul permanent virtual connection (PVC) service are approximately $275 at 56/64Kbps, $850 at 256Kbps, $1,370 for 512Kbps, and $2,300 for 1.544Mbps (note the distance independence). "Guaranteed" bandwidth (committed information rate, CIR) is charged in multiples of 8, 16, 32, or 64Kbps. Some carriers are now also in the process of introducing switched virtual channel (SVC) services and frame relay-to-ATM interworking.

As related to the "traditional" approach to voice support, in the recent past, long-distance carriers became involved in bidding contests that were driving down negotiated rates to as low as 5 cents per minute (as long as the organization was willing to channel all of its communication requirement to one provider). Reasons cited for this include anticipated concerns about the Regional Bell Operating Companies (RBOCs) entry into the long-haul market and the emergence of voice telephony over packet networks (IP and frame relay). The 5-cents-per-minute rate is available to customers with $20 million a year minimum annual commitment (MAC); customers with a $1 million per year can expect a 7.5 cents per-minute rate. Some fast-packet vendors claim that organizations can achieve voice transmission at $0.5 per minute over frame relay, ATM, or Internet (*Network World*, December 2, 1996, page 15).

6.2 Frame Relay Technology and Services

This section provides some fundamental information on frame relay service and technology.

6.2.1 Basic Frame Relay Service Concepts

Frame relay service is a connection-oriented "fast-packet"[1] service supporting bursty traffic at medium speeds. The service has evolved as an "improvement" of packet-switching service, supporting higher end-to-end throughput, lower delay, and less expensive user and network equipment. Frame relay accommodates applications such as wide area interconnection of LANs at the n × 56Kbps and 1.544Mbps rates. A frame relay interface (FRI) between the user and the network can support multiple sessions (specifically, multiple virtual channels, VCs) over a single physical access line, including data and voice. The term "relay" implies that the Layer 2 (data link layer) data frame is not terminated nor processed at the ends of each link in the network, but is relayed to the destination endpoint. Limiting Layer 2 functionality to the *core functions* required to achieve this relaying implies that forwarding functions can be implemented in hardware, rather than in software, thus improving throughput/delay characteristics at the switch and at the interface. Frame relay implements only the core functions on a link-by-link basis; the other functions, particularly error recovery, are done on an end-to-end basis. The data link layer core functions are:

- Frame delimiting, alignment, and transparency
- Frame multiplexing/demultiplexing using the address field
- Inspection of the frame to ensure that it consists of an integer number of octets prior to zero-bit insertion or following zero-bit extraction
- Inspection of the frame to ensure that it is neither too long nor too short
- Detection of transmission errors

Frames with errors are identified and discarded in the network, and user equipment is expected to recover higher-layer protocol data units (PDUs) using upper-layer protocols. Note that with cleaner fiber-based circuits, bit error rate (BER) is improved, thereby reducing the chance of transmission errors to a low probability. In a frame relay environment, the network can detect errors, but the correction is relegated to the endsystems (using TCP), which therefore must be appropriately configured to support these tasks. Error conditions include lost, duplicated, misdelivered, discarded, and out-of-sequence frames. Figure 6.2 shows a frame relay frame.

Frame relay enables the transmission of variable-length data units over an assigned virtual connection. Connection-oriented service involves a connection establishment phase, an information transfer phase, and a connection termination phase. A logical connection is set up between endsystems prior to exchanging data. This is accomplished using the signaling mechanism or by administrative arrangement. Sequencing of data, flow control, and transparent error handling are some of the capabilities supported by a generic connection-oriented service. Frame relay service initially provides a permanent virtual connection (PVC) service and later

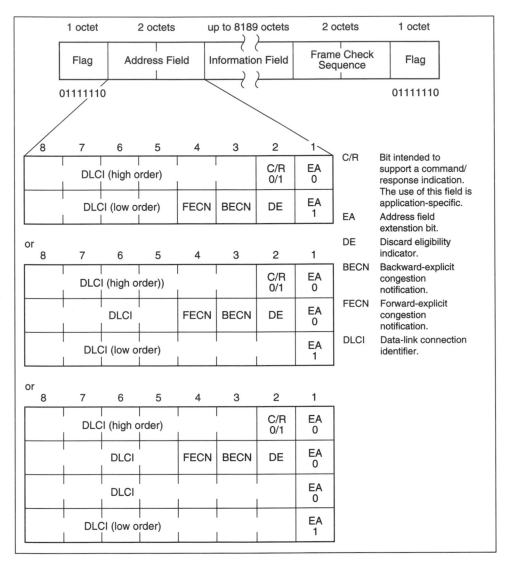

Figure 6.2   Frame relay frame.

on could support a switched virtual connection (SVC) service. A PVC implementation establishes a fixed path through the network for each source-destination pair, which remains defined for a long period of time (weeks, months, or years). Since the setup is done once, it implies the allocation of some resources, regardless of the real-time traffic requirements or lack thereof. In SVC, resources are put in place only for the duration of the actual session (minutes or hours).

Frame relay service was developed originally as an ISDN packet service, with logically separate control plane and user plane information. In the control plane, all signaling capabilities for call control, parameter negotiation, and so on, to support SVC service, were based on a set of protocols common to all ISDN services. However, until the late 1990s, the implementations did not support the control plane, they were not deployed in conjunction with ISDN, and they have been based on PVCs. Nearly all services now in place are PVC-based.

Frame relay can be obtained both as a private network technology or as a public network service. Early commercial impetus in the United States was toward the deployment of frame relay service within the context of enterprise corporate networks, particularly for LAN interconnection. However, although a customer can deploy private switches, to get maximum benefit from frame relay, the service should be provided by a carrier. Scores of carriers offer the service either LATA (local access and transport area)-wide, nationally or internationally.

Standards work for frame relay started in the mid-1980s, then accelerated in the late 1980s, after the publication of the first ITU-T frame relay standards. Table 6.1 compares key ITU-T and ANSI standards; Table 6.2 lists additional standards and requirements. A significant amount of work has been undertaken by the Frame Relay Forum. Table 6.3 lists the key FRF specifications in support of the service, as of the time of this writing. The basic frame relay protocol, described by the international standards committee, by the national standards committee, and even by the Frame Relay Forum, such as User to Network (UNI) and Network to Network (NNI) Implementation Agreements, has been augmented in recent years by the FRF via additional agreements that detail techniques for structuring application data over the basic frame relay information field. These techniques enabled successful support for data applications such as LAN bridging, IP routing, and SNA. Like X.25, frame relay specifies the interface between customer equipment and the network, whether public or private. This interface specification is described in generalities in ITU-T

Table 6.1   Formal Frame Relay Standards

STANDARD	ANSI NUMBER	ITU-T NUMBER
Framework		I.122
Service Description	T1.606	I.233
Congestion Management	T1.606 Addendum	I.370
Data Transfer Protocol	T1.618	Q.922 Annex A
Access Signaling	T1.617	Q.933

Table 6.2   Additional Recommendations and Documents

ITU-T Q.933	Digital Subscriber Signaling System No. 1 (DSS1). Signaling specification for frame mode bearer service.
ITU-T Q.939	Typical DSS1 service indicator coding examples.
ITU-T Q.950	Stage 3 description for number identification supplementary services using DSS1; supplementary services protocols; structure and general principles.
ITU-T Q.951	Stage 3 description for number identification supplementary services using DSS1; calling line identification presentation (CLIP); calling line identification restriction (CLIR); connected line identification presentation (COLP); connected line identification restriction (COLR).
ITU-T Q.952	Stage 3 service description for call-offering supplementary services using DSS1; diversion supplementary services.
ITU-T Q.953	Stage 3 description for call completion supplementary services using DSS1; call hold.
ITU-T Q.954	Stage 3 description for multiparty supplementary services using DSS1; conference calling; three-party service.
ITU-T Q.955	Stage 3 description for community-of-interest supplementary services using DSS1; multilevel precedence and preemption (MLPP).
ITU-T Q.957	Stage 3 description for additional information transfer supplementary services using DSS1; user-to-user signaling.
Bellcore TA-TSV-001240	Generic requirements for frame relay access to SMDS.
Bellcore TA-NWT-001327	Generic requirements for FR network elements operations.
Bellcore TR-TSV-001369	Generic requirements for frame relay PVC exchange service.
Bellcore TR-TSV-001370	Generic requirements for exchange access frame relay PVC service.
Bellcore TA-NWT-001371	Generic requirements for Phase 1 frame relay PVC CNM service.

Table 6.3 Frame Relay Forum Specifications

User-to-Network (UNI) Implementation Agreement	FRF.1.1, Date: January 19, 1996
Frame Relay Network-to-Network (NNI) Implementation Agreement Version 2.1	FRF.2.1, Date: July 10, 1995
Multiprotocol Encapsulation Implementation Agreement (MEI)	FRF.3.1, Date: June 22, 1995
Switched Virtual Circuit Implementation Agreement (SVC)	FRF.4, Date: N/A
Frame Relay/ATM Network Interworking Implementation Agreement	FRF.5, Date: December 20, 1994
Frame Relay Service Customer Network Management Implementation Agreement (MIB)	FRF.6 (FRFTC93.111R3), Date: March 1, 1994
Frame Relay PVC Multicast Service and Protocol Description	FRF.7, Date: October 21, 1994
Frame Relay/ATM PVC Service Interworking Implementation Agreement	FRF.8, Date: April 14, 1995
Data Compression over Frame Relay Implementation Agreement	FRF.9, Date: January 22, 1996
Frame Relay Network-to-Network SVC Implementation Agreement	FRF.10, Date: September 10, 1996
Voice-over Frame Relay Implementation Agreement	FRF.11, Date: May 5, 1997
Frame Relay Fragmentation Implementation Agreement	FRF.12, Date: December 15, 1997
Service Level Definitions Implementation Agreement	FRF.13, Date: August 4, 1998

Recommendation I.122, first published in 1988; it is also described in FRF1.1. ANSI T1.606 describes the frame relay service; the equivalent ITU-T recommendation is I.233. ANSI T1.606 Addendum describes congestion management; the equivalent ITU-T recommendation is I.370.

The frame format for data transfer is based on a subset of Q.921 (LAP-D), but extended with the flow control fields. The protocol is now known as Link Access Procedure F-Core (LAP-F Core) and is defined in ANSI T1.618-1991; it also defined in ITU-T's Q.922 Annex A adopted in 1992.[2] It also describes the data transfer protocol at the UNI. A 1992 ITU-T protocol extended from Q.931, called Q.933, was developed to support SVC service. In the United States, T1.617-1991 describes access signaling, along with FRF.4. PVC management functions are included in T1.617 Annex D; many

FRAME RELAY FORUM DIRECTIONS

The membership of the Frame Relay Forum (FRF) had several goals at the time of this writing.

- The Technical Committee and the membership (through ballot) were to finalize the first phase of the Voice over Frame Relay Implementation Agreement (IA), and continue to enhance this exciting application beyond the 1997 accomplishments. The North American Market Development and Education Committee (MD&E) released a white paper on Voice over Frame Relay (available at http://www.frforum.com).

- The European MD&E Committee was to continue to educate potential customers and providers about the benefits of implementing frame relay in Europe (e.g., the recent Frame Relay 2000 initiative in Europe, sponsored by the FRF).

- The board of directors was to begin the FRF's efforts to promote frame relay in the Pacific Rim, Asia, and China.

- The MD&E Committee was to work to bring frame relay into the mainstream of SNA business applications, through carrier services and advanced functionality in frame relay access devices (FRADs) and frame relay switches.

In 1997, FRF members participating on the Technical Committee and associated working groups focused on:

- FRF.10: Switched virtual circuits (SVCs) at the network-to-network interface (NNI). Ballot resolution had been completed and would be forwarded

of features of the (Interim) Local Management Interface ((I)LMI) specification contained in T1.617 were initially proposed by vendors and by the Frame Relay Forum. The (I)LMI makes it possible for the network to notify the end user of the addition, deletion, or presence of a PVC at a specified UNI (any such information received on a UNI applies to that particular UNI). Areas of standardization also include NNI protocols and interoffice signaling. The frame relay sidebar summarizes key standardization/specification activities at time of this writing.

6.2.2 Enterprise Networking Applications

Figure 6.3 depicts the use of frame relay services in the context of an enterprise network. As noted, frame relay was originally developed to support the bursty traffic generated by LANs interconnected over WANs. In the early 1990s, it was used as a cost-effective consolidation of distinct corpo-

to the board for ratification. FRF.10 was planned to be available to the public soon thereafter.

- FRF.11: Voice over Frame Relay (VoFR) specifies procedures for the transport of packetized low bit rate voice-over frame relay networks. This first-phase IA defines support for preconfigured connections allowing multivendor interoperability. The VoFR IA became available in mid-1997.

New efforts initiated by the membership that may lead to IAs in the future include:

- Frame Relay Fragmentation: This will enable fragmentation and reassembly of frames at the FR UNI. Work was completed in December 1997.

- Multilink Frame Relay at the User-to-Network Interface (UNI): This will enable frame relay devices to use multiple physical links; in essence, frame relay inverse muxing. This effort was expected to be completed by late 1997.

- Frame Relay-to-ATM (FR/ATM) Switched Virtual Connection (SVC) Service Interworking: This effort will define FR/ATM service interworking supporting SVCs, popular in ATM, and already defined for frame relay. This effort is expected to be completed by the time this book goes to press.

- Frame Relay Network Service Level Definitions: This effort will provide FR network performance definitions, to enable service providers to deliver service levels that are uniform across diverse networks. It will provide users with a metric for use when determining whether contracted service levels are rendered. The agreement was completed in August 1998.

rate networks, such as legacy SNA networks. Frame relay's low cost compared to meshing of dedicated lines, along with the first kind of traffic contracts available in the WAN market (ATM being the culmination in this respect) has made the service popular. For example, let's assume the user is on a T1/DS1 line, and contracts for 256Kbps of CIR with the carrier; the user could then try to burst to a much higher level and for a relatively long period of time. Users in general try to get away with the lowest possible CIR, even as low as 0, and then send more data, in which case, all of the relevant performance metrics, delay, jitter, and loss will be impacted.

The financial advantage of a frame relay network becomes more marked when the number of routers is high (half a dozen to a dozen or more), and when the distances between routers is considerable (hundreds or thousands of miles). If the routers are all located within a small geographic area, like a city, a county, or an LATA, the economic advantage of elimination lines is less conspicuous. The following list summarizes some of the benefits of frame relay:

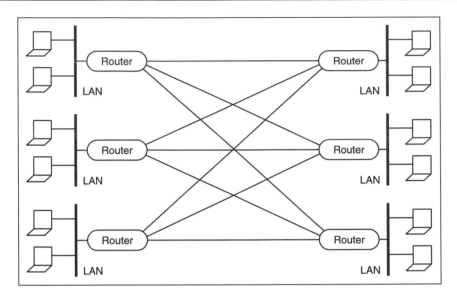

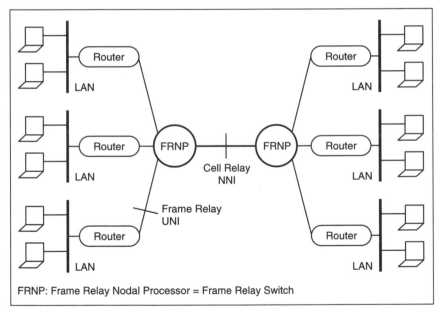

Figure 6.3   Use of frame relay in enterprise networks: (top) preframe relay; (bottom) with frame relay. (Note: Switches may be user- or carrier-owned.)

Port and Link Sharing

Bandwidth-on-Demand

High Throughput and Low Delay

Ease of Network Expansion

Ease of Transition from Existing Router Networks

Ease of Transition from Any Existing Network

Cohesiveness and Symbiosis with LANs

Simplified Network Administration

Standards-Based

Economic Advantages (in a variety of situations)

As discussed earlier, private networks based on dedicated lines tend to become impractical when a large number of remote data sources/sinks are generating bursty traffic. The number of links grows quadratically with the number of sites to be interconnected. In addition, the interconnection capacity needs to be higher; this increase in the speed is often dictated by applications requiring more data to be transacted, as well by the number of users invoking the service of interconnection. This implies that fairly expensive links are required. Five classes of solutions are available:

- Instead of connecting all routers with a fully interconnected network, connect some routers in tandem. While this reduces the number of links, it introduces extra end-to-end delay and increases nodal processing (requiring more machine cycles).

- Deploy a private frame relay network using frame relay switch(es). Instead of physical point-to-point links, this approach requires connecting only the routers to the switch(es) with a single physical link. Connection between various routers is accomplished with PVCs.

- Utilize a PVC-based carrier-provided frame relay network. Instead of many physical point-to-point links, this approach requires connecting only the routers to the carrier's switch with a single physical link. Connection between various routers is accomplished with PVCs, which are established at service subscription.

- Utilize a hybrid configuration. A cluster of sites employ private frame relay; other sites take advantage of public frame relay services.

- Utilize a SVC-based carrier-provided frame relay network. Instead of many physical point-to-point links, this approach requires connecting only the routers to the carrier's switch with a single physical link. Connection between various routers is accomplished as needed by establishing a real-time SVC, which is in existence only for the duration of the session.

The evolution in the private environment involves using switches that provide FRIs to the routers and use cell relay/ATM technology between nodes (as indicated, it would be technically possible to also use frame relay techniques between the switches, as in fact two frame relay routers connected by a dedicated T1 link use). Although frame relay remains a connection-oriented service, there still are advantages in connecting LANs through frame relay rather than X.25 packet switching. In particular, when utilizing X.25 service, routers had to encapsulate LAN traffic in the X.25 packet, imposing substantial performance degradation. Frame relay, on the other hand, incurs little overhead and allows for a number of protocols to be transported transparently.

Some users may deploy hybrid frame relay networks. These users could utilize their own frame relay backbone connecting major sites, and use a public frame relay network to connect secondary sites.

In view of the growth in popularity of LANs, carriers have realized the commercial opportunity to provide public PVC-based frame relay data services that support high-capacity access/throughput, coupled with the universal access, survivability, economies of scale, and efficiency available through resource sharing. SVC-based frame relay can have some advantages, but it also has some limitations. First, the service may become available only later in the decade. Second, a user who needs to send data to some remote user on another LAN may not be willing to incur the call setup time each time a session is required. Some people have gotten around the setup time issue in packet-switched networks by using long-duration SVCs: these are set up once and kept active for an appropriate amount of time, like a day.

As noted, frame relay services are also used by the ISPs. It is prudent for the communication manager to look at networking solutions that will not have to be discarded after a couple of years to keep up with network growth or higher speed networking needs or technologies. One answer to this problem is to rely on a public carrier and avoid setting up a private network and secure the WAN-switching hardware. Some private frame relay switches now on the market support only data. Other switches support data, voice, and video. Because switches based on cell switching better utilize backbone, the deployment of these mixed-media switches in a private network benefits users who need to connect LANs over integrated backbones supporting a variety of *other* traffic. Users with LAN traffic only may choose *data-only* switches. Other approaches, though, have evolved in the recent past. One is the use of campus ATM switches; another is to use Layer 2 switches (L2S—e.g., Ethernet switches). Planners now routinely run MPEG-1 (CD-ROM-based) video over LANs and L2Ss.

Although initially carrier frame relay networks were implemented as separate overlay networks, today many carriers' frame relay networks are integrated with ATM. This means that the switch supports a frame relay user-to-network (UNIs) interface to the user side, but internally is an

ATM switch. So input frames are cellularized (typically on the input card), and the ATM quality of service and traffic/buffer management mechanisms are used to handle the derivative cells. On the output side, cells are either converted back to frames for immediate delivery or are passed up to another switch for wide-area coverage. At the destination switch, cells are converted back to frames (having thereby achieved network interworking) or are delivered directly over an ATM link to the user. The user can in turn convert those cells back to frame relay (the advantage of this approach is that a high-speed link, such as 45Mbps or 155Mbps can be used, rather than just a T1 link, as would be the case in a frame relay NNI). Note that frame relay was not originally designed to support voice or QoS-based communications, while ATM has been developed from the beginning for this type of traffic mixing. In the frame-over ATM case, QoS can be guaranteed to the cell stream but not necessarily to the frame stream. Clearly, better edge-to-edge behavior obtained via the ATM core network's QoS is a step in the right direction.

6.2.3 Voice Considerations

The frame relay PVC enables the delivery of frames across a WAN in the proper order, and error checking prevents delivery of errored frames. However, frame relay service does not provide any intrinsic mechanisms for higher grades of service. In other words, there is no explicit method for establishing frame-level performance priorities. The only way to get any different traffic treatment is to:

1. Set up different PVCs from the router/FRAD to the other end, over the WAN.

2. Administratively inform the carrier that certain PVCs carry "higher-priority traffic."

3. Hope that the carrier has a switch that has some level of different grade-of-service treatment.

4. Hope that the carrier does not greatly overbook the bandwidth.

5. Hope that there are not too many hops in the network.

6. Acquire a CPE (router or FRAD) that can itself handle different inputs (e.g., LAN segment, PBX, etc.) differently (according to some priority scheme).

In May 1997, the Frame Relay Forum ratified a standard called FRF.11 for interoperable voice-over frame relay networks (see FRF.11 sidebar).

FRAME RELAY FORUM PRESS RELEASE ON FRF.11 (HTTP://WWW.FRFORUM.COM)

The Frame Relay Forum announced in May 1997 the ratification of FRF.11, an implementation agreement (IA) providing for voice-over frame relay (VoFR) communications.

Specifically, FRF.11, entitled "Voice over Frame Relay" provides for bandwidth-efficient networking of Voice and Group 3 fax communications over frame relay and defines multiplexed virtual connections (VCs). This latter function allows for up to 255 voice and data subchannels to be carried over a single VC through a frame relay network. Transparent relay of Group 3 fax communications is provided for in the IA by "spoofing" of the fax protocol, and transmission of fax traffic as a low bit-rate digital stream.

Two classes of voice compliance are supported, for maximum flexibility and worldwide applicability. Class 1 compliance calls for use of G.727 EADPCM, typically at 32Kbps (2:1 compression). Class 2 compliance specifies G.729/G.729A CS-ACELP at 8Kbps (8:1 compression). To maximize use of bandwidth, it is possible to carry multiple voice samples in a single frame, further minimizing overhead.

The new IA is significant in that it is the first step for true multivendor interoperability of voice and fax over frame relay. Already offering a streamlined, compatible method for interoperability of data applications over the wide area, the new IA bolsters frame relay's capability to support the full complement of corporate LAN and legacy data, voice, fax, and packetized video communications.

Prior to that, users had to rely on vendor-specific solutions. Implementation plans are unclear at this time; frame relay service providers have cautioned companies against implementing voice-over frame relay, most ostensibly because these carriers also stand to lose voice traffic revenues. Secondarily, it may be that their networks are unable to support the QoS required for voice. However, it is expected that equipment suppliers will implement the standard as time goes by.

To support voice, it is necessary to support priorities in the switch (organization- or carrier-owned). Hence, in looking at switch technology, one needs to ascertain how the priorities are allocated and managed. With top-of-the-line switches, such as Ascend/Cascade B-STDX 9000, Newbridge 36170, Cisco BPX/AXIS, Nortel Passport 160, Telematics NCX-1E6, and Sentient Ultimate 1000/2000, the frame relay priorities are supported via ATM priorities and qualities of service. Consequently, a good understanding of the latter is needed. The bottom line is, however, that since ATM has strong quality-of-service capabilities, it has become possible to support priorities in frame relay, thereby making the support of voice-over frame relay possible. Some switches support 2 frame relay priorities, others 4 or 8 priorities, others yet as much as 32 priorities (these are assigned by administrative provisioning of the PVC). The difference with ATM is that even when the priorities are implemented by the switch, the QoS is not "guaranteed," as would the case in the former. Table 6.4 lists some of the desirable features of a state-of-the-art frame relay switch, enabling it to support, among other services, voice. Some older and/or smaller switches do not support sophisticated priority mechanisms to handle PVCs in different ways (at the queue level).

Although frame relay is popular for its flexible bandwidth, its popularity has given rise to congestion on some networks, because carriers may not properly engineer their networks (to maximize their profitability); or carriers have had difficulty keeping up with the demands for new service. Given just the demand for higher bandwidth as additional organizations subscribe, it is a relatively simple step for the public carriers to add switches and capacity to the backbone to accommodate the growing demand. But now customers are requesting lower latency service for their carriers, so that voice and fax can be carried over frame relay. There is a perception that many carriers are struggling in their effort to increase capacity to meet this demand and/or to replace older switches with new ones that are ATM-based and support quality of service at the PVC level. These issues also impact use in an ISP context.

Carriers, central office switch manufacturers, and customer premises equipment vendors are addressing the voice-over frame relay opportunity simultaneously. Customer premises equipment (CPE) manufacturers have recently seen a growing interest in voice-over frame relay, and have followed up with fast-paced research and the development of voice-capable frame relay access devices. However, although the equipment choices are numerous, many of the carriers do not provide adequate support; only two companies at time of this writing, for example, provided service-level guarantees for voice-over frame relay. Issues related to voice-over frame relay are treated at length in Minoli's *Delivering Voice over Frame Relay and ATM* [1].

6.3 Additional Details on Frame Relay Technology and Services

Frame relay is a multiplexed data networking capability supporting connectivity between user equipment (routers and private frame relay

Table 6.4   Key Features of Frame Relay Switch

Frame relay to ATM network interworking	Critical
Frame relay to ATM service interworking	Critical
Channelized DS3 plug-ins	Critical
Channelized DS1 for frame relay	Critical
ATM UNI DS3	Critical
CO power (−48v)	Critical
Dual power source	Critical
Redundant switch processor	Critical
Frame relay point-to-point PVC support	Critical
Guaranteed committed information rate (CIR)	Critical
Performance reports	Critical
Billing reports	Critical
Telemetry access	Critical
Traps to multiple network management systems (NMSs)	Critical
Local configuration database	Critical
Modularity	Critical
High port density	Critical
High backplane capacity	Critical
NEBS compliance	Critical
Year 2000 compliance	Critical
Load sharing	Critical
Dual power feeds	Critical
Hot-swappable (all elements)	Critical
1 for N line redundancy	Critical
Support of standards (see Table 6.1), plus more)	Critical
Large number of PVCs per port	Important
Frame relay point-to-multipoint	Important
Unchannelized DS1 plug-ins	Important
Configurable peak rate	Important

Table 6.4   *(Continued)*

Oversubscription	Important
ATM traffic parameter support (PCR, SCR, MBS)	Important
ATM QoS classes	Important
NNI connectivity for frame relay	Important
External timing	Important
NMS support under HPOV	Important
Configuration GUIs	Important
SNMP support	Important

switches), and between frame relay switches, introduced in the late 1980s and early 1990s.[3] The frame relay protocol supports transmission over a connection-oriented path; it enables the transmission of variable-length data units over an assigned virtual connection. Compared to traditional packet-switched services, frame relay can reduce network delays, provide more efficient bandwidth utilization, and decrease communication equipment cost. Traditional packet services typically introduce a 200-millisecond (msec) network delay or more (40–60 milliseconds per hop to handle error correction and control on a hop-by-

SUMMARY OF KEY FEATURES OF A FRAME RELAY NETWORK

- Standardized by ITU-T, ANSI, and FRF standards.
- Only "core" functions are provided by the network.
- Network does not guarantee delivery of data.
- Protocols in user's equipment is responsible for retransmitting data that is lost, misrouted, or discarded by the network because of congestion.
- Frames are transported transparently (only label, congestion bits, and frame check sequence are modified by network).
- Network detects (but does not correct) transmission, format, and operational errors.
- Network does not acknowledge or retransmit frames.
- Delivers frames in sequence.
- Can be "service" and "network" interworked with ATM.

hop basis), whereas with frame relay that network delay can be reduced to about 20–40 msec.

As is the case in X.25, frame relay standards specify the user interface to a device or network supporting the service. This user-to-network interface (UNI) is called frame relay interface (FRI). A FRI supports access speeds of 56Kbps, N × 64Kbps and 1.544Mbps (2.048Mbps in Europe). The service can be deployed (i) in a point-to-point link fashion between two routers, (ii) using customer-owned frame relay switches (frame relay switches may employ cell relay on the trunk/NNI side), and (iii) utilizing a carrier-provided service. The following sidebar provides a summary of key features of a frame relay network.[4]

6.3.1 Recent Evolution of Enterprise Networks

Frame relay functions supporting the FRI need to be added to user equipment such as routers, front end processors (FEPs), legacy access multiplexers, and so on, in order to be connected to a private or public frame relay network.

At this time, frame relay technology is being applied mostly to enterprise network *interconnection environments.* Existing enterprise routers have been upgraded to support the FRI. Asynchronous terminals not on LANs may also be supported by a frame relay network; synchronous SNA terminals or other devices (for example, a front end processor) can also use frame relay. In these cases, an appropriate frame relay handler (similar to a packet assembler/dissassembler (PAD) but only supporting a Layer 2 FRI to the network) is required. This is called a *frame relay PAD,* or FRAD. In terms of quality of service, the delay incurred by the needed protocol conversion to support these devices (which is similar to the delay through a PAD in an X.25 environment) is not eliminated by frame relay technology, except possibly to reduce queuing time toward the switch, given lower network congestion. The delay through such a frame relay handler is determined by the access speed of the user's line, plus the handler's processing time. For example, if the user's frame from a synchronous terminal contained 262 octets, and the access line was 9,600 bps, the initial frame relay "framing" delay would be 219 milliseconds; the "deframing" delay would also be 219 milliseconds. If the access speed were 56Kbps, the figure would be 37 milliseconds. This framing/deframing delay is in addition to the frame relay network delay.[5] From the user perspective, any delay is important regardless of whether the delay is generated by the frame relay network or by the access apparatus to the frame relay network (whether in a PC, a terminal adapter, or a PAD-like device). This last issue was never properly appreciated by the packet-equipment vendors, and is the reason packet technology did not see much penetration in the mission-critical synchronous networks of the 1980s.

Performance characteristics to support voice include low delay, delay variation (jitter) and frame loss. Because in enterprise networks frame relay is typically secured via routers, voice/QoS performance must be seen in the context of the router and of the frame relay service proper.

To get maximum benefit from frame relay without having to incur large communication or equipment charges (i.e., for dedicated T1 links between sites, or for the deployment of user-owned frame relay switches), the *service must be provided by a carrier.* Many carriers now offer frame relay services. Carrier networks based on frame relay provide communications at up to 1.544Mbps (in the United States), shared bandwidth-on-demand, and multiple user sessions over a single access line. The use of a router equipped with a frame relay interface over a dedicated end-to-end T1 link is not economically advantageous compared to a nonframe relay solution, and in fact, may affect response time. A carrier, on the other hand, can multiplex the traffic of one user with that of other users, and can, therefore, pass back to the users the economic advantages of bandwidth sharing. Without carriers or private switches, dedicated T1 links between two sites to be interconnected are needed, regardless of the protocol used over the link. However, it should be noted that when using an IXC or VAN service, the user needs a dedicated T1 or 56Kbps link to the IXC's or VAN's POP. If the LEC serving the user's location provides the service, the dedicated T1 is required only to the serving CO.

A second way to benefit from frame relay is to secure it with *private frame relay* switches. Some corporate networks were already deploying this technology in the late 1980s, in the form of fast-packet *multiplexers*. In this case, the service can often be cost-effective compared to a non-packet-based backbone, since the user can obtain from the backbone bandwidth-on-demand, rather than on a preallocated (and inefficient) basis. The "saved" bandwidth is then available to other users of the same backbone, in theory minimizing the amount of new raw bandwidth the corporation needs to acquire from a carrier in the form of additional T1 or fractional T1 links. However, without a switch using cell relay principles internally and/or in the trunking, dynamic bandwidth allocation is not altogether achievable. Also, there is a strong desire for integration: having a single network that supports both the broadband needs as well as the lower (frame relay-level) needs. This is achievable by using an ATM switch that also has frame relay support. Some frame relay switches use frame relay on the NNI; fine-grain multiplexing is more difficult, particularly in mixed-media and multimedia applications. In the private network application, the user leases from a carrier private lines between the remote devices and the switches, and between the switches; the user employs frame relay to statistically multiplex traffic, in a standardized way, in order to achieve better utilization of the (now common) transmission resources. The switch must be housed in selected user locations.

The ultimate enterprise application is to use frame relay to access an ISP and then secure an IP tunnel (that is, VPN) service across the Internet.

Frame relay is a natural evolution of packet switching. Many of the principles still apply, although some of the error handling has changed and the switches are much faster, being ASIC-based and operating at the 1–10Gbps aggregate rate. Packet switching allows users to be easily added and interconnected, while following open international standards. But packet switching has traditionally been slow, and the throughput has been limited.[6] These limitations became more accentuated with the new LAN applications involving graphics, multimedia, desktop publishing, attachments transfer, and other data-intensive requirements. This has led to the development of two solutions specifically aimed at LANs: frame relay and ATM. Frame relay supports bursty traffic at medium speeds. The introduction of switched Ethernet, 100Mbps Ethernet, and gigabit Ethernet imply that for major locations frame relay is not enough. Organizations that have these kinds of desktop networks need to use ATM or ATM-based transparent LAN services (TLS) offered by a number of CLECs, notably TCG. But for branch locations, frame relay continues to be an adequate choice.

The business trend is toward *interconnection of all company resources* into a seamless enterprisewide network. The paradigm is now "the corporation is the network." However, such interconnection can become prohibitively expensive, unless it is done correctly. Corporations also see the emergence of new LAN applications in the 1990s, which must be supported by the enterprisewide network. QoS support is also required. New high-bandwidth applications dictate the introduction of new high-capacity digital services and technologies in the corporate network. Frame relay is a step in that direction. High end-to-end throughput, low latency, cost-effective bandwidth-on-demand, and any-to-any connectivity are the order of the day. A major evolution in the way corporations connect their computers and the ubiquitous PC is already evident in progressive companies. Now, new equipment and new communications services (e.g., Internet-based e-commerce) allow corporations to redesign their networks and save money, while at the same time increase their capabilities and workforce productivity. The key to achieve these communication goals in a private network environment is frame relay over a cell relay platform, or a high-capacity public-switched service like frame relay.

The new technologies needed to support the evolving corporate environment cannot, however, be introduced in a vacuum. It would be easy to deploy an optimal state-of-the-art network when the LAN manager could throw away everything and start from scratch. The transition steps to the new communication environment depend on the network currently in place in the company. Five generations of corporate networks have been deployed in the past decade. Some users moved from generation to generation; other users leapfrogged one or two generations. Still others were forced to retain a network until the payback could be achieved and then some. Usually, a network stays in place for a period corresponding to the useful life of the equipment, which can be five to eight years. A short review of the five generations of corporate networking aids the discussion of how frame relay evolved and the problems it solves; it can also establish the point of departure for the transition, which the LAN manager needs to undertake in order to implement frame relay.

First-generation corporate networks. In the early 1980s, this phase saw the introduction of unintegrated nationwide networks, which typically employed low-speed analog lines to support discrete mission-critical corporate functions. LANs were just being introduced in companies. Connectivity among LANs, for the few progressive companies that attempted it at that time, used its own point-to-point transmission facilities. Different departmental data applications (for example, a mainframe payroll application and a minicomputer supporting marketing) used separate networks. Not only was this solution expensive because of the duplicate transmission costs, but it also was difficult to manage and to grow. A number of mission-critical networks in place today still conform to this architecture. These companies have found that until now a backbone network was not cost-effective.

Second-generation corporate networks. In the mid-1980s, this phase saw the introduction of T1 multiplexers and supporting digital transmission facilities. The data applications were aggregated over a common backbone network, improving network management, simplifying the topology, and reducing the communications cost. A few traditional analog lines are enough to justify the cost of a high-speed digital link, as discussed elsewhere in this book, making this transition a popular upgrade in the recent past. Voice traffic was also carried by the backbone. One of the shortcomings of this approach, however, is that the LAN interconnection traffic, now growing, usually remained separate, perpetuating the problem of overlay networks. This was typically due to restrictions of the byte-interleaved multiplexer, namely, the inability to support dynamic traffic for bursty users, and interface problems. A number of mission-critical networks in place today still conform to this architecture.

Third-generation corporate networks.   In the late 1980s, T1 multiplexers started to support LAN interconnection traffic. The traffic was assigned a fixed amount of TDM bandwidth over the corporate backbone network. Although this approach to LAN interconnection had several advantages compared to the previous arrangement, it also had a number of disadvantages. Consider N nodes with high peak-to-average (bursty) traffic that need to be supported by an enterprise network. A mesh network providing full interconnection between key nodes may have been installed in many companies. This arrangement can be expensive due to the number of communications links. For example, five locations require 10 T1 links; six locations require 15 links. The addition of a new backbone node also requires the introduction of many new links. Less than fully interconnected routers networks are usually not the best answer to the interconnection requirement, since this tandem arrangement affects the end-to-end delay and complicates network management. Additionally, and perhaps equally important, the bandwidth is not efficiently allocated by using the TDM technique common to the equipment supporting this type of network. As a short-term solution, companies sought to keep the number of designated first-tier locations, which need full interconnection, down to a small number, typically between three and six, hence limiting the number of required links. Some companies still have these types of networks today, particularly for mission-critical applications. Some LAN managers, understanding the intuitive advantage of packet switching, chose to rely on a private (or public) packet-switched network to interconnect the multitude of user routers. These packet networks typically introduce a router-to-router delay on the order of 200 milliseconds or more. This delay is due to, one, protocol processing at intermediary nodes, and, two, the hop-by-hop error correction and control utilized by packet networks. In addition to the delay, the throughput of these networks is not sufficient to support today's applications. That is why a new technology was needed.

Fourth-generation corporate networks. Managers soon realized that ubiquitous connectivity using the existing technology would lead to highly meshed networks. What is needed is a technology for high end-to-end throughput, low latency, cost-effective bandwidth-on-demand, and any-to-any connectivity. The restrictions discussed previously of many of the existing unintegrated networks or of the integrated networks that use TDM technology, has led to the development of the frame relay. Since corporate resources are increasingly being deployed on LANs, including the users, the mainframes, and the data bases, and since routers have taken on the function of the T1 multiplexers of the late 1980s, this interconnection solution is the one that has been and is being deployed in the enterprisewide networks of the 1990s. Fewer and shorter T1 or fractional T1 links can be used between the users and the switch, thereby reducing communication costs.

Fifth-generation corporate networks. As noted, the introduction of switched Ethernet, 100Mbps Ethernet, and gigabit Ethernet is beginning to require interconnection between subnets at speeds higher than 1.544Mbps possible with frame relay. Speed requirements range from 6–10 Mbps (achievable with inverse multiplexers and TLS), to as much as 45, 155, and 622Mbps on ATM UNIs. Many progressive companies and early adopters are now introducing ATM in their campuses and WANs. The issue, however, is how to secure broadband connectivity over the long haul.

A new generation of corporate networks now use Internet and/or Internet or ISP-provided private-IP-network VPN services. As noted, frame relay plays somewhat of a role on the access side, although dedicated DS1, DS3, or ATM access is also now becoming prevalent.

6.3.2 Key Frame Relay and Cell Relay Concepts

The following "mini-glossary" defines key frame relay terms. As this discussion proceeds, keep in mind that all high-speed lines used in frame relay, either for access or between switches are unchannelized FT1, T1 or T3 lines.

Frames

A frame is a block of user data, as created by the data link layer (Layer 2). It consists of a flag, a header, an information field, and a trailer. Different

MINI-GLOSSARY OF FRAME RELAY TERMS

Access Rate.   The rate of the access channel employed by the user's equipment, measured in bits per second. The speed of the access channel determines how rapidly the end user can send data to the switch or network.

American National Standards Institute (ANSI).   An organization that accredits groups developing U.S. standards required for commerce. One such group is the Exchange Carriers Standards Association, which developed the T1.606, T1.617, and T1.618 for frame relay.

Asynchronous Transfer Mode (ATM).   A packet-switching technique developed by ITU-T, which uses packets of fixed length, resulting in lower processing and higher speeds. Also known as cell relay.

Backward-Explicit Congestion Notification Indicator.   A bit in the frame set by the network to notify the user's equipment that congestion avoidance procedures should be initiated, so as to limit the amount of traffic injected into the network or sent to the switch. The field is set in a frame going in the opposite direction of the congestion (i.e., it is sent to the origination). It is similar to a "slowdown" signal.

Bandwidth.   The communications capacity (measured in bits per second) of a transmission line or a path through a network.

Bursty Traffic.   Traffic where the ratio of the maximum intensity to the average intensity is very high (>10). Typical of some LAN environments.

Cell Relay.   A high-bandwidth, low-delay switching and multiplexing packet technology required to implement a frame relay network in an efficient manner. Trunk transmission technique used by switches. Also known as ATM.

Cell.   A fixed-length packet of user data (payload) plus an overhead. A cell is usually small, 53 octets or fewer.

Committed Information Rate (CIR).   A measure that specifies the amount of bandwidth promised to a user, between any two points; CIR can be as high as the access rate. If the CIR is exceeded, the frame relay device can send the data, but it should set the DE bit to indicate the data can be discarded if necessary.

Core Functions.   Data link layer functions supported by frame relay. Core functions include frame delimiting, alignment, and transparency; frame multiplexing/demultiplexing using the address field; and detection of transmission errors.

Data Link Connection Identifier (DLCI).   A field in the frame indicating a particular logical link over which the frame should be transmitted. The field has local significance, since it can be changed by the switches as the frame traverses a single-node network (the input DLCI is mapped to an output DLCI). Multinode networks may "pipeline" cells to the network edges. In this case, virtual channel identifiers (VCIs) are used and remapped. Access DLCIs are assigned by the network manager, while trunk VCIs are allocated dynamically. Toward the network, the switch associates each VCI with the physical address of the trunk, over which the frame needs to be transmitted to reach its ultimate destination. Toward the user, VCIs are associated with the physical line supporting the DLCI identifying the user.

Data Link Layer.   OSIRM Layer 2 functionality, responsible for reliable transmission over a single communication link. It combines data bits into a block called a frame, and adds a frame check sequence to allow detection of bit errors at the remote point.

Discard Eligibility Indicator.   A field in the frame set by the user's equipment to indicate that the frame can be discarded if needed in case of congestion, in order to maintain the committed throughput.

Error Correction.   In frame relay, error correction and retransmission are done in the user equipment. The network can detect errors, but the correction is relegated to the endsystems.

Fast Packet.   A term for various streamlined packet technologies now synonymous with cell relay. Supports reduced functionality compared to X.25 packet switching so that it can operate at much higher speeds.

Forward Explicit Congestion Notification Indicator.   A field in the frame set by the network or switch to notify downstream equipment and/or the destination equipment that congestion avoidance procedures should be initiated. The field is set in a frame in the direction of the destination. It is similar to a "holdon" signal for received frames, as well as a destination "slowdown" signal for traffic from the destination.

Frame Relay Assembler/Disassembler.   A device or capability that allows nonframe relay terminals, typically in a non-LAN environment (e.g., SNA) to be carried in a frame relay network.

Frame Relay Interface.   A standardized interface between customer equipment and a switch or a frame relay network. A two-layer protocol stack interface capability implemented at both endpoints of a link.

Frame Relay Switch.   A frame relay processor is a switch that "connects" users, facilitating any-to-any connectivity. Connections are accomplished in real time over the PVC. Tables are maintained by the node to facilitate the connections.

Frame Relay.   A 1990's packet-based T1-speed technology that provides for dynamic bandwidth allocation with high throughput and low delay to support the increasing amount of bursty traffic in the corporate environment. Frame relay defines a standardized format for data link layer frames, which are transmitted over a network of interconnected LANs.

Frame.   A block of user data, as created by the data link layer. It consists of a flag, a header, an information field, and a trailer.

International Telecommunications Union-Telecommunications (ITU-T).   A United Nations organization that develops international standards and

continues

MINI-GLOSSARY OF FRAME RELAY TERMS *(Continued)*

interfaces for telecommunications. The frame relay standards are based on underlying ITU-T standards.

Link Access Procedure F-Core.   Subset of LAP-F utilized in frame relay.

Link Access Procedure F.   The data link layer protocol used in frame relay. It is specified by ANSI T1.618-1991; it is similar to ITU-T Q.922 Annex A. It is a slimmed-down protocol supporting only core functions. It is based on ISDN's LAP-D protocol.

Local Management Interface (LMI).   A specification for use by frame relay products that defines a method of exchanging status information between the user device and the network. It is used to manage PVCs. It is specified in ANSI's T1.617.

Multicast.   An LMI option that allows a frame relay device to broadcast frames to multiple destinations.

Open Systems Interconnection Reference Model (OSTRM).   A model for data communications interconnection that maps functions necessary to undertake orderly communication to one of seven hierarchical layers.

Permanent Virtual Circuits (PVC).   A logical link or path between the originating and terminating routers. No resources are allocated to the link unless data is actually being sent. The link is set up by the administrator and remains in place for however long as needed (days, months, or years).

Router.   A device operating at the network layer of the OSIRM used by a LAN to access other LANs across a variety of wide area networks.

Switched Virtual Circuit.   A virtual circuit set up on a call-by-call basis. A future frame relay service, of particular importance to public frame relay networks.

Systems Network Architecture (SNA).   A network architecture used in IBM networks in support of mission-critical functions. Originally, the architecture was strictly hierarchical and employed front-end processors and cluster controllers. It is not moving toward a peer-to-peer architecture, supporting LAN access to the mainframe.

Time Division Multiplexing (TDM).   A traditional method of combining multiple simultaneous channels over a single transmission path by assigning discrete time slots to each channel. It results in inefficient bandwidth allocation in bursty environments.

Virtual Circuit Identifier (VCI).   A label used by a cell switch to identify cells belonging to a given user. VCIs have local significance.

Virtual Circuit.   A logical connection established through a frame relay or packet network. Frames or packets are routed through the network in an order-preserving transfer. The connection is similar to a dedicated line between the endpoints.

data link layers create different frames; differences manifest themselves in terms of the fields, their position, and their length. The Logical Link Control/Subnetwork Access Protocol sublayer of a LAN creates a frame of particular interest, since it is the frame that is involved in the transmission of data over a network of interconnected LANs. The frame relay frame format was shown in Figure 6.2; the fields shown in the figure are described here.

Flag sequence.   All frames start and end with the flag sequence consisting of one 0 bit followed by six contiguous 1 bits and one 0 bit. The flag preceding the address field is defined as the opening flag. The flag following the FCS field is defined as the closing flag. The closing flag may also serve as the opening flag of the next frame, but the protocol engine must be able to accommodate reception of one or more consecutive flags.

Address Field.   The address field (more precisely, the routing label) consists of at least 10 bits over 2 octets, but may optionally be extended up to 4 octets. To support a larger DLCI address range, the 3-octet or 4-octet address fields may be supported at the user-network interface or the network-network interface based on bilateral agreement.

Control field (C/R).   There is no control function for frame relay core services. The field is not used by the network and is passed transparently between user equipment, for application-specific uses. This bit is used in protocols like LAP-D to indicate that the frame is a command or a response.

FECN.   This bit is set to 1 by the network to notify the user receiving the frame that the frame has been delivered through a congested path in the network. This implies that insufficient network resources are available to continue handling the traffic at the current rate. Two actions could ensue (depending on the user's equipment capabilities):

1. The inbound traffic, if any, from the destination (i.e. the traffic going in the opposite direction of the received frame) should be temporarily reduced.

2. The destination should be willing to enter a "holdon" or "wait" state, since traffic may arrive at longer intervals than otherwise expected.

BECN.   This bit is set to 1 by the network to notify the user that traffic sent in the opposite direction to the frame with the bit set may pass through a congested path. Consequently, the sending equipment should reduce its inbound traffic to the destination, if there is any. Figure 6.4 depicts the operation of the FECN and BECN.

EA.   Used as an expansion bit to indicate that the DLCI is longer than 10 bits.

DE.   The discard eligibility bit set by the user to inform the network that in case of congestion this frame can be dropped before other not-so-indicated frames are touched.

Frame Relay Information Field.   Follows the address field and precedes the frame check sequence. The contents of the user data field consist of an integral number of octets (no partial octets). The default information field size to be supported by networks is 262 octets; other values are negotiated between users and networks and between networks. The support of a maximum value of 8,189 octets is suggested by the standards for applications such as LAN interconnection, to prevent the need for segmentation and reassembly by the user equipment (however, the usage of a cell-based switch runs counter to this philosophy). The frame length can be variable. Since the 16-bit FCS specified for frame relay can detect errors in frames of lengths up to 4,096 octets, some are recommending that only this maximum be actually allowed, otherwise the network cannot even detect errored frames.

Frame Checking Sequence (FCS) Field.   A 16-bit CRC sequence used to determine the integrity of the information.

Transparency.   A transmitting data link layer entity must examine the frame content between the opening and closing flag sequences, (address, frame relay information, and FCS fields) and must insert a 0 bit after all sequences of five contiguous 1 bits (including the last five bits of the FCS) to ensure that a flag or an abort sequence is not

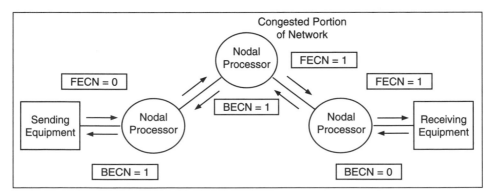

Figure 6.4   FECN and BECN action.

simulated within the frame. A receiving data link layer entity must examine the frame contents between the opening and closing flag directly following five contiguous 1 bits.

Order of Bit Transmission.   The octets are transmitted in ascending numerical order; inside an octet, bit 1 is the first bit to be transmitted.

Invalid Frames

An invalid frame is a frame that:

1. Is not properly bounded by two flags (e.g., a frame abort).
2. Has fewer than 5 octets between flags. (Note: if there is no information field, the frame has 4 octets and the frame will be considered invalid.)
3. Contains more than 8,193 octets between flags.
4. Does not consist of an integral number of octets prior to zero-bit insertion or following zero-bit extraction.
5. Contains a frame check sequence error.
6. Contains a single octet address field.
7. Contains a data link connection identifier not recognized by the network.

If the frame received by the network is too long, the network may either:

- Discard the frame.
- Send part of the frame toward the destination user, then abort the frame.
- Send the frame toward the destination user with invalid FCS.

Selection of one or more of these behaviors is an option for designers of frame relay network equipment, and is not subject to further standardization. Users cannot not make assumptions as to which of these actions the network will take. Furthermore, the network, optionally, may clear the frame relay call if the number or frequency of excessively long frames exceeds a network-specified threshold. Invalid frames are discarded without notification to the sender. No action is taken as a result of that frame.

Frame Abort

Receipt of seven or more contiguous 1 bits is interpreted as an abort, and the data link layer ignores the frame currently being received.

Error Correction

In frame relay, error correction and retransmission are done in the user equipment. The network can detect errors, but the correction is relegated to the endsystems. Error conditions include lost, duplicated, misdelivered, discarded, and out-of-sequence frames; recovery from these error conditions must be performed by the user's equipment, which must be appropriately configured to support these tasks. This does not require any additional functionality than most intelligent equipment, like LAN routers, has today. Furthermore, with today's higher-quality digital transmission facilities and the migration to fiber, it is unlikely that many frames will be received in error, requiring end-to-end retransmission. Error-prone circuits of the past necessitated complex error checking and recovery procedures at each node of a network. The X.25 packet standards assume that the transmission media is intrinsically error-prone, and in order to guarantee an acceptable level of end-to-end quality, error management is performed at every link, by a fairly sophisticated but resource-intensive data link protocol. With a high-quality fiber-based communication infrastructure becoming commonplace, many of the error-correction and retransmission capabilities of X.25 can be safely eliminated.

Since error correction and flow control are handled at the endpoints, frame relay expedites the process of routing packets through a series of switches to a remote location by eliminating the need for each switch to check each packet and correct those in error. This error treatment increases performance and reduces bandwidth requirements, which in turn can reduce communications costs.

In the past when transmission errors were common, it was not efficient to require the transport layer (whose job is to guarantee ultimate end-to-end reliability) to keep track of unacknowledged PDUs. Instead, the data link layer, closer where the problem had its roots, was responsible for the correction task. It turns out that, in the final analysis, when the probability of error over a link is relatively high, it is better to do error correction on a link-by-link basis (i.e., at the data link layer), as measured by the amount of network bandwidth required to successfully send a PDU (although it may, in fact, have been faster to do it end to end). When the probability of error is low, it is better to do error correction end to end, that is, at the transport layer. In other words, for the same amount of network bandwidth, the PDU gets delivered faster by doing the error management end to end; in addition, the switches can be cheaper since they need to undertake fewer tasks.

Public frame relay networks have been designed with quality of service in mind. Some of the parameters being discussed are:

```
Ratio of Nondelivered PDUs to total PDUs < 10⁻⁴;
Ratio of errored PDUs to total PDUs < 10⁻¹³;
Ratio of misdelivered PDUs to total PDUs < 10⁻⁸;
Ratio of duplicate PDUs to total PDUs < 10⁻⁹
```

Today's frame relay networks do not yet meet all of these goals, and there are no guarantees. If the network is not properly engineered from a traffic perspective (i.e., insufficient trunk bandwidth is provided), and unreliable flow control procedures are used, the number of network-discarded frames could become significant. In addition to the quality-of-service measures with reference to error conditions, carriers aim at an end-to-end delay of about 250 milliseconds per average frame (1,000 octets) over a DS0 access line and 20 milliseconds over a DS1 access line.

Frame Relay Switches

A frame relay switch "connects" users, facilitating any-to-any connectivity. Connections are accomplished in real time over the PVC (the PVC itself, however, must be previously established). The frame relay interface is only a definition of what the data stream into the frame relay network looks like. Equipment in the form of switches is needed in the network (private or public) to make the frame relay concept a reality. Like a packet or an ATM switch, a frame relay switch supports a virtual connection. Tables are maintained by the switch to tell the switch the physical port on which an incoming frame must be transmitted. For users terminating on the same switch, the frames are directly sent to the destination by checking the address and determining which physical port needs to receive the data. For users terminating on two different switches, the data must be sent over the appropriate trunk to the destination node, for ultimate delivery. Centralized administration of the backbone network routing tables and the natural port sharing and multiplexing attributes of frame relay make network growth manageable and simple.

As noted, frame relay networks can be private, public, or hybrid. A network consists of (i) user equipment that supports the frame relay interface, (ii) one or more frame relay processors owned by the user or a carrier, and (iii) communication links between the users and the switches and between the processors (links between the switches are owned by the carrier in a public network). The user equipment typically consists of appropriately configured LAN routers. The switches interpret the frame and transmit them (using cells, or in some cases, frames), making the concept of frame relay a reality. Figure 6.5 shows an example of a (public) frame relay network where frames traverse a fixed PVC path through the network, although transmission resources (including bandwidth) are not dedicated to each virtual connection. Figure 6.6 shows another view of a frame relay network; here, a core ATM network supports backbone connectivity, while the frame relay switch (with ATM uplink) services the edge-protocol adaptation function. For ISP applications, the frame relay network must be public or hybrid.

Transmission Mode

Traditionally, ITU-T, the original frame relay standardization body, has pursued a connection-oriented philosophy. Connection-oriented service involves a connection establishment phase, a data transfer phase, and a connection termination phase. A logical connection is set up between

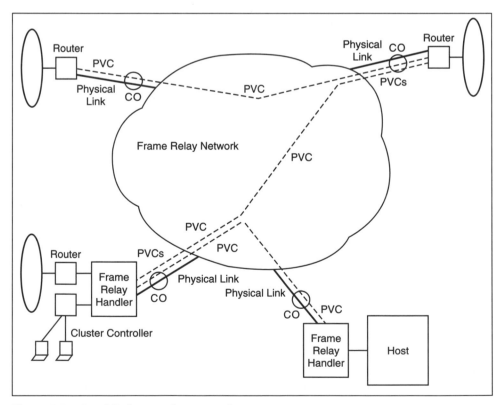

Figure 6.5   A public frame relay network.

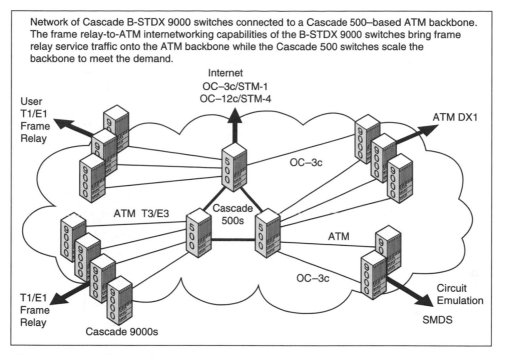

Network of Cascade B-STDX 9000 switches connected to a Cascade 500–based ATM backbone. The frame relay-to-ATM internetworking capabilities of the B-STDX 9000 switches bring frame relay service traffic onto the ATM backbone while the Cascade 500 switches scale the backbone to meet the demand.

Figure 6.6   ATM frame relay network.
(Courtesy of Ascend/Cascade)

endsystems prior to exchanging data. These phases define the sequence of events to ensure successful data transmission. Sequencing of data, flow control, and transparent error handling are some of the capabilities typically inherent with the service. The call setup phase (as would be the case in the SVC environment) adds some delay to each call, but facilitates dynamic connectivity. For today's permanent virtual circuit-based frame relay, setup is done once by the system administration on behalf of the user. The PVC approach implies the allocation of some resources—like table entries—regardless of the real-time user traffic condition). Since the PVC is established at subscription time, there is no need for real-time signaling in this type of service (there may be status signaling, but this is unrelated to the establishment of the channel). Given the need for any-to-any connectivity, SVC services may yet evolve.

In a connectionless service, such as IP, each data unit is independently routed to the destination; no connection-establishment activities are required, since each data unit is independent of the previous or subsequent one. Connectionless-mode service provides for unit data transfer without regard to the establishment or maintenance of connections. This is advantageous in interenterprise applications. Each unit of data contains the addressing information and the data itself. Responsibility for assuring that the message gets to the other end is shifted up from the data link layer to higher layers, where the integrity check is done only once, instead of at (every) lower layer. In the frame relay environment, the VCs are used by the router as a logical point-to-point connection between it and one or more remote routers. The IP datagrams move in a connectionless fashion over these VCs.

The backbone frame relay switches typically have a centralized network management terminal to provision connections. The manager specifies the endpoints (i.e., the two routers for which a PVC is desired). The network management system will then automatically build a path between the nodes (and, hence, the endpoints), and will inform all nodes in the network of the route. Some processors require a manual entry of the entire forwarding path in the various tables. This path will be used for all subsequent transmission between the specified endpoints. The manager can also specify alternate logical/physical routers to deal with node or trunk failure (user-access line failure cannot be dealt with by this method) (see Figure 6.7). Figure 6.8 depicts a typical frame relay network protocol architecture. These stacks must be implemented in the user equipment and in the switches in order to implement frame relay. In the example of Figure 6.9, there are two PC users on two geographically separate LANs. These LANs would access the frame relay node via routers configured to terminate the frame relay interface. There are two PC users on the two remote LANs. Three network nodes have been provisioned to logically interconnect the end-user equipment via permanent virtual circuits. Node 1 and node 3 terminate the end-user equipment directly over the link with a frame relay interface. They must support ATM/cell segmentation functions, as discussed earlier.

Frame Relay Protocol Stack and Protocols

A total of 1,021 PVCs per UNI are supported. Logical channel 0, 1, and 1023 are reserved; channel 1023 is used to send link-layer management messages from the network to the user's device; other logical channels (up to 45) may be reserved by some carriers.

One of the goals of ITU-T work has been to align some of the available data communications protocols and offer recommendations for a set of efficient network services that can then be built upon by user equipment. One aspect of these new services is the separation of the control informa-

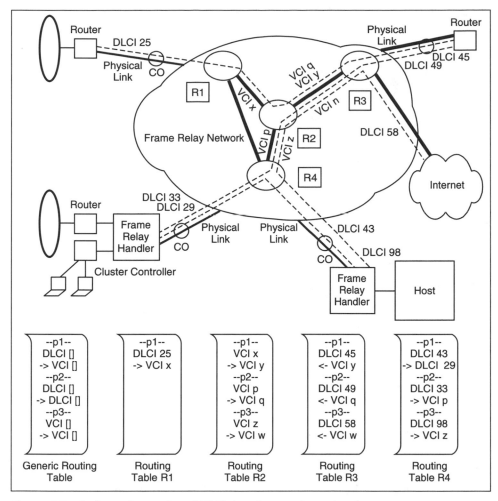

Figure 6.7 Paths and mapping of DLCIs in a frame relay network.

tion from the user information into logically separate (but not necessarily physically separate) paths, as is the case in ISDN. Another aspect of the goal was to simplify the network protocols. Simplification, as provided by frame relay, allows the realization of services that are superior in terms of delay and throughput than existing services since there is much less per-frame processing on the part of the network.

In most legacy networks (e.g., X.25s, SNAs, analog voices, etc.), there is no clear end-to-end distinction between the logical control path and the data path. A close coupling between information and control limits the flexibility needed to support new services and new signaling and transport needs. Separation, the goal of frame relay as originally conceived, has the following benefits:

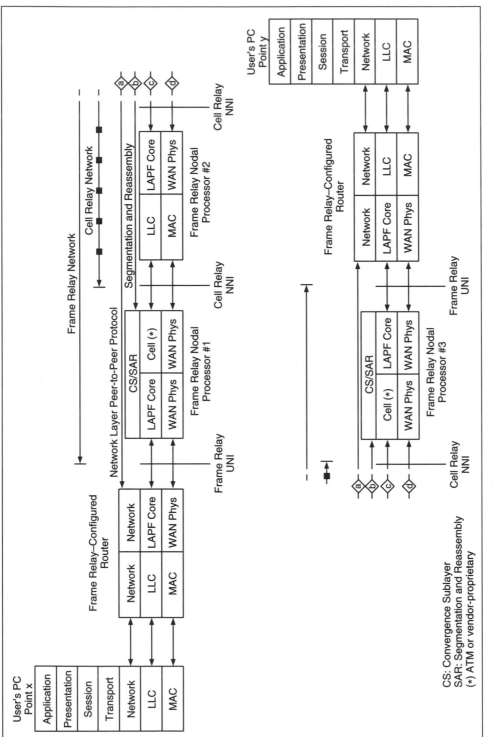

Figure 6.8 Protocol stacks in a frame relay/cell relay network.

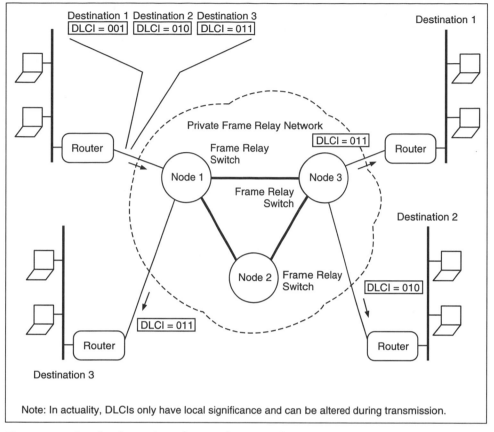

Figure 6.9 Routing in a private frame relay network.

- There is the potential for the integration of signaling for voice, data, and other media. This is important for future multimedia services.

- Since the information path does not have to support control, its logic can be substantially simplified. This implies that the hardware will be cheaper and faster.

- Independent optimization of the two paths can be accommodated.

The major characteristics of frame relay are out-of-band call control and link-layer multiplexing. Although, as noted, frame relay today is not deployed in conjunction with ISDN, under ISDN, all the new packet services, particularly the SVC services, have the following characteristics:

- All control procedures, if needed, are performed in a logically separate manner (channel) using protocol procedures that are integrated across all telecommunications services. Consequently, Recommendations I.430 or I.431 provide the Layer 1 protocol for the control channel; Recommendations I.441 and I.451 are extended as the Layer 2 and 3 protocols, respectively (LAP-F/Q.922 and Q.933). In the case of PVCs, no real-time call establishment is necessary, and any parameters are agreed upon at subscription time.

- The data transfer procedures share the same Layer 1 functions based on Recommendations I.430/I.431. The data transfer may use any channel on which the user implements LAP-F.

The separation can occur in a number of ways, including on a physically separate interface, and on another logical channel within the same interface (for example, a time slot, the D-channel, or other).

ITU-T I.122 recognizes two frame relay implementations: a switched implementation under the auspices of ISDN, using the ITU-T Q.933 protocol for call setup, and a PVC implementation. The PVC does not require call setup and call termination, but is obviously not as efficient in resource utilization as SVC. I.122 is an access standard; on the trunk side, no restriction is imposed (same as in ISDN); as discussed, the trunk side is typically cell-based.

As noted, the term "relay" implies that the Layer 2 data frame is not terminated nor processed at the endpoints of each link in the network, but is relayed to the destination, as is the case in a LAN. In contrast with X.25-based packet switching, in frame relay, the physical line between nodes consists of multiple data links, each identifiable by information in the data link frame. In X.25, multiplexing is achieved through the use of logical packet layer channels; hence, the network layer provides switching. In contrast, X.25 multiplexing takes place at the packet layer (Layer 3). It is interesting to note the renewed interest in network layer switching embodied by newer technologies such as MPOA and MPLS. In frame relay, switching is accomplished at the data link layer, and link-layer multiplexing is used in user's plane to facilitate sharing of bandwidth among multiple users. Switching in the data link layer is achieved by binding the DLCIs to forward information at intermediary nodes to form a set of network edge-to-network edge logical paths. Multiplexing is done through the statistical multiplexing of different data link connections on the same physical channel, as specified in LAP-F Core/Q.922. Frame relay service is based on the frame structure originally employed by the ISDN D-channel LAP-D, which provides statistical multiplexing of different user data streams within the data link layer (Layer 2). Interestingly, having to reach all the way into the network layer is also a problem of IP; hence, the new proposals for MPLS, tag switching, IP switching, and so on.

Put slightly differently, a feature of frame relay is to have the virtual circuit identifier, originally implemented in the network layer of X.25, positioned at the data link layer so that switching can be accomplished more easily. In the X.25 environment, when a data call is established, the virtual circuit indicator is negotiated and used for the duration of the call to route packets through the network. In a layered protocol environment, layer $n + 1$ protocol information is enveloped inside layer n information. The network layer routing indicator is enveloped within the Layer 2 header/trailers, which must be processed before it can be exposed. This processing involves more than just stripping the header/trailer; for example, error detection and correction. In LANs, the routing of the actual packets is accomplished directly at Layer 2: The data packets are supplied with a 48-bit destination address, which is readily available and which is used to physically route the data to the intended destination. Also, there is no error recovery in a LAN as a packet flows by a station on its way along the bus or ring. In frame relay, only the lower sublayer of Layer 2, consisting of such core functions as frame delimiting, multiplexing, and error detection, are terminated by a network at the user-network interface. The upper procedural sublayer of Layer 2, with functions such as error recovery and flow control, operates between users on an end-to-end basis. In this sense, a user's data transfer protocol is transparent to a network.

Frame relay implements only the core functions on a link-by-link basis; the other functions, particularly error recovery, are done on an end-to-end basis. Indeed, the capabilities provided by the transport layer protocol accommodate this transfer of responsibilities to the boundaries of the network. On the user side, beyond the frame relay interface with the network, the user can employ any endsystem-to-endsystem protocol.

Transmission Mechanism across a Frame Relay Network

Every network needs to assure that traffic is forwarded reliably from the source to the destination. In a frame relay network, forwarding of the frames from the various routers is determined by the DLCI of the frame on a given user-network interface. Nodes use the DLCI to determine the frame's destination. The DLCI is not an address of the destination, since it may change as the frame travels through the network (i.e., the DLCI has local significance only); rather, it identifies the logical connection between an element in the network and the next element in the network (i.e., endpoint and switch and switch and endpoint; forwarding between switches is accomplished through the VCI when ATM principles are employed).

The forwarding table entries for permanent virtual circuit service are populated via the network management system, and forwarding is not determined on a "per-call" basis.

When using the frame relay interface, the router on a LAN selects the required remote router by specifying the permanent virtual circuit via a data link connection identifier contained in the frame relay frame it builds prior to transmitting the data. The mapping of IP datagrams is done according to RFC 1490, Multiprotocol Interconnect over frame relay (July, 1993). If the system is well designed, there should be no segmentation of the LAN frames into multiple frame relay frames, although this could happen in theory, adding delay and overhead. The switch accepts the frame it receives on one of its incoming ports, segments it into cells, while appending a sequence number for remote-switch cell-to-frame reassembly, and delivers it over the trunk connecting to that remote switch. Initially, trunk interfaces used a packetlike protocol; more recently, products are moving in the direction of ATM cells standards. The switch must segment incoming frame relay frames for delivery through the cell format, because these frames can be long, while cells are much shorter. Switches do, however, check the frame check sequence (FCS) code of a received frame. If the frame is found in error, it is dropped without further processing.

In the example of Figure 6.9:

- The network layer in the sending PC (typically part of TCP/IP stack) looks in the routing table for the address associated with the destination application, known at the sending end by some logical name, say y. The table indicates that the local router must be specifically addressed for the selected destination.

- Upon reception of the frame, the router checks its routing tables to determine the local DLCI needed to be appended to the frame in order to reach the remote destination. The datagram is mapped with RFC 1490.

- The router's data link layer places the information in a frame relay frame and sends it to node 1 with the DLCI label properly appended to the information.

- Node 1 recognizes the DLCI associated with an existing logical path through the network. If the frame is not in error and it has a valid DLCI, it is segmented into cells, which are subsequently identified by a node-assigned VCI and other segmentation/reassembly mechanisms (some switches forward entire frames without segmentation, but there are advantages in using cell relay NNIs over frame relay NNIs). The cells are sent on to node 2 and then to node 3. Otherwise, it discards the frame.

- Node 3 reassembles the cells into the frame using the VCI and other Segmentation and Reassembly (SAR) mechanisms; the node then passes the frame over the access line that terminates in the equipment supporting application *y*.

- Upon receipt, the router forwards the information to the PC. In turn, the data is sent from the PC's data link layer to the application via the transport, session, and presentation layers.

The switches do not have to read the variable-length frame to achieve switching; instead, the DLCI is sufficient to allow the edge processors to make the necessary forwarding decisions. The DLCI may be reused by virtual circuits that do not share one or both endpoints. Figure 6.7 implies that the routing is more complex than the short discussion just given, since in modern ATM-based frame relay networks, there is an interplay between DLCI, the cell's VCI (or equivalent vendor-proprietary indicator), and ultimate trunks. Three aspects of Layer 2 "routing" exist:

- Association between the locally significant DLCI and the cell's VCI (and the other way around). This occurs at origination and destination switches.

- Remapping of a VCI to another VCI. This occurs whenever there are ATM switching points or cross-connect nodes (a specific VCI has no end-to-end significance if the virtual channel connection is switched; the VCI could remain the same end to end if the virtual connection is provided on a semipermanent basis). This occurs at intermediate nodes.

- Association between a local DLCI and a DLCI of a user connected to the same switch.

This in turn raises several questions pertaining to vendors' implementation of the frame relay/cell relay switches.

- Are tandem switches allowed, or must switches be connected with direct trunks?

- Does a tandem switch have to reassemble cells back into frames, or are the cells relayed ("pipelined") directly as needed?

■ How does a switch treat an incoming frame destined for a user directly connected to the same processors? Namely, is segmentation required?

These questions have critical impact on the end-to-end delay of the frame relay network. Just the initial segmentation and the remote reassembly can already be significant; any intermediary reassembly impacts the grade of service further. Figure 6.9 depicted a scenario where the frame is segmented by the first processor handling it (node 1), and then is sent downstream to a tandem processor (node 2), which accepts cells as such and transmits them along individually and discretely, without intermediary reassembly. The frame is reassembled only by the destination node (node 3). Note that Figure 6.9 did not show segmentation/reassembly function at node 2. This would happen if the switch followed cell relay/switching ATM principles; such a process typically would serve a variety of end-user streams, some of which could be digitized video, digitized voice, or frame relay information. Notice that, at the very least, the use of tandems implies having to incur the trunk transmission time twice. Recently deployed frame relay networks (e.g., TCG's) utilize this approach. It is conceivable that if a switch does not follow cell relay/switching principles, each frame must be assembled and disassembled by each switch in the path; some of the early frame relay networks that used (proprietary) cell-based trunking (but not ATM) used this approach. Some frame relay networks are still non-ATM based. Here, the various switches are connected over frame relay NNI (FRF2.1), which is frame-based.

Congestion Management

Congestion management is important, particularly for voice and/or QoS-based applications. Frame relay has (in principle) a way to manage and control congestion. However, this control is not explicitly tied to a QoS mechanism (in terms of meeting a stipulated service level agreement). The frame relay network composed of the switches, private or public, attends to this first by using congestion notification strategies and then by selectively discarding frames when needed to relieve congestion. Congestion control mechanisms are used to treat users fairly and to protect the network and users by localizing the congestion within the network.

The congestion notification takes place when a network node determines that it is becoming congested. It sets the Forward Explicit Congestion Notification (FECN) bit in the frames as it sends them to the destination router. It also sets the Backward Explicit Congestion Notification (BECN) bit in the frames destined for the source router. Upon receipt of these frames, the source and destination routers are expected to initiate procedures to throttle back the traffic offered to the network. If congestion continues to increase despite using congestion notification, the network will begin to discard eligible frames and will put the congestion localization procedures into effect. The network of switches selects frames for discard by looking at the Discard Eligibility (DE) bit in each frame to see if it has been set by the router. If it has been set, then the network discards the associated frame. These procedures continue until the congestion subsides. These techniques are congestion-avoidance techniques.

One issue, however, is if and how the router can enforce throttling back to the PCs originating the traffic. Hence, the important question to ask about a frame relay router, a switch, and a carrier service is whether the full congestion control apparatus specified by the standard is implemented in each of these devices.

Congestion Control Issues for Public Networks

As indicated, in frame relay, the entire bandwidth, up to the maximum access speed, can be made available to a single user during peak periods. A problem may arise in the network if many users require this bandwidth simultaneously, as might be the case when LANs from multiple organizations (or departments within an organization) are terminated on the network. The frame relay network must be able to detect any overload condition and quickly initiate corrective actions.

Congestion control (also known as *flow control*) is already necessary in traditional public packet networks, but in a frame relay network, its need is more critical due to the performance objectives of the latter and the greater access speed. In X.25 networks of the early 1980s, the access speed is normally much lower than the speed and capacity of the backbone. It was unlikely that a single device would ever monopolize the backbone. In a LAN interconnection/frame relay environment, the routers seen as an ensemble may transmit a combined rate, which exceeds the capacity of the backbone itself. A single router may flood the backbone; this in turn will starve other circuits of bandwidth.

Temporary conditions of overload occur in any well-utilized network. Networks that never experience temporary overloads may in fact be underutilized. Overengineering, however, is not a desirable way to handle congestion control because it is not cost-effective. Ignoring the issue of congestion is also undesirable since, in effect, it means not capitalizing on the full potential of frame relay. In private networks, transmission costs are a major component of any design evaluation, and most of the benefits of frame relay technology are lost if implementing it demands the leasing of excessive amounts of bandwidth. The challenge is not how to preclude any temporary congestion, but how to react to it when it occurs. Overengineering, or better yet, relying on statistical averaging to obtain the most efficient utilization of deployed resources may be an approach that is viable in a public network environment, given the large population of potential users.

The ANSI standards specify explicit congestion control notification bits and a congestion notification control message. The important fields in the address portion of the frame relay format are the FECN, BECN, and DE just described. In the ANSI standard, each of the individual virtual circuits in a frame relay connection (if the user and/or topological implementation calls for multiple PVCs over a physical link) can be independently throttled back. To be fair, the sources that contribute the most to the congestion should be slowed down the most, while sources contributing less traffic should be slowed down less. Hence, the network must be able to identify which PVCs over a physical link, or beyond the access portion, in the network are responsible for monopolizing resources. There also is an interplay between the frame relay congestion mechanism and the ATM congestion mechanism when ATM is used at the core of the network.

Both the user's equipment and the switch should be able to respond to congestion control actions implied by the congestion control fields. For example, during periods of heavy load, the network could signal the user's equipment by setting the congestion bit to reduce the traffic arrival rate; when the overload situation dissipates, the opposite action could be achieved by setting the congestion bit back to normal. In some situations, the user's equipment could be overloaded; for example, a LAN gateway may be servicing another user and may not be able to absorb heavy loads of traffic coming from the network. Here, the user's equipment must be able to throttle back the network.

The ANSI standards also provide for a DE capability, to discard some frames if the initial congestion control actions do not correct the situation. The network should not be designed to discard frames indiscriminately; rather, it is fairer to discard frames from the users who contributed the most to the congestion. If the implementation supports the DE field, this can be accomplished equitably, since the user's equipment can indicate which frames should be discarded first. The DE capability makes it possible for the user to temporarily send more frames than it is allowed on the average. The network will forward these frames if it has the capacity to do so; but if the network is overloaded, frames with the DE bit set will be discarded first. With ATM cores, some switches support early packet discard (EPD) and partial packet discard (PPD); these aim at ameliorating over all throughput and service quality.[7]

Some network/equipment vendors may implement a simple flow control procedure, rather than the full ANSI capability. For routers incapable of implementing the control mechanism of the ANSI Annex D spec, a simplified X-on/X-off form of flow control is allowed by (I)LMI. The optional flow control limits transmission in the direction of the network, but not the reciprocal way. While this approach is useful, in the view of observers, backbone frame relay networks must also implement the full ANSI mechanisms, otherwise the network will not be able to control effectively overloads from these devices.

Implicit congestion notification (to the transport layer of the ultimate user equipment, i.e., the PC) occurs when the user's end-to-end protocol determines that data been lost. Actions to deal with implicit congestion notifications usually take higher priority than *explicit congestion notifications*. The former is normally handled by the ultimate equipment; the latter is handled first by the router and subsequently by the ultimate equipment. The network may indicate to the user router that the data may be about to traverse a congested path by the FECN/BECN bits previously discussed. The user response to these congestion notifications is dependent on the type of notification and the frequency with which they are received.

To reduce oscillations possibly due to transient congestion conditions, a congestion monitoring period (CMP) can be established by the user's router to track the frequency of explicit congestion notifications received. This CMP is typically defined as four times the round-trip delay through the network. The CMP starts upon receipt of a frame with the BECN or FECN bit set, or if the logical link is currently recovering from a congestion state. In a windowing environment, two window rotations may be used to measure the CMP instead of four times the round-trip delay. The user's router receiving the FECN bit set in half or more of the frames received during the CMP should start throttling data in the direction of the received frame. Since data at any given time is typically weighted in the direction opposite the frame with the BECN bit set, the BECN indication is likely to occur less frequently than the FECN indication. The user's equipment should therefore start throttling data in the opposite direction of the received frame when the first indication of BECN is received.

During data transfer, one of the following four states is active. Typical carrier-suggested actions are:

Data throttling due to implicit congestion notification.   When a frame has been lost, as seen from the end-to-end protocols, typically the data flow should be reduced by approximately one-fourth of current flow. Data should not be throttled below the minimum end-to-end protocol flow (e.g., minimum window size).

Data throttling due to explicit congestion notification.   When data has not been lost during the CMP, and the criteria for FECN or BECN frequency during the CMP has been fulfilled (i.e., half or more of the received frames have the FECN bit set, or one or more of the received frames have the BECN bit set), then the data flow should be reduced by approximately one-eighth of the current flow. Data should not be throttled below the minimum end-to-end protocol flow (e.g., minimum window size).

Data flow recovery.   If the criteria for FECN or BECN frequency has not been fulfilled during the CMP (e.g., fewer than half of the received frames have the FECN bit set or no more received frames have the BECN bit set), then the data flow should be gradually returned to normal flow at a rate of one-sixteenth of the normal end-to-end protocol flow.

Normal data flow.   No congestion notification occurs and data throttling is not necessary (i.e., no congestion action is taken).

Class of Service Parameters

Carriers are specifying various class of service parameters for the PVC frame relay service. These include:

Committed burst size (CBS) (also called Bc).   The maximum amount of user data (in bits) that the network agrees to transfer, under normal conditions, during one second.

Excess burst size (EBS) (also called Be).   Represents the maximum amount of uncommitted data exceeding the CBS that the network will attempt to deliver during one second.

Committed information rate (CIR).   Represents the user's throughput that the network commits (but does not absolutely guarantee) to support under normal network conditions. CIR is measured in bits per second.

Committed rate measurement interval (CRMI) (also called T).   The time interval during which the user is allowed to send information at the CBS rate or at the CBS + EBS rate. Hence, T = CBS/CIR.

These quantities are important as they are the basis of the services the carriers provide, and for the supporting tariffs. Frame relay carriers will enforce the subscribed CBS, EBS, and CIR in the network in order to meet the grade of service. The user must allocate some minimum CIR to every possible device-to-device relationship (i.e., PVC); this implies that frame relay service, as currently available, is not the optimal solution to inter-enterprise applications. These issues have to be taken into account when using frame relay as an access service to an ISP.

As data is received over time interval T, a determination is made as to whether the frame is:

- Under the committed burst size

- Over the committed burst size but under the excess burst size

- Over the burst size

Recently, some vendors (e.g., Cascade/Ascend) have suggested that ATM-like classes of service should also be added to frame relay to better handle time-sensitive traffic. They support:

Guaranteed packets.   Packets to be delivered according to some time constraint and with high probability.

Best-effort packets.   Packets to be delivered to the best of the network's capability after meeting the requirement for delivering guaranteed packets.

Cascade/Ascend uses three colors, green, amber, and red, to describe and categorize packet frames for monitoring and enforcement (note that these are not FRF constructs):

- If the number of bits received during the current time interval, including the current frame, is less than CBS, then the frame is designated as a green frame. Green frames are never discarded by the network, except under extreme congestion conditions.

- If the number of bits received during the current time interval, including the current frame, is greater than CBS but less than EBS, the frame is designated as an amber frame. Amber frames are forwarded with the DE bit set, and are eligible for discard if they pass through a congested switch.

- If the number of bits received during the current time interval, including the current frame, is greater than EBS, the frame is designated as a red frame. Red frames are forwarded with the DE bit set when Cascade's special Graceful Discard is enabled, and are dropped when the feature is not enabled (as would be the case under the baseline FRF specifications). See Figure 6.10.

Cell Relay Usage in Frame Relay

A cell is a fixed-length packet of user data (payload) plus an overhead, usually small, 53 bytes or less. Cell relay is a high-bandwidth, low-delay switching and multiplexing packet technology (discussed in Chapter 7), which is *required to implement a frame relay network in an efficient manner,* particularly for mixed-media and multimedia applications. With cell relay, information to be transferred is packetized into fixed-size cells.

NOTE Vendors tend to use the term *cell relay switch* (or node) when their equipment does not implement the ITU-T ATM standard, but a proprietary standard. If the ITU-T standard is implemented they typically refer to the equipment as an *ATM switch.*

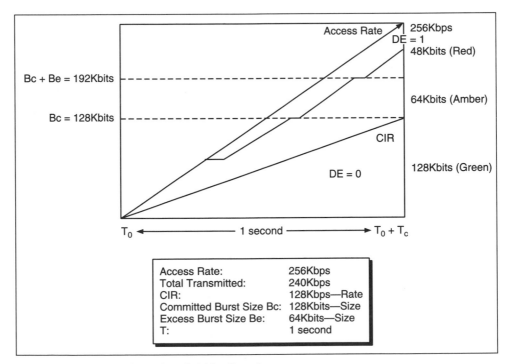

Figure 6.10   Determining bandwidth allocation.

As noted, most modem frame relay switches use cell relay methods at the NNI. Cells are identified and switched by means of a VCI/VPI label in the header. A number of functions of the Layer 2 protocol are removed to the edge of the backbone, while "core capabilities," are supported directly by the cell switches, in addition to Layer 1 functions (clocking, bit encoding, physical medium connection). Cells allocated to the same connection may exhibit an irregular recurrence pattern since they are filled according to the actual demand. Cell relay allows for capacity allocation on demand, so the bit rate per connection can be chosen flexibly. In addition, the actual "channel mix" at the interface can change dynamically. The cell header (such as the ATM's header) typically contains a label and an error-detection field; error detection is confined to the header. The label is used for channel identification, in place of the positional methodology for assignment of octets, inherent in the traditional TDM T1/T3 systems. Cell relay is similar to packet switching but with the following differences: Protocols are simplified; cells (packets) have a fixed and small length, allowing high-speed switching nodes; switching decisions are straightforward and many functions are implemented in hardware. Cell relay is critical to the deployment of frame relay, and only those switches that implement it give the users the full advantages of the new technology.

One complication of using cell relay instead of frame relay at the NNI has to do with network discard options. A packet-based frame-switching device can discard a *frame* found to be in error, or in case of overload, a *frame* designated as eligible for discard by the user. In fast-packet/cell relay platforms, the frame loses its identity in transit (since it is pipelined and only reassembled at the remote switch, not an intermediary processor). The issue then arises as to what to "throw away" in case of congestion: Although a frame might have been segmented into, say, 30 cells, throwing away 30 random cells might imply corrupting the integrity of 30 frames, not (just) one frame, as might have been the intention of the network. As a practical solution, manufacturers of cell-based switches put greater emphasis on designing their processors to avoid a congestion state, rather than on how to deal with congestion after it arises (systems with frame relay-based NNIs tend to do the opposite). Hence, these switches have enough buffering to absorb a user's input data during an interval of network congestion, rather than start forwarding that data into the network, only to find later that some cells were lost, and therefore having to take some remedial action. (This is similar to the airline industry principle of holding planes on the ground if congestion exists, rather than launching the plane and then having to hold it while in transit.) Another approach is to utilize EPD/PPD.

It is critical that a frame relay switch supports a dynamic view of the data being transferred through it, otherwise the user will not obtain the full benefit possible with the technology. Without a cell-based switch, dynamic bandwidth allocation is not easily achievable. The simplest way is to upgrade the routers with a frame relay board and retain the existing point-to-point infrastructure. This approach does not provide any consequential advantage over the existing environment.

The frame relay-to-ATM interworking is defined in ITU-T I.555 and FRF.8. The planner should note, however, that the edge frame relay switch typically buffers the incoming frame until it is totally received. This allows the switch to determine if the frame should exit from the same card (which could, for example, support 28 DS1s on a DS3 access card, or 672 DS0s, and/or many virtual channels), where there would be no cellularization involved; or if the frame must be segmented to be put onto the internal bus to reach another card that is also connected on the local side (this segmentation may or may not be ATM-based; e.g., it could be into 64-byte words); or if it is meant for remote (NNI) delivery. Only in the latter case would the I.555 mechanism come into play. Note that this has buffering delay implications.

Many customers deploy high-capacity circuits to meet peak traffic (and performance goals); however, DS1 lines used exclusively for data are reported by some to be loaded only at 15 percent or less. Dynamic bandwidth allocation requires the incorporation of cell relay in the switch to handle communication over the trunks (another way would be to employ a frame-switching nodal fabric, but the granularity or efficiency of the multiplexing can be significantly lower). Dynamic bandwidth allocation is done by designing the switch from the ground up and eliminating any fixed-bandwidth constraints imposed by a TDM nodal architecture. No internal blocking should be allowed in the switch, and queuing must be eliminated or at least minimized. Vendors that have experimented with these architectures over the past few years are in a position to incorporate these advanced architectures in the products they manufacture. TDM and cell relay can be viewed at two ends of a spectrum: One cannot take full advantage of cell relay if the node has internal and/or external TDM structural restrictions. Because of the efficient multiplexing possible with cell relay, dynamic bandwidth allocation, so important to bursty users, particularly in the LAN router environment, is achieved.

When a network is properly designed, the full bandwidth of the frame relay interface can be available to any application that requires it for relatively long-duration bursts of data, as may be the case for interconnected LANs. These applications may require that the network nodes support bursts occupying the full-access bandwidth for intervals of up to 10 seconds or more in order to support transfer of large files or interactive traffic.

There are economic advantages to using the combination of frame relay access and a cell-based backbone network. Using frame relay technology in conjunction with a cell-based backbone multiplexer as an upgrade to an existing private corporate backbone can be cost-effective, since the user can obtain needed bandwidth-on-demand from the backbone, rather than on a fixed (and inefficient) basis. The "saved" bandwidth is then available to other users of the same backbone, in theory *minimizing* the amount of new raw bandwidth the firm needs to acquire from a carrier in the form of additional T1 or fractional T1 links. As an alternative strategy, the service from a carrier can be utilized. Although switches can also support nonframe relay traffic (for example, voice or video), the two technologies together, cell relay and frame relay, promise to increase throughput between locations that have large amounts of bursty traffic.

One may wonder why is it beneficial to utilize segmentation of a frame into many (up to 133) cells and, consequently, why a cell-based platform is superior to a frame-switching technology in the switch. The explanation is that frame relay is a data-only protocol; it is intended to support HDLC-type traffic—for example LAN packets; its main focus is on data services. Cell relay (fast-packet) switches, on the other hand, can also handle voice and video. For example, voice "frames" may be as small as 1 octet. Therefore, if a user needs a strictly LAN interconnection, then a frame-switching technology with FRIs on both the access and on the trunk side might, in fact, be superior in terms of performance. However, if the user also contemplates supporting voice and video, the best solution is to use a cell relay platform that supports FRI for LAN access, some other access protocol for voice and for video, and a cell method on the trunk side. The ATM cell procedure is being introduced to support *all* media, including voice, data, and video. Multiplexer vendors view frame relay as an access protocol; the cell relay/fast packet backbone is viewed as giving the user better control over the quality of service of the path, and for facilitating a mix of traffic.

In the previous discussion it is important to keep in mind that the frame relay network supports the Access Subnetwork (ASN) as shown in Figure 2.9.

(I)LMI

The (I)LMI specification defines a protocol and a set of messages to make the configuration and maintenance of PVCs easier. The protocol describes an (I)LMI that is applicable between the network and the user's equipment (i.e., at the UNI see Figure 6.11). The (I)LMI transfers messages that provide notification by the network to the user of the presence of an active DLCI, notification of the removal or failure of a DLCI, and real-time monitoring of the status of the physical and logical link between the network and each user device. In other words, the (I)LMI solves the issue of a "keep alive signal" between the network and the user's equipment. It also provides capabilities for downloading logical link addresses from the network to the user's equipment. Also, as indicated, a multicast facility for ease of address resolution by bridges and routers is included. These features are now included in the ANSI standards.

Many elements of the vendors' extensions for network management, particularly the (I)LMI's local in-channel signaling, have subsequently been incorporated in the ANSI standards (ANSI T1.617 Annex D, Additional Procedures for PVC's Using Unnumbered Information Frames). The (I)LMI specification describes a protocol and associated procedures

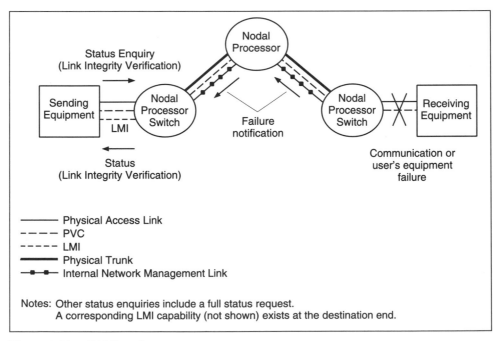

Figure 6.11 (I)LMI environment.

operating at the UNI to handle network management functions. The features of a network that supports (I)LMI include: notification to the user of the addition, deletion, and presence of a PVC in the network, and notification to the user of end-to-end availability of a PVC. Vendors are working on implementing support of Annex D. In addition, a standard to support X.25 over a public frame relay network has evolved.

The (I)LMI protocol consists of an exchange of messages between the user and the local access node of the network. The (I)LMI protocol is based on a polling scheme: The user's equipment (router) polls the network to obtain status information for the PVCs defined over a given UNI interface. The user device issues a status enquiry message, and the network responds with a status message. The (I)LMI uses a connectionless data link protocol based on Q.921/LAP-D, making the procedure easy to implement; at Layer 3, Q.931 messages are used, similarly to ISDN.

Annex D of T1.617 specifies procedures for the following tasks:

- Addition or deletion of a PVC
- Status determination (availability/unavailability) of a configured PVC
- Local in-channel signaling for link reliability errors
- Local in-channel signaling for link protocol errors

Data Link Layer

The (I)LMI data link layer conforms to a subset of LAP-D. Only unnumbered information frames are used; the poll bit is set to 0; the control field is coded as 00000011. The DLCI is set to 0. See Figure 6.12. The DLCI is specified in bits 3 through 8 of the second octet, and bits 5 through 8 of the third octet (the leftmost bit is bit 8; the rightmost bit is bit 1). The message field must contain the (I)LMI protocol discriminator, set to 00001001 in the LAP-D frame; it is used by the user-network call control to distinguish this message from other messages. The call reference is set to the dummy 00000000. A locking shift field is also required; it is used to identify codesets (currently only codeset 5 is supported).

Management Layer

This layer consists of two facets: the format of the message field, including information elements, and the message functional description. An entire (I) LMI message always fits an entire LAP-D frame. The information elements have specific formats, specified by the bit mappings for various functions.

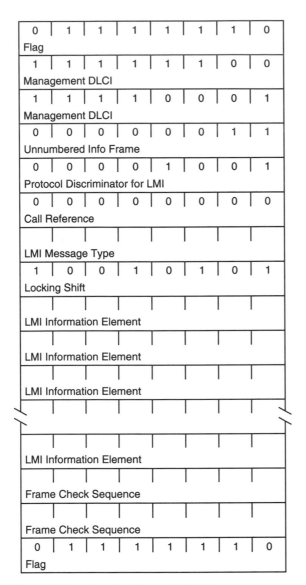

0	1	1	1	1	1	1	0
Flag							
1	1	1	1	1	1	0	0
Management DLCI							
1	1	1	1	0	0	0	1
Management DLCI							
0	0	0	0	0	0	1	1
Unnumbered Info Frame							
0	0	0	0	1	0	0	1
Protocol Discriminator for LMI							
0	0	0	0	0	0	0	0
Call Reference							
LMI Message Type							
1	0	0	1	0	1	0	1
Locking Shift							
LMI Information Element							
LMI Information Element							
LMI Information Element							
LMI Information Element							
Frame Check Sequence							
Frame Check Sequence							
0	1	1	1	1	1	1	0
Flag							

Figure 6.12   Data link layer of (I)LMI messages.

The link integrity verification status enquiry from the user and the status message from the network allow both the user and the network to determine link reliability errors (physical faults) and protocol errors. The full status report has a PVC status information element that allows the user to detect the addition of a PVC, the deletion of a PVC, the availability of a configured PVC, and the unavailability of a configured PVC. A user's frame relay device (for example, a frame relay capable router) periodically issues a status enquiry message for the network's full status report to determine when a PVC has become active or inactive. The reports are exchanged using DLCI 0. Full status reporting (PVC status and link integrity verification information element) is employed to report communication or remote user equipment failure to the local user. This procedure can also be used to signal a trunk or switch failure.

The (I)LMI messages and some related information elements are shown in Table 6.5. These procedures are driven by a set of parameters established at subscription. Table 6.6 depicts some key parameters. Additional procedural details, not covered here, are required to undertake the network management functions.

Table 6.5 (I)LMI Messages

MESSAGES	DESCRIPTION
STATUS	Sent from the network to user device in response to a STATUS ENQUIRY. Has Message Type field of 01111101.
STATUS ENQUIRY	Used by the router or frame relay device to request status information. Actual configuration and status information is contained in the information elements. Has Message Type file of 01110101.
INFORMATION ELEMENTS	**DESCRIPTION**
REPORT TYPE	Used to indicate either the type of enquiry requested by the user's frame relay device or the contents of the STATUS message returned by the network. It can be a full status or a link integrity verification only.
LINK INTEGRITY VERIFICATION	Used to exchange sequence numbers between network and user equipment on a periodic basis to indicate to each other that they are active and operational.
PVC STATUS	Present in a STATUS message and sent by the network to notify the user's frame relay device of the configuration and status of an existing PVC; the PVC is identified at the (I)LMI UNI by the DLCI.

Table 6.6   (I)LMI Parameters

Full Polling Cycle	Describes the number of polling cycles between full status reports. It is set by the user and has a default value of 6 with range 1–255.
Error Threshold	Number of reliability or protocol errors before a PVC or a user device is declared inactive. It is set by both the network and the user, and has a default value of 3 and can range from 1–10.
Monitored Events Count	Specifies the size of the window employed by the network or user to determine if a PVC or user device is active. After a PVC or device is declared inactive, the network waits a number of successful poll cycles specified by this parameter before declaring them active again. Has a default value of 4 and ranges from 1–10.
Link Integrity	Indicates how frequently the user should send a status.
Verification Time Enquiry	Set by the user. Ranges from 5–30 seconds, with a default value of 10.
Polling Verification Timer	Indicates the interval of time the network should wait between status enquiry messages; if no messages are received, the network posts an error. It is set by the network; it can range from 5–30 seconds and has a default value of 15 seconds.

References

1. D. Minoli, E. Minoli. *Delivering Voice over Frame Relay and ATM* (New York: John Wiley & Sons, Inc.), 1998.

Notes

[1] This term is a colloquialism used to refer to communication where the information is packaged in blocks (packets, frames, or cells) and is transferred through the network at a higher access and delivery speed than would be in a traditional packet network.

[2] Q.922/LAP-F (ISDN Data Link Layer Specification for Frame Mode Bearer Services) is a full data link layer protocol in its own merit; it was adopted in 1991. Frame relay uses a subset called LAP-F Core.

LAP-F functions like windowing; error correction is not included in the core subset.

[3] This discussion is based in part on D. Minoli, *Enterprise Networking: Fractional T1 to SONET, Frame Relay to BISDN* (Artech House). Norwood, Mass, 1992.

[4] Instead of using cell relay on the trunk side, some switches use frame relay. In the long run, most switches will probably migrate to the cell relay NNI.

[5] In a cell-based switching/transport platform, as soon as a frame starts to arrive at a switch, it can immediately be segmented to cells "on the fly."

[6] Packet switching and other statistical multiplexing schemes do fulfill the role of supporting error-free transmission of asynchronous traffic from "dumb" terminals (or from devices and PCs emulating "dumb" terminals), which have no error protection of their own. A frame relay service would be a mismatch in this environment.

[7] EPD triggers if the switch detects that congestion is about to occur and discards the entire incoming packet (except for the end-of-packet cell; this is doable via the AAL5 mechanism). PPD triggers to discard incoming packets when congestion occurs too abruptly for EPD to respond.

CHAPTER 7

ATM Technology for ISPs and QoS Support Capabilities

In using the Internet for extranet and enterprise network support (e.g., VPN, SOHO), corporations need QoS-enabled communications. To support QoS on the Internet, ISPs need to rely on new technologies and protocols, including, among others, asynchronous transfer mode. This chapter focuses on ATM, which, as it is well known, is a broadband switched service supporting WAN (and LAN) applications; cell relay service deliverable over an ATM platform is the QoS-enabled communication service par excellence.[1] Given its design goals, in abstract, ATM supports QoS very well, for example, in an end-to-end pure ATM network. However, ATM must be used in the context of other embedded protocols, such as, IP; hence, QoS has to be ultimately understood in that environment. The material included in this chapter may be useful to the corporate planner in posing inquiries to the prospective ISPs as to the QoS capabilities that might be available and exactly how they are using ATM to deliver QoS (if they are doing so at all).

As covered in the previous chapter, an Internet-based connection is composed of various network components, where different technologies are applicable. Hence, as already stated in previous chapters, contrary to the provincial view of some techno-religionists, all technologies eventually find a place on the Internet. In general, one can identify three major elements in an Internet connection: the access subnetwork (ASN), the ISP aggregation subnetwork (IASN), and the NSP backbone network (NBN).

Each of these elements can make use of a number of distinct technologies, including ATM. Leading-edge ISPs/NSPs use ATM in the access subnetwork to provide corporations with burstable-speed access, currently up to DS3 speeds, but soon up to OC-3c. Many DSLAM systems supporting xDSL use ATM as an uplink. Also, high-end routers use ATM uplinks, to reach the OC-3c and OC-12c speeds required in the backbone. Many Internet backbones are ATM-based. This chapter addresses the use of ATM and the delivery of QoS through ATM for these three elements.

> **NOTE** Readers interested in ATM/cell relay features should pay particular attention to section 7.1. Readers interested in a more complete description of cell relay services may find the entire chapter of interest, particularly if the QoS question is paramount in their minds, and in preparation for the discussion of Chapter 9 where the direct support of IP over ATM is discussed.

In addition to use on the Internet, ATM services are being contemplated by chief technology officers (CTOs) in many organizations to support traditional corporate enterprise networks and to provide increased bandwidth and functionality. In particular, there is an increased need to connect all sites of an organization via a network of sufficient capacity to allow the corporation to conduct its business in an effective manner, at speeds exceeding 1.544Mbps. As noted in Chapter 4, there is increasing interest in multimedia. In addition, there are increased interenterprise connectivity demands (e.g., as possible over the Internet). Furthermore, the logical topology of the interconnected parties must be customizable to changing business needs; for example, to support virtual corporation concepts and mobile workers.

In reference to traditional enterprise networks, as covered in the previous chapter, until recently, customers' networks have consisted mostly of a mesh of dedicated point-to-point lines. These dedicated lines have been migrated from analog and 56Kbps digital lines, up to T1/DS1 and even T3/DS3 lines; these lines were traditionally terminated on T1/T3 multiplexers or directly on routers. One disadvantage of this approach is the cost of the mesh network of dedicated lines. ISDN services, frame relay, and cell relay are *switched* high-speed services operating at 1.5Mbps (ISDN, FM, and ATM), 45Mbps (ATM), and 155Mbps (ATM),[2] that enable users to eliminate multiple dedicated lines and obtain not only more cost-effective connectivity, but also increase their reach (since more destinations can be connected without having to install organization-maintained

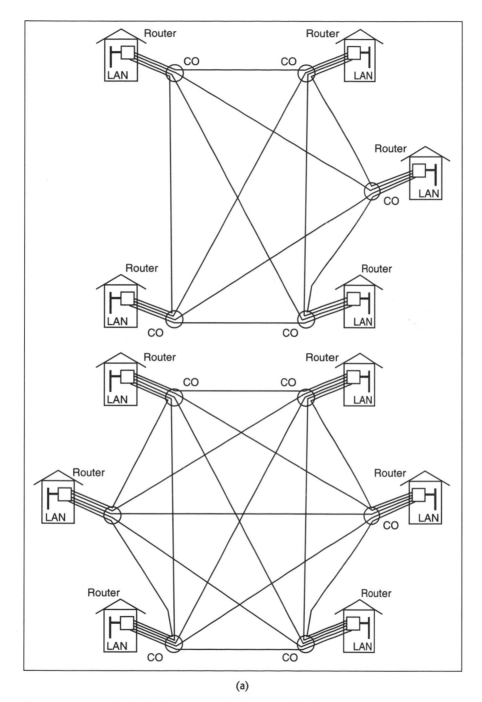

(a)

Figure 7.1   Topological advantages of using a switched service: (a) enterprise networks composed of dedicated lines, and the difficulty of adding a new site to the network; *continues.*

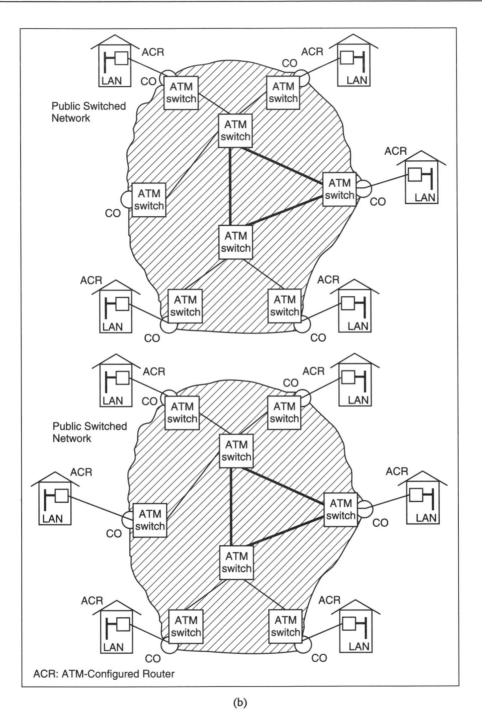

(b)

Figure 7.1 (Continued) Topological advantages of using a switched service: (b) enterprise networks utilizing public switched networks.

facilities), and improve availability (since the network can afford alternate routing via a large number of available carrier facilities). Figure 7.1 shows the topological advantages of using a switched service such as cell relay: Reduced circuit mileage implies reduced costs to the user. Additionally, the reduced number of facilities implies simpler network management. This kind of topological simplification is also possible for ISPs in connecting dispersed backbone routers, although certain considerations related to bandwidth efficiency have to be taken into account.

One key advantage of ATM is the possibility of integrated support of all of a customer's media (data, voice, video, image), in a QoS-based manner. In addition, ATM can support classical IP-based applications in a variety of ways, as covered in Chapter 9. This makes ATM a good candidate for network support, including voice communication.

7.1 ATM Basics

ATM supports the deployment of integrated intranets, enterprise, and Internet/VPN networks that allow corporations and organizations to access their voice, video, and data from across town as easily as across the hall, using one network. High throughput applications are now entering the corporate mainstream. Examples include scanned documents and imaging, hypermedia documents, multimedia, and desktop video and videoconferencing. In addition, 100Mbps LANs are entering the corporation, and gigabit Ethernet systems are just around the corner. Unconnected islands of users are no longer acceptable either across geographic or technology barriers. Hence, high-throughput WAN/interworking systems are needed.

In particular for enterprise applications, ATM platforms and cell relay services are now being considered as the vehicle to support a variety of evolving applications such as:

- LAN interconnection over a WAN (bridged) link, particularly for high-speed 100Mbps LANs, including carrier-provided TLS service
- Legacy-to-broadband interworking via LAN Emulation (LANE)[3]
- Multimedia conferencing, collaborative computing, and similar applications
- Image-based workflow systems
- (On-demand) video distribution using Motion Pictures Expert Group Standard 2 (MPEG-2) over ATM

- Carriage of transport/network protocols (such as TCP/IP) over ATM

- Circuit emulation (the realization of a service similar to private lines, without installation of the physical facility end to end)

- Support of intranets, Internet high-capacity backbones, and VPNs

For ISP applications, ATM can be used in all subelements of the Internet: access, aggregation, and backbone.

Routed internets at DS1 speeds or less are "running out of steam," as is Internet access at T1 or fractional T1 speeds. DS1 private lines do not scale well to DS3, due to the bandwidth granularities. Also, DS3 does not scale seamlessly to OC-3c. Figure 7.2 depicts the technology evolution over the years, in terms of the ubiquitous penetration of complex technologies throughout the corporation.

In recent years, LAN segmentation has been used at the LAN level to increase per-user bandwidth. However, unless other elements of the enterprise network are appropriately upgraded, the end-to-end through-put will be compromised. Layer 2 switches (L2Ss) used in LAN segmenta-tion are fast, but if the routers, building/campus backbone, WAN backbone, or Internet backbone are inadequate, the actual end-to-end QoS and throughput will suffer.

ATM uses cellularization to make the most effective use of available network bandwidth. Because the cells are small, it is easy to get the maxi-mum use of transmission resources. Long PDUs could imply that there are unfilled gaps between transmissions. Short standardized packets (cells) allow the multiplexing equipment at the link's endpoints to fully pack the link. Figure 7.3 diagrammatically represents this. Furthermore,

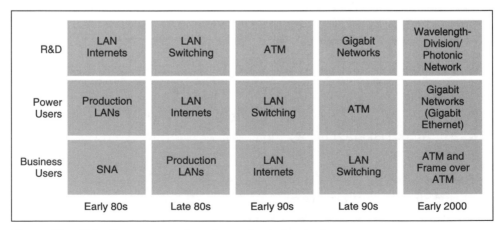

	Early 80s	Late 80s	Early 90s	Late 90s	Early 2000
R&D	LAN Internets	LAN Switching	ATM	Gigabit Networks	Wavelength-Division/ Photonic Network
Power Users	Production LANs	LAN Internets	LAN Switching	ATM	Gigabit Networks (Gigabit Ethernet)
Business Users	SNA	Production LANs	LAN Internets	LAN Switching	ATM and Frame over ATM

Figure 7.2   Ubiquitous permeation of complex technologies.

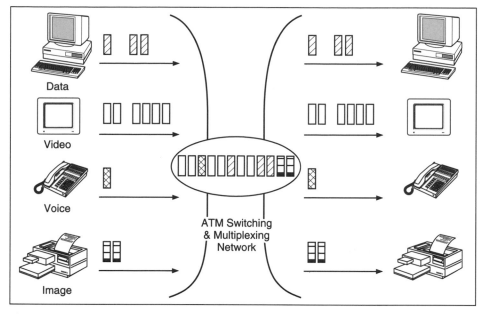

Figure 7.3 ATM's multimedia potential.

cells of constant length improve the delay performance through the switch, as illustrated in Figure 7.4. However, in an IP environment, this cellularization also implies an overhead. The trade-off of the length of a PDU's header versus the PDU's payload is a well understood issue, which researchers have studied for a long time [4].

ATM took shape through the international consultative process as well through industry initiatives (e.g., the ATM Forum) and grew out of other well-established ISDN standards, although the standard specifications have not yet resolved every possible issue related to WAN or LAN networking. This process has taken about 13 years (1985–1998), and is ongoing. Researchers in the 1980s were looking at the best method to achieve high-speed packetized data transmission. Their work began with ISDN standards activities. ISDN is a digital service, but is characteristic of its generation. Its physical layer (layer 1) is based on copper wire, and its bandwidth is limited to hundreds of thousands of bits per second. ISDN allocates the available bandwidth into channels using time division multiplexing (also known as synchronous transfer mode) technology: two 64Kbps channels for data transport and one 16Kbps channel for signaling. The signaling channel is used to establish a connection; the data transport channel then supports transfer of the information. ISDN is strictly a circuit-switched service of defined bandwidth capabilities ($n \times 64$, with n up to 30). Frame relay moves in the direction of statistical TDM at T1 and sub-T1 rates.

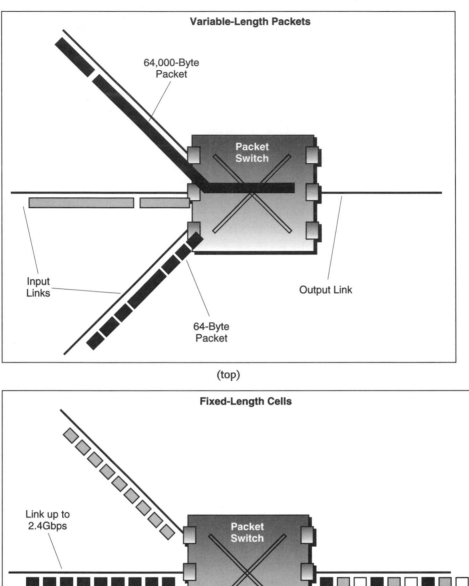

(top)

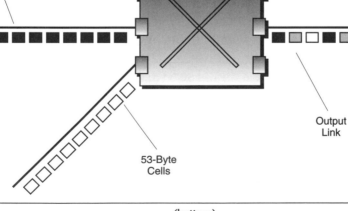

(bottom)

Figure 7.4 Advantages of cell relay: (top) variable-length packets; (bottom) fixed-length cells.

A decision was made in the mid-1980s to seek a new standard that could be based to some extent on ISDN principles, but at the same time support optical fiber; because of the media used, the supported speeds are much higher. The standard became known as B-ISDN (for Broadband ISDN). Although both are digital, ATM technology differs from ISDN in so far that ISDN is a synchronous transfer mode technology (namely, ISDN is a circuit-switched technology without any statistical multiplexing and statistical gains); ATM, on the other hand, is an asynchronous transfer packet technology with statistical multiplexing and gain. Because the user and the carrier "gamble" on statistical multiplexing, sophisticated traffic management capabilities are required on the network switches.

Several entities have published relevant ATM standards, specifications, and requirements including the International Telecommunication Union, Telecommunications (ITU-T) and ANSI (ATIS). The ATM Forum (ATMF), the Frame Relay Forum (FRF), and Bellcore have published relevant documentation. Carriers require the support of the ATMF User-to-Network Interface Specification version 3.1 or 4.0, Broadband Intercarrier Interface (B-ICI) version 2, and (for internal connectivity only) Private Network Node Interface (P-NNI) version 1.0 or higher. UNI 3.1 supports the ITU-T Q.2931, which is important. LAN Emulation (LANE) version 2.0 and MPOA standards are also required for some applications. Table 7.1 lists some key ATM standards and specifications.

The ATM Forum has focused on issues of interoperability. It appears that ATM will resolve vendor interoperability issues more quickly than its predecessors, primarily due to two factors: focus and commitment. The ATM Forum consists of a plethora of vendor, user, government, and academic representatives whose commitment to the success of ATM is, in some people's view, unparalleled. FDDI, for example, encountered early difficulties in linking workstations from different manufacturers. Token ring also had problems of this kind, due to the lack of an organization focusing efforts on implementation and deployment issues.

For high-bandwidth networks based on fiber, ATM is frequently employed with SONET.[4] SONET defines a series of bandwidth levels for transmission over fiber networks. SONET rates consist of multiples of a base of 51.840Mbps. Current ATM technology supports bandwidths at the OC-1 (Optical Carrier-1) level (51.840Mbps), OC-3c level (155.520Mbps), and OC-12c level (622.08Mbps). SONET levels now targeted by systems developers would deliver 1244.160Mbps (OC-24c) and 2488.320Mbps (OC-48c). SONET standards are now nearly ready for OC-192c (about 10Gbps) speeds. Alternatively, developers are looking at dense wavelength division multiplexing (DWDM) technology. For user access, current ATM technology supports 155.520Mbps and 622.080Mbps. OC-24c

Table 7.1 Key ATM Documents

ITU-T	I.113: B-ISDN Vocabulary of Terms
	I.121R: Broadband Aspects of ISDN
	I.150: B-ISDN ATM Functional Characteristics
	I.211: B-ISDN Service Aspects
	I.311: B-ISDN General Network Aspects
	I.321: B-ISDN Protocol Reference Model and Its Applications
	I.327: B-ISDN Functional Architecture Aspects
	I.361: B-ISDN ATM Layer Specification
	I.362: B-ISDN ATM Adaptation Layer Functional Description
	I.363: B-ISDN ATM Adaptation Layer Specification
	I.371: B-ISDN Traffic Control and Congestion Control
	I.413: B-ISDN User-Network Interface
	I.432: B-ISDN User-Network Interface—Physical Layer
	I.555: ATM-FR Interworking
	I.610: B-ISDN UNI Operations and Maintenance Principles
	Q.2931: ATM SVC Signaling
Bellcore	TA-NWT-001110: Broadband ISDN Switching System Generic Requirements
	TA-NWT-001111: Broadband ISDN Access Signaling Generic Requirements
	TA-NWT-001112: Broadband ISDN User-to-Network Interface and Network Node Interface Physical Layer Generic Requirements
	TA-NWT-001113: Asynchronous Transfer Mode (ATM) and ATM Adaptation Layer (AAL) Protocols Generic Requirements
	TA-TSV-001408: Generic Requirements for Exchange PVC Cell Relay Service
	TA-TSV-001409: Generic Requirements for Exchange Access PVC Cell Relay Service
	TA-TSV-001501: Generic Requirements for Exchange SVC Cell Relay Service

Table 7.1   *(Continued)*

ATM Forum	User-to-Network Interface 3.1 and 4.0
	LANE version 1.0 and 2.0
	Traffic Management 4.0
	MPOA Version 1.0
	P-NNI Version 1.0

and OC-48c would represent the gigabit network concept mentioned so often in public discussion in the context of "information superhighways." Applied with ATM technology, these bandwidth levels should be achievable later in this decade.

ATM can be delivered over dedicated private networks (e.g., an enterprise network, an ISP's backbone network), or over a Layer-2 carrier's service.

Fiber media, used with the SONET Physical Layer protocol, makes available high capacity to the connected users. Still, there is a need to support statistical multiplexing and bandwidth overbooking, to obtain transmission efficiencies, particularly in the long haul. The question is how much overbooking makes sense; generally, overbooking should be no more than 200 to 400 percent. Overbooking also drives QoS. It follows that, in ATM, sophisticated congestion control is needed in order to "guarantee" a very small probability of cell loss even under significant traffic levels. These characteristics add up to a technology that can permit users and applications developers to explore possibilities that have not been feasible until now.

From an ISP point of view, ATM provides a multiplexed Layer 2 service that can be used almost like a private line service. In fact, studies have shown that, currently, backbone links shorter than 500 miles are best served by dedicated circuits (in so far that these are cheaper), while links longer than 500 miles are more cost-effective when delivered over an ATM service. One of the problems associated with ATM, is, however, the "cell tax," which is also compounded when one sends small PDUs (e.g., 64 bytes) that are split into two cells (hence, having to send 106 bytes to carry just 64 bytes of information). Fortunately, a lot of the Internet traffic is TCP PDUs, which tend to be of full size. These considerations sometimes drive ISPs to look into POS as a way to support backbone connectivity.

7.2 Overview of Key ATM Features

This section outlines some of the key features of ATM, including:

- The structure of its 53-byte cells, or labeled information containers.
- The physical layer, ATM layer, and ATM adaptation layer, which organize appropriate service data units (SDUs)/PDUs for transmission. Special attention is given to the adaptation layer, which is used to accommodate the special requirements of voice, video, and data traffic. The service layer sits on top of the AAL and uses specific AALs (e.g., AAL 1, AAL 2, AAL 5, etc.) to provide the appropriate services to the legacy protocols (e.g., IP) residing at the network layer.

The ITU-T standards for ATM specify the cell size and structure and the UNI. Note that there are two kinds of UNIs: one for access to public networks, and one, called Private UNI, for access to a customer-owned ATM network (specifically to a hub, router, or switch). As already discussed, for the public UNI, the physical layer is defined for data rates of 1.544Mbps, 45Mbps, 155Mbps (SONET OC-3c), and 622Mbps. For the private UNI, a number of physical layers for different media (UTP, STP, single-mode fiber, multimode fiber) are defined. ISPs may use both public and private UNIs, depending on whether they develop their own ATM backbone or use that of a Layer 2 service provider.

ATM can be described as a packet transfer mode based on asynchronous time division multiplexing and a protocol engine that uses small fixed-length data units, namely, cells. ATM provides a connection-oriented service. Note that LANs such as Ethernet, FDDI, and token ring support a connectionless service. IP is also connectionless. Hence, interworking must take this into account. Each ATM connection is assigned its own set of transmission resources; however, these resources have to be taken out of a shared pool, which is generally smaller than the maximum needed to support the entire population—this is the reason for the much talked-about traffic management problem in ATM. ATM nevertheless makes it possible to share bandwidth through multiplexing (multiple messages transmitted over the same physical circuit). Multiple virtual channels can be supported on the access link, and the aggregate bandwidth of these channels can be overbooked (ATM relies on statistical multiplexing to carry the load). Within the network, expensive resources, such as communication links and supportive switch buffers, are "rationed," and bandwidth must be allocated dynamically. ATM is thus able to maximize resource (bandwidth) utilization.

ATM supports two kinds of channels in the network: virtual channels and virtual paths. VCs are communication channels of specified service capabilities between two (intermediary) ATM peers. Virtual channel connections (VCCs) are concatenations of VCs to support endsystem-to-endsystem communication. VPs are groups ("bundles") of VCs. Virtual path connections (VPCs) are concatenations of VPs to support endsystem-to-endsystem communication. In VC switching, each VC is switched and routed independently and separately. VP switching allows a group of VCs to be switched and routed as a single entity.

A virtual circuit can be either switched (temporary) or permanent. A connection is established through preprovisioning with the carrier or private devices (thereby establishing permanent virtual channels—PVCs—and/or permanent virtual paths—PVPs), or through signaling mechanisms (thereby establishing switched virtual channels—SVCs). Connections supported by these channels (PVCs or SVCs) enable a router or other system on the network to communicate with another. More specifically, as covered, communication in ATM occurs over a concatenation of virtual data links called virtual channels; this concatenation is called a virtual channel connection. VCCs can be permanently established by an external provisioning process, entailing a service order (with desired traffic contract information) and manual switch configuration. Such a VCC is called a PVC.

Figure 7.5 depicts a functional reference model that is utilized when developing recommendations and deploying equipment. It shows a user plane, where user communication takes place, and a control plane, where user signaling takes place. Switched cell relay service requires signaling to

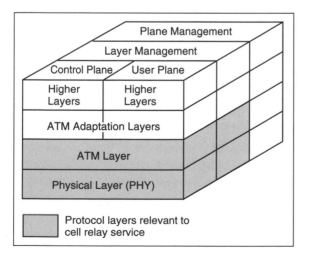

Figure 7.5 A B-ISDN functional reference model.

specify the details of the connection, such as the forward and backward bandwidth, the quality of service class, the type of adaptation and inter-working, subaddressing, point-to-multipoint connectivity, and other user-to-user information. When the control plane mechanisms are implemented in both the user equipment and in the switch (specifically, ITU-T Q.2931 and/or ATMF UNI 3.1/4.0), the user will be able to establish connections automatically on an as-needed basis. This type of connection is called SVC.

Network resources such as inbound speed, outbound speed, quality of service, multipoint capabilities, and so on are requested as a connection is established. A connection is established if the network is able to meet the request; if not, the request is rejected. Once the virtual circuit is defined, the call connection control assigns an interface-specific virtual channel identifier (VCI) and virtual path identifier (VPI) to identify the connection. These labels have only interface-specific meaning. Two different sets of VPIs/VCIs are assigned to the two endpoints of the connection. Inside the network, as many sets of VPIs/VCIs as needed (along the path) are used by the network, invisibly to the end users. As long as the connection remains active, the assigned VCI and VPI represent valid pointers into routing tables in the network; the tables (accessed via the VPI/VCI) are used to accomplish cell routing through the network. Figure 7.6 depicts a simple example of cell switching using VPI/VCI lookup.

7.2.1 Cell Format

ATM cell has a 48-byte payload, accompanied by a 5-byte header that is divided into fields. Headers are of two types: the UNI and the network-to-network interface (NNI). See Figure 7.7.

Fields within the UNI cell are:

- *The first, of 4 bits, provides for generic flow control (GFC).* It is not currently used, and is intended to support a local bus ("extension") function to connect multiple broadband terminal equipment to the same UNI as equal peers (note that multiple users can be connected to the UNI today by using a multiplexing—not peer—function).

- *A 24-bit routing pointing field subdivided into an 8-bit VPI subfield and a 16-bit subfield for VCI.* It indirectly identifies the specific route laid out for traffic over a specific connection, by providing a pointing function into switch tables that contain the actual route.

- *Three bits allocated to the payload type identifier (PTI).* Identifies whether each cell is a user or a control cell, used for network management.

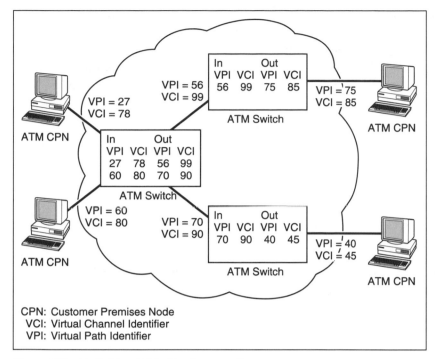

Figure 7.6   Switching ATM virtual connections.

- *A single-bit cell loss priority (CLP) marker.* Used to distinguish two levels of cell-loss priority. Zero identifies a higher-priority cell that should receive preferred loss treatment if cells are discarded due to network congestion. One indicates lower-priority cells whose loss is less critical. This bit is used in the context of traffic "policing," which in turn is used in the context of QoS support.

8	7	6	5	4	3	2	1
Generic Flow Control				Virtual Path Identifier			
Virtual Path Identifier (continued)				Virtual Channel Identifier			
Virtual Channel Identifier (continued)							
Virtual Channel Identifier (continued)				Payload Type Identifier			Cell-loss Priority
Header Error Control							
Payload							

Figure 7.7   ATM cell structure.

- *Header error control (HEC), an 8-bit cyclic redundancy code (CRC) computed over the ATM cell header.* The HEC is capable of detecting all single-bit errors and certain multiple-bit errors. It can be used to correct all single-bit errors, but this is not mandatory. This mechanism is employed by a receiving device to infer that the cell is in error and should simply be discarded. It is also used for cell-boundary recovery at the physical layer.

- *The remaining 48 bytes are devoted to payload.* (In case of interworking, some of the payload bytes have to be used for network-used AAL protocol control information.)

- *The NNI cell structure has one difference.* The 4-bit GFC field is dropped, and the VPI field is expanded from 8 bits to 12.

As already noted, cellularization leads to bandwidth overhead. In addition, "odd"-size PDUs (e.g., a PDU of 64 bytes), has even higher bottom-line overhead since it needs two cells to be sent. This issue has received considerable attention, as noted in Chapter 2. It is a problem that is the focus mostly of newly formed bandwidth-starved ISPs. ISPs that are facilities-based can make effective use of ATM to secure ATM's advantages (including fine-grain QoS) without letting the overhead become the driving factor. For example, many CLECs offer transparent LAN services that provide native-speed support of 10Mbps Ethernets over DS-3 tails provisioned through a switch, in conjunction with premises-based adaptation devices; similarly, they support native-speed 100Mbps Ethernets over OC-3c tails. These examples show that bandwidth efficiency is not always the be all and end all, and if a useful service can be provided, there will be a market.

7.2.2 Addressing

Addressing is a fundamental need in any network. The ITU-T ATM protocols calls for a hierarchical ISDN telephone numbering scheme, specified in ITU-T E.164, to be used in ATM. (There also are private network addressing schemes, but these would typically not be used by ISPs, unless they just set up a small, stable private network arrangement for their backbone; they should avoid using private addressing if they can plan ahead and realize that a larger hybrid private backbone/public services network may eventually be required.) The standard permits the ATM address to be divided into an address and a subaddress. The ATM Forum recommends that the address describe the point of attachment to the public network (if connected to the public network) and that the subaddress identify a particular endstation within a private network [5]. Note that the VPI/VCI are just labels, not E.164 addresses; they are table pointers for the "relaying of cells" to their destination, based on switch routing tables. As noted, the ATM Forum specification permits two address formats to be used as an ATM address in private networks. One is the E.164 format and the other is a 20-byte address modeled after the address format of an OSI network service access point (NSAP).

7.2.3 The Protocol Model

An extension of the conventional OSI seven-layer stack can be used to describe the structure of the ATM protocol; a reference model specific to ATM depicts its structure more clearly. Figure 7.8 depicts an interface reference model, while Figure 7.9 depicts the protocol stack used in a simple ATM network. The protocol reference model (Figure 7.5) distinguishes three basic layers. Beginning from the bottom, these are the physical layer, the ATM layer, and the AAL. Each is divided further into sublayers, as seen in Figure 7.10. To further elaborate the protocol stack, Figure 7.11 shows both the data flow plane and the signaling plane required to support switched connections.

The physical layer includes two sublayers:

- Like any other data link layer protocol, ATM is not defined in terms of a specific type of physical carrying medium; but it is necessary to define appropriate physical layer protocols for cell transmission. The

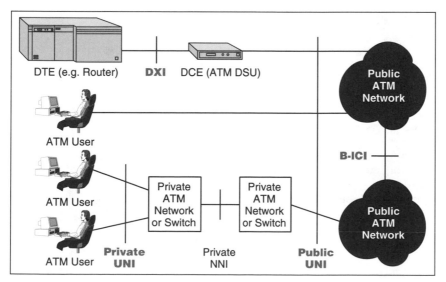

Figure 7.8 An interface reference model.

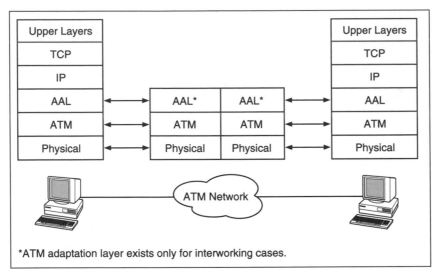

Figure 7.9 The protocol stack used in a simple ATM network.

physical medium (PM) sublayer interfaces with the physical medium and provides transmission and reception of bits over the physical facility. It also provides the physical medium with proper bit timing and line coding. There will be different manifestations of this layer based on the specifics of the underlying medium (e.g., for WAN/Internet applications on a DS1 link, a DS3 link, a SONET link, etc.)

Convergence	CS	AAL
Segmentation and Reassembly	SAR	
Generic Flow Control (if/when implemented) Cell VPI/VCI Translation Cell Multiplex and Demultiplex		ATM
Cell Rate Decoupling HEC Header Sequence Generation/Verification Cell Delineation Transmission Frame Adaptation Transmission Frame Generation/Recovery	TC	PHY
Bit Timing Physical Medium	PM	

Figure 7.10 ATM reference model.

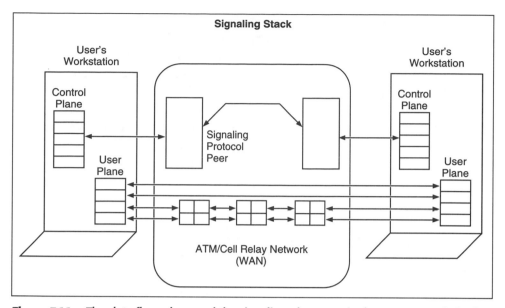

Figure 7.11   The data flow plane and the signaling plane required to support switched connections.

- The transmission convergence (TC) sublayer receives a bit stream from the PM sublayer and passes it in cell form to the ATM layer. Its functions include cell-rate decoupling, cell delineation, generation and verification of the HEC sequence, transmission frame adaptation, and the generation/recovery of transmission frames.

The ATM layer, in the middle of the ATM stack, is responsible for one of ATM's most "trivial" functions: to encapsulate downward-coming data into cells from a number of sources and multiplex the cell stream; conversely, it is responsible to deencapsulate upward-coming cells and demultiplex the resulting stream out to a number of sources.

The ATM layer controls multiplexing (the transmission of cells belonging to different connections over a single cell stream) and demultiplexing (distinguishing cells of various connections as they are pulled off the flow of cells.) ATM, as a data link layer protocol, is medium-independent: It is capable of performing these functions on a wide variety of physical media. In addition, the ATM layer acts as an intermediary between the layer above it and the physical layer below. It generates cell headers, attaches them to the data delivered to it by the adaptation layer and then delivers the properly tagged cells to the physical layer. Conversely, it strips headers from cells containing data arriving on the physical layer before hoisting the data to the application layer.

VCs and VPs are identified by their VCI/VPI tags.[5] The ATM layer assures that cells are arranged in the proper sequence, but it does not identify and retransmit damaged cells. If this is to be done, it must be accomplished by higher-level procedures. The ATM layer also translates VCI/VPI information. As noted earlier, each ATM switch has its own routing table to identify each connection. In transit between switches, VPI/VCI identifiers (routing table pointers) will be different. Switches translate identifiers as they transfer cells onward to other switches. Finally, the ATM layer performs management functions. If the payload type identifier (PTI) identifies a cell as a control packet, the ATM layer responds by carrying out the appropriate functions.

7.2.4 Support of Existing Protocols over ATM

The ATM adaptation layer allows various network layer protocols to utilize the service of the ATM layer. As discussed earlier, the ATM layer only supports the lower portion of the data link layer. Hence, in order for the network layer (e.g., IP) to use ATM, a "filler sublayer" is required. This is analogous to IP use over a LAN: the media access control layer only supports the lower portion of the data link layer; consequently, the subnetwork access protocol/logical link control (SNAP/LLC) layer is sandwiched in between.

Fundamentally, the AAL keeps the network layer "happy" by enabling it to use ATM transparently. The basic function of the AAL is to segment the downward-coming data (network layer PDU) into cells, and to reassemble upward-coming data into a PDU acceptable to the network layer. It is critical to understand that AALs are end-to-end functions (endsystem-to-endsystem). A network providing pure ATM will not be cognizant of, or act upon, AAL information (but in case of service interworking in the network, there has to be network interpretation of the AAL information). The design goal of an AAL protocol is to keep it simple enough so that it does not add any overhead.

In one classical view of the ATM protocol model, a "service" layer resides above the AAL, in the endsystems. Hence, by further elaboration one can say that, in a coincidental manner, the AAL differentiates in the endsystem the treatment of different categories of cells and permits responses to user-to-user quality-of-service issues. A number of AALs has been defined to meet different user-to-user quality of service requirements. Again, however, a backbone providing pure ATM will not be aware of, or act upon AAL information (but in case of service interworking in the network, there has to be network interpretation of the AAL information). Therefore, the AAL-supported service differentiation is among endsystem peers, and is not the mechanism used by the ATM network to support network quality of service. We use the term "user-to-user quality of service" to describe the kind of endsystem-to-endsystem peer-to-peer connection service differentiation (this connection being viewed as "external" to the ATM network). In an ISP environment, the router will deal with the AAL, since IP packets have to be reassembled before they can be inspected. Generally, routers use AAL 5.

For example, an endsystem TV monitor needs a continuous bit stream from a remote codec in order to paint a picture; it may have been decided that an ATM network is to be used to transport the bits. Because of the codec/monitor requirements, the bits have to be enveloped in such a manner that clock information is carried end to end in such a fashion that jitter is less than some specified value. To accomplish this, the bits are enveloped using AAL 1. From the ATM network's point of view, this is totally immaterial: the ATM network receives cells and carries them to the other end; the network delivers cells. The network does not render any different type of QoS to these cells based solely on the fact that the cell had AAL 1 information in them; the network was not even aware of the content. Naturally, it would be desirable if the network provided reasonable QoS to this stream, based on some kind of knowledge or arrangement. How is that accomplished?

It is important to understand that the different QoSes obtained via an ATM network are based on user-to-network negotiation, not by the content of the cell. In PVC, this negotiation is via a service order. Here, the user would tell the network (with paper) that the user wanted to get reasonable service for a certain stream carrying codec video. The network provider would make arrangements to terminate this stream on a switch line card where, for example, a lot of buffers were allocated. The network provider then tells the user (with paper) to employ a certain VPI/VCI combination (say 22/33) for this specific stream. Here is what happens: The user sends cells over the physical interface terminated at the card's port. Certain cells arriving on the interface have VPI/VCI = 44/66; these get some kind of QoS treatment. Then some cells arrive on the interface with VPI/VCI = 22/33; these cells get the agreed-to QoS by receiving specific treatment by the switch. In SVC, a similar mechanism is in place, except that instead of communicating the information using paper, the call-setup message is used (with automatic call negotiation).

In any event, the QoS in the ATM network is not based on the fact that the cells carried a certain AAL. It is the other way around. The user needs a certain endsystem-to-endsystem QoS. The user then needs to do two things: (1) select its (network-invisible) AAL, and (2) separately inform the carrier of the type of QoS needed.

AALs utilize a (small) portion of the 48-byte payload field of the ATM cell by inserting additional control bits. In all AALs, the ATM header retains its usual configuration and functions. Notice that the data coming down the protocol stack is first treated by the AAL by adding its own header (protocol control information). This AAL PDU must naturally fit inside the ATM PDU. Hence, the AAL header must fit inside the payload of the lower layer, here ATM. To say that "quality of service definitions are obtained at the cost of reductions in payload" is not exactly correct: AAL provides an appropriate segmentation and reassembly function—QoS is supported by the network switch; as discussed, AAL classes support peer-to-peer connection differentiation.

In some instances, users determine that the ATM layer service is sufficient for their requirements, so the AAL protocol remains empty. This occurs, for example, if the network layer protocol can ride directly on ATM (this is unlikely for legacy protocols and for IP), or if the two endsystems do not need additional coordination. In the majority of cases, however, this AAL layer is crucial to the endsystem protocol stack because it enables ATM to accommodate the requirements of voice, image/video, and data traffic while providing different classes of service to meet the distinctive requirements of each type of traffic.

Two sublayers make up the AAL: the segmentation and reassembly sublayer (SAR) and the convergence sublayer (CS). The SAR sublayer segments higher-layer information into a size suitable for cell payloads through a virtual connection. It also reassembles the contents of cells in a virtual connection into data units that can be delivered to higher layers. Functions like message identification and time/clock recovery are performed by the CS sublayer.

AAL 5 is specifically designed to offer a service for data communication with lower overhead and better error detection. AAL 5 is the protocol that is used by ISPs. It was developed because computer vendors realized that AAL 3/4 was not suited to their needs. In addition to the header, AAL 3/4 takes an additional four bytes for control information from the payload field, reducing its capacity by 8.4 percent. They also maintain that the error detection method of AAL 3/4 does not cope adequately with issues of lost or corrupted cells. See Table 7.2.

Table 7.2   AAL Type 5 CS-PDU

INFORMATION PAYLOAD	PAD	CONTROL	LENGTH	CRC-32
0–64K	0–47	1 byte	2 bytes	4 bytes

With AAL 5, the CS sublayer creates a CS protocol data unit (CS-PDU) when it receives a packet from the higher application layer. The first field is the CS Information Payload field, containing user data. The PAD field assures that the CS-PDU is 48 bytes aligned. A 1-byte control field remains undefined, reserved for further use. The 2-byte Length field indicates the length of information payload, and the CRC field is used to detect errors.

When the CS sublayer passes the CS-PDU to the SAR sublayer, it is divided into many SAR protocol data units (SAR-PDUs). The SAR sublayer then passes SAR-PDUs to the ATM layer, which carries out transmission of the cell.

When passing on the final SAR-PDU within the CS-PDU, SAR indicates the end of the CS-PDU transfer by setting to 1 the payload type identifier (PTI) in the header. By using the CS length field and the cyclic loss redundancy code (CRC) in the header's HEC (header error control), the AAL can detect the loss or corruption of cells.

Figure 7.12 depicts in simplified form the functionality needed to support legacy systems over ATM. As seen in this figure, AALs are utilized to

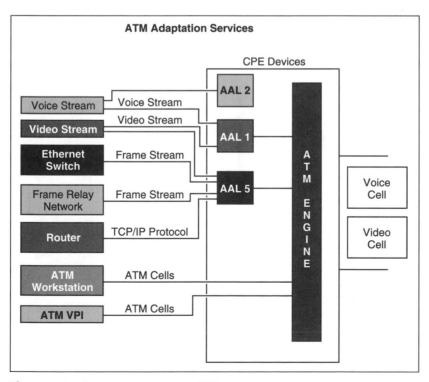

Figure 7.12   Legacy systems over ATM.

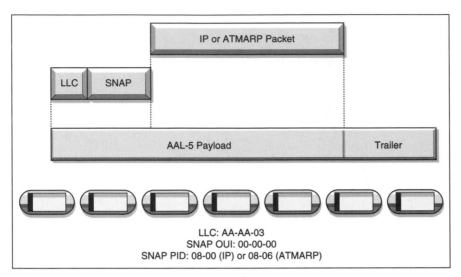

Figure 7.13 Encapsulation of an Ethernet frame into cells.

this end. Building on the AAL 5 format, Figure 7.13 shows the encapsulation of an Ethernet frame into cells. Figure 7.14 takes an even more general view of how LAN would work (in LANE 1.0, the "encapsulation" actually uses VC muxing; in LANE 2.0, SNAP/LLC is utilized).[6] Figure 7.15 shows how AALs can be utilized to support video applications.

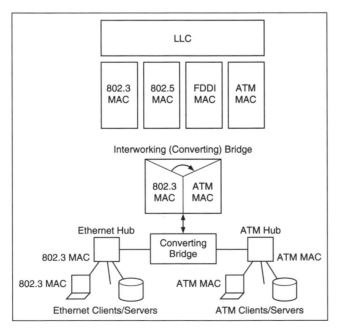

Figure 7.14 Simplified view of LAN emulation.

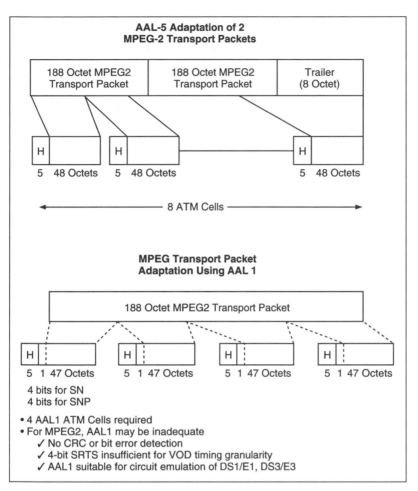

Figure 7.15 AALs can be used to support video applications.

7.2.5 Classes of Service

The ITU-T specifications apply three broad criteria to distinguish four ATM classes of service (CoS), tagged as A, B, C, and D. These end-to-end (network-external) criteria are (see Figure 7.16):

- Time relation between source and destination
- Bit rate
- Connection mode

The four end-to-end (network-external) classes of service are:

Class A. For example, clear-channel voice and fixed bit-rate video, such as movies or high-resolution teleconferencing. A time relation

	Class A	Class B	Class C	Class D
Application	Voice Clear Channel	Packet Video	Data	
Timing (source-destination)	Needed		Not Needed	
Mode	Connection-oriented			Connectionless
Bit Rate	Constant	Variable		

Figure 7.16   ATM class of service.

exists between source and destination. The bit rate is constant, and the network layer-level service is connection-oriented.

Class B.   As in Class A, there is a time relation between source and destination, and network layer-level service is connection-oriented, but the bit rate can be varied. Examples include audio and video with variable bit rates (e.g., unbuffered video codecs with motion compensation).

Class C.   The network layer-level service is connection-oriented, but there is no time relation between source and destination, and the bit rate is variable. This can, for example, meet the requirements of connection-oriented data transfer and signaling.

Class D.   Intended for applications like connectionless data transport (at the network layer); none of the three parameters applies: Service is connectionless, there is no time relation between source and destination, and the bit rate is variable.

These classes are general descriptions of types of user traffic. They do not set specific parameters or establish values. Thus, equipment from multiple vendors based on different parameters may theoretically find it difficult to establish connections. AALs are end to end and generally external to the ATM network; considerations on AALs relate to consideration of end-user equipment. AALs are considered by the network only when there is service interworking. Examples include frame relay-to-ATM interworking in the network; legacy LAN-to-ATM interworking (specifically, LANE) in the network; private line-to-ATM interworking in the network. For example, in the first case, frames come in and cells go out. There is another case where AALs are used in the network, but this is totally transparent to the user. This situation (called by some *network interworking*) is when the network supports a "carriage function" over

ATM. Examples include frame relay carriage over an ATM network; Ethernet carriage over ATM network (e.g., Ethernet bridging); and line carriage over an ATM network. For example, the frame relay user gives a frame relay frame to the (ATM-based) network; the network takes the frame and segments it into a stream of cells utilizing AAL 5 protocols; the stream is carried across the network, and in proximity of the destination, the cells are reassembled into a frame relay frame using AAL 5; the destination is handed a frame—this type of service is called frame relay carriage over ATM or frame relay-to-ATM network interworking. Another even more "involved" use of AALs occurs in networks supporting *service interworking*. Service interworking could be used by ISPs in the aggregation portion of their network, where several low-speed frame relay connections are mapped into an ATM connection.

As already discussed, four AAL protocols have been defined to support the three classes of service in the endsystem: AAL 1, AAL 2, AAL 3/4, and AAL 5. Computers routers and other devices must employ the same AAL in order to communicate with one another on an ATM network.

AAL 1.   Meets the performance requirements of service class A. It is intended for voice, video, and other constant bit-rate traffic, and its performance, to the upper layers of the endsystem stack, is similar to today's digital private lines. Four bits in the payload are allocated to sequence number (SN) and sequence number protection (SNP) functions.

AAL 2.   Aims at class B requirements. AAL 2 allows high efficiency for the transport of small packets. It is specifically designed to carry low-bit rate, variable-length, delay-sensitive packets such as would be required for packet telephony applications over an ATM network. AAL 2 (common part) provides what are termed logical link connections (LLCs) riding over an ATM PVC. These LLCs are provided by the smaller variable-length packets contained in the ATM cells. Each of these smaller packets contains an LLC identifier and length indicator. These LLCs are point-to-point in nature in the same manner as the PVC that carries them. There is also interest in an "LLC switch," which would provide LLC-level switching and allow multiplexing of LLCs destined for different locations to be carried in the same PVC. This would achieve even more bandwidth efficiency. The traffic parameters of the PVC are envisioned to be adjustable, for example, via signaling, so that the peak cell rate can be adjusted up or down as the offered voice traffic changes. Also, there is no need for a segmentation and reassembly sublayer in AAL 2. It should be noted that the principles of AAL 2 are applicable to non-ATM environments—for example, frame relay and IP—and multiplexing protocols similar to AAL 2 for carrying low-bit rate voice are being investigated as solutions in these areas. Final approval of the AAL 2 common part was scheduled for early 1998, and work is underway on the specification of a number of service specific convergence sublayers [7].

AAL 3/4.   Intended for connectionless data services (e.g., for support of switched multimegabit data service). Four bytes are devoted to control functions, including a multiplexing identifier as well as segment type (ST) and SNP indicators.

AAL 5.   Also intended for data communications, including services like frame relay, support of IP, LANE, and MPOA. The ATM Forum and the Internet Engineering Task Force (IETF) recommend that AAL 5 also be used to encapsulate IP packets in the user's endsystem.

Most likely, ISPs will be interested in Class D/AAL 5 applications.

Another way of looking at different ATM services is to talk about continuous bit rate (CBR), variable bit rate (VBR), available bit rate (ABR), and unspecified bit rate (UBR) services. These native ATM services support different user requirements, in a fashion related to the previous service class discussion. CBR provides constant bit rate in support of a service that provides the equivalent of a private line at DS1 or DS3 rates. VBR is a variable bit rate service in support of data applications such as frame relay and LAN interconnection. ABR provides available bit rate service at a discount basis; here the amount of bandwidth in the network is not guaranteed, and is managed via a feedback mechanism. UBR is an unspecified bit rate with only best-effort characteristics. The following sidebar defines the classes supported in the TM 4.0/UNI 4.0 specification of the ATM Forum. Per earlier discussion, the switch is made aware of what stream it is carrying for a specific VC, and the buffers and internal cell treatment are correlated to the type of traffic (CBR, VBR, etc.). Table 7.3 provides additional information on these services, based directly on the ATMF specification. ISPs will likely be interested in VBR, UBR, and perhaps ABR services (see sidebar).

One of the key features of ATM is that it supports negotiated connections for specified QoS. Service is obtained via traffic contract (per VC basis). Parameters include traffic characteristics, peak cell rate, and sustainable cell rate. QoS includes delay and cell loss. For ATM services, the customer can specify (the equivalent of) the sustainable cell rate (SCR), the peak cell rate (PCR), and other traffic parameters. The switch allocates various resources (e.g., trunk capacity, buffers) on a statistical basis using call admission control (CAC), as illustrated in Figure 7.17. This involves the use of traffic

CLASSES SUPPORTED IN UNI 4.0

- **Constant Bit Rate (CBR). A deterministic bandwidth requirement that makes it easy to provision/engineer. Sources that can make use of CBR generate cells at a fairly consistent rate, fully occupying the allocated bandwidth most of the time. The source rate corresponds to a known peak emission rate measured in cells per second. Conforming cells are typically guaranteed high priority because they are the product of latency-sensitive traffic such as video, voice, and circuit emulation. Loss of cells, or significant delays, will have a substantially negative impact on these applications.**

- **Variable Bit Rate Real-time (VBR-rt). Bursty data with delay sensitivity.**

- **Variable Bit Rate Nonreal-time (VBR-nrt). Bursty data without delay sensitivity.**

- **Available Bit Rate (ABR). ATM Forum cell-based adaptive flow control.**

- **Unspecified Bit Rate (UBR). Best-effort category.**

shapers, traffic policers, and tagging for discard. The carrier has the obligation to deploy enough resources in the network to guarantee the type of quality of service and the kind of service required (e.g., constant bit rate, variable bit rate, available bit rate, unspecified bit rate, etc.). Non-ATM services are allocated in a similar manner, but the user has no direct control on the (ATM) traffic parameters. This topic is covered in more detail later.

Related to QoS, one may ask if ATM supports voice and multimedia; and if so, how? Although on a campus, voice, video, and multimedia information can be carried over a variety of technologies (e.g., ATM, FDDI, shared/switched 10/100Mbps Ethernet interface), at the WAN level, ATM is one of the few, if not the only, technology that can support such a mix in an effective manner. ATM's fine-grain QoS makes it a good platform for these media. More specifically, the ATM Forum started work on voice transport in 1993, and in early 1995 the VTOA (Voice and Telephony over ATM) working group published its first document, addressing both unstructured and structured circuit emulation specifications. Unstructured circuit emulation maps an entire T1 (1.544Mbps) circuit to a single ATM VC, thus limiting it to point-to-point applications. Structured circuit emulation allows switches to map individual 64Kbps circuits in a T1 line to ATM VCs, and it can be used for point-to-multipoint connections. An update to the circuit emulation specification was published in early 1997[7] [7] [8].

One can also ask if ATM supports multipoint services; and if so, how? ATM supports multipoint connections. The ATFM UNI 3.1 specifies the use of signaling messages to establish such connections. Many ATM

Table 7.3   ATM Service in ATMF UNI 4.0

CONSTANT BIT RATE (CBR) SERVICE

The constant bit rate service category is used by connections that request a static amount of bandwidth that is continuously available during the connection lifetime. This amount of bandwidth is characterized by a peak cell rate (PCR) value.

The basic commitment made by the network to a user who reserves resources via the CBR capability is that once the connection is established, the negotiated ATM layer QoS is assured to all cells when all cells are conforming to the relevant conformance tests. In the CBR capability, the source can emit cells at the peak cell rate at any time and for any duration and the QoS commitments still pertain.

CBR service is intended to support real-time applications requiring tightly constrained delay variation (e.g., voice, video, circuit emulation) but is not restricted to these applications. In the CBR capability, the source may emit cells at or below the negotiated peak cell rate (and may also even be silent) for periods of time. Cells that are delayed beyond the value specified by the maximum cell transfer delay (maxCTD) are assumed to be of significantly reduced value to the application.

The CBR service category may be used for both VPCs and VCCs.

REAL-TIME VARIABLE BIT RATE (RT-VBR) SERVICE

The real-time VBR service category is intended for real-time applications, those requiring tightly constrained delay and delay variation, as would be appropriate for voice and video applications. rt-VBR connections are characterized in terms of a peak cell rate (PCR), sustainable cell rate (SCR), and maximum burst size (MBS). Sources are expected to transmit at a rate that varies with time. Equivalently, the source can be described as "bursty." Cells that are delayed beyond the value specified by maxCTD are assumed to be of significantly reduced value to the application. Real-time VBR service may support statistical multiplexing of real-time sources.

NONREAL-TIME (NRT-VBR) SERVICE

The nonreal-time VBR service category is intended for nonreal-time applications that have bursty traffic characteristics and are characterized in terms of a PCR, SCR, and MBS. For those cells that are transferred within the traffic contract, the application expects a low cell-loss ratio. Nonreal-time VBR service may support statistical multiplexing of connections. No delay bounds are associated with this service category.

UNSPECIFIED BIT RATE (UBR) SERVICE

The unspecified bit rate (UBR) service category is intended for nonreal-time applications, those not requiring tightly constrained delay and delay variation. Examples of such applications are traditional computer communications applications, such as file transfer and e-mail.

UBR service does not specify traffic-related service guarantees. No numerical commitments are made with respect to the CLR experienced by a UBR connection, or as to the CTD experienced by cells on the connection. A network may or may not apply PCR to the CAC and UPC functions. In the case where the network does not enforce PCR, the value of PCR is informational only. When PCR is not enforced, it is still useful to have PCR negotiated, since this may allow the source to discover the smallest bandwidth limitation along the path of the connection. Congestion control for UBR may be performed at a higher layer on an end-to-end basis.

Table 7.3   (*Continued*)

The UBR service is indicated by use of the best effort indicator in the ATM user cell rate information element. MCR will be supported in the next release.

AVAILABLE BIT RATE (ABR) SERVICE

ABR is an ATM layer service category for which the limiting ATM layer transfer characteristics provided by the network may change subsequent to connection establishment. A flow control mechanism is specified that supports several types of feedback to control the source rate in response to changing ATM layer transfer characteristics. This feedback is conveyed to the source through specific control cells called resource management cells, or RM-cells. It is expected that an endsystem that adapts its traffic in accordance with the feedback will experience a low cell-loss ratio and obtain a fair share of the available bandwidth according to a network specific allocation policy. The ABR service does not require bounding the delay or the delay variation experienced by a given connection. ABR service is not intended to support real-time applications.

On the establishment of an ABR connection, the endsystem specifies to the network both a maximum required bandwidth and a minimum usable bandwidth. These are designated as peak cell rate (PCR), and the minimum cell rate (MCR), respectively. The MCR may be specified as zero. The bandwidth available from the network may vary, but will not become less than MCR.

switches do not currently support ATM UNI multiconnections (it does support a kind of internal multipoint service for LAN support).

7.2.6 Traffic Management Version and Congestion Control

An ATM network simultaneously transports a wide variety of network traffic—voice, data, image, and video.[8] It provides users with a guaranteed QoS, monitors network traffic congestion, and controls traffic flow to ease congestion. Traffic management allows an ATM network to support traffic flows not readily supported by other LAN technologies. A carefully planned ATM network can guarantee quality of service to each type of traffic as the network grows. This section discusses traffic management and congestion control.

Traffic management in ATM networks consists of those functions that ensure that each connection receives the quality of service it needs, and that the flow of information is monitored and controlled within the ATM network (see Table 7.4 and Figure 7.18 [9]). As an organization grows, its business operations become more sophisticated and so its information systems requirements must reflect that change. Networks that support a wider variety of traffic types are needed by these organizations. Understanding traffic management in an ATM network requires an appreciation

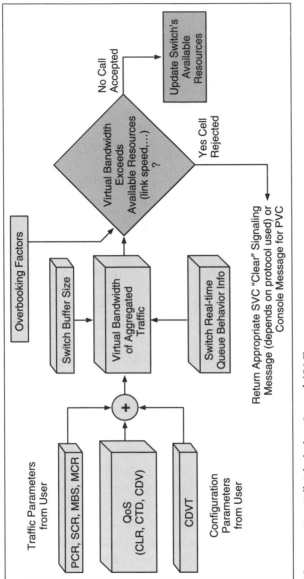

Figure 7.17 Call Admission Control (CAC).

Table 7.4   Traffic Management Tools and Methods Used in ATMF TM 4.0

Connection Admission Control (CAC)	Set of actions taken by the network during the call set-up phase in order to determine whether a connection request can be accepted or should be rejected (or whether a request for reallocation can be accommodated).
Feedback Controls	Set of actions taken by the network and by endsystems to regulate the traffic submitted on ATM connections according to the state of network elements.
Usage Parameter Control (UPC)	Set of actions taken by the network to monitor and control traffic, in terms of traffic offered and validity of the ATM connection, at the endsystem access. Its main purpose is to protect network resources from malicious as well as unintentional misbehavior, which can affect the QoS of other already established connections, by detecting violations of negotiated parameters and taking appropriate actions. Such actions may include cell discard and cell tagging.
Cell Loss Priority Control	For some service categories the endsystem may generate traffic flows of cells with cell loss priority (CLP) marking. The network may follow models that treat this marking as transparent or as significant. If treated as significant, the network may selectively discard cells marked with a low priority to protect, as far as possible, the QoS objectives of cells with high priority.
Traffic Shaping	Mechanisms that may be used to achieve a desired modification of the traffic characteristics.
Network Resource Management (NRM)	The service architecture allows logical separation of connections according to service characteristics. Although cell scheduling and resource provisioning are implementation- and network-specific, they can be utilized to provide appropriate isolation and access to resources. Virtual paths are useful for resource management.
Frame Discard	A congested network that needs to discard cells may discard at the frame level rather than at the cell level.
ABR Flow Control	The ABR flow control protocol may be used to adaptively share the available bandwidth among participating users.

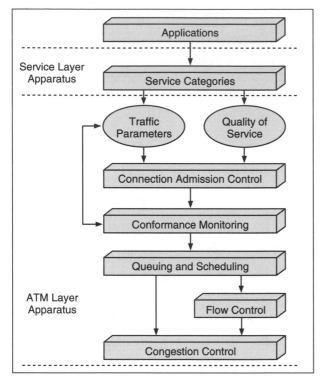

Figure 7.18   Traffic management elements in ATM networks.

of the differences in the types of traffic it carries, both in enterprise network applications and in Internet backbone applications.

Classifying ATM Network Traffic

As discussed, the types of traffic supported by an ATM network can be classified by three characteristics: bandwidth, latency, and cell delay variation. Bandwidth is the amount of network capacity required to support a connection. Latency is the amount of delay associated with a connection. Requesting low latency in the QoS profile, for example, means the cells need to travel very quickly from one specific point in the network to another. Cell delay variation is the range of the delays experienced by each group of cells associated with a given transmission. Requesting low cell delay variation means this group of cells must travel through the network without getting too far apart from each other.

As discussed earlier, ATM networks carry three types of traffic: CBR, VBR, and ABR. CBR traffic includes transmissions such as voice and video traffic. To handle this type of traffic, the ATM network can be configured to act like a dedicated circuit. It provides a sustained amount of bandwidth,

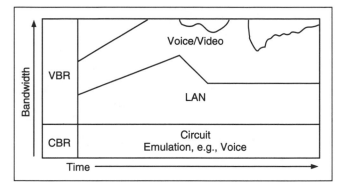

Figure 7.19   Link capacity allocated to different traffic types.

low latency, and low cell delay variation. VBR traffic is handled similarly to CBR except that the bandwidth requirement is not constant. For example, an ATM network supporting a videoconferencing application guarantees bandwidth during the videoconference. During the videoconference, however, the actual amount of bandwidth used can vary. ABR traffic does not require a specific amount of bandwidth or specific delay parameters, and is quite acceptable for many of today's applications. Applications such as electronic mail and file transfers are usually supported by ABR connections. LANE and TCP will also use ABR connections. Figure 7.19 shows why and illustrates how link capacity is allocated to each different traffic type. While CBR reserves a constant amount of the total available bandwidth, VBR requires that a large amount of spare capacity be available. ABR defines a way to use this very valuable spare capacity. It can provide service that is no worse, and in many cases is better, than most of today's networks, but it requires only a very low amount of bandwidth.

ATM networks are usually architected to provide the performance guarantees required by CBR and VBR traffic, and allow ABR traffic to use the remaining bandwidth.

Establishing ATM Network Connections

To establish an ATM connection, the ATM endstation (i.e., the calling party) asks the ATM network for a connection to another ATM endstation (i.e., the called party or destination) by initiating a connection request. The connection request leads to a negotiation between the calling party and the ATM network (a connection establishment procedure). The parameters being negotiated are specified by the ATM Forum User-Network Interface and include sustained and peak bandwidth, burst length, and QoS class. As a result of this connection establishment procedure, a "contract" is secured between the ATM network and the ATM endstation. The ATM network promises to deliver a guaranteed QoS, and the ATM endstation promises not to send more traffic than it requested in the connection establishment procedure.

To have meaning, of course, contracts must be enforced. Traffic management functions include all the techniques used to ensure that users receive the QoS guaranteed to them during the connection establishment procedure. Further, when congestion does occur, traffic management provides the mechanism that allows the network to recover.

Traffic Management Functions

ATM networks use three techniques to manage traffic: traffic shaping, traffic policing, and congestion control.

Traffic Shaping

Traffic shaping is a management function performed at the user-network interface of the ATM network. It ensures that traffic matches the contract negotiated between the user and the network during connection establishment. Traffic is shaped according to the generic cell rate algorithm (GCRA) as specified by the ATM Forum UNI standard. Devices implementing traffic shaping are typically those connected to an ATM network and include ATM network adapters in PCs or workstations, hubs, bridges, routers, and DSUs.

Traffic Policing

Traffic policing is a management function performed by the ATM network (i.e., ATM switches); it ensures that traffic on each connection remains within the parameters negotiated at connection establishment. To police traffic, ATM switches use a buffering technique called a *leaky bucket,* which is a system in which traffic flows (leaks) out of a buffer (bucket) at a constant rate (the negotiated rate), regardless of how fast it flows into the buffer. The need for policing occurs when traffic flow exceeds the negotiated rate and the buffer overflows. The ATM switches must then take action to control (police) it. In the header of each ATM cell is a bit called the CLP bit. The ATM switches use this bit to identify cells as either conforming (to the contract) or nonconforming. If cells are nonconforming (for example, there are more cells than the contract allows), the ATM switch sets the CLP bit to 1. This cell may now be transferred through the network, only if the current network capacity is sufficient. If not, the cell is discarded and must be retransmitted by the sending device.

CBR traffic requires a single buffer (leaky bucket) to police the traffic because CBR traffic uses only a sustained (average) rate parameter in its network contract. VBR traffic uses two buffers (dual leaky buckets) to monitor both the sustained rate over a discrete time period and the maximum (peak) bandwidth used during the connection. If either value exceeds the contract parameters, the ATM switch polices the VBR traffic by manipulating the CLP bit.

The next two subsections cover policing in more detail by way of an example (how a carrier actually handles it). In general ISPs will be more interested in VBR policing than CBR policing; the latter is included for completeness.

CBR Policing[9]

Figure 7.20 shows a CBR traffic profile. As can be seen, CBR stream is just this: constant; it does not vary. In this scenario, there is a burst of constant cells for a short duration. The traffic burst exceeded the PCR and the constant CDVT settings, and thus are in violation of the traffic contract.

The CBR policing actions taken:

- The ATM carrier admits the cells within PCR and CDVT.
- The ATM carrier immediately discards noncompliant cells (> PCR and CDVT).

Traffic management factor(s) to be considered for CBR are buffering and the service algorithm. First, CBR cells are not buffered at all. Upon admission, the UPC function kicks in and cells go through the selective discarding function to determine whether they are compliant, so they are either admitted or discarded/tagged.

In addition, since CBR is not oversubscribed at any trunk(s) and egress queue(s), the CBR cell stream is always served immediately, first, ahead

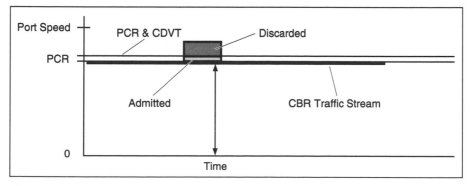

Figure 7.20 CBR policing.

of VBR and ABR cells. In other words, the CBR has a much tighter delay guarantee than any other class of service because it does not get buffered at all throughout the ATM network. Therefore, the delay (i.e., end-to-end response) is close to a constant value at all times. The ATM carrier aims for an objective value for cell transfer delay (CTD), which includes among other things, the CDVT value inherent in ATM networks. CTD is mainly based on mileage.

Moreover, since CBR does not get oversubscribed, the ATM carrier has to preserve the entire bandwidth across the trunks, and to engineer enough additional capacity for rerouting purposes in case of a trunk failure.

VBR-nrt Policing

Figure 7.21 shows a VBR-nrt traffic profile. In this scenario, there are two bursts of cells that occurred above the SCR: the first one (B1) at a rate above the PCR, and the second one (B2) at the PCR. No matter how long the duration of the first burst (B1), it exceeded the PCR and the constant CDVT settings, and thus is a violation of the traffic contract. Those cells are therefore immediately discarded.

The second burst of cell (B2) occurs at the PCR, for a long duration. As long as the burst does not exceed the MBS associated with this connection, it is admitted to the network. Once the MBS is exceeded, then the cells remaining within that burst are tagged with a cell loss priority one (CLP = 1) and passed into the network. Tagged traffic is similar to the FR's DE bit, as discussed in Chapter 6. In the event of downstream congestion within the network, cells with CLP = 1 are discarded immediately.

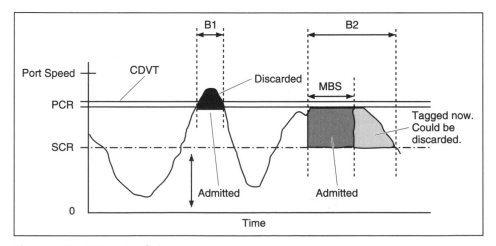

Figure 7.21   VBR-nrt policing.

VBR-nrt policing actions taken:

- The ATM carrier admits the cells up to SCR.
- The ATM carrier admits the cells within SCR and PCR, during the MBS.
- The ATM carrier labels noncompliant cells (> MBS) with CLP = 1 and admits it into the network.
- The ATM carrier admits the cells within PCR and CDVT.
- The ATM carrier immediately discards noncompliant cells (> PCR and CDVT).

Another way to look at the SCR in a VBR connection is in terms of an average rate available to the application. In Figure 7.22, a VBR-nrt application has a 10Mbps PCR and a 3Mbps SCR. Since SCR is an average, the source has to expect 3Mbps as a "sustained" throughput for the duration of the connection. Sure, it can burst, up to the PCR, but if it does this for the total allowed MBS, then it has to wait for a long time to burst back up again. In other words, the gaps between the bursts would be further apart. On the other hand, it can burst up to another rate less than PCR, more frequently, with all bursts within the allowed MBS (see Figure 7.23).

Some people think of this as credit accumulation. But no matter how it is viewed, the average must be maintained, otherwise cells will violate the traffic contract, and the application throughput will be impacted. Therefore, it is advantageous for application throughout to have the SCR fairly close to the PCR.

Traffic management functions to be considered for VBR-nrt are buffering and service algorithm. Similar to CBR, the VBR-nrt CoS is not buffered at all within the ATM network. The UPC algorithm handles the

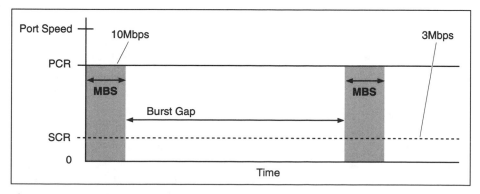

Figure 7.22   SCR as an average rate: scenario 1.

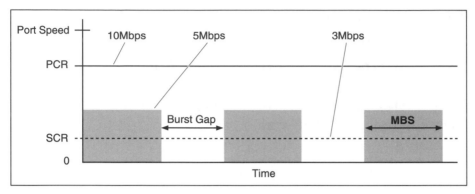

Figure 7.23 SCR as an average rate: scenario 2.

cell conformance to the negotiated traffic contract. The delay (i.e., end-to-end response) is no longer a constant value. Even though VBR-nrt cells do not go through buffers, the delay is variable because the traffic stream is variable and bursty.

Congestion Control

In a well-designed ATM network, CBR and VBR traffic experience the low-latency service they negotiated at setup, while ABR traffic might experience congestion, depending upon the current loading of the network. Since the applications that use ABR connections are less sensitive to delay, all applications run as planned. Congestion control is needed because the ABR traffic is likely to experience congestion at some point in time. If the congestion is controlled, the ABR service still provides value. CBR and VBR are designed to require no complex congestion management schemes. Several schemes have been proposed, and the two leading schemes involve controlling traffic flow on either a link-by-link basis or an end-to-end basis. The ATM Forum has been working on a solution that will integrate the best features of each.

End-to-End Flow Control

End-to-end flow control is readily available from most vendors and at a relatively low price. But it has two major drawbacks: First, recent studies show that cells can be lost during congestion; second, it requires a lot of buffer space. End-to-end schemes control the transmission rate at the edge of the network—where the LAN meets the ATM device. If the ATM-to-LAN connection is Ethernet to the WAN, at which point an access device will convert your traffic to ATM, then this is a low-cost method of connecting to the WAN. Because little of the LAN beyond the backbone uses ATM technology at this time, precise control may not be required, and the few extra buffers will not substantially increase the cost. As ATM equipment prices continue to drop, ATM technology will be used more. Paying for the extra buffer space that will be needed will be expensive, making precise control over more complex networks a very important issue; thus, the compromise to include the option to provide more precise link-by-link control.

Link-by-Link Flow Control

Link-by-link flow control supports more users but uses less buffer space, all without losing cells. Link-by-link has two major drawbacks: At first, it will be more expensive, and, second, equipment that implements link-by-link is not yet available. Link-by-link schemes, besides providing control on a per-link basis, also control each VC separately. This allows the network of ATM switches to control a particularly active device, while other devices continue to receive a fair share of the available network capacity. This control is more precise and can be implemented in either of two ways: a rate-based or a credit-based method. The rate-based method controls the flow of traffic by communicating to the sending device the rate at which it can transmit (the allowed rate). The credit-based method controls traffic flow by communicating to the sending device the remaining buffer space (credits) the downstream device (receiver) has to receive traffic, on a per-VC and per-link basis.

Integrated Control

The integrated proposal considered by the ATM Forum provides an end-to-end, rate-based scheme as the default method, with the link-by-link scheme as an option. Because most equipment can provide this level of control immediately, users will have a standards-based ABR congestion control scheme very quickly. If the network requires a more precise congestion management scheme, the optional scheme can be used to increase the control of the ABR resources. This would still be a standards-based solution, with end-to-end and link-by-link equipment coexisting in the same network. When a connection is made from an end-to-end device, the link-by-link device would simply perform the end-to-end control scheme when talking to that device. This would preserve the existing investment in equipment, while providing for future growth.

7.2.7 Call Admission Control in UNI 4.0

As discussed in the previous section, traffic management in ATM (which is needed to support QoS) has two major components: traffic shaping (by sending devices) and policing (by switching devices). To ensure that the traffic arriving at a switch is conforming and is, therefore, not impacted by the usage parameter control function, a traffic source must (should) schedule traffic into the network according to the conformance definition. Two types of shaping are used: *ingress shaping*, which is performed by the CPE source on the traffic before it enters the network, and *egress shaping*, which is performed as traffic leaves the switch and enters another network. To be able to support the stated QoS, it is necessary to "police" the traffic according to the conformance definition to ascertain that nonconforming cells are discarded or tagged as low-priority cells. This "guarantees" that one connection is not able to affect the QoS of another connection. At the UNI, policing is done by a UPC function, which implements one or two instances of the CGRA (also known as leaky bucket) with the peak cell rate or peak cell rate and the sustainable cell rate. At the NNI, policing is done by the network parameter control (NPC).

So, ATM switches that support QoS by policing their input traffic implement the leaky bucket algorithm, which provides a method of describing the rate of traffic when data is transmitted into the network in a frame or cell format. Each leaky bucket has an input rate and a limit parameter. The actual policing is done via vendor-specific code; the leaky bucket is just a concept to help visualize the algorithm of policing (see Figure 7.24 for a pictorial representation) [2].

Call admission control for SVC service uses the traffic parameters discussed shortly to make a best estimate if the switch, or switches, can carry data between clients at the desired bandwidth. ATM QoS is specified to the software implementing the call admission control as the performance that can be realized by the end devices via the negotiation of the following traffic description parameters (see Table 7.5 from ATMF TM 4.0, and Figure 7.25)[10]:

Peak Cell Rate (PCR).   The maximum number of cells that can be transmitted over a unit time.

Cell Delay Variation Tolerance (CDVT).   The amount of "clumping" that can be tolerated before a series of cells exceeding the PCR is deemed as violating the traffic contract.

Sustainable Cell Rate (SCR).   A rate of cells that is near or slightly higher than the average over a unit time.

Maximum Burst Size (MBS).   The amount of cells on a virtual circuit that can burst at the PCR.

Minimum Cell Rate (MCR).   The minimum rate at which a host using the available bit rate service category will always be able to transmit

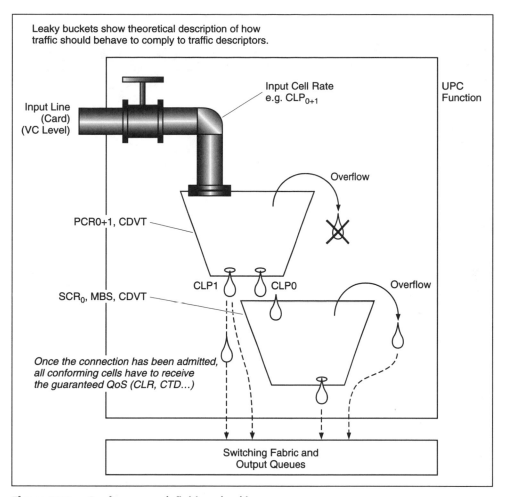

Leaky buckets show theoretical description of how traffic should behave to comply to traffic descriptors.

Input Line (Card) (VC Level)

Input Cell Rate e.g. CLP_{0+1}

UPC Function

Overflow

$PCR0+1$, CDVT

SCR_0, MBS, CDVT

CLP1   CLP0

Overflow

Once the connection has been admitted, all conforming cells have to receive the guaranteed QoS (CLR, CTD...)

Switching Fabric and Output Queues

Figure 7.24   Conformance definition checking.

data. The default value is 0. When the minimum rate is set to 0, the network does not always promise that bandwidth will be available.

These mechanisms are important for ISPs to understand and for corporate planners to have an appreciation of what the ISPs are doing when an ATM backbone is used. A successful call setup, and subsequent virtual circuit creation, involves selecting a set of values from the preceding parameters that are acceptable to the call admission control software running on the switches. If the desired resources exist, then the switch will respond to the end devices that the call was established. The successful set of parameters is called the traffic contract because it specifies that the network will make some guarantees about performance if the network resources utilized are less than or equal to those specified in the call setup request [2].

Table 7.5 ATM Service Category Attributes Defined in ATMF UNI 4.0

| ATTRIBUTE | ATM LAYER SERVICE CATEGORY | | | | |
| | DELAY SENSITIVE | | NON-DELAY SENSITIVE | | |
	CBR	RT-VBR	NRT-VBR	UBR	ABR
Traffic Parameters:					
PCR and CDVT (See Notes 4 and 5)	specified			specified$_2$	specified$_3$
SCR, MBS, CDVT (See Notes 4 and 5)	n/a	specified		n/a	
MCR (See Note 4)	n/a			n/a (See Note 6)	specified
QoS Parameters:					
Peak-to-Peak CDV	specified		unspecified		
maxCTD	specified		unspecified		
CLR (See Note 4)	specified			unspecified	(See Note 1)
Other Attributes:					
Feedback	unspecified				specified

Notes:
1. CLR is low for sources that adjust cell flow in response to control information. Whether a quantitative value for CLR is specified is network-specific.
2. May not be subject to CAC and UPC procedures.
3. Represents the maximum rate at which the ABR source may send. The actual rate is subject to the control information.
4. These parameters are either explicitly or implicitly specified for PVCs or SVCs.
5. CDVT refers to the cell delay variation tolerance. CDVT is not signaled. In general, CDVT need not have a unique value for a connection. Different values may apply at each interface along the path of a connection.
6. Work is underway in the ATMF to support MCR for UBR.

After the call has been established, the usage parameter control software on the switch monitors the resources being used to determine if the traffic contract is being adhered to. For example, the combination of the PCR and CDVT are used by any usage parameter control algorithm that is policing the maximum offered load of the traffic contract. The policing done on the values of the PCR and MBS is done in the first leaky bucket. This bucket is allowed to accept logical cells until it overflows, in which case the overload feeds into subsequent measurement buckets.

In some cases, selecting the values for the traffic parameters can be difficult because most applications, like legacy LAN traffic, are not traditionally specified by these metrics. And in many cases, network managers either

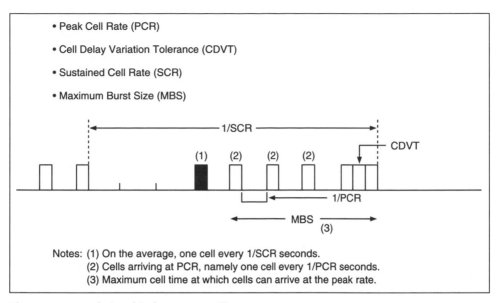

Figure 7.25   Relationship between traffic contract parameters.

specify no policing of LAN traffic or set the values of PCR/SCR only because their Internet provider is selling limited bandwidth. In that case, the Internet service provider can utilize ingress policing on the ATM ports serving customers to check that only the allocated bandwidth is used [2].

For a virtual circuit requiring high QoS, or at least a very consistent stream of cells, the peak rate could be nearly identical to the bandwidth allocated. If the virtual circuit is carrying bursty data, the peak rate requested is typically somewhat lower than the actually maximum because the call is more likely to be accepted, and the transmitting host's ATM layer should be able to shape the egress cell stream.

The SCR and MBS are the parameters used in constructing the second leaky bucket measurement device. The SCR is always chosen by the endsystem when signaling for the creation of the virtual circuit, and is by definition lower than the PCR. MCR is used only with ABR. When considering SCR values, the network manager should evaluate those that will provide consistent good performance to applications over long periods of time. That way the data rate will be able to burst to the PCR for short periods but always be able to depend on SCR performance [2].

The preceding traffic parameters are used by the network to determine which resources are required for the virtual circuit. In addition to those already listed, the following QoS parameters are signaled in a call setup message:

Cell Loss Ratio (CLR). A measure that quantifies how much traffic has been lost compared to the total amount transmitted. The loss can be attributed to any cell-corrupting event like congestion or line-encoding errors.

Cell Transfer Delay (CTD). The measure of the time required for the cell to cross certain points in the ATM network. The primary concern to end users is the time required for the last bit of the cell to leave the transmitter until the first bit arrives at the receiver. CTD can be affected by processing in the ATM switches or, more likely, by buffering in the switch.

Cell Delay Variation (CDV). The measure of how the latency varies from cell to cell as they cross the network. Variation is caused by queuing and variation in switching that speed cells encounter as they are transmitted. CDV is of concern in ATM networks because as the temporal pattern of cells is modified in the network, so is their traffic profile. If the modification is too large, then the traffic has the potential of exceeding the bounds of the traffic profile, and some cells may be dropped, at no fault of the transmitter.

These signaled QoS parameters are used in the following fashion when requesting service:

- CLR applies to CBR, real-time VBR, nonreal-time VBR.
- For ABR, a value of CLR may be associated with the service, but it is not signaled.
- CTD is carried in the call setup messages for CBR and real-time VBR services.
- CDV is carried in the call setup messages for CBR and real-time VBR services.

Compared with ATMF UNI 3.1, the UNI 4.0 specification supports the following additional features [2]:

Traffic Parameter Negotiation. Allows the SETUP to contain multiple IEs for the same object, with the intent of reducing call admission control failures. If the first information element (IE) is unacceptable for call completion, the switch has the option of retrying the call admission control with the second IE.

Available Bit Rate. Utilizes ATM's closed-loop flow control by requesting in the signaling message that the service be associated with the new circuit. ABR also functions as a means of traffic parameter negotiation because it allows the user to establish a baseline, then requests modification after the circuit is in service; applications can learn from the network how much data can be transmitted.

Virtual Path Switching.   Permits the signaling of an entire virtual path instead of the usual VPI/VCI granularity.

Frame Discard Service.   Allows signaling to request this service be associated with a circuit so that during congestion the partial packet discard algorithms are employed.

Signaling of Individual QoS Parameters.   The UNI 4.0 specification diverges from the UNI 3.1 philosophy by selecting a QoS service category.

Multicast Extensions.   Supports multicast capabilities.

With these features comes a set of new IEs that evoke and control their behavior. The new IEs used when establishing a virtual circuit on a UNI 4.0 capable switch are [2]:

Minimum Acceptable ATM Traffic Descriptor.   Field used with the ABR service category. It sets the baseline for the ABR service and specifies the lowest bit/second that can be transmitted. ABR setup parameters include the various objects used to initialize ABR:

- Initial cell rate

- RM (resource management) round-trip time

- Data rate increment factor

- Data rate decrement factor

- Transient buffer exposure

Alternative ATM Traffic Descriptor.   Field used with the new feature of multiple IEs for the same parameter. If the ABR service is being selected, the alternative traffic descriptors are prohibited.

ATM Traffic Category (CBR, VBR-nt, etc.).   Selected by a new field, transfer capability in the broadband bearer capability information element. This IE also specifies the signaling message as point-to-point or multicast.

Extended QoS Parameters.   Used to specify the values of cell delay variation and cell loss ratios. The QoS parameters are not directly specified by the IEFT.

End-to-End Transit Delay.   Specifiable as a QoS parameter.

7.2.8 Specific ATM Layer QoS Mechanisms

As implied by the previous discussion, ATM's claim to fame is its support of QoS. This is done via expansive use of resource-sharing techniques, so that communications resources (specifically, broadband communication channels) are available on a per-VC basis, without having to allocate the maximum number of resources, which would grow linearly on the number of VCs or ports. ATM is a statistical multiplexing technology par excellence; yet the statistical multiplexing is done in such an intelligent way that QoS is "guaranteed" to the user. Statistical multiplexing allows higher utilization of resources based both on allocating unused bandwidth to those who need it and on the intrinsic higher efficiency of pooled traffic.[11] Furthermore, the judicious use of overbooking increases efficiency. The good news is that not only have standards been developed (e.g., UNI 3.1 and UNI/TM 4.0), but that *switches have been brought to the market* by many vendors that support these standards [7]. In general, support of QoS implies *buffer management*; in addition to algorithmic resources, this implies the presence of relatively large buffers. Besides the photonics (specifically, long-reach lasers), the bulk of the cost in an ATM switch is in memory.

This subsection amplifies some of the concepts introduced earlier, to further explain how QoS can be negotiated and monitored in ATM.

Traffic management allows ATM networks to have well-behaved operations in terms of predictable performance, matching the expected (negotiated) level, thereby minimizing congestion and maximizing efficiency. ATM's QoS support is useful not only in pure ATM networks, but in IP/RSVP-based networks that rely ATM for Layer 2 transport. Although today applications are not QoS-aware, new voice, video, multimedia, and CTI applications may be developed with QoS in mind. As discussed earlier, in the future, tiered-service with priority support in the Internet, intranets, and enterprise networks is likely.

In spite of the benefits, QoS and the switches' approach to supporting it (e.g., dropping cells), have to be clearly understood, because some applications such as TCP may not operate well in a scenario of high cell loss; the cell loss naturally depends on the CoS that is selected (with CBR having the lowest and UBR having the highest).

Approaches to QoS in ATM

QoS is achieved by managing the traffic intelligently. Controls monitor the rate at which the traffic enters the network, at a VC level. The parameters used by ATM (specifically from the ATM-layer pacing mechanism) to do traffic management are obtained at SVC or PVC setup time.

As noted, the host signals its requirements to the network via the signaling mechanism (Figure 7.26). Each ATM switch in the path uses the traffic parameters to determine via the call admission control mechanism if sufficient resources are available to set up the connection at the requested QoS level. In private networks, the Private Network Node Interface (P-NNI) protocol is responsible for determining if the required resources are available across the network (end to end).[12] The CAC is used in each individual switch to determine if locally controlled resources are available, consistent with the request of the SETUP message. If the switch does have resources to support the call request, it then reroutes the message to the next switch along a possible (best) path to the destination.[13]

To convey QoS requests, there has to be a capability for the endsystem to signal its requirements to the connecting ATM switch. In turn, this switch must propagate that request across the network. The former is done via UNI signaling (e.g., ATMF UNI 4.0); the latter is done via NNI signaling (e.g., PNNI 1.0). (Neither PNNI signaling nor UNI signaling are

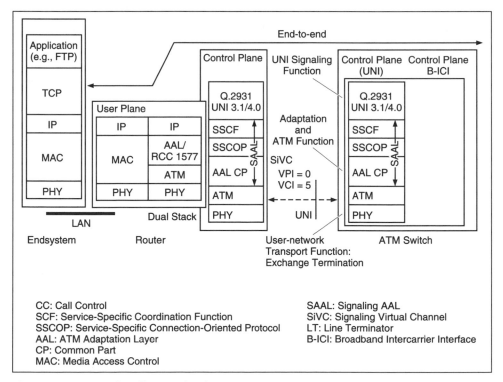

Figure 7.26   ATM signaling mechanism.

covered here; for this information, the interested reader may consult [2] and [6], respectively.) The signaling mechanism, where the various QoS parameters are coded into the SETUP message, supplements the "QoS class" procedures defined in ATMF UNI 3.1 and ITU-T I.356, briefly discussed shortly. It is worth noting that many switches and carriers actually supported UNI 3.1 (rather than 4.0) at the time of this writing. In practice, however, many networks will continue to offer discrete, class-based values for services, although the "vocabulary" is now available for the user to communicate the QoS values. The specification indicates that "implementations capable of stating QoS in terms of individual numeric parameter values may do so using the procedures defined in UNI Signaling 4.0 and PNNI 1.0; implementations must at a minimum support QoS indication via QoS classes."

An important aspect of QoS is to exactly define measurements, cell events, outcomes, and so on, and to have a reference model (Figure 7.27). For example, a lost cell outcome is defined as the situation when no cell is received, corresponding to the transmitted cell within a specified time, *Tmax*. Another important point is that quantitative values for performance objectives are not defined in the specifications; rather, the document specifies means to measure or estimate the values of defined performance metrics[14]. This is too bad, although it is clear why no numbers were specified: No one wanted to commit to some specific goal. This is not the case with other transmission standards. For example, ANSI and Bellcore standards define exact jitter, BER values, and so on, for DS1 lines, DS3 lines, and others. The consequence is that the VBR service from one carrier may be different from the service obtained from another carrier, even though the main of the service is the same. Somewhat mitigating this possibility for inconsistency is that carriers may all use a few kinds of switches (say, Cisco LS1010, Fore ASX1000, etc.). Hence, to a degree, there may be some derivative commonality. However, different carriers may set the "knobs" of the switches differently—for example, oversubscription limits, buffer depths, different buffer allocation to different classes out of the total pool of available buffers. For example, a carrier with a Cisco LS1010 may allocate 256 buffers to CoS while another carrier could allocate 512; in some cases, the buffer pool for a given class of service is for every active VC (e.g., Cisco LS1010), while in other cases the pool is allocable for the exclusive use of a VC. In turn, this has implications on the QoS, for example, cells lost—Figure 7.28 for an example.

It is to be understood that the measurement of the network performance on a VC is likely to be different from the negotiated objective at any given time, for two reasons: the negotiated objective is the worst case

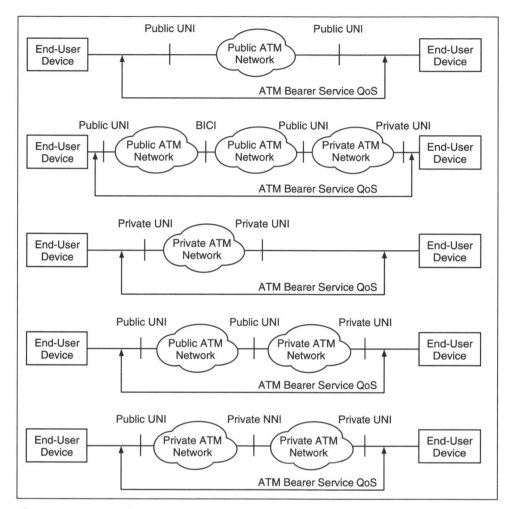

Figure 7.27   QoS reference model.

of network performance that the network will allow, including peak intervals (hopefully, the QoS measures will exceed these numbers in many cases); and transient events may cause the measured performance to be worse than the negotiated objective (if/when a measurement is taken over a small time base).

QoS commitments are probabilistic in nature; therefore, both users and carriers have to realize that statements like "guaranteed QoS" are incorrect. The stated QoS is only an *approximation* of the performance that the network plans to offer over the duration of the connection. Specifically, since there is no limit to the length of the connection, and the network only makes resource decisions based on information available at the time

```
NYC01A#show atm int resource atm 0/0/0
Resource Management configuration:
  Output queues:
    Max sizes(explicit cfg): none cbr, none vbr-rt, none vbr-nrt, none abr-u
      br
    Max sizes(installed): 256 cbr, 256 vbr-rt, 4096 vbr-nrt, 12032 abr-ubr
    Efci threshold: 25% cbr, 25% vbr-rt, 25% vbr-nrt, 25% abr, 25% ubr
    Discard threshold: 87% cbr, 87% vbr-rt, 87% vbr-nrt, 87% abr, 87% ubr
    Abr-relative-rate threshold: 25% abr
  Pacing: disabled 0 Kbps rate configured, 0 Kbps rate installed
  Link Distance: 0 kilometers
  Controlled Link sharing:
    Max aggregate guaranteed services: none RX, none TX
    Max bandwidth: none cbr RX, none cbr TX, none vbr RX, none vbr TX
    Min bandwidth: none cbr RX, none cbr TX, none vbr RX, none vbr TX
  Best effort connection limit: disabled 0 max connections
  Max traffic parameters by service (rate in Kbps, tolerance in cell-times):
    Peak-cell-rate RX: none cbr, none vbr, none abr, none ubr
    Peak-cell-rate TX: none cbr, none vbr, none abr, none ubr
    Sustained-cell-rate: none vbr RX, none vbr TX,
    Tolerance RX: none cbr, none vbr, none abr, none ubr
    Tolerance TX: none cbr, none vbr, none abr, none ubr
Resource Management state:
  Cell-counts: 0 cbr, 0 vbr-rt, 0 vbr-nrt, 0 abr-ubr
  Available bit rates (in Kbps):
    137436 cbr RX, 137436 cbr TX, 137436 vbr RX, 137436 vbr TX,
  Allocated bit rates:
    0 cbr RX, 0 cbr TX, 10307 vbr RX, 10307 vbr TX,
  Best effort connections: 0 pvcs, 0 svcs
NYC01A#
```

Figure 7.28   Snapshot of a node (LS1010) in TCG's network showing some of the available carrier knobs (e.g., buffers, thresholds, etc.).

the connection is established, the actual QoS may well vary over the course of time. Transient events such as intermittent physical trunk failure, higher transient bit error rate (e.g., for circuits over microwave links), and even bursts of traffic from other sources when the UPC parameters (including switch-specific "fudge knobs") are not properly set by the switch administrator can all impact QoS. Thus, the ATMF TM 4.0 document indicates that "QoS commitments can only be evaluated over a long period of time and over multiple connections with similar QoS commitments." Although this implies that in the long term the QoS is met, it could also mean temporary problems with real-time traffic such as voice, particularly if CBR services are not used. Figure 7.29 shows some of the factors that can degrade an ATM network's QoS.

Attribute	CER	SECBR	CLR	CMR	CTD	CDV
Propagation Delay					X	
Media Error Statistics	X	X	X	X		
Switch Architecture			X	X	X	
Buffer Capacity		X	X		X	X
Number of Tandem Nodes	X	X	X	X	X	X
Traffic Load			X	X	X	X
Failures	X	X	X			
Resource Allocation			X		X	X

CER = Cell Error Ratio
SECBR = Severely Errored Cell Block Ratio
CLR = Cell Loss Ratio
CMR = Cell Misinsertion Rate
CTD = Cell Transfer Delay
CDV = Cell Delay Variation

Figure 7.29   Factors that can degrade an ATM network's QoS.

Quality-of-Service Parameters

The ATMF TM 4.0 supports six QoS parameters already described:

- Peak-to-peak Cell Delay Variation (ptpCDV)
- Maximum Cell Transfer Delay (MaxCTD)
- Cell Loss Ratio (CLR)
- Cell Error Ratio (CER)
- Severely Errored Cell Block Ratio (SECBR)
- Cell Misinsertion Rate (CMR)

The first three can be negotiated as part of the call setup, while the last three are more network-intrinsic. Negotiation may entail specifying one or more of the parameters in question; also, the QoS could be set up differently for the two directions (or multiple legs) of a VC. By definition of call setup, QoS can be established on a per-call per-VC basis. In the network, QoS support is achieved by appropriate dynamic routing of the connection or by implementation-specific mechanisms. What may well fit in this last category is the current tendency of carriers to overengineer the network to make sure that QoS can be achieved and sustained. It should be noted, however, that carriers may provide a small set of discrete choices for the negotiable parameters, rather than accept a continuum of request values. For example, there may be a low (10 to the minus 9), medium (10 to the minus 8), and high (10 to the minus 7) CLR to choose from, and so on.

Maximum cell transfer delay and peak-to-peak cell delay variation (both of which are negotiable) have to be defined very exactly, also using the reference model (as done in ATMF TM 4.0 [10]). The following lists some of the "dependability" measures that can be defined by formula:

CLR = Lost cells/total transmitted cells

CER = Errored cells/(successfully transferred cells + errored cells)

SECBR = Severely errored cell blocks/total transmitted cell blocks

CMR = Misinserted cells/time interval

NOTE CLR is negotiable in UNI 4.0; the other metrics are not.

A service agreement for ATM services involves a traffic contract.[15] The user's traffic is described via traffic parameters already described (PCR, SCR, MBS, and MCR).

7.3 QoS by Menu

As noted, carriers may support only a QoS-class service level (i.e., "select from a menu"), rather than a continuum of values for the parameters in question. Also, various parameters may be bundled, to arrive at classes, such as:

Gold Bundle   ptpCDV < 250 microseconds; MaxCTD = 30 milliseconds; CLR = 10 in 1 billion

Silver Bundle   ptpCDV < 350 microseconds; MaxCTD = 40 milliseconds; CLR = 10 in 0.1 billion

Bronze Bundle   ptpCDV < 450 microseconds; MaxCTD = 40 milliseconds; CLR = 10 in 0.01 billion

According to the standards (e.g., ITU-T Recommendations I.150, I.37, Q.2931), a user of an ATM connection (a VCC or a VPC) is provided with one of a number of QoS classes supported by the network. It should be noted that a VPC may carry VC links of various QoS classes; here the QoS of the VPC must meet the most demanding QoS of the VC links carried.

The QoS class associated with a given ATM connection is indicated to the network at the time of connection establishment and will not change for the duration of that ATM connection.

QoS class (which may be thought of as "packaged menus") can have specified performance parameters (called specified QoS class) or no specified performance parameters (called unspecified QoS class). A specified QoS class specifies a set of performance parameters and the objective values for each performance parameter identified. Examples of performance parameters in a QoS class are all or a subset of cell transfer delay, cell delay variation, and cell loss ratio.

Within a specified QoS class, at most two cell loss ratio parameters may be specified. If a specified QoS class does contain two cell loss ratio parameters, then one parameter is for all CLP = 0 cells, and the other parameter is for all CLP = 1 cells of the ATM connection. As presently foreseen, other performance parameters besides the cell loss ratio would apply to the aggregate cell flow of the ATM connection. A QoS class could contain, for example, the following performance parameters: maximum cell transfer delay, a cell delay variation, and a cell loss ratio on CLP = 0 cells. The performance provided by the network should meet (or exceed) performance parameter objectives of the QoS class requested by the ATM endpoint.

7.3.1 Specified QoS Classes

A specified QoS class provides a quality of service to an ATM connection in terms of a subset of the ATM performance parameters just discussed. For each specified QoS class, there is one specified objective value for each performance parameter. Initially, each network should define objective values for a subset of the ATM performance parameters for at least one of the following service classes from ITU-T Recommendation I.362 in a reference configuration that may depend on propagation delay and other factors:[16]

Service Class A.   Circuit emulation, constant bit rate video

Service Class B.   Variable bit rate audio and video

Service Class C.   Connection-oriented data transfer

Service Class D.   Connectionless data transfer

The following specified QoS Classes are currently defined:

Specified QoS Class 1.   Supports a QoS that will meet service class A performance requirements; specified QoS class 1 should yield performance comparable to current digital private line performance.

Specified QoS Class 2. Support a QoS that will meet service class B performance requirements; specified QoS class 2 is intended for packetized video and audio in teleconferencing and multimedia applications.

Specified QoS Class 3. Supports a QoS that will meet service class C performance requirements; specified QoS class 3 is intended for interoperation of connection-oriented protocols, such as frame relay.

Specified QoS Class 4. Supports a QoS that will meet service class D performance requirements; specified QoS class 4 is intended for interoperation of connectionless protocols, such as IP or SMDS.

7.3.2 Unspecified QoS Class

In the unspecified QoS class, no objective is specified for the performance parameters. However, the network may determine a set of internal objectives for the performance parameters. In fact, these internal performance parameter objectives need not be constant during the duration of a connection. Thus, for the unspecified QoS class, there is no explicitly specified QoS commitment on either the CLP = 0 or the CLP = 1 cell flow. Services using the unspecified QoS class may have explicitly specified traffic parameters. An example application of the unspecified QoS class is the support of a best-effort service (i.e., UBR). For this type of service, the user selects the best-effort capability, the unspecified QoS class, and only the traffic parameter for the PCR on CLP = 0 + 1. This capability can be used to support users capable of regulating the traffic flow into the network and to adapt to time-variable available resources.

7.4 Additional Features Supported in TM 4.0

This section highlights some of the new features introduced by the ATM Forum and some mechanisms to support these features.

Available bit rate may be used to carry IP traffic (which may carry voice-over IP), although some feel that UBR with early packet discard (EPD) and MCR may be better for traditional TCP/IP applications. ABR uses a rate-based flow control protocol. Resource management (RM) cells are sent at regular intervals. When the network elements (e.g., switches) detect congestion, the EFCI bit is set in the RM cell. The destination reacts to this by setting the congestion indication bit (CI) in the return RM cell.

Once the cell is received by the origination of the traffic (see Figure 7.30), it reacts by slowing down. PCR and MCR parameters are supported by the UPC algorithm for ABR, implying that a minimum cell rate is "guaranteed," if the source appropriately shapes the traffic (in a dynamic manner). Sources and destinations must be suitably equipped to support this behavior. The virtual source/virtual destination (VS/VD) concept at the edge of the network also helps in this regard either by acting on behalf of the real source/destination when these do not support the feedback mechanism (and the VSs and/or VDs can throttle back to the degree possible; i.e., be more severe in the tagging/discard mechanism) or by creating shorter loops, as shown in Figure 7.31 [9].

ABR allows switch developers to minimize the amount of buffering required in high-speed links with high-speed sources (e.g. 155 or 622 Mbps) and high-source/trunk-speed mismatch (e.g., 622 Mbps sources and OC3 trunks). In well-designed ABR systems, the CLR will be low; there will be efficient use of resources; and it will be possible to absorb transient congestion without requiring the action of TCP. The overheat in ABR is relatively small (6 percent when using default RM generation rate of 1 RM cell every 32 information cells). Some implementations, particularly for DS1 links, can lead to lower performance. In order to support ABR, there has to be conformant end-to-end implementation, including at the CPE router (and NIC) level. Note that when the ATM closed loop terminates at the VS/VD, there may be excessive buffering and, eventually, PDU loss (with TCP intervention).

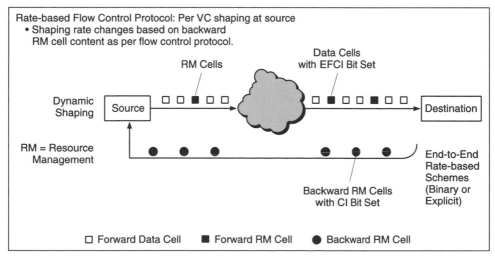

Figure 7.30   ABR flow control.

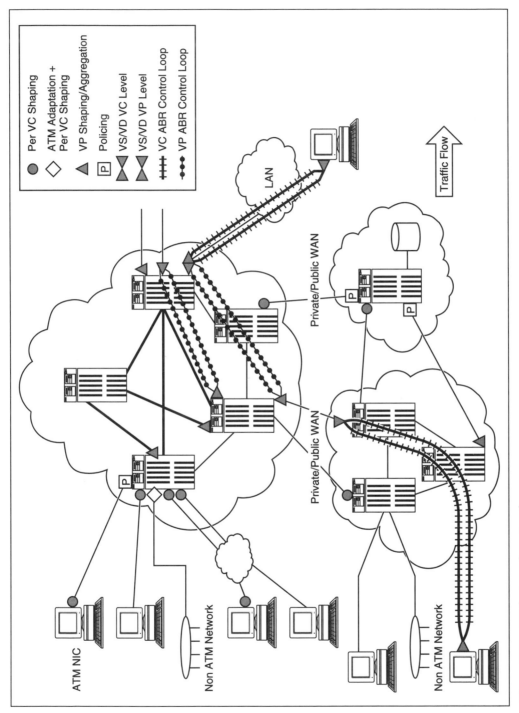

Figure 7.31 TM features in networks.

Another useful feature is frame discard (in a variety of flavors such as early packet discard [EPD], partial packet discard [PPD], and intelligent packet discard [IPD]). With this feature, network elements can discard all cells of an AAL 5 packet when congestion develops. Random cell discard would result in potentially many partial PDUs, which have to be thrown away by the destination after incurring the effort of network delivery. Frame discard, therefore, provides higher network efficiency and higher "goodput," and cuts down TCP retransmits and removes the requirement for extremely low cell loss for data applications. It conveys congestion notification to the application layer quicker by discarding frames. Early packet discard is particularly useful in UBR. It is simple to engineer and is insensitive to traffic parameters. It provides the highest performance (with sufficient layer buffers); no overhead is involved, and performance is a function of the buffer size (although delay may become an issue). QoS guarantees (in the form of MCR in the next release of UBR) can be obtained with WFQ.

In spite of these recent developments in ABR and UBR, designers of ATM applications now usually expect VBR services from the network [13]. "Field experience" with data applications using UBR and ABR shows that these services suffer from the same behavior as data in best-effort IP networks, particularly when run over ATM switches with limited buffering, whose shallow queue depths were designed to anticipate only CBR traffic (first- and second-generation ATM switches of the 1990–1993 and 1994–1996 vintage, respectively, tend to fall in this category).

Voice and video, initially carried with CBR service, are also being targeted to VBR-rt and VBR-nrt services. We say targeted, because products appearing at the time of this writing that implemented the VTOA specification still relied on circuit emulation service with AAL 1 (although some proprietary systems using AAL 2 were also available). VBR service aims at minimizing the effects of jitter, but also permits an application to consume extra bandwidth up to a negotiated PCR limit. In handling VBR applications, however, the network is more susceptible to oscillating queue depths; this in turn necessitates more sophisticated queuing algorithms to provide a consistent service.

CBR was designed to service legacy TDM applications that could accept no network variation (hence the shallow queues). CBR services can and have been used to support traditional voice and video applications, but evolving applications-based, variable-length encoding and variable-rate compression technologies (mentioned in passing in Chapter 1), are ideally suited for VBR network services, while at the same time enjoy QoS support.

In summary, ATM (UNI 4.0/TM 4.0) offers flexible service based on five categories, including bandwidth-on-demand services with QoS guarantees

(ABR and UBR). The CAC allocates resources in the switch to "guarantee" QoS to conforming traffic. Policing ensures that only "conforming traffic" exiting a router (for example) is conforming to the UPC contract/function. Efficient queuing (e.g., weighted fair queuing [WFQ]) enables the network to achieve QoS requirements with optimal resource allocation. ABR offers increased control of traffic entering the network, while discard can provide optimized management of congestion for AAL 5 streams.

One final issue of QoS in ATM (and other networks for that matter) is the need to develop ATM application programming interfaces (APIs) that allow the applications to have direct control of the underlying communication services, features, and options. More work is needed in this area, since not enough attention has been paid to it by the industry in recent years.

7.5 Conclusion

ATM services for local access and for long-haul applications are now increasingly becoming available to companies and ISPs. Understanding the nuances associated with ATM (e.g., cell tax, service classes, QoS support, traffic management approaches), helps the planner determine whether ATM is an applicable solution. Questions ISPs and their customers should ask include: What services are supported? What is the overbooking percentage? What is the peak and sustainable cell rate? Will PVCs and PVPs be supported, and will SVC be supported?

References

1. D. Minoli, M. Vitella. *Cell Relay Service and ATM for Corporate Environments.* (New York: McGraw-Hill), 1994.
2. A. Schmidt, D. Minoli. *MPOA.* (Greenwich, CT: Prentice-Hall/ Manning Pubs.), 1998.
3. D. Minoli, A. Schmidt, *Network Layer Switched Services.* (New York: John Wiley & Sons, Inc.), 1998.
4. D. Minoli, "Optimal Packet Length for Packet Voice Communication." IEEE Transactions on Communications, March 1979, Vol COMM-27, pp. 607–611.
5. Peter Newman, "ATM Local Area Network." *IEEE Communications Magazine,* March 1994, pp. 86 ff.
6. D. Minoli, G. Dobrowski, *Principles of Signaling for Cell Relay and Frame Relay.* (Norwood, MA: Artech House), 1995.

7. D. Minoli, J. Amoss. *IP Applications with ATM.* (New York: McGraw-Hill), 1998.
8. D. Minoli, E. Minoli. *Voice over Packet Networks* (New York: John Wiley & Sons, Inc.), 1998.
9. N. Giroux, "ATM Traffic Management for Efficient Multi-Service Networks." Network & Service Management for ATM, ICM-sponsored Conference, Chicago, IL, August 1997.
10. The ATM Forum, Traffic Management Specification 4.0, af-tm-0056.000, April 1996.
11. Fred Baker, "Lies, Damned Lies and RSVP," *Business Communications Review,* March 1997, pp. 30 ff.

Notes

[1] The chapter provides only a summary view of the topic; readers who want more details can refer to any number of texts, including those listed in the References at the end of this chapter [1], [2], and [3]. (Portions of this chapter are based on the authors' *Network Layer-switched Services.*)

[2] In the future, some of these services, such as cell relay, may operate at a higher speed (622Mbps or higher).

[3] LAN emulation entails emulating MAC layer functionality of specific LAN protocols such as Ethernet, or token ring. This allows endstations on the traditional LANs to communicate with endstations on ATM LANs without requiring any hardware or software changes to the endstations on the traditional LANs. But this requires separate MAC emulators for each of the previously mentioned LAN protocols, to be deployed in endstations connected to ATM LANs and in bridges connecting ATM LANs with traditional LANs.

[4] Outside the United States, the SONET concept is described in the context of the synchronous digital hierarchy (SDH); effectively, this hierarchy uses building blocks of 155.520Mbps rather than building blocks of 51.840. However, they are basically consistent for appropriate values of the aggregate bandwidth.

[5] Do not confuse VCs/VPs with connections. VCs are channels; connections are instances of end-to-end communications. Connections are identified by call reference and connection identifiers included in the setup message used in signaling. See [6] for a more extensive description.

[6] Specifically, LANE is an interworking capability that allows Ethernet/token ring stations to communicate directly with ATM sta-

tions (and vice versa) as if they were using the same protocol. The interworking equipment supports the conversion between the two protocols. Traditional LANs use the 48-bit MAC address. The MAC address is globally unique. This nonhierarchical LAN address assigned by the manufacturer identifies a network interface in the endstation. The use of a MAC address is practical in a single LAN segment or in a small internet. However, large bridged networks become difficult to manage and experience large amounts of broadcast traffic for the purpose of attempting to locate endstations. The address space of a large network is preferably hierarchical. This makes it easier to locate a particular point on the network; such an address, however, restricts the mobility of the network users. The E.164 address used in (public) ATM is hierarchical.

To emulate a LAN, the ATM network must support addressing using MAC address scheme: Each ATM MAC entity must be assigned a 48-bit MAC address, from the same address space, to facilitate its identification. As noted, an ATM network, whether public or private, uses a hierarchical address. The address resolution operation in LANE binds the endstation MAC address to the physical address of the ATM port to which the endstation is currently connected. When an endstation is attached to an ATM switch port, a registration protocol exchanges the MAC address between the ATM network and the endstation. SVCs are set up to the intended destinations. The LAN emulation service consists of several pieces of software and hardware operating on one or more platforms:

LAN Emulation Client (LEC).   Software that resides at the edge device, which is where the emulated service is rendered in terms of the conversion between protocols.

LAN Emulation Server (LES).   Provides initialization and configuration functions, address registration, and address resolution. Since ATM and legacy LANs use very different addressing schemes, a way to map the two is important, particularly with a view to "subnetworks," where the addressing capabilities of ATM may be lacking.

In a traditional LAN, all frames (unicast, multicast, and broadcast) are broadcast to all stations on the shared physical medium; each station selects the frames it wants to receive. A LAN segment can be emulated by connecting a set of stations on the ATM network via an ATM multicast virtual connection. The multicast virtual connection emulates the broadcast physical medium of the LAN. This connection becomes the broadcast channel of the ATM LAN segment. With this capability, any station may broadcast to all others on the ATM LAN segment by transmitting on the shared ATM multicast virtual connection.

[7] Specifications in the VTOA family currently require voice to be treated as CBR traffic over a channel emulation service (CES). A problem with CBR traffic, however, is that it forces customers to reserve bandwidth for voice even when no information is being sent. Sending voice as VBR traffic is the obvious alternative; however, VBR for voice has not yet been standardized. Silence suppression and voice compression will be a part of a new AAL specification, AAL 2, that would provide more efficient use of bandwidth. As noted, AAL 2 defines a VBR service for low-bit rate voice traffic, and is expected to be used initially between a wireless base station and mobile switch center. When fully defined, AAL 2 will provide silence suppression and voice compression. Some vendors offer prestandard equipment. Work in this group has generally been split into two areas [7]:

VTOA Trunking for Narrowband Services.   Targeted primarily at applications in private voice networks and potentially public networks.

VTOA Legacy Voice Services at a Native ATM Terminal.   Targeted at applications in private and public networks, where interworking and interoperation of ATM and non-ATM networks and services for voice is needed. Other VTOA specifications include the following [9]:

Trunking for Narrowband Services.   Based on the use of an interworking function (IWF) between the ATM network and each interconnected narrowband network.

Voice and Telephony over ATM to the Desktop Specification. Specifies the functions required to provide voice and telephony services over ATM to the desktop. It describes the functions of the interworking function (IWF) and a native ATM terminal. This version covers only the transport of a single 64Kbit/s A-law or mu-law-encoded voiceband signal.

[8] This section is based on Fore Systems promotional material, and is used with permission.

[9] This subsection is based on a personal communication with Julian Crizaldy, May 27, 1998.

[10] The traffic parameters are defined by the ATM Forum in the User Network Interface Specification.

[11] For example, pooling the tellers at a bank and merging the queue into one queue is more efficient than having multiple servers and multiple queues behind them. Similarly, pooling the voice, video, and data traffic is intrinsically more efficient because of the teletraffic/queuing principles than having separate networks.

[12] PNNI is used for global QoS support in a private ATM network. This is accomplished via hierarchical, link-state, source-based QoS-driven routing, where the information is propagated using the ATMF UNI signaling mechanism (rather than, for example, being based on the Broadband ISDN User Part of the Common Channel Signaling System No. 7).

[13] The PNNI interswitch routing protocol is used to identify the shortest path between the current location and the destination; the switch then computes the probability of successfully completing the call (based on available resources to supported the requested QoS) over all available paths. The path with the highest likelihood for completion is selected.

[14] The only exception to this is the Circuit Emulation Service, where jitter, wonder, and BER values are specified by the ATMF.

[15] Formally, the negotiated characteristics of a connection. The traffic contract at the public UNI consists of a connection traffic descriptor and a set of QoS parameters for each direction of the connection. The connection traffic descriptor consists of parameters such as PCR, SCR, MBS, and MCR, along with the cell delay variation tolerance and the conformance definition used to unambiguously specify the conforming cells in the connection. Refer to [11] for more discussion and definition.

[16] As noted, though, the standards do not specify the numerical values of these parameters. This discussion only makes the point about the structure of the QoS request (i.e., that it ought to be based on a predefined menulike mechanism).

CHAPTER 8

Layer 3 Fundamentals with an Eye to QoS: IP, IPv6, Internet Routing, and BGP

8.1 Overview

As covered in the previous chapter, ATM was designed from the start as a multimedia, multiservice, multipoint Layer 2 technology; hence, ATM supports extensive QoS and service class capabilities, allowing time-sensitive traffic, such as voice, to be transported across the network in a reliable jitter-free manner. And switches have been designed with effective traffic management capabilities to support the QoS and service classes needed for the various applications, including voice.

The issue, however, is that ATM is not widely deployed by ISPs or corporate planners, and is still relatively expensive, whereas IP-based Layer 3 networks are ubiquitous in the corporate landscape and in the Internet. Consequently, there is keen interest in trying to secure QoS support in the IP space, including in the Internet and in IP VPNs. IP has already become the backbone for nearly all corporate data applications. Planners are looking at voice-over IP for intranet/enterprise network applications, and voice-over the Internet for geographically dispersed applications. Bandwidth efficiency and quality are the principal trade-offs in this arena. For example, products for voice-over IP are emerging because organizations have significant investments in private data facilities that have the capacity to carry additional on-net traffic with what is perceived to be little initial incremental expense.

IP by itself has limited QoS support. Thus one needs to look at other supplementary methods, such as ATM support of IP, or more to the point, RSVP.

The Internet now has several million hosts connecting hundreds of millions people worldwide. It is used by many people: educators, telecommuters, librarians, hobbyists, researchers, government officials, and business personnel, to name just a few. It is used for a variety of purposes, from people-to-people communication to enabling corporate workers to access valuable information and resources. The Internet provides connectivity for a wide range of application processes called network services: one can exchange electronic mail, access and participate in discussion forums, search databases, browse indexes, transfer files, and so forth. Use of the Internet for multimedia applications, including voice and for mission-critical, time-sensitive applications is a relatively new development, driving QoS requirements, as noted in Chapters 4 and 5. The capability to carry voice (and fax) across an IP network or the Internet creates a cost-effective way of managing intracorporate communications. In addition, obviously it can support intercorporate communications.

This chapter provides a fundamental review of all the Layer 3 issues relevant to a discussion of Internet-based communication, to establish a baseline of discussion. It covers IP, IPv6, and BGP among other topics [1][2]. All of these issues are important in terms of how an ISP would architect its access, aggregation, and backbone network; it also impacts peering with other segments of the Internet. In addition, this chapter covers two of the key principles used in Internet routing: classless interdomain routing and autonomous systems. These two technologies have been used to control the explosive growth of routing tables and to help implement scalable network designs. The QoS applications and solutions are treated in the next two chapters.

8.2 IP/Internet Background

Network communications can de divided into two basic types: circuit-switched (sometimes called connection-oriented) and packet/fast-packet-switched (these can be connectionless or connection-oriented). Circuit-switched networks operate by forming a dedicated connection (circuit) between two points. In packet-switched networks, data to be transferred across a network is segmented into small pieces called segments that are multiplexed onto high-capacity intermachine connections. A packet, which usually contains few hundred bytes of data, carries identification that enables the network hardware to know how to send it to the specified destination. In frame relay, the basic transfer unit is the (data link layer) frame; in cell relay, this basic unit is the (data link layer) cell. In IP, this is a datagram. Services such as frame relay and ATM use circuit-switching principles; namely, they use the call setup mechanism similar to that of a circuit-switched (ISDN) call. Packet communication takes place at Layer 2 and at Layer 3. Layer 2 includes frame and cell relay.

The most well-known Layer 3 packet protocol is IP (and people call the resulting service "IP dialtone"). IP has become the standard connection-less packet network layer protocol for both LANs and WANs. Enterprise networks based on IP are now ubiquitous: Users range from small home office operators to large multinationals.

8.2.1 Internet Protocol Suite

At the network level, an IP internet provides two broad types of service that all application programs use:

Connectionless Packet Delivery Service. A Transmission Control Protocol/Internet Protocol (TCP/IP) internet routes small messages from one endsystem to another, based on address information carried in the message. Because it usually maps directly onto the underlying hardware, the connectionless service is relatively efficient; and, more important, it makes the TCP/IP protocols adaptable to a wide range of network hardware.

Reliable Stream Transport Service. The reliable transport service in TCP/IP protocols (specifically in TCP) handles problems such as transmission errors, lost packets, and so on. It allows an application on one computer to establish a "connection" with another application as if it were a permanent, direct hardware connection.

TCP/IP is the de facto term for a family of more than 100 data communications protocols used to organize computers and data-communications equipment into practical computer networks. The most accurate name, however, for the set of protocols is the "Internet protocol suite"; TCP and IP are only two of the protocols in this suite, but because TCP and IP are the best known of the protocols, it has become common to use the term TCP/IP to refer to the whole family. Some of the protocols in the TCP/IP suite of protocols provide "low-level" functions needed for many applications. These include IP, TCP, User Datagram Protocol (UDP), and Internet Control Message Protocol (ICMP). Other protocols are for undertaking specific tasks, for example, transferring files between computers, sending mail, or finding out who is logged in on another computer. The primary features that distinguish TCP/IP are:

Network Technology Independence.   While TCP/IP is based on conventional packet-switching technology, it is independent of any particular vendor's hardware.

Universal Interconnection.   TCP/IP allows any pairs of computers with appropriate drivers to communicate. Each computer is assigned an address that is universally recognized throughout the internet/Internet.

End-to-End Acknowledgments.   The TCP/IP internet protocols (specifically TCP) provide acknowledgments between the source and the destination, even when they do not connect to a common physical network.

Application-Level Protocol Standards.   The TCP/IP protocols include standards for many common applications including electronic mail, file transfer, and remote login.

TCP/IP protocols are normally deployed in layers, with each layer responsible for a different facet of the communications. TCP/IP is normally considered to be a four-layer system. Each layer has a different responsibility (see Table 8.1):

- The *link layer,* sometimes called the network interface layer, normally includes the device driver in the operating system and the corresponding network interface card in the computer. Together, they handle all the hardware details of physically interfacing with the cable.

- The *network layer* (sometimes called the internet layer) handles the movement of packets in the network. Routing of packets, for example, takes place here. IP and ICMP provide the network layer in the TCP/IP protocol suite.

- The *transport layer* provides a flow of data between two endsystem hosts, for the application layer above. In the Internet protocol suite there are two vastly different transport protocols: TCP and UDP. TCP provides a reliable flow of data between two hosts. It is concerned with things such as partitioning the data passed to it from the application into appropriately sized frames for the network layer

Table 8.1   Functionality of the TCP/IP Suite Layers

Network Interface Layer	Responsible for accepting and transmitting IP datagrams. This layer may consist of a device driver (e.g., when the network is a local network to which the machine attaches directly) or a complex subsystem that uses its own data link protocol.
Network Layer (Internet Layer)	Handles communication from one machine to the other. It accepts a request to send data from the transport layer along with the identification of the destination. It encapsulates the transport layer data unit in an IP datagram, and uses the datagram routing algorithm to determine whether to send the datagram directly onto a router. The internet layer also handles the incoming datagrams, and uses the routing algorithm to determine whether the datagram is to be processed locally or forwarded.
Transport Layer	The software segments the stream of data being transmitted into small data units and passes each packet along with a destination address to the next layer for transmission. The software adds information to the packets, including codes that identify which application program sent it, as well as a checksum. This layer also regulates the flow of information and provides reliable transport, ensuring that data arrives in sequence and with no errors.
Application Layer	Users invoke application programs to access available services across the TCP/IP Internet. The application program chooses the kind of transport needed, which can either be messages or stream of bytes, and passes it to the transport level.

below, acknowledging received packets and setting time-outs to make certain the other end acknowledges packets that are sent. Because this reliable flow of data is provided by the transport layer, the application layer can ignore all those details. UDP, on the other hand, provides a much simpler service to the application layer. It sends packets of data called datagrams from one host to the other, but there is no guarantee that the datagrams will be delivered to the other end. Any desired reliability must be added by the application layer.

- The *application layer* handles the details of the particular application. There are many common TCP/IP applications that almost every implementation provides:

  TELNET for remote login

  FTP, the file transfer protocol

  SMTP, the Simple Mail Transfer Protocol for electronic mail

  SNMP, the Simple Network Management Protocol

  Many more

In this architecture, IP is responsible for relaying packets of data (protocol data units—PDUs—, or datagrams) from node to node. TCP is responsible for verifying the correct delivery of data from the sender to the receiver. TCP allows a process on one endsystem to send a stream of data to a process on another endsystem. It is connection-oriented: Before transmitting data, participants must establish a connection. Data can be lost in the intermediate network(s). TCP adds support to detect lost data and to trigger retransmission until the data is correctly and completely received.

So, TCP and IP are distinct protocols with separate jobs. TCP's job is to provide a reliable mechanism for computers to transmit data over one or more interconnected networks; data must be delivered reliably, in sequence, completely, and with no duplication, in spite of the fact that there may be multiple networks along the way. IP's job is to move, specifically route, blocks of data over each of the networks that sits between the computers that want to communicate. IP provides for the carriage of datagrams from a source host to destination hosts, possibly passing through one or more gateways (routers) and networks in the process. An IP protocol data unit (datagram) is a sequence of bits containing a header and a payload. The header information identifies the source, destination, length, handling advice, and characteristics of the payload contents. The payload is the actual data transported. Both endsystems' hosts and routers in an internet are involved in the processing of the IP headers. The hosts must create and transmit them, and process them on receipt; the routers must examine them for the purpose of making routing decisions, and modify them as the IP packets make their way from the source to the destination.

The IP service, also called "IP dialtone" by some, as mentioned earlier, is provided by ISPs; TCP is used end to end, between the user's PC and the web site being accessed. IP has been the staple of network interconnection. Although the Internet is the most well-known IP network, as noted in Chapter 1, it is just one of the millions of such networks now deployed, public or private. IP protocols are supported over a variety of underlying media such as ATM, frame relay, dedicated lines, ISDN, Ethernet, token ring, and others. As IP networks have become ubiquitous, the business community has become sophisticated about utilizing IP networks as a cost-effective corporate tool, first in data communications, and now for other applications. Organizations favor networks based on IP because of the flexibility and vendor support: IP networks run under the most widely used network operating systems; they are scalable to a large degree; and they enjoy extensive implementation across product lines (e.g., in the routers, PC clients, servers switches, etc.).

A relatively new IP application now in demand is high-quality, low-bandwidth voice (and fax) transmission over IP networks.

8.2.2 TCP/IP in the Internet

The same IP technology now used extensively in corporate internets is used in (in fact, originated from) the Internet. A person at a computer terminal or personal computer with the proper software communicates across the Internet by placing data in an IP packet and "addressing" the packet to a particular destination on the Internet; TCP guarantees end-to-end integrity. Communications software on the intervening networks between the source and destination networks "read" the addresses on packets moving through the Internet and forward the packets toward their destinations. From a thousand or so networks in the mid-1980s, the Internet has grown to millions of connected networks with hundreds of millions people having access to it. Currently, the majority of these Internet users live in the United States or Europe, but the Internet is expected to achieve ubiquitous global reach over the next few years. Chapter 1 provided a history of the development of the Internet. In this chapter, the Internet-Related Activities sidebar provides a chronological snapshot of these developments, and Figure 8.1 provides yet another topological/architectural view of the Internet, to provide some systemization of concept.

As noted earlier, TCP and IP were developed for basic control of information delivery across the Internet. Application layer protocols, such as TELNET (Network Terminal), FTP (File Transfer Protocol), SMTP (Simple Mail Transfer Protocol), HTTP (HyperText Transfer Protocol), have been added to the TCP/IP suite of protocols to provide specific network services. Access and backbone speeds have increased from 56Kbps, to 1.5Mbps (most common now), to 45Mbps and beyond, for most of the

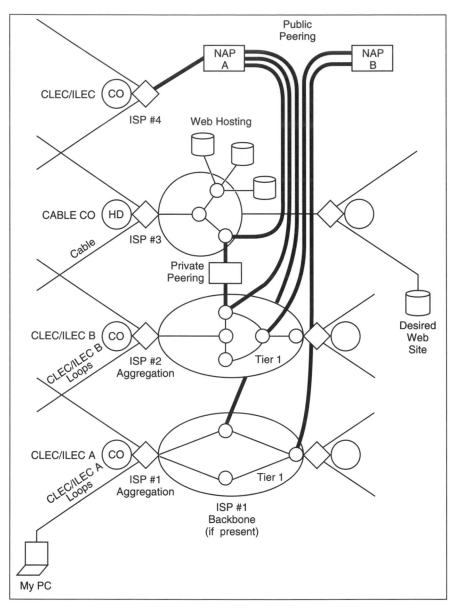

Figure 8.1   Topological/architectural view of the Internet.

backbones. Intranets use the same Web/HTML/HTTP and TCP/IP technology used for the Internet.

Over the years, people who have somehow been associated with the development of the Internet continue to want to portray it anachronistically as some kind of special entity. This is not the case. The idea of having a parallel Public Switched Data Network to the PSTN based on packet technology (specifically X.25 Packet Layer Protocol, which is not, after all, that much different from IP) was already being pursued in the mid to late 1970s. The idea of having a set of standards, so that the data on any computer can be accessed in the same manner (e.g., HTTP/HTML) is self-evident, and the idea of using what are called in other venues network graphical user interfaces (NGUIs, specifically in the form of browsers) is also pretty straightforward. All of these same principles have applied to the PSTN for decades: a network accessible by all; standards enabling a person in Siberia to dial up a person in Chile; and a common interface to the network (a pretty-much standardized dial pad).

8.3 A Technical Primer of IP and Routing

One of the common ways to interconnect IP networks at this time is through the use of routers. Routers are found at the boundary point between two logical or physical subnetworks. (In general parlance, these are known as network layer relays [3]; however, we use the more commonly accepted terminology.) Routing is a more sophisticated, and hence more effective, method of achieving internetworking compared to bridging. In theory, a router can translate between a subnetwork with a physical layer protocol P1, a data link layer protocol DL1, and a network layer protocol N1, to a subnetwork with physical layer protocol P2, data link layer protocol DL2, and network layer protocol N2. In practice, however, a router is used for internetworking two (sub)networks that use the same network layer but have different data link layer protocols [4].

Internetworking products, including routers, represent a large fraction of the sunk enterprise network cost, as well as a large fraction of the yearly network deployment and operating budget. This is due to the fact that the routers themselves are relatively expensive, particularly at the high end and/or for newer protocols, and because the number of such devices in the network has increased over the last few years. Routing entered the enterprise networking scene in the mid-1980s, and has supplanted a major portion of the previous multiplexer-based technology. Today, network administrators spend a lot of time deciding which routing technology to use, by way of the products they purchase, and analyzing how to refine the router's metrics to consistently support optimal routes. Furthermore, network design tuning follows from topology changes, such as adding locations, links, access technologies, and so on [5].

It is, therefore, fair to say that, at this juncture, routers have become the fundamental and the predominant building technology for data internet-

A SNAPSHOT OF INTERNET-RELATED ACTIVITIES OVER THE YEARS

- Late 1960s: DARPA (think tank of DoD) introduces ARPANET.

- During the 1970s, ARPANET expands geographically and functionally (allows nonmilitary traffic; e.g., universities and defense contractors).

- By late 1970s, realization takes hold that ARPANET cannot scale.

- TCP/IP is developed for heterogeneous networking, interenterprise connectivity. Protocols to support global addressing and scalability are developed.

- Early 1980s (1983), TCP/IP is a standard operating environment for all attached systems.

- Network splits into a military component (MILNET) and a civilian component (ARPANET).

- In 1986, six supercomputer centers are established by the NSF.

- Interagency dynamics and funding considerations lead to creation of NSFNET by the NSF. IP protocol and newer equipment utilized in NSFNET. NSFNET and ARPANET intersect at Carnegie Mellon University.

- Late 1980s, ARPANET is absorbed into NSFNET.

- "Phase 1": Three-tiered architecture is developed:
  1. NSF undertakes overall management; funds the backbone operationally and in terms of technology upgrades.
  2. Regional and state network providers arise; supply Internet services between universities and the backbone; become self-supportive on service fees.
  3. Campus networks, organizations, colleges and universities use TCP/IP-based system to provide widespread access to researchers and students.

- Six supercomputer sites interconnect in 1987 using DEC routers and 56Kbps links.

- Traffic congestion begins to be felt.

- "Phase 2": Merit partnership forms with IBM and MCI to upgrade network.

- By mid-1988, a DS1-line (1.544Mbps) network connects over a dozen sites. IBM-based switches are used.

- Reengineering begins in 1989 due to fast growth (15 percent/month); new routers and additional T1 links (MCI) are installed.

- "Phase 3": Third redesign of NSFNET takes an outsourcing approach, whereby NSFNET is "overlaid" over a public Internet (NSF relieved from responsibility of upgrading the network on an ongoing basis). Lines upgraded to DS-3 rates (45Mbps).

- Merit, IBM, and MCI form Advanced Network Services Inc. (ANS). The not-for-profit organization is to build/manage a commercial Internet.
- DS3 lines are provided by MCI; routers by IBM (RS/6000-based). Network also called ANSNET. NSFNET is now a virtual network in the ANSNET (migration is accomplished in two years).
- In 1992, original NSFNET is dismantled.
- ANS launches for-profit subsidiary (ANS CORE) to address costs.
- Debates are sparked by commercial Internet providers.
  - PSINET, CERFNET, and AlterNet form Commercial Internet Exchange (CIX) as a backbone and bypass to the NSFNET; 155 other members join, including NEARNet, JvNCNet, SprintLink, and InfoLAN.
  - Based on CIX approach, CICNet, NEARNet, BARRNet, North WestNet, NYSERNet WestNet, and MIDNet form the Corporation for Regional & Enterprise Networking (CoREN).
  - Regional commercial providers (not in CoREN) compete against CoREN.
- "Phase 4": Rapid increase requires NSF to redesign the backbone.
- Two years of bidding and planning leads to two awards to replace current NSFNet: MCI to deploy Very High-Speed Backbone Network Service (vBNS) based on 155Mbps, and SONET/ATM to connect NFS supercomputing centers; Merit and USC Information Sciences Institute to do routing coordination.
- Network access points/providers (NAPs) to provide access to the vBNS; NAP functions go to Ameritech, Sprint, MFS, and PacTel
- NFS institute is the routing arbiter for fair treatment among various Internet service providers with regard to routing administration; database of route information, network topology, routing path preferences, interconnection information; deployment of routing that supports type of service, precedence routing, bandwidth-on-demand, and multicasting (accomplished by "route servers" using Border Gateway Protocol and Interdomain Routing Protocol).
- Fund is established to support Network Information Center (NIC)
  - Registration Services (by Network Solutions Inc.): IP and Domain Names, whois, and white pages.
  - Directory Services (by AT&T): Directory of directories, white pages, yellow pages
  - Information Services (by General Atomics): coordination services, clearinghouse for information, training, workshops, reference desk, education (General Atmonics operated CERFnet—now owned by AT&T—and San Diego Supercomputer Center)
- Shakeout of ISP is predicted in the next few years, reducing the number from thousands to hundreds.

working. Routers permit the physical as well as the logical interconnection of two networks. With the introduction of ATM, however, the role of routers in enterprise networks could theoretically change, so as to no longer require hop-by-hop datagram handling, but perhaps just edge-to-edge handling. For example, devices enabling connectivity between locations based on router technology may conceivably no longer be obligatory elements—though the concept of routing (forwarding frames at the network layer of the protocol model) will certainly continue to exist. In addition, routers work well for traditional data applications; but new broadband video and multimedia applications need different forwarding treatment, higher throughput, and tighter QoS control.

The connectivity provided by routers is supported at the network layer of the OSIRM. Routing entails the use of network-layer (topology) information as part of the process of deciding how to forward network-layer PDUs and which PDUs to forward (and where). Source and destination addresses within the network-layer PDU identify the sending and receiving networks. The use of routers allows the establishment of distinct physical and logical networks, each having its own network address space. Routing methodologies are becoming increasingly sophisticated as topologies become larger and more complex. A variety of protocols are supported by various LAN subnetworks that need to interwork to make end-to-end connectivity feasible. The more common network layer protocols are IP, IPX, and AppleTalk, with IP widely in command. Routers can be used to connect networks in building/campus proximity, or to support wide area connections. The communication technologies that can be used include low-speed, high-speed, and broadband dedicated-line services, as well as low-speed, high-speed, and broadband switched services.

Routers are the key element of the Internet at the network element level. They show up in the access, aggregation, and backbone components.

8.3.1 Routing Functions

Routing deals with techniques to move PDUs to distinguishable Layer 3 entities [4]. The issue of distinguishability relates to the address assignment, which is covered later in the chapter. This section describes support of two key underlying functions: determination of (optimal) routes, and movement (forwarding) of information through the internet.

Determination of (Optimal) Route

Routers build their routing tables through information obtained via routing protocols; these protocols allow routers on an internet to learn about one another, and to stay current as to the optimal way to reach all attached networks. Routers interconnect different types of networks and embody the capability to determine the best route to reach the destination. Path determination is accomplished through the use of algorithmic metrics that are functions of network parameters such as path length, available bandwidth, security level of path, path cost, path QoS, and so on. Generally, these metrics are implemented in software. Values required by the path determination algorithm are stored in router-resident "routing tables" of appropriate depth; the entries of the table are populated through local as well as remote information that is circulated around the network. Routing protocols are the adjunct mechanism by which routers obtain information about the status of the network. That is to say, routing protocols are used to populate routing tables and calculate costs.

Conceptually, routers operate by distributing, often through broadcast, advertisement PDUs, signaling their presence to all pertinent network nodes. These advertisement PDUs also signal to the other routers destinations that are reachable through the advertising router, or links to neighbors. They communicate with other routers for the purpose of propagating the view of the network connections they have, the cost of connections, and the utilization levels.

A number of techniques are available to populate the routing tables, and thereby support routing of information PDUs. This applies to enterprise routers as well as to Internet routers. *Static routing* requires the network manager to build and maintain the routing tables at each router or at a central route server. This implies that once configured, the network paths used for the PDUs must not change. A router using static routing can issue alarms when it recognizes that a communication link has failed, but it will not automatically update the routing table to reroute the traffic around the failure. Static routing is, therefore, typically used in limited-distance internets—for example, in a building's backbone or in a campus. *Dynamic routing* allows the router to automatically update the routing table and recalculate the optimal path, based on real-time network conditions (e.g., link failures, congestion, etc.). Routers implementing dynamic routing exchange information about the network's topology with other routers. Dynamic routing capabilities are the most desirable, because they allow internets to adapt to changing network conditions. (Note: Dynamic routing mechanisms can coexist in networks that use static routing on certain routers.) (See the sidebar, Use of Dynamic Routing for more on this.)

The process of reconfiguring the routing tables (called *convergence*), must occur rapidly to prevent routers with dated information to misroute PDUs. Dynamic routing is nearly always used when internetwork-

---

TRADITIONAL REASONS FOR USING DYNAMIC ROUTING

- Networks grow to such an extent that maintenenace of a statitically configured tables becomes unmanageable.

- Communication links experience outages either in the local access, local service switch, or interexchange service switch, which necessitates PDU rerouting over a different service facility.

- New communication links can be added to the internet. This necessitates propagation of routing information related to the new routes to the other routers.

- Additional communication links between two given routers can be established. This necessitates updates so that the routers will use the new facilities.

- Communication links supporting the internet can become congested, which necessitates that (certain) routing protocols adapt their routing tables to avoid the congested paths.

- Communication links can become degraded from a QoS point of view. This necessitates that (certain) routing protocols adapt their routing tables to avoid the degraded paths.

---

ing across WANs. Dynamic routers regularly update the view of the entire network; this view includes a map of devices operating at or below the network layer. Some dynamic routers also support traffic balancing.

The specifics of the various routing algorithms differ, but there are common goals:

- Determine the optimal path to a destination and collect values for metrics (e.g., hop count, latency, bandwidth capacity, and path QoS) that consistently result in the best route selection for PDU transfer.

- Minimize network bandwidth required for routing information propagation and minimize router processing required to determine optimal routes.

- Converge rapidly on new optimal routes following a network topology change.

The issue of dissemination of network topology/status information via the "routing protocol" mechanism is discussed further shortly.

Movement of Information through the Internetwork

It is the responsibility of routers, whether in a private network or in the ISP/NSP network, to forward PDUs belonging to a given set of protocols to appropriate subnetworks. The router forwards these PDUs based on parameters that are assigned weighted values. A router analyzes and selectively forwards network-layer PDUs to specific destinations (see Figure 8.2). This is accomplished by:

- Stripping off data link-level protocol control information (PCI) (headers and trailers).
- Examining the network layer destination address field and determining the PDU's destination.
- Determining where to forward the PDU (parochially: over which physical router port to transmit the information).
- Enveloping the data in an appropriate data-link frame.
- Enveloping the data in a physical layer frame (when needed).
- Transmitting the PDU thus generated onto the transmission medium.

When a router is able to interpret a routed or network protocol's format (which is determined by appropriate hardware and software configura-

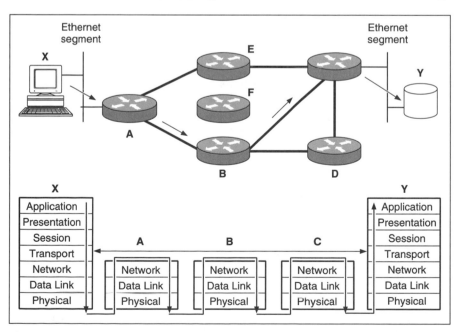

Figure 8.2   A router analyzes and selectively forwards network-layer PDUs to specific destinations.

tion), it is able to switch or route this traffic between networks directly. This process is known as *native* or *direct protocol* routing. If the format of a protocol is not known (e.g., is not enabled at configuration and/or hardware/software capabilities are not available, so that the protocol is not supported), then the router silently discards the packet. If the protocol is not routable, one may configure certain routers to treat all router hops between any two routers as a single "hop" or "tunnel." This technique, known as *encapsulation* or *tunneling*, is used to pass these PDUs through the subnetwork.

Many routers now are of the "multiprotocol" type. These have the ability to interpret (i.e., route) different protocols. This implies that interface ports on these routers, when configured, have the capability to route PDUs for various protocols simultaneously to the correct subnetwork and destination. In these routers, routing tables (per supported routing protocol) are maintained and updated.

Within the router are two distinct processes referred to as routing and forwarding. Routing refers to the process of choosing a path over which to send datagrams, and involves the operation of routing protocols. Forwarding is the process of moving datagrams within the router, utilizing the information gathered from the routing protocols. Routers are nothing more than high-end specialized computers running routing software that performs the routing process; they contain specialized hardware that has been optimized for the forwarding process.

All IP datagrams contain a source and destination address, as we cover later on. Routing in the Internet uses the source and destination address as the primary means for selecting routes. Ideally, or in next-generation internets, the routing decisions will take into consideration type of service, network congestion, or network costs; for the most part, these capabilities do not exist today. Forwarding packets based on the IP destination address alone, while efficient, has some undesirable consequences. The most obvious from an ISP's perspective is that all traffic follows the same path. This means that if there are multiple paths to the destination it is very difficult to utilize this capacity.

Related to the path selection process is the problem that data flowing in the reverse direction may be routed along a different path. This can lead to problems if underlying protocols anticipate symmetric performance. Finally, forwarding based on IP address destination does not allow for end-to-end resource negotiation or for determination that the destination even exists. That is, a host on the conventional Internet may be transmitting packets to a destination that does not exist.

Within the IP router, the routing table that is consulted by the forwarding hardware is constructed. The routing table contains pairs of the IP address of a destination network and the IP address of the next hop router along the path toward the destination. Each entry in a routing table points to a router that is physically connected to one of the segments on the router. That is, the next hop router must be accessible over a local area network or a wide area network connection and must not reside on a network with an intermediate router in between.

There are two types of routing protocols used to create routing tables: Interior Gateway Protocols (IGP) and Exterior Gateway Protocols (EGP). This chapter primarily focuses on EGP because they are the protocols most often used for interprovider communication. For now, it is best to consider each as a unique application for interior topology control and exterior reachability communication. Regardless whether the protocol is an interior or exterior routing protocol, its principal job is to populate the routing tables. When a datagram is ready to be transmitted, IP routing software locates the best-match entry in the routing table. From the IP address, the forwarding process determines where to send the packet next and utilizes whatever the physical media may be to transmit the packet to the next hop router.

8.3.2 Routing Modes: Dynamic, Default, and Static Routes

Understanding routing protocols and how to correctly configure IP routers is not a trivial task. One of the most important things for network engineers to understand is when and when not to use the tools they have been given. Many of the protocols described throughout this chapter are powerful and flexibly configurable. This is a double-edged sword because while it allows ISPs to create ingenious ways of solving their problems, it also has historically caused some very difficult-to-diagnose problems.

There are some clear examples in the Internet when these protocols are unnecessary. They can be found in networks that do not have multiple paths for data to traverse. In these cases, the designer can create what is called a default or a static route. Static routing refers to routes to destinations listed manually in the router. Default routing refers to a route of last resort to a destination that the router will use as an outlet for all networks for which it does not have reachability information.

These terms are used to define the technique whereby the router is instructed that it only has one possible path, the default, to forward packets. This type of configuration is useful in sites with only one connection to the rest of the Internet: for example, a small business with one LAN connected to a single ISP via a single router. That router has only one possible choice for forwarding packets; therefore, it does not need to be involved in complicated routing topology updates.

Static routes are also used in small ISP networks because the address space that has been allocated throughout the network can be manually disseminated throughout the ISP's routers. For example, if a small ISP has only six routers and a dozen subnetworks, it is unlikely that there will be many topological changes. For this reason, the ISP may not require running a routing protocol, and it would be best served with static routing. In many cases, for smaller ISPs, the most stable configurations utilize static routing; thus, it would be best that these customers not use BGP.

Finally, dynamic routing is a term used to describe the implementation of routing protocols that enable the network to automatically learn routes. Dynamic routing implements either an internal or an external routing protocol and can be realized by running, for example, BGP or Open Shortest Path First (OSPF) [6].

8.3.3 Dissemination of Network Status Information via Routing Protocols

As discussed, there are two routing protocol types for status dissemination: protocols that operate within an autonomous network (typically an administrative domain) called Interior Gateway Protocols (IGPs), and protocols that operate between autonomous networks, or Exterior Gateway Protocols (EGPs). (The term "gateway" to refer to a router is based on traditional Internet nomenclature.)

In order to modernize the parlance, here we refer to "autonomous networks" or "autonomous subnetworks" rather than "autonomous systems." Systems, in the English sense of the word, represent collections of entities. Therefore, a network can be viewed as a system, namely a collection of links, routers, gateways, and so on. However, within the computer industry, the term system has become almost synonymous with computer (this also being a collection of entities; e.g., central processing unit, random access memory, hard-drive memory, etc.). To eliminate the possible ambiguity, we therefore prefer the term "autonomous (sub)networks."

Within an autonomous network, any suitable protocol may be (independently) used for route discovery, propagation, and validation, but autonomous networks must make routing information available to other autonomous networks using a systemwide protocol. So, within an autonomous network, an interior routing protocol is used, and between autonomous networks, an exterior routing protocol is used.

Key IGPs include:

Routing Information Protocol (RIP)

Open Shortest Path First (OSPF)

Cisco's Interior Gateway Routing Protocol (IGRP)

Intermediate-System to Intermediate-System (IS-IS) Protocol

Key EGPs include:

Exterior Gateway Protocol (EGP)

Border Gateway Protocol (BGP) (discussed later)

To support effective communication, the exchange of appropriate routing and status information among routers is required. The routers exchange information about the state of the network's links and interfaces and available paths, based on different metrics. Metrics used to calculate optimal paths through the network include cost, bandwidth, distance, delay, load, congestion, security, QoS, and reliability. Routing protocols are used as the means to exchange this vital information. The three common protocols used in the TCP/IP context for private enterprise (on intra-ISP) networks are RIP, IGRP, and OSPF, listed above.

Two methodologies are used for information dissemination: *distance vector* and *link-state*. Routers that employ distance vector techniques create a network map by exchanging information in a periodic and progressive sequence. Each router maintains a table of relative costs (hop count or other weights such as bandwidth availability) from itself to each destination. The information exchanged is used to determine the scope of the network via a series of router hops. After a router has calculated each of its distance vectors, it propagates the information to each of its neighboring routers on a periodic basis, say, once every 60 seconds. (More pedantically, periodic updates are not a property of distance vector routing; they are the mechanisms of choice [over unreliable links]; broadcast is used to provide reliability through retransmission.) If any changes have occurred in the network, as inferred from these vectors, the receiving router modifies its routing table and propagates it to each of its own neighbors. The process continues until all routers in the network have converged on the new topology.

Distance vector routing was the early kind of dynamic routing. Distance vector protocols include RIP, IGRP, and DECnet Phase IV, and they can be implemented in a reasonably simple manner. However, they suffer from a number of limitations, including:

- Periodic broadcast of routing information, using up network bandwidth
- Susceptibility to routing loops
- Slow convergence, particularly in enterprise large networks

Enhancements to the distance vector method have been developed to speed convergence and reduce the chance of routing loops. These enhancements are *holddown, split-horizon,* and *poison-reverse,* and are defined in Table 8.2.

Routers using link-state protocols learn the topology of the internetwork infrastructure and update each other's tables by periodically flooding the network with link-state information. This information includes the identification of the links or subnetworks directly connected to each router and the "cost" of the connection. Routers using the *shortest path first* algorithm send link-state information to all routers on the internet; in turn, these routers use the information to populate a table of routers and link/subnet-

Table 8.2 Enhancements to the Distance Vector Method

Holddown	After receiving a destination-unreachable indication from a neighbor router, the router in question will not accept new routing information from that router for a specified period of time (specifically, longer than it takes for the distance vector routing protocol to count to infinity). With this process, routing loops are avoided. The process also prevents a situation where routers begin to oscillate, attempting to converge (which can occur where a circuit transitions from operable to inoperable condition in a short period of time).
Split-horizon	Routing information cannot be sent back to the source from which it came, in order to reduce the chance of routing loops*. Split-horizon aims at stopping routing loops between adjacent routers.
Poison-reverse	Once a router determines that it has lost contact to a neighboring router, it immediatly propagates a routing update with the inoperable route metric set to infinity. The router also broadcasts the same information for several update periods to ascertain that all routers receive the notification. Poison-reverse aims at stopping routing loops between multiple routers.

*Split-horizon must be used with care when connecting routers to a PVC-based service such as frame relay or cell relay. These networks allow multiple PVCs to be mapped to a single physical circuit; hence, the router must disseminate routing information over each virtual circuit. It follows that if split-horizon is implemented such that updates cannot return over the physical link from which they came, it would be blocking routing updates to the other virtual circuits.

work connections. After this, each router calculates the optimal path from itself to each link: Indirect paths are discarded in favor of the shortest path. Link-state protocols include OSPF and the Intermediate-System to Intermediate-System (IS-IS) protocol.

Link-state routing is a newer form of dynamic routing, whereby routers broadcast their routing updates to all routers within the administrative domain. Since routing information is flooded, rather than just sent between neighboring routers as in the case in distance vector environments, each router can develop a complete map of the network topology. Given the topology map, each router can then calculate the best path to each destination.

Link-state protocols transfer routing information using link-state packets (LSPs). The transmission of an LSP is also called *route advertisement*. LSPs are broadcast periodically, typically every 15 or 30 minutes. An LSP is also broadcasted when: a communication link to a neighboring router is lost or gained; the assigned cost (in general, any metric) of a link changes (e.g., due to QoS); or when a new router is added to the network.

Link-state routing may well be the preferred choice in the future because it requires less bandwidth than distance vector routing and converges much faster following a topology change. The higher processing requirement for link-state routing algorithms becomes less important as processor performance increases and price per (millions of) operations per second continues to go down. Link-state protocols are indicated for rules-based routing and support of type of service or quality of service features. These protocols tend to be resistant to the creation of routing loops. In addition, they enjoy low overhead to support the routing function; bandwidth frugality is achieved through the use of more intensive computing resources and higher memory requirements for the router. Table 8.3 provides a comparison between the two routing methods.

Table 8.3   Distance Vector versus Link-State Routing Algorithms

DISTANCE VECTOR	LINK-STATE
Loops	Loops not formed since each router has the complete network topology.
Slow convergence	Faster convergence.
Bandwidth-intensive: distance vector routing sends routing updates every 60 seconds.	Link-state routing only sends routing updates every 15–30 minutes, or when there is a change in network topology.
Low processing overhead.	Increased route calculation processing.

Routing Information Protocol

RIP is an internal gateway protocol developed at the Xerox Palo Alto Research Center (PARC). It is a distance vector routing protocol initially targeted to the Xerox Network Systems (XNS) protocol, then was subsequently implemented for the TCP/IP protocol suite in the early 1980s. RIP has also been implemented on AppleTalk networks, where it has been called Routing Table Maintenance Protocol (RTMP), as well as on Novell's NetWare. Given the penetration of TCP/IP in enterprise networks, it is not surprising that RIP is fairly common and that many products today have RIP implementations. It uses a datagram protocol for proliferating routing tables. RIP's characteristic features are:

- A hop count representing the number of routers the PDU needs to pass through to reach a destination (subnetwork) is employed to assess the distance between a source and a destination. A router is defined to be one hop in distance from directly connected networks, two hops in distance from networks that are reachable from one other router, and so on. The maximum number of hops allowed is 15 (a destination/subnetwork is considered unreachable if it has 16 or more hops).

- RIP recognizes two types of user devices: active and passive. Active users, (e.g., routers), advertise their view of the routes via a broadcast over their networks. Passive users (e.g., hosts, servers), receive and update their route information based on the RIP broadcasts, but do not themselves advertise routes. Updates to routing tables are sent by active users (e.g., routers) every 30 seconds. A routing update, however, is sent immediately in case of a network topology change, such as a communications link outage. A RIP broadcast is a listing of pairs showing (a) every network the sender of the RIP message can reach, and (b) the distance, in hops, to that network. Note that if route information is received indicating a lower count hop than the current route, the new route through the neighboring router that issued the update is designated to be the actual path to be used from that instance onward.

- Routes are considered disconnected (timed-out after 180 seconds) from a given router's point of view, unless an update for that path is received by the router. In other words, route information received by RIP is considered valid for only 180 seconds. By implication, the inference is that when a route fails, the internetwork is "made aware" of this occurrence by the lack of a route update. The implicit assumption is that routes fail very frequently. This may or may not be the case in modern internetworks, although one can make the argument that the condition of the route (e.g., available bandwidth and/or ability to support a specified QoS, particularly in an ATM network) changes over time; this could occur in support of switched virtual connection (SVC) routes over ATM.

RIP has a number of limitations. For example, because RIP was originally developed to be used for LANs, and therefore uses broadcast techniques, it becomes inefficient for internetworks (particularly those involving WANs) because it requires a nontrivial amount of bandwidth to operate. Even within an Ethernet it increases the traffic and, consequently, the MAC-level contention. Furthermore, if/when a destination becomes unreachable, the time required for this status information to propagate to all routers in the network can be significant. Additionally, incorrect route information may be propagated in case of link failure. As noted, the number of allowed hops is kept to less than 16, in an effort to alleviate some of the difficulties just described. In turn, this implies that RIP is unsuitable for networks of medium-to-large diameters. Finally, some vendors offer extensions that are not uniformly supported or implemented.

Interior Gateway Routing Protocol

IGRP is a Cisco-proprietary distance vector internal gateway protocol, intended as a RIP enhancement. Though only Cisco routers support IGRP, IGRP routing information can be redistributed to other routing protocols. Because RIP uses just hop count as its routing metric, it often cannot select the best route. IGRP addresses this limitation by defining a routing metric that includes:

- Bandwidth of route
- Congestion of the route
- Latency along the route
- Maximum Transfer Unit (MTU) of the network in the route
- Reliability of the links in the route

IGRP is a popular protocol for routing IP because of the vendor's market share. (Cisco has also brought forth an enhanced version called EIGRP, now broadly deployed.)

Exterior Gateway Protocol

EGP is a distance vector protocol that does not employ routing metrics. Hence, it only propagates reachability information; it advertises which networks are available through which routers. EGP is used when two or more autonomous networks need to exchange routing information. EGP uses point-to-point communication, rather than broadcast. When a router employs EGP to communicate with another autonomous network, the router is called an *exterior gateway*. EGP (RFC 904) was developed by the IETF in the mid-1980s; it is used on the Internet to exchange reachability information between routers forming the Internet backbone. (Note: EGP is being phased out in favor of the BGP.) EGP supports the following functions:

Neighbor acquisition.   Enables handshaking between two exterior gateways to exchange reachability data.

Polling neighbors for responses.   This refers to neighbors in logical proximity, not necessarily (but not excluding) neighbors in topological proximity. It entails request and confirmation of the "acquisition" of a neighbor. EGP uses a "Hello" message to test neighbors. Specifically, EGP uses the poll function to force a reachability update of its tables.

Transfer of reachability information.   EGP only transfers information (e.g., distance metrics) related to its own autonomous network. It is now being replaced because of its limitations.

Border Gateway Protocol

BGP (RFC 1163, 1990) is a distance vector exterior routing protocol (technically, it is a path vector protocol) developed by the IETF as an enhancement to EGP for interdomain applications such as the Internet. In effect, BGP aims at replacing EGP by providing additional features to address some of EGP's limitations. The enhanced capabilities include: support for policy-based routing, and use of an authentication apparatus to guard against unauthorized updates to routing tables. BGP was designed so that the exchange of reachability information takes place only with other BGP gateways, limiting the amount of traffic that has to go across the internet. Also, the protocol supports the maintenance of a virtual connection between two endsystems for the exchange of entire routing tables and table updates.

BGP routing updates consist of a pair composed of a network number and an autonomous system path (this path is simply a list of all autonomous systems that must be traversed to reach a specific network). Given that BGP enumerates the complete route to the destination, routing loops are avoided and convergence is expedited. To ensure reliable transfer of routing information, BGP utilizes TCP as its transport mechanism.

This most-important Internet protocol is discussed in greater detail later in the chapter.

Open Shortest Path First

OSPF is a link-state internal gateway protocol developed by the IETF. It is an open protocol specification defined in RFC 1247; it has full Internet-standard protocol status. OSPF aims at allowing more optimized routing compared to distance vector protocols by supporting user-definable, least-cost, multipath routing. Each router contains a routing directory that identifies the router's active interfaces, along with status information about adjacent routers. OSPF supports the definition of contiguous networks and systems as isolated network segments ("areas"), to reduce the amount of information required at each router related to its autonomous network. A router using OSPF calculates the shortest path to the other routers in the autonomous network by considering itself as the root. This information is periodically proliferated to all routers in the same autonomous network. OSPF:

- Authenticates routing update information to ascertain it is valid.
- Converges rapidly upon network topology changes.
- Is resilient to routing loops.
- Supports load balancing across multiple communication links/services, because it can store multiple routes for a destination.
- Supports type-of-service routing, such as link bandwidth or expected link latency.

OSPF routers use a number of "advertisement" techniques [7]:

Router links advertisement. An area-specific advertisement carrying information about links in one area; the advertisement is flooded only throughout that area.

Networks links advertisement. Employed by a broadcast network to transmit a list of all routers connected to a network; the advertisement is flooded only throughout an area.

Summary links advertisement. Employed by border routers to proliferate information on routes inside an autonomous network; the advertisement is flooded only throughout an area.

Autonomous system extended links advertisement. These advertisements used by boundary routers contain information on routes in other autonomous systems; they are flooded throughout an autonomous network.

Multiprotocol Routing

As already described, many of today's routers fall in the multiprotocol category. This implies that these devices can route PDU-form multiple protocols suites simultaneously (e.g., TCP/IP, DECnet, IPX, and AppleTalk). Typically, separate routing protocols are used to build the tables needed to route the specific suite-dependent PDUs. For example, a router routing four distinct protocols may have to use that many distinct routing protocols, one for each suite. Routing protocols do not share routing information or otherwise interact with each other, which is why this approach is called "ships in the night." The advantage of such an approach is that modifications to any protocol do not affect any other protocol being routed; the disadvantage is increased communication bandwidth and router processing requirements. Efforts are underway to develop integrated routing schemes where a single routing protocol can be used.

8.3.4 A Synopsis of IPv4

In a TCP/IP environment, IP provides the underlying mechanism to transfer information from one endsystem on one LAN to another endsystem on the same or different LAN.[1] The current version of IP is known as IPv4. IP makes the underlying network transparent to the upper layers, TCP in particular. It is a connectionless protocol, whereby each IP PDU is treated independently. In this context, PDUs are also called datagrams. IP provides two basic services: addressing and fragmentation/reassembly of long TCP PDUs. IP adds no guarantee of delivery, reliability, flow control, or error recovery to the underlying network other than the data link layer mechanism already provided. IP expects the higher layers to handle such functions. IP may lose PDUs, deliver them out of order, or duplicate them; IP defers these problems to the higher layers (TCP, in particular). Effectively, IP delivers PDUs on a best-effort basis. There are no network connections, physical or virtual, maintained by IP.

To provide its services, IP employs key header fields for the PCI:

Addresses (source and destination).   IP address of sending and receiving entity.

Data Unit ID.   Unique integer that identifies the datagram, allowing the destination to collect datagram fragments into an integral datagram.

Type of service.   Parameters set by the endstation specifying, for example, expected delay characteristics, expected reliability of path, and so on.

Time-to-Live.   Parameter used to determine the PDU's lifetime in the interconnected system.

Options.   Parameters to specify security, timestamps, and special routing.

Header checksum.   A two-octet field used by IP to determine PDU integrity (however, no corrective action is supported).

The full format of the IP PDU is covered in a later section.

IP Addresses

IP addressing provides a way to identify a device on an internet. A PDU that is coming down the stack of a PC or host connected to the network contains the IP address of the origination as well as the address of the destination. If the destination device is on the same network as the originating device, the PDU will be directly "absorbed" by the destination. If the network is different from the network of the originating device, the PDU must first be routed to that remote network (or some intermediate network), where it will be "absorbed" by the intended device.

An IP address consists of a network address used to identify the network to which a device (also called a host) such as a PC, terminal, or computer is connected, and an identifier for the device itself. It is 32 bits in length. An IP address can be represented as:

```
AdrType|netID|hostID.
```

Each "official" IP address must be unique, because of the requirement to interconnect a multitude of networks with a worldwide backbone (the Internet). Overall responsibility for IP addresses administration rests with the Internet Assigned Number Authority (IANA).

Traditionally there have been five standardized ways to describe how the 32 bits are to be allocated; these are referred to as Classes A, B, C, D, and E. These classes are used to accommodate different requirements in terms of enterprise size.

Address Class A.   Utilizes the first bit of the 32-bit space (bit 0) to identify it as a Class A address; this bit is set to 0. Bits 1 to 7 represent the network ID, and bits 8 to 31 identify the PC, terminal, or host on the network. Clearly, every device and every network has a unique identifier. This address supports $2^7 - 2 = 126$ networks and approximately 16 million ($2^{24} - 2$) devices on each network. IP prohibits the use of an all ones or all zeroes address for both the network and the device ID (which is the reason for subtracting 2).

Address Class B. Utilizes the first two bits (bit 0 and 1) to identify it as a Class B address. These bits are set to 10. Bits 2 to 15 are used for network IDs, and bits 16 to 31 are used for device IDs. This address supports $2^{14} - 2 = 16,382$ networks and $2^{16} - 2 = 65,134$ devices on each network.

Address Class C. Utilizes the first three bits to identify it as a Class C address. These bits are set to 110. Bits 3 to 23 are used for network IDs, and bits 24 to 31 are used for device IDs. This address supports more than 2 million ($2^{21} - 2$) networks and $2^8 - 2 = 254$ devices on each network.

Address Class D. Used for multicasting (multiple devices receive the same IP-level PDU).

Address Class E. Reserved for "future use."

An address with all bits equal to 0 represents "this" (this network or local host); an address with all bits equal to 1 stands for "all" (all networks or hosts). Large organizations have typically been granted Class B addresses (universities, Fortune 100 companies, etc.). Organizations with a large number of networks are assigned Class C. Early participants in the Internet have Class A addresses. Class A addresses are assigned to networks with a large number of devices; Class C addresses are assigned to networks with a small number of devices. An extension mechanism (i.e., IPv6) will be required in the future when the address space may become exhausted. One drawback of this addressing scheme is that if a device or host moves from one network to another, its IP address must be changed.

NOTE Organizations that do not connect to the Internet, or connect only via a network firewall, do not need an official assignment in order to use the IP address scheme within the confines of their organization.

IP utilizes a simplified notation to represent, for ease of use and reference, the 32 binary bits. This notation is known as dotted decimal notation (DDN). Consider the example:

```
IP Address = 01111110011000011111111000111001 (Class A)
```

This number is broken down into four octets, as follows:

```
01111110-01100001-11111110-00111001
```

In turn, the octet is assumed to be the representation of a decimal number (between 0 and 255). In this example, one has:

```
01111110 = 126
01100001 = 97
11111110 = 254
00111001 = 57
```

Finally, the IP address is represented as 126.97.254.57. In fact, this notation can be used directly when specifying routing tables, since there is an internal translation function, so that the DDN number is automatically translated to binary.

Subnetwork Addressing

Usually, organizations have subnetworks that subtend the larger network (independent of the address class they may have). This is done for performance or administrative reasons. The establishment of subnetworks can be done locally, while the whole network still appears to be one IP network to the outside world. As discussed, the IP addresses consist of the pair:

```
<network address><host address>
```

IP allows a portion of the host/device field to be used to specify a subnetwork (the network ID portion cannot be changed). Subnetworks are an extension to this scheme by considering a part of the <host address> to be a "local network address," that is, the subnetwork address. IP addresses are then interpreted as:

```
<network address><subnetwork address><host address>.
```

For example, in Class A addressing, a subset of the bits from 8 to 31 could be employed for subnetwork identification. The partitioning of the original <host address> into a <subnetwork address> and <host address> can be done by the local administrator without restriction. However, once this partition has been established, it must be used consistently throughout the whole local network. Also, whereas bits can in theory be used freely, it is best to employ a contiguous set to represent the subnetwork.

Subnet masks are used to describe subnetworks; they tell devices residing on the network how to interpret the device ID portion of the IP address. The address-checking software in each device is informed via the subnet mask not to treat the device ID exclusively as a device identifier, but as a subnetwork identifier followed by a (smaller) device identifier.

Naturally, since the address space is finite, there is a trade-off between the number of subnetworks that can be supported and the number of devices on each subnetwork.

The mask contains a bit for each bit in the IP address, although the "active ingredients" portion of the mask is really contained only in the section describing the device ID. If the bit is set in the IP address mask, the corresponding bit is to be treated as a subnetwork address. All unaffected bits in the left portion of the mask are set to 1. Bits set to 0 represent the actual extent of the device address. For example, consider the Class B IP address:

```
IP Address = 10|11111001100001|1111111000111001
```

where the symbol | is used only for visual convenience—it is not part of the address. Normally, the last 16 bits are used to identify devices on the (single) network (whose identity is 11111001100001). A mask of the form:

```
11|1111111111111|1111111111000000
```

implies that the first 10 binary positions of the device ID field are used to represent subnetworks. In addition to using the DDN as an address-representation scheme, it is also used to describe the subnet masks. Here, though, the representation is only a shorthand for the bit pattern of the mask, and clearly not an address. A LAN manager would specify the mask just described as:

```
11111111-11111111-11111111-11000000
```

or, compactly:

```
255.255.255.192
```

Class A addresses allow only the following masks: 255.xyz.abc.ghi (as seen later, not all 255 combinations actually make sense). Specifically, bits 0 to 7 cannot be altered to represent subnetworks, and so are shown in the mask as a string of eight ones. This arrangement allows considerable flexibility in terms of the number of subnetworks that can be defined. Class B addresses allow only the following subnet masks: 255.255.xyz.abc. This class affords a fair degree of flexibility in terms of subnetworks. Class C addresses allow only the mask 255.255.255.xyz. It offers limited flexibility in terms of subnetworks; however, it still allows a balance between subnetworks and the number of devices per subnetwork.

With Class B, a typical subnet mask is 255.255.255.0. This corresponds to 11111111-11111111-11111111-00000000, meaning that the first two octets represent the network ID; the next octet represents a subnetwork ID; and the last octet represents a device ID. Up to 254 subnetworks, each with up to 254 devices, are supported. This octet-based partition for the network ID, the subnetwork ID, and the device ID is easy to parse, making routing decisions simple. An example of a network address could be 128.79.xyz.abc. If one wanted only the last six bits to represent device addresses, then the encoding would be 255.255.252.192 (i.e., the last octet would be 11000000).

As hinted earlier, not all masks are easy to or useful to deal with. In the example just given, a mask of 255.255.255.17 would imply the following binary pattern:

```
11111111-11111111-11111111-00010001
```

This would imply that bits 27 and 31 represent the subnetwork ID. Such an address would be difficult to parse. It is preferable to use representations that result in a contiguous stream of zeroes and ones.

All the devices in a subnetwork must use and implement the same address mask. However, an IP router node uses the full four-octet address to route to the destination network, and so it is not required to interpret the subnetwork field on the transmit side.

Due to the way IP addresses are segmented into classes of networks, much of the address space is "wasted." In particular, addresses for Class B networks are largely used up. The Internet community has adopted a scheme, called classless interdomain routing (CIDR) that will preserve addresses by abandoning the old class rules. CIDR is expected to provide relief in the foreseeable future. The IETF is working on the next generation of the IP suite of protocols, specifically IPv6. The class-based scheme may continue to be used in enterprise networks.

Classless Interdomain Routing (CIDR)

Tightly coupled to routing are the issues involving IP address allocation and management. Throughout the Internet's history, until approximately 1992, IP address use has been associated with *classfull allocations* discussed in the previous section. Classfull allocation is typically referred to as Class A, Class B, and Class C, and is a way of looking at the address space where each class has a predefined number of addresses and is easily identified by its prefix. For example, a class C address is restricted to a single octet, and therefore can accommodate 254 hosts.

Classfull IP addresses posed two critical problems to the Internet. First, by 1991, the rate and way addresses were being consumed were accelerating dramatically, and there was fear that the pool of free addresses would disappear. The second problem posed by classfull IP addresses is that each requires an entry in the routers forwarding table. This is a critical problem for ISPs because, until 1995, routing tables were growing at an alarming rate (see Figure 8.3).

To cope with the problems associated with classfull address allocation, a new means of utilizing addresses was required. CIDR allows a network in the Internet to be represented by a prefix and a number representing the subnet mask length. CIDR's allocation scheme creates the capability for address aggregation, the practice of aggregating a contiguous block of addresses into a single routing table entry.

The CIDR allocation of IP addresses then is very different from IP Classes A, B, and C. For example 198.100.0.0/16, is the notation for a CIDR allocation in which 198.100 is the beginning of a collection of aggregated Class C networks. The /16 notation designates that the subnetwork mask contains 16 bits, and therefore, a total of 256 traditional Class C networks will be aggregated into this block.

When a traditional classfull IP address is allocated into a larger aggregate than is legally possible in the classless domain, as a product of CIDR's use, the result is called a supernetwork. Supernetworks are only possible with a CIDR allocation, and are easily identifiable because the new CIDR network mask is larger than the classfull allocation's natural mask.

One of the key advantages of CIDR supernetwork aggregation that can be seen in the previous example is that the ISP routing table entry for the

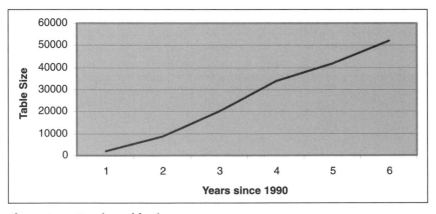

Figure 8.3   Routing table sizes.

individual classfull networks would be substantially larger than without CIDR aggregation. Networks that are subsets of an aggregate are sometimes called *more specific* because they provide greater detail for routing reachability. If there were more than one entry in the IP routing table for the subnetwork, then the forwarding process would always select the longest match; that is, it would select the most specific routing entry.

This efficiency of routing table utilization in this example, replacing 256 entries with just one, has successfully curbed the growth of Internet backbone routing tables. However, there are two potential pitfalls to CIDR aggregation. First, the IP addresses used by customers must be taken from their ISP's address space. If a customer subscribes to one ISP service and is allocated IP addresses, and then decides to change to a different provider, while keeping the same addresses, the CIDR block will no longer be aggregated. The second possible problem with CIDR involves customers who are connected to multiple ISPs. Because they are *multihomed*—that is, connected more than once—each ISP must advertise reachability to the customer, and this may lead to routes that are not in aggregated blocks.

IP Routing Tables

A key function of the internetworking layer is to support routing. Basic IP routers (also known as gateways with partial routing information) only have information about the devices directly attached to the physical networks to which this gateway is attached. The IP routing table contains information about the locally attached networks and IP addresses of other gateways located on these networks, in addition to the networks they attach to. The table can be extended with information on IP networks that are further away, and can contain a default route, but it still remains a table with limited information. Hence, this kind of gateway is called a gateway with partial routing information. Gateways (routers) with partial information are characterized by the following:

- They do not have knowledge about all interconnected networks.

- They allow local autonomy in establishing and modifying routes.

- Routing entry errors in one gateway may introduce inconsistencies, thereby making part of the network unreachable.

Some configurations require more than just the basic routing function; these configurations require a gateway-to-gateway (i.e., router-to-router) communication mechanism to relay routing information. A more sophisticated gateway (router) system is required if:

- The gateway (router) needs to know routes to all possible IP networks.

- The gateway (router) needs to have dynamic routing tables. Dynamic routing tables are kept up to date with minimal or no manual intervention.

- The gateway (router) has to be able to convey local changes to other gateways.

If the destination device is attached to a network to which the source host is also attached, information can be sent directly by encapsulating the IP PDU in the physical network frame. This is called *direct delivery/ direct routing*. When the destination device is not on a network directly accessible to the source host, indirect routing occurs. Here, the indented destination must be reached via one or more IP routers (i.e., hop-by-hop routing). The address of the first of these gateways (the first hop) is called an indirect route. The address of the first gateway is needed by the source device in order to initiate the delivery of the information.

This simple view of the world makes the routing table relatively straightforward. A router keeps tracks of two sets of addresses in the IP routing table:

1. Devices attached to networks that are directly accessible. These devices have the same IP network ID address as the IP network ID of the source gateway/host itself.

2. For "indirect" hosts, the only knowledge required is the IP address of the "next gateway," a gateway leading to the destination "IP network."

Additionally, the table contains a default route, which contains the (direct or indirect) route to be used in case the destination IP network is not otherwise identified.

IP relaying is based on the network ID portion of the destination IP address. The device ID portion of the address plays no part at this stage. On the incoming side, arriving IP PDUs are checked to determine if the IP address on the PDU coincides with the IP address of the local network (that address can be thought as being assigned to the IP router, rather than something more abstract as a network). If the addresses match, the PDU is passed up to the upper portions of the protocol stack. If the address does not match, the IP router checks its routing tables to determine on which physical outgoing path the PDU should be directed.

The fundamental operation for gateways is as follows: An incoming IP PDU that contains a "destination IP address," other than the local host or gateway IP address (or addresses), is treated as a normal outgoing IP PDU. Any outgoing IP PDU is subject to the IP routing algorithm of the gateway/host in question. The host/gateway selects the next hop for the PDU (the next device/gateway/host to send it to) by checking its routing table. This new destination can be attached to any of the physical networks to which the gateway/host is connected. If this network is a different physical network from the one on which the gateway/host originally received the IP PDU, then the net result is that the local gateway/host has forwarded the IP PDU from one physical network to another.

IP Protocol Data Unit

The format of an IP PDU is shown in Figure 8.4. It is 20 or more octets long. A partial discussion of the fields, their purpose, and format follows.

The VERS field describes the version of the IP protocol, for example, version 4. The LEN field is the length of the IP header counted in 32-bit

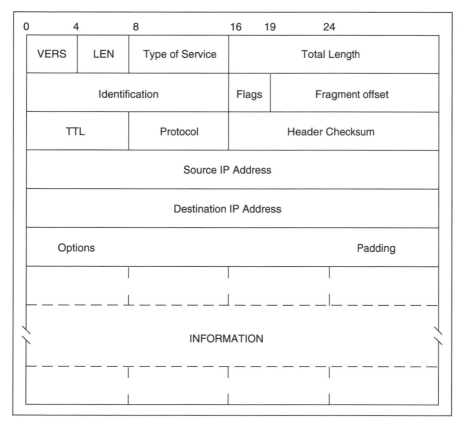

Figure 8.4 IP PDU.

units. The Type-of-Service field describes the quality of service requested by the sender for this IP PDU. It has the format:

```
Precedence|D|T|R|xxx
```

where Precedence is an indication of the priority of the IP PDU; D specifies whether this IP PDU can be delayed (0) or cannot be delayed (1); T indicates the type of throughput desired (0 = normal, 1 = high); R specifies whether reliable subnetwork is required (1) or not (0); and xxx is reserved for future use. The precedence options are: Routine (000), Priority (001), Immediate (010), Flash (011), Flash Override (100), Critical (101), Internetwork Control (110), and Network Control (111). This field could be used to support CoS, if routers implemented appropriate parsing and handling (in general they do not).

The Total-Length field specifies the length of the entire IP PDU. Since the IP PDU is encapsulated in the underlying network frame (e.g., LLC and then MAC), its length is constrained by the frame size of the underlying network. For example, as mentioned, the Ethernet limitation is 1,500 octets. However, IP itself deals with this limitation by using segmentation and reassembly (SAR) (also called fragmentation and defragmentation). IP does require, however, that all underlying networks be able to handle IP PDUs up to 576 octets in length without having to use SAR capabilities. Fragments of an IP PDU all have a header, basically copied from the original IP PDU, and segments of the data. They are treated as normal IP PDUs while being transported to the destination. However, if one of the fragments gets lost, the entire IP PDU is declared lost since IP does not support an acknowledgment mechanism; any fragments that have been delivered will be discarded by the destination. More information on segmentation is provided later.

The Identification field contains a unique number assigned by the sender to aid in reassembling a fragmented IP PDU (all fragments of an initial IP PDU have the same and unique identification number). The Flags field is of the form 0 | DF | MF, where DF specifies if the IP PDU can be segmented (0) or not (1); and MF specifies if there are more segments (1) or no more segments, the present one being the last (0).

The Fragment-Offset field is used with fragmented IP PDUs and aids in the reassembly process. The value represents the number of 64-bit blocks (excluding header octets) that are contained in earlier fragments. In the first segment (or if the IP PDU consists of a single segment), the value is set to 0.

The Time-to-Live (TTL) field specifies the time in seconds that this IP PDU is allowed to remain in circulation. Each IP gateway (router) through which this IP PDU passes subtracts from this field the processing time expended on this IP PDU (each gateway is requested to subtract at least one unit from this counter). When the value of the field reaches 0, it is assumed that this IP PDU has been traveling in a loop and is therefore discarded.

The Protocol field indicates the higher-level protocols to which this gateway should deliver the data. A large number of protocols are defined. For example, a code of decimal 6 (= 00000110) means TCP; 29 is for ISP TP4; 10 is for BBN's RCC; 22 is for Xerox's IDP; 66 MIT's RVD; and so on.

The Header-Checksum field is a checksum covering the header (only). It is calculated as the 16-bit ones complement of the ones complement sum of all 16-bit words in the header (for the purpose of the calculation, the Header-Checksum field is assumed to be all zeroes).

The Source IP Address field contains the 32-bit IP address of the device sending this IP PDU. The Destination IP Address field contains the destination for this IP PDU. These addresses conform with the format described earlier.

The Options field (which must be processed by all devices in the interconnected network, although not all devices must be able to generate such field) defines additional specific capabilities. These include explicit routing information, record route traveled, and timestamping.

IP Segmentation

As IP PDUs travel from one network to another, they may run across networks that have a maximum frame size smaller than the length of the IP PDU. This precludes the placement of an IP PDU into a single network frame. A procedure is required to fragment long IP PDUs and reassemble them at the receiving end. An unfragmented IP PDU has the More Segments flag bit set to 0; the fragment offset is also set to 0. A router is not required to reassemble a fragmented PDU, unless the PDU carries the address of that router.

When fragmentation is required, the following tasks are undertaken.

1. The "DF flag" is checked to determine if fragmentation is allowed. If it is not allowed, the IP PDU is discarded.

2. The "Information field" is segmented into two or more parts, each having a length, in octets, that is a multiple of 8 (the last fragment is padded, if needed, to meet this criterion).

3. All information portions are placed in the IP PDU. The header of the "Continuation of Message" PDU is the same as the "Begin of Message" PDU, with the following modifications:

   3.1. The "More Fragments" flag is set to 1, except for the last fragment.

3.2. The "Fragment Offset" field is set to the location this data portion occupied in the original IP PDU, relative to the beginning of the original unfragmented IP PDU.

3.3. If "Options" were included in the original IP PDU, the type of option determines whether or not these options will be copied into all fragment IP PDUs or just to the first one.

3.4. The "Header Checksum" field is recomputed.

4. Each of these fragmented IP PDUs is now transmitted as a normal IP PDU.

At the destination, the information has to be reassembled into one IP PDU. The "identification field" of the IP PDU was set by the sending device as a unique number, from that sending device's perspective. The fragmentation process does not alter this field. Incoming fragments can, therefore, be identified and associated (this ID must be used in conjunction with the source and destination IP address in the IP PDU). A buffer, managed by a timer, is employed at the destination to undertake the reassembly process.

NOTE The length field in each fragment refers only to the size of that segment, not the entire PDU. The receiving end has an understanding of the length of the PDU by way of a prenegotiated MTU size (which specifies nominal, actually maximum size), as well as using the OFFSET and "more segments" flag mechanism. That is accomplished at the TCP layer (using the SYN bit) when a TCP session is started—usually, most hosts limit this to 576 bytes. The IP fragmentation should therefore only occur when an expected lower MTU is found in a subnet (say following a rerouted occurrence) than initially negotiated. For UDP, applications such as SNMP typically prelimit the MTU to 576.

Address Resolution Protocol

The Address Resolution Protocol (ARP) performs a key function: It is responsible for binding higher-level addresses (IP addresses) to physical network addresses. Individual hosts or devices are identified on the network by their physical hardware address.

As discussed, higher-layer processes (and protocols) address destinations use a symbolic IP address. When such a higher-layer process needs to send a PDU to a destination, it uses its IP address expressed as w.x.y.z, discussed earlier. The device driver does not know how to interpret this address. Consequently, the ARP module is provided to take care of the translation of the IP address to the physical address of the destination device. ARP uses a table (also known as the ARP cache) to perform this translation.

When the address is not found in the ARP cache, a broadcast message, called the ARP request, is sent over the network. If one of the devices on the network recognizes its own IP address in the request, it sends an ARP reply to the requesting entity. The reply contains the physical hardware address of the destination. This newly received address is then placed in the ARP cache of the requesting device. All subsequent PDUs to this destination IP address can now be directly translated to a physical address, which is used by the sender's device driver to transmit the PDU on the network.

Reverse Address Resolution Protocol

Some network devices, such as diskless workstations, do not immediately know their own IP address when they are booted. To determine their own IP address, they must use a mechanism similar to ARP. In this case, the hardware address of the device is the known parameter and the IP address the required parameter. This protocol differs from ARP in that a "RARP server" must exist on the network, which maintains database mappings from the hardware address to the protocol address.

8.3.5 SLIP/PPP: Extending Routing Capabilities Off-Net

There has been an increasing interest in defining methods for achieving IP host connections over dial-up lines rather than leased lines or other more complex WAN services. This requirement is in support of access to the Internet, or as a way to extend an enterprise network to smaller sites; for example, for telecommuting purposes [8]. There are now two schemes for transmission over serial point-to-point lines, which were introduced in Chapter 2: the Serial Line Interface Protocol (SLIP) and the Point-to-Point Protocol (PPP). SLIP is limited for use with IP; PPP, on the other hand, may be used for IP as well as for other network layer protocols. SLIP and PPP are used in Internet (access subnetwork) applications.

Point-to-point dial-up links between LANs, PCs, and routers can provide adequate connectivity in some application environments. Increasingly, commercial services provider support access to the Internet, and point-to-point links are a practical way to connect to the local provider. Until recently, what held back the introduction of this kind of connectivity for point-to-point IP links was the lack of an encapsulation protocol that was accepted either as a de facto or Internet standard. To solve this requirement, the Internet community has adopted two approaches for the transmission of IP PDUs over serial point-to-point lines, namely, SLIP and PPP.

SLIP

SLIP (RFC1055) is a widely used protocol. It is included in Berkeley Unix, Digital Equipment Corporation's Ultrix, Sun Microsystems' Unix, and a number of TCP/IP implementations for PCs. SLIP has been developed to support host-to-host, host-to-router, router-to-router, or PC-to-host communications over asynchronous or synchronous, leased or dial-up lines. It typically operates at speeds from 1.2 to 19.2Kbps, but can also be used at higher speeds.

The majority of SLIP implementations accept IP datagrams up to 1,006 octets in length. The datagrams are transmitted octet by octet over the serial line, preceded by a character called ESCAPE, octal 333, (not the same as the ASCII ESCAPE character) and followed by a character called END, octal 300. If a data octet in the IP datagram has the value octal 300, it is replaced with the two-octet sequence ESCAPE, octal 333, and octal 334. If a data octet in the IP datagram has the value octal 333, it is replaced with the two-octet sequence ESCAPE, octal 333, and octal 335. Because of its simplicity, however, SLIP has a number of limitations, including the following:

- SLIP does not provide a mechanism to communicate addressing information; hence, both ends in a SLIP connection must know each other's IP addresses to accomplish routing.

- SLIP has no protocol identification mechanism and, therefore, only a single protocol may be used over a SLIP connection. SLIP was designed for use with IP; however, SLIP frames are not constricted to contain a IP datagram; any higher-layer PDU can be carried, but only a single network layer protocol may be used over a single SLIP connection.

- SLIP does not provides error-correction or error-detection mechanisms, leaving the burden to the higher layers.

- SLIP does not provide a mechanism for PDU compression, which would be desirable in low-speed lines.

PPP

PPP is specified in RFC 1331 and ancillary, early 1990's documents (RFC 1220, 1332, 1333, 1334, 1334, 1376, 1377, and 1378). It defines a standardized encapsulation protocol for the transport of a variety of network layer protocols across serial, point-to-point links. The protocol also describes mechanisms for network-protocol multiplexing, link configuration, link-quality testing, authentication, header compression, error detection, and link-option negotiation [9]. PPP has three elements:

- A method for encapsulating datagrams over serial links, using the ISO High-level Data-Link Control (HDLC) protocol.

- A Link-Control Protocol (LCP) used for establishing, configuring, authenticating, and testing the data link connection.

- A set of Network-Control Protocols (NCPs) used for establishing and configuring different network layer protocols.

Figure 8.5 depicts the components of the PPP protocol stack. At the physical layer, PPP is designed to work over any asynchronous or synchronous (EIA-232-E, EIA-422, EIA-423, EIA-530, and ITU-T V.24 and V.35), dedicated or dial-up, full-duplex bit-serial circuit. PPP's data-link layer is based on HDLC for both the synchronous and asynchronous communications environments. An intermediary layer, the LCP, is used by the two communicating PPP devices to establish, configure, and terminate the data-link connection. Specifically, LCP procedures have been defined to allow agreement on the encapsulation format options, to handle vary-

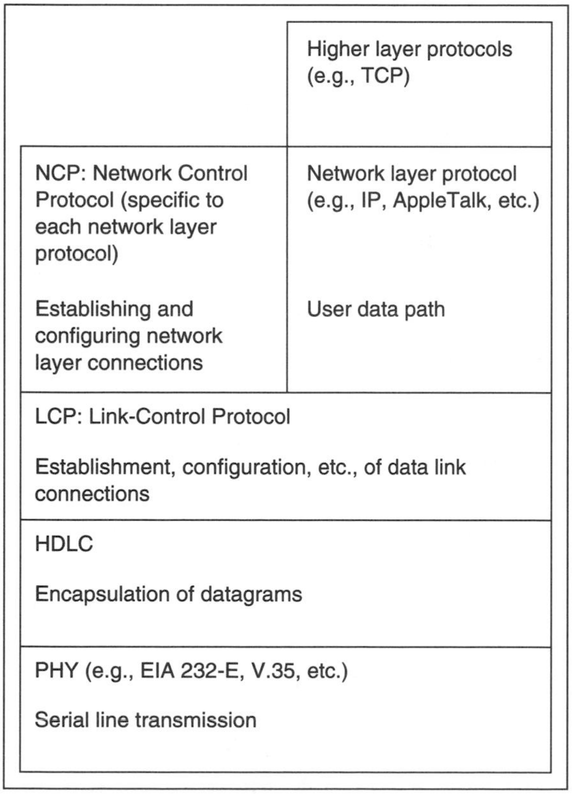

	Higher layer protocols (e.g., TCP)
NCP: Network Control Protocol (specific to each network layer protocol)	Network layer protocol (e.g., IP, AppleTalk, etc.)
Establishing and configuring network layer connections	User data path
LCP: Link-Control Protocol Establishment, configuration, etc., of data link connections	
HDLC Encapsulation of datagrams	
PHY (e.g., EIA 232-E, V.35, etc.) Serial line transmission	

Figure 8.5 PPP protocol stack.

Table 8.4   PPP Frame

Flag	Bit pattern 01111110, utilized to indicate the beginning and end of the frame.
Address	HDLC all-station address: Octet 11111111 (PPP does not assign individual station addresses).
Control	HDLC field indicating the frame type; contains any associated sequence numbers. In PPP, only HDLC unnumbered information frames (value 00000011) are used.
Protocol	Two-octet field used by PPP to identify the protocol encapsulated in the Information field.*
Information	A PDU consistent with the protocol identified in the Protocol field (default maximum size of this field is 1,500 octets, though larger PDUs may be supported).
Frame Check Sequence (FCS)	Cyclic redundancy check to detect bit errors (usually 16 bits in length, but may be extended by agreement between the users).

*To comply with HDLC's rules, the first octet must end with a 0 and the second octet must end with a 1.

ing limits on PDU size, to authenticate the identity of the hosts, to determine when a link is functioning properly and when it has failed, to detect a looped-back link, and to identify other common configuration problems [9]. LCP information is carried in the PPP/HDLC frame. Finally, two protocol stacks reside on top of the LCP: Network layer PDUs containing higher-layer information, are used to exchange user information; in parallel, NCP PDUs are utilized to exchange information to control the network layer protocol connections.

The PPP frame contains an opening flag field, an address field, a control field, a protocol field, the information field, a FCS field, and a closing flag field (see Table 8.4).

LCP PDUs are classified into one of three types according to function. The first type is Link-Configuration PDU, used to establish and configure a PPP link. The second type is Link-Termination PDU, used to terminate a PPP link. The third type is Link-Maintenance PDU, used to manage and debug a link. All LCP PDUs used to support configuration requests, link establishment/termination requests, and so on, have the same general format, as follows: a one-octet code field identifies the type of PDU (configure-request, configure-ack, configure-nak, configure-reject, terminate-request, terminate-ack, code-reject, protocol-reject, echo-request, echo-reply, and discard request); a one-octet identifier field is a number selected at random and used to associate requests and replies (any PDU sent in response to a request must contain the identical identifier-field value as the request); a two-octet length field indicating the length in octets of the entire LCP. Any other information, such as configuration options, follows the length field.

8.3.6 IPv6

The interest explosion in Internet-based communication, the plethora of web sites being established on a daily basis, the introduction of electronic commerce, and the proliferation of networked resources around the world may in the next few years exhaust the address space of IPv4.

Although the 32-bit address mechanism in IPv4 can handle more than 4 billion devices on about 16.7 million networks, the usable address space is more limited, particularly given the original address classification into Class A, B, and C. For example, an organization might have received a Class B address, but is not making full use of it. Figure 8.6 shows an example of this address inefficiency. Any time the administrator decides to subnet, a price must be paid in available devices. As is obvious from the examples and some calculation, the total number of devices under subnets is always less than the number of devices without subnetting.

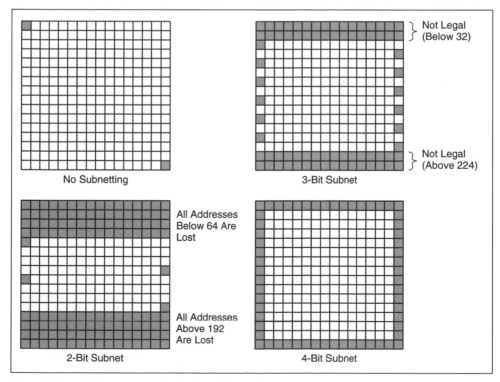

Figure 8.6   Address space limitations (Class C).

That is the trade-off for the ability to manage to network more easily. The lost addresses are all zeroes and all ones addresses for each subnet, and the all ones and all zeroes values for the subnet field itself. As one can see, the price of subnetting varies with the numbers of subnet bits and the class of network used.

The IETF started to look at this problem in 1991. Part of its 1992 recommendation was to consider "bigger Internet addresses." IPv6 has a 128-bit address. Preserving the current IP routing and addressing architecture while increasing the total size of the IP address space is just one possible way of supporting growth of the Internet. If the restriction on uniqueness of IP addresses within a private internet is relaxed, then the size of an internet (for example, the Internet) would no longer be bound by the size of the available IP address space. This would change the current architecture, but would also allow for the continued use of IPv4 without being constrained by the size of the IPv4 address space. One technology that supports connectivity in the presence of nonunique addresses is Network Address Translation (NAT) (RFC 1631). NAT technology allows each organization connected to the Internet to reuse the same block of addresses (for example, the addresses defined in RFC 1918), while requiring only a small number (relative to the total number of addresses used by the organization) of globally unique addresses for external connectivity. The case can be made that use of NAT devices represents a significant departure from the current IP routing and addressing architecture. However, widespread deployment of mediating gateways indicates that the traditional IP-level connectivity may not be that crucial, and that the connectivity provided by such gateways could be sufficient [10].

What is now called IPv6 originated from work known as Simple Internet Protocol Plus (SIPP). The group working on the protocol, also known at times as the SIPP Group, included the "working" IPv4 functions (though in some different locations in the IP header or by different names), and removed (or made optional) infrequently used or "nonworking" functions. Figure 8.7 depicts some highlights of IPv6 [11]. The protocol is described in RFC 1883; additional information on transition mechanisms can be found in RFC 1993 (see ds.InterNIC.net) [12]. The protocol has also been called IPng (IP Next Generation).

The IPv4 address space problem is just one factor motivating the development of IPv6. Some argue that today's IPv4 host implementations lack such features as autoconfiguration, network layer security, and others. IPv6 is intended to address most of the inadequacies in the existing IPv4 implementations, which will require the introduction of a new network layer header (IPv6). IPv6 removes the Header field, the IP Header checksum and changes the Time-to-Live field to become a Hop Count limit. See

Feature	Benefit
128-bit, Fixed-Length, Address	More levels of addressing hierarchy
Authentication Extension	Data integrity
Autoconfiguration Support	Ease of installation
Encryption Extension	Data confidentiality
Extended Option Headers	More and longer options available
Multicast Scope Field	Improved multicast routing scale ability
Option Encoding	Incremental deployment with minimum disruption
Quality of Service	Special router handling via flow label
Regional Cluster Addressing	Extra source, path control
Simplified Header Format	Reduce common processing and bandwidth
Source Demand Route Support	Source directed routing
Transition Plan	Incremental migration

Figure 8.7   Highlights of IPv6.

Figure 8.8. IPv6 is identified in the Ethertype field in the SNAP/LLC with the siglum 86dd hex instead of 0800 hex.

Although IPv6 significantly increases the total size of the available IP address space, the challenge is: Is this increased space sufficient to enable the continuous growth of the Internet? Within the current IP routing and addressing architecture, IP addressing must be unambiguous, but this is not sufficient to guarantee IP-level reachability within an internet. Within the current architecture, the role of IP addresses is not just to enumerate all the nodes (hosts and routers) within an internet, but to provide a capability for routing (IP-level reachability) to all the nodes within the internet. Therefore, in order to support an uninterrupted growth of the Internet while maintaining the current IP routing and addressing architecture, not only is a larger IP address space needed, but the assignment of addresses must also enable scalable routing [10].

4 bits	4 bits	3 Bytes	2 Bytes	1 Byte	1 Byte	16 Bytes	16 Bytes
Version	Priority	Flow Label	Length	Next Header	Hop Limit	Source	Target

Figure 8.8   New network layer header (IPv6).

Specifically, minimizing routing overhead, and thus making the IP address space routable, is one the fundamental problems in the current Internet. As the Internet grows, this problem is likely to become even more onerous. Without providing an adequate solution to this problem, increasing the total size of the available IP address space (by introducing IPv6) may not be adequate, because this would not increase the total amount of the routable IP address space, and thus would not help to sustain the growth of the Internet. Fortunately, hierarchical routing is expected to scale even for the size of the Internet that could be realized with the IPv6 address space. Therefore, for the foreseeable future, the Internet routing system (both for IPv4 and IPv6 address space) will rely on the technique of hierarchical routing [10]. However, the use of hierarchical routing mandates the use of routers. While this is good for the technology providers, it may not in the end be all that great for the organization, since routers have traditionally been expensive.

IPv6 Addressing

IPv6 supports three types of addresses in the target field: unicast, multicast, and anycast (the source field must be a unicast address). A unicast address is unique to the interface/device it names. In IPv6, there is no broadcast IP address. A multicast address identifies a group of interfaces.

Each of these interfaces/devices also has a unicast address. The multicast address is utilized to send information to sets of interfaces (e.g., in support of a videoconference). One can designate a multicast address for every interface/device in a network or subnetwork. The anycast address is new to IPv6. The network assumes the responsibility of delivering the PDU, with this target address, to any one in an anycast group/set of addresses. Examples could be the DHCP server, an Internet relay chat server, and so on.

IPv4 used the byte-dot-byte, or dotted decimal notation. In IPv6, colons are used to separate the address into eight 16-bit segments, as shown in Figure 8.9. A compact notation is also in use:

- If any segment has a value less than 1000 hex, the leading zeroes are omitted.
- If any of the segments has a value of 0, the address is written without anything between the pertinent colons. Note: The double-colon abbreviation can be used only once in an address.

IPv6 utilizes a hierarchy of bits in the address range (from most significant to least significant). The leftmost bits in the address signify a variable length address prefix; this variable length currently ranges between 3 and 10 bits. Figure 8.10 shows the prefixes that have been assigned (other pre-

```
1234:0567:0089:000A:0000:000B:00CD:0EF0
```
                                                      IPv6 Standard Written Format

```
        1234:567:89:A:0:B:CD:EF0
```
                                                      IPv6 16-Byte Read Format

```
        1234:567:89:A::B:CD:EF0
```
                                                      IPv6 Compact Format

Figure 8.9   Colons separate the address into eight 16-bit segments.

fixes have the status of "unassigned"). Some of the reserved addresses have special meaning, as described in Table 8.5.

Currently defined IPv6 address allocation architecture (RFC 1887) is similar, if not identical, to the IPv4 address allocation architecture; both are based on hierarchical hop-by-hop routing, and specifically, on CIDR (RFC 1518, RFC 1519). As a result, the IPv6 routing architecture does not offer any significant improvements over the IPv4 hop-by-hop routing architecture. At the same time, if the technique of hierarchical routing can provide enough scalability to the larger Internet than could be created using the IPv6 address space, then one can argue that the IPv6 routing architecture does not need to offer any significant improvement over the IPv4 routing architecture with respect to its capability to scale—the IPv4 routing architecture could be used by IPv6 as well. Therefore, by combining hierarchical routing and very large IP address spaces, IPv6 would make it possible to sustain the growth of the Internet for the foreseeable future [10].

Binary	Allocation
0000 0000	Reserved
0000 001	ISO Network Address
0000 010	Novell (IPX) Network Addresses
010	Provider-based Unicast Addresses
100	Geographic-based Unicast Addresses
1111 1110 10	Link Local Addresses
1111 1110 11	Site Local Address
1111 1111	Multicast Address

Figure 8.10   Prefixes assigned.

Table 8.5   Special IPv6 Addresses

FUNCTION	ADDRESS	PURPOSE
Unspecified Address	0:0:0:0:0:0:0:0	Used when one does not have the true address. Example: A device requests a server for an IP address; while waiting, the device can use the unspecified address as the source address for any message it must send (the unspecified address is not allowed as a target).
Loopback Address	0:0:0:0:0:0:0:1	Used for diagnostic purposes. The message never leaves the system, but can be used to test the protocol stack without having to rely on the network (the system sees a message leave and one arrive, but in fact it is the same loopback message).
Subnet-Router Address		An anycast address that IPv6 builds by using a nonzero subnet prefix followed by zeroes. The prefix identifies a particular subnet.
IPv4 Compatible Address	Example: If IPv4 address is 192.153.185.101 dec. or C0 99 B9 65 hex, then IPv4-compatible address is 0000:0000:0000:0000:0000:0000:C099:B965.	Used to support transition between IPv4 and IPv6. IPv6 devices can communicate with each other over an IPv4 network. The IPv4-compatible address system uses routers at the crossover point between the IPv4 and the IPv6 domains. The dual-IP router will convert the IPv4-compatible address to a normal IPv4 address to travel over the IPv4 network. At the entry point of the remote IPv6 network, another dual-IP router reverses the address substitution process.
IPv4 Mapped Address	Example: If IPv4 address is 192.153.185.101 dec. or C0 99 B9 65 hex, then IPv4-mapped address is 0000:0000:0000:0000:0000:FFFF:C099:B965.	These addresses identify systems that do not support IPv6. Routers may convert these addresses, but IPv6-addresses systems utilize them to communicate with IPv4-only systems.

Header Format

The header for IPv6 is the same length as the header of IPv4, but since the addresses (source and destination) are much longer, the rest of the header has to be simpler, so that the protocol is also simpler. Many of the IPv4 header functions are carried as extension headers. The fields are as follows:

Version.   The version of the protocol, now 6.

Priority.   This 4-bit nibble replaces the functions of the Precedence field in IPv4. The lower the priority value, the more willing the source is to have a router discard the PDU.

Flow Label.   This 3-byte field is used to request special handling of the PDU in the router(s). The designers see this field as important for running TCP/IP over high-speed networks, such as ATM. The source IP address and the Flow Label define a flow. This is a sequence of PDUs, for which the source wants special handing (typically in terms of QoS and performance) is the flow that the label defines. The routers that recognize the Flow Label can avoid routing tasks at the network layer (e.g., looking up a routing table), and simply follow the previous calculations/assignments that it made in forwarding previous PDUs in this flow. This is the concept of tag switching/net-flows/MPLS discussed in Chapter 5. Typically, the Flow Label is used to reserve resources on the target/destination system. By using the same Flow Label for all the PDUs during the session, the routers and endsystems reserve network and endsystem resources. By looking up only the Flow Label (clearly a less complex function on 3 bytes than looking up the entire address on 16 bytes), the router can decide how to forward the PDU. A system that does not support the Flow Label function must set this field to 0 for originating PDU, pass/route PDUs without changing the field when forwarding PDUs, and ignore the field when receiving PDUs. All PDUs with the same (no-zero) Flow Label must have the same destination address, hop-by-hop options header, routing header, and source address content.

Payload Length.   This 2-byte unsigned integer field specifies the length (in octets), of the PDU after the IPv6 header (by specification, the IPv6 header is fixed at 40 bytes, so the IPv4 Header length field is no longer needed).

Next Header Values.   This 1-byte field performs the same function as the IPv4 Protocol field. The listing in Figure 8.11 shows the currently defined values. Protocols shown in parentheses follow the order shown, based on the specification (RFC 1883); all other protocols (those without parentheses) follow that order (the exception is value 59: No Next Header). By following the recommendation's header order, the routers in the path can process the PDU more efficiently [11].

Hop Limit. This is the maximum number of nodes that may forward the PDU. Being an octet, the integer can be up to 255.

Source/Target Address. A 16-octet address of the sender/recipient of the PDU. (If a routing header is present, it may not be the ultimate destination.)

Transition Mechanisms: Host Address Autoconfiguration

The goal of IPv6 address autoconfiguration is to enable an IPv6 host to configure its IPv6 address without human intervention. Specifically, there is a desire to simplify configuration of new hosts and to enable existing hosts to

Value	Next Header	Order
00	Hop-by-Hop Option Header	1
04	Internet Protocol (IP)	
06	Transmission Control Protocol (TCP)	
17	User Datagram Protocol (UDP)	
43	Routing Header	3
44	Fragment	4
45	Interdomain Routing Protocol (IDRP)	
46	Resource Reservation Protocol (RSVP)	
50	Encapsulating Security Payload (ESP)	5
51	Authentication Header	6
58	Internet Control Message Protocol (ICMPv6)	
59	No Next Header	7
60	End-to-End Options Header	2 & 8

Figure 8.11 Currently defined values.

change (renumber) their addresses with the minimum amount of intervention in a minimally disruptive manner (graceful host renumbering).

To minimize disruption during host renumbering, it is important to take steps that would avoid (or at least minimize) forceful termination of established communications between the host that has to be renumbered and other hosts. Because TCP/IP communications are bound to a particular IP address of a host, one way to minimize the disruption is to avoid binding new communications to an old address, while at the same time allowing the existing communications to use the old address for as long as possible [10]. This is the approach adopted by IPv6.

IPv6 requires IPv6 hosts to be able to support multiple IPv6 addresses per interface. Moreover, IPv6 enables the capability to identify an IPv6 address assigned to an interface per interface as either "valid," "deprecated," or "invalid." A host can use a valid address both for the existing communication and for establishing new communications. In contrast, the host could use a deprecated address only for the existing communications; but is not allowed to use such an address for new communications. Finally, if a host has an address that is invalid, that address cannot be used for any of the new or existing communications. In the process of renumbering, a host's current IPv6 address would become deprecated, and the host would acquire (through one of the IPv6 address autoconfigurations mechanisms) a new (valid) address. As a result, all the new communications would be bound to the new address.

Transition to IPv6 routing assumes deployment of routers that would be able to support both IPv4 and IPv6 routing protocols and packet forwarding. The routing protocols expected to be used with IPv6 (at least initially) are mostly straightforward extensions of the existing IPv4 routing protocols; thus, one should not expect significant problems within the IPv6 routing system. To minimize interdependencies, transition to IPv6 routing assumes that there will be noncontiguous IPv6 segments throughout the Internet. These segments could be as large as a collection of many routing domains or as small as a single IP subnet or even a single host. IPv6 connectivity among hosts in different segments will be supported by tunneling IPv6 over IPv4. IPv6 allows for two types of tunnels: automatic and manually configured. For automatic tunnels to be available, IPv6 addresses of the hosts that are reachable in this manner have to be IPv4 compatible; also, IPv4 addresses that are used to form IPv6 addresses of those hosts (IPv4-compatible addresses) have to be routable. In addition, the use of automatic tunnels is currently defined only when the remote endpoint of a tunnel is a host [10]. The following list summarizes the transition challenges:

- IPv6 provides a reasonable answer to some, but not all, of the Internet scaling challenges.

- The increase in the available address space provided by IPv6 is useful.

- Hierarchical routing supports scaling sufficient for the size of the Internet, which could be realized with the IPv6 address space. Therefore, IPv6 has adopted hierarchical routing (using the IPv4 routing architecture).

- IPv6 address autoconfiguration is an important step in developing such technologies.

- Currently defined IPv6 host renumbering attempts to minimize the disruption of applications during renumbering, but it does not guarantee totally nondisruptive behavior.

- It will take some time to develop mature IPv6 host products.

- Supporting IPv6 will have less impact on routers than on hosts, and is not expected to pose unforeseen problems.

Common Subnet Interaction

IPv6 makes improvements in the area of interaction among hosts and routers on a common data-link subnetwork. All the mechanisms related to the interaction among hosts and routers on a common subnetwork are consolidated into a single protocol: Neighbor Discovery Protocol (ND). ND replaces functionality provided in IPv4 by the Address Resolution Protocol (ARP), Internet Control Message Protocol (ICMP) Router Discovery, and ICMP Redirect. Furthermore, ND provides a number of enhancements over the functionality available with the former protocols. For example, in contrast to IPv4, where the IP-to-link-layer address resolution is based on using link-layer broadcasts (ARP), the IP-to-link-layer address resolution in IPv6 uses multicast. This results in a reduction in the number of address resolution-related activities (e.g., interrupts) on nodes other than the target of the resolution.

8.4 Border Gateway Protocol Background

In previous chapters, we described how Internet services and the underlying architectures are designed to move and transfer TCP/IP datagrams. This section focuses on the details of data movement in the Internet by describing how routers forward IP datagrams and the protocols that are used to communicate network reachability information. Earlier in this chapter, we described how routing takes place in an internet, the concepts of table-driven IP routing, and different IP routing algorithms. In this section, we cover the most common protocols for IP routing in Internet service provider backbones, the Border Gateway Protocol [12].

8.4.1 Routing Protocol Architectures

Earlier we described that, from a high level of abstraction, routing protocols can be segregated into two categories, interior and exterior. One reason that a single protocol is not used globally is scalability. From the categories of interior and exterior, it is possible to perform further segregation into the two main categories of routing protocol architectures called distance vector protocols and link-state protocols.

Distance vector protocols were designed for small networks; the name is derived from the fact that the protocol utilizes updates containing vectors of distances. These distances are actually the number of intermediate routers between subnetworks. The protocol operates by exchanging routing updates that contain tables showing which networks are reachable and how far the network is from the router. After this information has been flooded throughout the network, each router can calculate a new routing table [13].

There are several problems associated with distance vector protocols. First, because the routers are calculating reachability information based on the flooded routing tables, the total topological distance of the network cannot be huge because it would become difficult to flood the tables, and it would become overly computational-intensive to calculate reachability. An additional problem with the distance vector protocols is that, as the topological size of the network grows, the hop count can exceed the protocol's maximum value of 15, as specified in the standards document.

Link-state protocols were designed after distance vector and have addressed some of their deficiencies. The link-state protocols are driven by routers exchanging information called link-states that inform adjacent routers about the physical link and node conditions. The advantage of an update that contains only link- and node-conditional information is that, as opposed to distance vector protocols, entire routing tables are not exchanged.

Link-state protocols pose some clear advantages over distance vector protocols. A few of the more important examples to Internet service providers are: lack of reliance on hop count values, ability to better represent network bandwidth topology and delay, smaller load caused by routing information updates, and better support for network hierarchy.

8.4.2 Autonomous Systems

The final topic that needs to be reviewed prior to discussing Internet routing technology is the concept of autonomous systems (AS) (which we referred to earlier as autonomous subnetwork). An AS is a technique used to segregate the Internet into subsections with clear administrative and technical autonomy. ASes are collections of routers that maintain a single routing policy and are under the control of a single administrative entity. The Internet is then constructed of a series of several autonomous systems where each autonomous system, from the outsider's perspective, is unique. Routing protocols, like the BGP, are used to exchange reachability information between autonomous systems. AS numbers, like IP addresses, are acquired from an Internet registry.

There are three different types of autonomous systems (Figure 8.12) that correspond to the three different possible ISP architectures:

Single-homed autonomous systems.   These correspond to ISPs or corporations that have only one possible outbound route; that is, static or default routing usually will suffice.

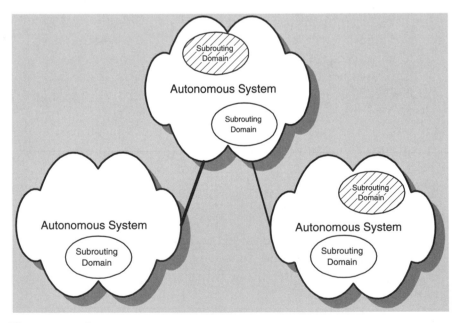

Figure 8.12   Autonomous system types.

Multihomed nontransit autonomous systems.   These autonomous systems are utilized by ISPs or corporations that have Internet connectivity to either two different ISPs or two different locations on the Internet. The autonomous system is called nontransit because it only advertises reachability to IP addresses that are within its domain.

Multihomed transit autonomous systems.   These autonomous systems correspond to national ISP networks because they contain multiple entry and exit points and are used to carry transit traffic. The traffic is called transit because it contains source and destination addresses that are not within the transit provider's domain.

Strictly speaking, a single-homed autonomous system, sometimes called a stub AS, does require dynamic routing protocols because it typically does not need to learn Internet routes. There are examples, however, when a dynamic routing protocol may be used to make the network administrator's job easier. For example, if the domain contained several noncontiguous networks, it would be easier to distribute this information with a dynamic protocol than to do manual table entries. Single-homed autonomous systems that do utilize BGP can optionally use an autonomous system number from a private pool that does not need to be registered on the Internet. The pool's values range from 65412 to 65535.

A nontransit autonomous system does not need to advertise its own routes and would not need to transmit routes learned from other autonomous systems outside of its domain. Therefore, a multihome nontransit autonomous system also does not need to run BGP with its provider and would only do so in situations where some of BGP's functionality for routing policy control (i.e., route filtering) was beneficial.

8.4.3 BGP Routing

The Border Gateway Protocol is the de facto standard for the dynamic routing protocol on the Internet. Currently, the version widely used is called Border Gateway Protocol version 4, or BGP4; it went into production in 1993. BGP4 is widely used because it allows ISPs to control routing policy and support scalable routing calculations, and it understands techniques to reduce routing tables' size, such as CIDR aggregation. BGP4 obsoleted the previous versions of the protocol—BGP1, BGP2, and BGP3.

BGP is somewhat similar to distance vector protocols. It operates by exchanging, or advertising, reachability information in the form of autonomous system path vectors. When BGP routers exchange collections of the autonomous systems they can reach and the metrics associated with those systems, each router can subsequently construct a directed graph corresponding to the total topology of the Internet. Autonomous system path vectors provide the capability to aggregate domains; therefore, the directed graph's scalability can be scoped.

When two BGP routers form an adjacency, they are called peers, or neighbors. Routers running the BGP protocol exchange routing information utilizing TCP. Therefore, the exchange of routing information is reliable and the protocol does not need to provide transport layer error correction. BGP message types that initialize routing tables are only generated at the beginning of a BGP session. Therefore, the protocol is much more efficient than its predecessors because after transmitting the initial full routing tables, only routing additions or withdrawals are communicated.

The actual operation of BGP centers on the exchange of four fundamental message types. When two routers have been configured to be BGP peers, they follow a predefined set of phases. The process proceeds as follows: Initially, a peer enters an initialization state; next it exchanges routing updates and/or keeps alive messages to determine if a peer still exists; and, finally, the peer may enter an error-reporting or session termination state.

As with static and dynamic routing protocols, within BGP is the concept of routing updates being created dynamically or statically. Dynamically created routes, sometimes referred to as *injected routes,* depend upon the status of the network and are susceptible to route fluctuations and the instability of the operational Internet. Statically injected routes are created manually by the network engineer and will remain in place regardless of the state of the network. Two ramifications of these techniques are that BGP provides the ISP with the ability to utilize the protocol to inject static information into the global routing database, and dynamic routing is acceptable; however, routes that change too frequently can be dampened and prevented from being advertised.

Finally, one of the key strengths of BGP4 over its predecessors BGP3 and BGP2 is its capability to accept routes from downstream autonomous systems and aggregate those advertisements into a single supernetwork (see Figure 8.13).

8.4.4 BGP Message Types

The first message type described is also the first message that is used to establish neighbors between BGP peers. A BGP peering session begins with TCP session initialization that includes TCP's three-way handshake.

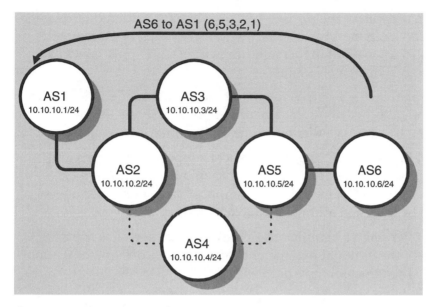

Figure 8.13   BGP4 aggregation.

After the TCP session is established, the BGP peers will transmit OPEN messages.

BGP OPEN and NOTIFICATION

The OPEN message is intended to establish identity and, optionally, authenticate the other end of the connection. Following the BGP OPEN message, routing updates can be exchanged between BGP neighbors. After the OPEN messages have been exchanged, the routers will examine the autonomous system numbers to determine if they are within the same logical autonomous system. If they are, then the peers consider the inter-action as an Internet BGP session.

A BGP OPEN message contains six fields:

Version.   Used to specify the version number, typically BGP4. When two BGP peers are establishing a neighboring relationship, they will attempt to negotiate the highest version number.

Autonomous System.   A 2-byte field used to transmit the source autonomous system number.

Hold Time.   Specifies a value for a timer that is used to determine if the neighbor is still functional; in that, if the neighbor does not transmit a routing update or a KEEPALIVE message before this timer value has expired, the peering session will be considered terminated. A KEEPALIVE message is typically transmitted at approximately one-third to one-half of the hold time interval and only contains a 19-byte BGP message header.

BGP Identifier. A 4-byte value that indicates the sender's identification and, in order to be globally unique, is usually the highest numeric IP address assigned to one of the router's interfaces.

Optional Parameters. the BGP protocol supports extensions and exchanges of optional parameters specified in the standard type, length, value (TLV) format. An example of an optional parameter would be a session authentication key value or password.

Optional Parameter Length. A single octet that specifies the total length of the optional parameter field; if set to 0, designates that no optional parameters have been specified.

If for any reason during the OPEN process an error should occur, or some condition after the OPEN has successfully completed should force termination, a NOTIFICATION message will be generated. A NOTIFICATION message is composed of three fields: error code, error subcode, and a variable-length error-data field.

The NOTIFICATION message is one of the key tools for diagnosing BGP peering session problems, because it provides, via the error code, a major category of failure, followed by the error subcode, which provides information in a subcategory to help isolate the offending parameter. The variable-length error-data section is used to convey information that may have caused the error; for example, a bad TLV value used as an optional parameter.

BGP UPDATE

The heart of the BGP protocol centers on the exchange of UPDATE messages, which contain all the information necessary for the neighbor to determine which routes are being newly advertised, which routes are having their advertisement withdrawn, and which CIDR aggregates are accessible (see Figure 8.14). This information is conveyed via three basic components of the UPDATE message: the Network Layer Reachability Information (NLRI), the Path attributes, and the unreachable route section. An UPDATE message can advertise at most one route, which is described by multiple path attributes; but it can contain multiple routes to be withdrawn.

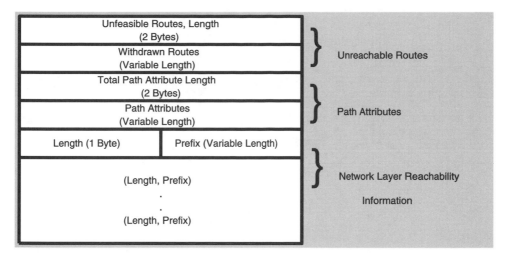

Figure 8.14 UPDATE Message Format.

NLRIs are critical to BGP's functionality because they are mechanisms for expressing reachability and for avoiding routing loops. NLRI updates contain an IP route prefix and the path attribute's list. The path attribute lists the autonomous systems that are traversed to get from the present location to the advertised prefix. In other words, when a prefix is announced at one end of the Internet, that advertisement may traverse other autonomous systems as the advertisement crosses the Internet.

When the advertisement is passed from autonomous system to autonomous system, the NLRI is augmented to contain the list of traversed autonomous systems. This information can subsequently be used to determine if a routing loop, or circular route, exists because an AS number would appear multiple times in the AS path list.

All BGP UPDATE messages contain a sequence of path attributes (see Figure 8.15). Path attributes are used to monitor route-specific information such as next hop value, routes preference, and CIDR aggregation. In addition, path attributes are used to facilitate making routing decisions and in the implementation of route filters. Path attributes are made up of a type, length, and value.

BGP Attributes

There are four categories of path attributes, differentiated by the first two bits of the path attribute's Type field.

- Well-known mandatory attributes are required in BGP UPDATE messages, and all routers are required to recognize this attribute.

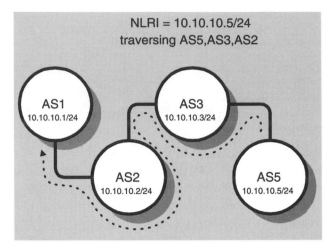

Figure 8.15 BGP routing update.

- Well-known discretionary attributes are required to be recognized by all BGP-capable routers but are not required in every UPDATE message.

- Optional transitive attribute implementation is optional. If the router does not recognize the attribute, it can pass the attribute on in subsequent UPDATE messages.

- Optional nontransitive attributes are optional and not required to be recognized by every BGP speaker; however, if the router does not understand a nontransitive attribute that it has received, it should not repeat the attribute to other BGP neighbors.

In addition to communicating feasible routes via NLRIs, BGP4 has the capability of communicating with drawn routes or routes that are no longer feasible. Withdrawn routes take the format of a CIDR announcement, in that they are expressed as a subnet mask length and an IP address. A BGP UPDATE message may contain multiple routes that need to be a withdrawn; and in its simplest form, the UPDATE message will not contain any NLRI advertisements, only routes to be withdrawn.

There are currently 10 path attribute types used to control routing in the Internet. The most common are listed here:

NEXT_hop (well-known mandatory attribute). The next hop attribute contains the IP address of the neighbor that is announcing the route.

ORIGIN (well-known mandatory attribute). Used to convey where the network layer reachability information was created. BGP uses this information when constructing its routing tables to determine if the information originated within the autonomous system or outside of the autonomous system. BGP prefers internally generated information over externally generated information.

AS_path (well-known mandatory attribute). Contains a list of autonomous system numbers that the routes traversed before reaching this destination. As the routing information propagates through the Internet, each autonomous system is responsible for prepending the local autonomous system number into the AS path list.

Multiexit discriminator (MED) (optional nontransitive attribute). Used to convey preference for data flow between two ISPs interconnected at multiple locations. The MED can be utilized to express preferences over EGP information so that both providers and customers can load balance traffic over multiple links between their autonomous systems. Multiexit discriminators are transmitted out of an autonomous system, but do not traverse more than one autonomous system before being deleted.

Local preference attribute (well-known discretionary). Used to manage traffic flows leaving an autonomous system when there are clear preferences on which path is best to exit a multihome network. For example, if an autonomous system were multihome to the same ISP with a primary high-speed link and a backup low-speed link, the routers within the autonomous system can be configured with the local preference attributes to prefer routes learned from the high-speed link. The local preference attribute is communicated within the autonomous system.

Atomic_aggregate (well-known discretionary attribute). When a downstream autonomous system is performing aggregation of multiple address blocks, specificity of where those blocks originated is lost. This attribute is required to be transmitted when that aggregation causes loss of information, and is implemented to communicate the loss to the next autonomous system.

Aggregator (optional transitive attribute). Goes hand in hand with atomic_aggregates and is used to notify a neighboring autonomous system of the router that has performed an aggregation. The attribute contains an AS number and the IP address of the router.

8.4.5 BGP Operation

With the preceding basic review of BGP components in mind, we can now review the BGP routing process from initialization through routing table establishment (Figure 8.16). BGP routing messages are exchanged between BGP neighbors in UPDATE messages. The UPDATE message can contain a series of routes that are being withdrawn—that is, no longer reachable—or a route that is being advertised as reachable. BGP UPDATE messages that are advertising reachability to a network do so by specifying the CIDR block and the autonomous system path list between the current router and the original subnetwork.

When a router running the BGP protocol receives an UPDATE message, it may optionally implement its own policy for routing modifications or rejections and then forward the BGP message to other adjacent neighbors. This is a subtle point, but one of BGP's greatest strengths, in that the protocol is capable of applying policy decisions to input routes and then of generating unique policy-based routing decisions for advertised outbound routing information. The router that has received multiple BGP UPDATE messages will then examine the different messages, which may have come from different upstream routers, and it will determine which are the best routes to be included in the local routing table, which will be consulted when forwarding packets.

8.5 Conclusion

This chapter described basic principles used by routers in the Internet. The Internet backbone routers are specialized high-performance comput-

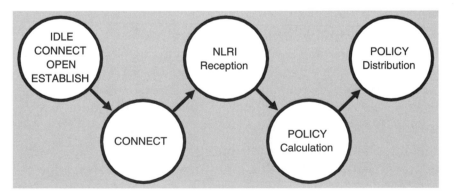

Figure 8.16   BGP operation.

ers with interfaces that have been optimized to forward IP datagrams at very high speeds. The process of routing involves the exchange of messages in a routing protocol and subsequently determining the topology of the Internet so that forwarding tables within the router can be populated. The de facto standard for an exterior routing protocol on the Internet is the BGP version 4. This protocol provides network engineers with the ability to capitalize on innovative technologies like CIDR and autonomous systems that produce manageable, loop-free, routing tables. BGP's main strengths are the rich diversity of attributes that can be used to control the way routes are advertised and the way inbound advertisements are interpreted. BGP also supports strong route-filtering capabilities that, when combined with the attributes, provide a flexible network management tool.

References

1. D. Minoli, A. Alles. *LAN, ATM, and LAN Emulation.* (Norwood, MA: Artech House), 1997.
2. D. Minoli. *Internet and Intranet Engineering.* (New York: McGraw-Hill), 1997.
3. D. Minoli. *Telecommunication Technology Handbook.* (Norwood, MA: Artech House), 1991.
4. R. Perlman. *Interconnections: The Theory of Bridges and Routers.* (Reading, MA: Addison Wesley) 1997.
5. D. Minoli. *Designing Broadband Networks.* (Norwood, MA: Artech House), 1993.
6. RFC 1583 OSPF version 2. playground.sun.com/ipng; also, ftp.parc.xerox.com:/pub/ipng; also, majordomo@sunroof.eng.sun.com
7. Uyless Black. *TCP/IP and Related Protocols.* (New York: McGraw-Hill, Inc), 1992.
8. O. Eldib, D. Minoli. *Telecommuting.* (Norwood, MA: Artech House), 1995.
9. Gary Kessler. "PPP: Getting to the Point," *LAN Magazine,* Vol. 8, No. 7, pp. 60–71, July 1993.
10. Cisco, Internet Protocol Version 6, cisco/warp/public/732/ipv6/ipv6_wp.html.
11. ARG, Hands-on Internetworking with TCP/IP, Morristown, NJ, Spring 1997.
12. RFC 1771, a Border Gateway Protocol for (BGP4)

13. D. Comer. *Internetworking with TCP/IP.* (Upper Saddle River, NJ: Prentice-Hall), 1995.

Note

[1] This section is redacted from a more extensive treatment found in the book *1st, 2nd, and Next-Generation LANs,* by Dan Minoli (New York: McGraw-Hill), 1993. For original references, credits, and acknowledgments, the reader should refer to that text.

CHAPTER 9

IP-Based Communication in ATM Environments: One ISP Approach to QoS

As covered in the previous chapter, IP is important in any discussion of enterprise networking and the Internet, because of its ubiquitous deployment and because specification and technology developers use it as their point of departure for many enhanced communication systems. Basic ATM technology was covered in Chapter 7, along with its QoS capabilities. This chapter covers:

- Carriage of IP PDUs over an ATM network[1,2]
- Network layer switching technology for improved support of IP

All of these techniques come into play in Internet applications in general and in multimedia-over-IP in particular, where the planner is seeking a more powerful engine at Layer 2 to secure better performance. At this time, many ATM applications used the ISPs are classical IP-over-ATM (CIOA) techniques in all three segments of the Internet, namely in the access, the aggregation, and the backbone segments.

Prospective corporate users may find it helpful to learn which IP-over-ATM techniques the ISP is using; the kind of policing/traffic-shaping the ISP is applying; the overbooking; and the ATM service chosen, as all these impact some aspect of QoS, whether in terms of dropped PDUs or in end-to-end delay. Traffic-shaping and policing is a "nasty" and complicated business. As an example, as this chapter was being written, one of the authors and his team had to take emergency measures to investigate why a certain IP-over-ATM route (using CIOA) over the company's ATM-based Internet backup backbone was experiencing high-latency ping times. As an example of IP carriage over ATM, CERFnet's Internet backbone is based on an OC-3c/OC-12c router-to-router dedicated line backbone, but its backup Internet backbone is based on a shared ATM network (shared with other company applications; e.g., telemetry, video, etc.) that uses CIOA thru OC-3c/OC-12c links. [2] The apparent reason was that the switch supplier did not seem to know how to do traffic shaping for a VBR contract when the output was into a public ATM carrier, rather than onto a dedicated switch-to-switch link. A convoluted emergency patch had to be installed, until the switch vendor redeveloped a better CAC. Clearly, ISPs need networks of quality.

9.1 Need for IP Support in ATM Networks

One of the key considerations regarding ATM technology in recent years has been support of IP. This requirement is driven by, one, the desire to support the embedded base of applications and enterprise networks (including intranets); and, two, the desire to have access to the Internet, including securing VPNs over it. Beyond basic support of IP-over-ATM, the industry has looked at ways to use the advantages of ATM to simplify IP-level Layer 3 PDU forwarding. In view of increased corporate dependence on information, including data, video, graphics, and distributed resources (web access), users and planners want faster, larger, and better-performing networks; namely: higher speeds, scalability, and better performance and management. Specifically, companies need all-points broadband networks that interconnect major corporate locations as well as remote branch locations. ATM has the potential of meeting these customer expectations when used in conjunction with IP and routers. Others are advocating entirely new approaches—for example, RSVP.

   This chapter examines a number of issues related to network migrations and use/support of ATM to bring about design improvements. Some approaches could entirely eliminate the use of routers (e.g., end-to-end ATM with IP route selection in the endsystem); other approaches use ATM as a "fat pipe"; still other approaches either diminish the dependence on hop-by-hop routing or make better use of routing by introducing new paradigms; some approaches are more conventional and make little use of ATM. The first approach is the most daring and controversial, and probably will not see much deployment. An obvious use of ATM is to connect dispersed routers via a mesh of PVCs using multiprotocol encapsulation. This entails upgrading the network-side hardware of the routers with an ATM access board that supports encapsulation of IP PDUs, segmentation, and basic ATM features, such as cell generation, cell relay, and possibly traffic shaping, signaling, and maintenance cell generation. However, this still requires conventional routers in support of the enterprise network. Radical redesigns that reduce the number of IP subnets and nearly eliminate the obligatory use of routers (and thereby have the potential of greatly reducing costs) are possible. However, the focus of recent research has been along more "traditional" lines.

ATM use in IP networks is being addressed by the ATM Forum and by the IETF, sometimes in cooperation, sometimes in competition. Issues under discussion include:

- Cost-effective deployment of broadband connectivity to all corporate locations

- QoS support (RFC 2205 Resource Reservation Protocol [RSVP] by the IETF; UNI 4.0 signaling by the ATM Forum)

- Traffic management (Classifier/Scheduler/FlowSpecs by the IETF; Traffic Management 4.0 Spec and traffic contracts by the ATM Forum)

- Addressing (Flow IDs and PIM by the IETF; VPI/VCIs and NHRP by the ATM Forum)

- Routing (IGP/EGP by the IETF; PNNI by the ATM Forum)

- Interneting (Routing over Large Clouds [ROLC] and NHS by the IETF; MPOA and I-PNNI by the ATM Forum)

Some of the challenges being addressed are [3]:

- Support for more than best-effort and constant bit rate services on the same router-based network

- Support for best-effort service over ATM

- Support for circuitlike service via IP on a router-based network

- Support for service levels regardless of physical media and network discipline (e.g., ATM/LAN switching, traditional IP routing, IP routing over ATM)

- A way to request QoS, to deliver it over various lower layers, and to find routes that support the needed QoS on a router-based network

- New designs/technologies that are easier to deploy in router-based networks

When Ipsilon Networks introduced the IP switching concept in 1996, the announcement attracted a lot of attention, although the ATM Forum and the IETF were already working on ways to route IP over ATM. Ipsilon argued that emerging standards were too complex, that interoperability and scalability might suffer, and that its IP switching was simpler and more robust. A number of vendors lent support to IP switching, including Digital Equipment Corporation, General DataComm, Hitachi, Ltd., ECI/Telematics, and NEC Corporation. Cisco Systems, IBM, Cascade/Ascend, Toshiba, and 3Com came up with alternative solutions based on similar principles. At time of this writing, the idea of generic IP switching, the forwarding/routing function that seeks to directly and cohesively switch and forward frames without having to do Layer 3 processing unless absolutely needed, had become well accepted. Other vendors—for example Cisco—promote their own "optimized solutions" (e.g., tag switching/netflows for large internetworks), but still support MPOA for smaller networks. The industry is now working toward a standard (MultiProtocols Label Switching [MPLS]). These issues are expanded upon in this chapter.

9.1.1 Key Motivations

It is acknowledged that networks based on "routers at *every node*" do not scale as the number of points increases (e.g., for the Internet of the year 2001). The fundamental problem is simple to state: How does a network planner interconnect, say, 1,000 users who (a) need a considerable amount of bandwidth because of evolving graphics/video-based applications (QoS support), and (b) who may be geographically dispersed?

We started out in the mid-1980s with an obligatory need to create small Layer 2 groups (what have been called *bridge groups*), because of the performance restrictions of shared-media LANs, including the generation of broadcast traffic across related communities of users. Because of the performance restrictions, network planners may have formed, say, 20 groups of 50 users each. The feudalistic fragmentation at Layer 2 reflected itself with a similar fragmentation at Layer 3. Network planners soon discovered plausible arguments to support this fragmentation. Private network technologists soon afforded justifications along the following lines: "Isn't it obvious that the marketing department should have a separate subnetwork from the support department?" "Isn't it obvious that the centralized East Coast support department should have a separate subnetwork from the colocated West Coast support department?" "Isn't it obvious that the academic department should have a separate subnetwork from the administration department?" "Isn't it obvious that the small cars manufacturing department should have a separate subnetwork from the medium-size cars manufacturing department?" The answer is: No! Why are separate subnetworks necessary? Corporations now more than ever need to work as a team. If people in marketing cannot trust people in support, then something is unhealthy about the company. There is no reason that the East Coast support department should keep separate data from the West Coast support department (unless geographically separate), because at some point, all of this information has to be merged, reported, and acted upon. Having created this myriad of subnetworks, there is an a posteriori need to provide a connection among the various subnetworks.

Enter the need for enterprise routers. Now corporations that want to save money in their networking budgets recognize that such segmentation was imposed by the immaturity of the 1980's technology, and is not a sacrosanct overall architectural imperative or an untouchable construct of perennial merit. The deficiencies of the technology of the 1980s, which originally gave rise to the need for routers have been overcome, and this allows corporations that want to take advantage of these technological improvements to reduce their costs as much as three-fourths. Instead of spending $80,000 on a router, they can get the same functionality from a $20,000 switch. But there is a caveat to this benefit: Enterprise networks would have to be redesigned to make use of such equipment. So the router vendors are right: You cannot just throw away the router; you have to first redesign the network to eliminate the need for routers, and then secure the benefits [4].[3] Corporations should look to embrace switching endsystem to endsystem, or at least edge to edge.

In the public Internet, the situation is less malleable: The ISP and NSP networks out there are all solidly based on IP and provide "IP dialtone" capabilities. However, at the same time routers are becoming bottlenecks. Hence, what ISPs need to do is to continue to support IP while at the same time diminishing their absolute dependence of "routers-at-every-node" paradigm, and shift more to "route-at-the-edge-switch-at-the-core" paradigm. Here is precisely where ATM can help.

9.1.2 The Need for Routers in Enterprise Networks

In the mid-1980s, designers of (then small) data networks needed a service that enabled them to

1. Forward IP PDUs toward the destination (in an effective manner).

2. Provide reliable concatenated-link-by-link connectivity.

3. Have a knowledge of the topology of the network, in order to accomplish point 1.

4. Support point 1 by introducing an addressing mechanism at Layer 3, which enabled the sender to pipeline data in real time (without appreciable setup latency) to any entity on the network (i.e., support any-to-any communication, rather than just fixed-point A to fixed-point B communication).

No such service was available at that time; therefore, these designers developed a box to do all four of these functions. They invented routers. Routers forward IP PDU, collect and maintain topology information, and support reliable concatenated-link-by-link connectivity, but do so by recomputing the IP decision at each endpoint of a Layer 2 link. But this is inefficient for these reasons:

- Each router must have a complex apparatus to generate, aggregate, distribute, and verify topology information.

- Each router must process PDUs through the physical, data link, and IP protocol engines. This becomes a bottleneck.

The challenge then is to relegate routers to do just job function 1. In particular, there has to be a decoupling between IP processing and the movement of information along a trajectory close to the destination.

More recently, unlike the mid-1980s, there are communication services that can support functions 2, 3, and 4 (in same cases even 1), so routers do not have to be obligated to support these other functions anymore. In effect, the goal is to push the routers to the edges of the network, to provide an interworking function with a legacy application, but without having the routers in the core of the network to handle basic heavy-duty (industrial-grade) data-forwarding functions, since they are no longer needed there (which makes it possible to use a $20,000 switch instead of an $80,000 router inside the network). Topology maintenance and calculation can also be centralized (as apparent with the route servers in the MPOA model) to eliminate having to replicate this intelligence at each hop-end—questions of reliability can be addressed as has been done for decades with the Common Channel Signaling System No. 7 and in the 800 translation databases. Figure 9.1 depicts the first stage of the desired migration, where routers have been relegated to the edges of the network.

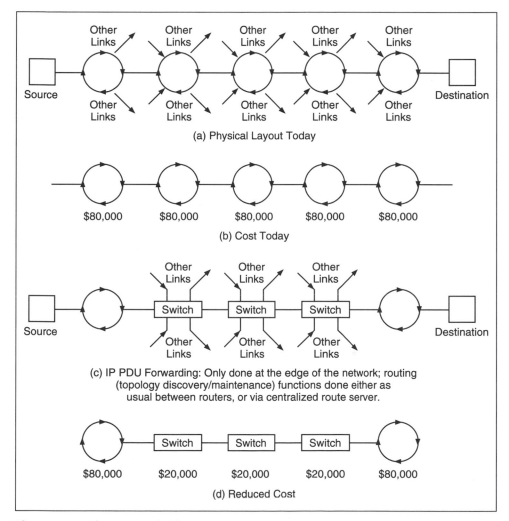

Figure 9.1   Advantages of using ATM.

9.2 A Baseline for Discussion: Dynamics in Enterprise/Backbone Networking Designs

New major market forces are at work in the enterprise and Internet backbone as well as at the desktop/hub level, with a barrage of new solutions (e.g., IP switching, MPOA, MPLS, etc.). At the desktop level, new solutions seem to be emerging all the time; however, new solutions are hard to come by and/or to be implemented where the real expenditures are, namely at the backbone and WAN level.

9.2.1 Internetworking Level

How can planners (both in corporate space and in the ISP space) make some sense out of all the available proposed networking alternatives? Are these alternatives real and fundamental, or are they just vendor-advanced variances of the same radical or reactionary solution? Observers note that, "There is widespread excitement on Wall Street, while at the same time there is confusion on Main Street." Clearly, there are new trends in networking. So corporate planners must try to guess as to which technologies are likely to be winners or losers. R&D users in a corporation tend to look at all new technologies. Eventually, these technologies find themselves being adopted by technical/power users. Ultimately, all users will dabble in a technology, on the assumption that it leads to success (some technologies, such as DQBD, SMDS, packet-over-ISDN, FDDI II, IEEE 802.9 never make it to market). See Figure 9.2.

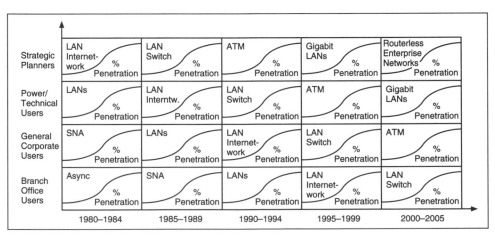

Figure 9.2 Promulgation of new technologies in the networking chain.

It is always important to understand the embedded base. At this time, the technology deployments listed in Table 9.1 are predominant.

The following are well-recognized trends of the late 1990s, modulating the embedded base.

- Apparent desire to retain widespread use of fairly mature technologies such as Ethernet and TCP/IP in the endsystem space (hosts and desk-proximity networks)

- Desire to upgrade rather than replace (e.g., upgrade 10Mbps Ethernet to switched Ethernet; upgrade 10Mbps Ethernet to 100Mbps Ethernet)

- Low price (e.g., less than $100 per desk)

- Businesses' critical dependence on computing and communication

- Consolidation of equipment vendors, carriers, and ISPs

- Operations and network management expenditure concerns

- An avalanche of new technologies that may well confuse the market. Vendors quote fast time-to-market as a must, since 50 percent of the profits come in the first 12 months of a new product's life.

The confusing, often self-serving, message from the technology providers has done nothing to shed light on the fact that newer architectures can indeed save money. Table 9.2 depicts some of the evolutionary "half-steps" in the right direction. The most critical, revolutionary change would be to

Table 9.1 Embedded Enterprise Network Technology (Late 1990s)

PCs	Intel (Pentium II or better)
Desktop OSes	Microsoft Workgroup/Windows 98/NT
Enterprise Connectivity	Physical: NICs/Switched Ethernet/100Mbps Ethernet (e.g., 3Com) Logical: TCP/IP Applications: Web/intranet/Internet (e.g., Microsoft, Netscape)
Servers	Unix, NT
Internetworking	Router-based technologies (e.g., Cisco)
Access	SOHO networking: dial-up, frame relay (e.g., Ascend) Internet Access (e.g., Ascend), Voice over IP
Carriers	LECs, CLECs, IXCs, ISPs, NSPs

Table 9.2 Evolutionary Steps

REQUIREMENT	LAN APPROACH	WAN APPROACH
Higher speed	Use switched Ethernet 100Mbps Ethernet Gigabit LANs	Use ATM (frame relay is not enough)
Dedicated bandwidth/ improved performance	Use switched Ethernet	Use service with QoS guarantees (such as ATM)
Multimedia	Isochronous Ethernet or higher-speed LANs	ATM
Improved Management	Use virtual LANs	Use TLS (Transparent LAN Service)
Multicast and Reservation	IP multicast RSVP	IP/RSVP-over-ATM

redesign the network to operate without core routers. Just making a router operate faster does not alleviate the inefficiency and inelegance of the way data is carried across an enterprise network. Having to read each PDU and make an individual decision is a brute-force method of solving a problem, and it is like doing an exhaustive search to solve an optimization problem, rather than using a rapidly converging analytical algorithm.

9.2.2 WAN/Backbone Level

Technologies have been more stable on the WAN side than on the LAN side. Specifically, frame relay has been commercially successful in the past decade, proving the utility of a switched service. ATM is viewed as being a couple of years behind frame relay. Some of the factors that have helped frame relay are as follows:

- Early support by canonical networks of the late 1980s, namely, SNA
- Generally, a software upgrade of routers
- Existing access mechanisms (e.g., T1 tails)
- Support of a range of speeds per need-at-the-time (e.g., 56Kbps)
- Economic savings, compared to meshes of dedicated lines

Now there is a need for speeds higher than T1, but some of the same principles are at play. Table 9.3 depicts some transitions in views as related to frame relay.

One of the reasons frame relay was so successful is that it supported a move toward all-points connectivity; also, it enabled data to be relayed

Table 9.3 Views on Frame Relay

EARLY 1990s VIEW	LATE 1990s VIEW
Limited in speed, does not scale	In spite of speed limitations, will continue to be important.
No QoS support	Vendor extension will include QoS.
Data Only	Voice now also carried in standardized form.
Frame relay a feeder to ATM	Frame relay will be carried over ATM.
Full upgrade to cell-based technology	Eventual upgrade to cell-based technology.

between points in the network without necessarily requiring hop-by-hop routing. Where it fell short was in supporting broadband and QoS (although some are now proposing ATM-like service classes for it). (Even if specs were published by the Frame Relay Forum, it is not clear that manufacturers would develop hardware—perhaps frame relay-over-ATM is a pragmatic compromise.) ATM is the broadband WAN technology of choice at this time, particularly because it supports QoS.

There are clear expectations that TCP/IP-based applications should run well over ATM as the data link layer technology. The problem is that there is duplication of addressing and routing functions between these two layers; further, the LAN Emulation (LANE) and Classical IP-over-ATM (CIOA) approaches hide ATM's QoS aspects. The latter is a concern as related to the support of multimedia. Also, there is increased interest in supporting multicast communication.

The plethora of technologies and choices has led (in the late 1990s) to a hybrid situation, where enterprise networks continue: to use routers in a traditional manner; to use routers connected to ATM switches and/or public ATM networks; to use routers connected directly to SONET-based private lines; or to use ATM switches that run router software (e.g., Ipsilon's IP Switching). Table 9.4 gives a late 1990s view of the two technologies.

Although not exclusively, the path to higher speed is generally via cell switching, whether directly at the ATM level or via network layer switching technologies. The exception is for the local environment, where Ethernet switching at the 10, 100, or 1000Mbps level is often based on frame technology.

The current commercial outlook is that ATM will not operate end to end (desktop to desktop), but will be focused in the WAN backbone for broadband applications. This use is consistent with how the technology

Table 9.4 Late 1990s View of Switching and Routing Technologies

FEATURE	SWITCHES (ORIGINAL)	SWITCHES (MORE RECENT)	ROUTERS (ORIGINAL)	ROUTERS (MORE RECENT)
Connections	PVCs	PVCs and SVCs	None	Flows
Unit of processing	Cells	Cells, FR frames, LAN frames	LAN frames	Cells, FR frames, LAN frames
Traffic Control	Service/QoS guarantees for CBR, VBR	Service/QoS guarantees for CBR, nrt-VBR, rt-VBR	Best effort	QoS support
Cost Implementation	Low Hardware	Low Hardware+ software support of functions (e.g., MPOA, LANE)	High Mostly software	Improving More hardware-based support
Scalability	Good	Better (with MPOA)	Somewhat limited	Improving
Speed	Single-digit gigabits per second	Double-digit gigabit per second	Megabits per second	Near-gigabit per second
Standards	Open, ATM	Open, IETF	Proprietary	More open (e.g., OSPF, MPOA/MPLS)
Customers	Telcos	Carriers, ISPs, large users	ISPs, corporate users	Carriers, ISPs, corporate users

was originally conceived in the late 1980s (frame relay will also continue to play a useful role for the foreseeable future). Must there be a single end-to-end technology? Not necessarily, although this would clearly be the ideal. However, this misses the point; specifically, that ATM could reduce overall networking costs. The issue of the value of ATM end-to-end is more related to the ability for endsystem routing (i.e., being able to automatically select an end-to-end path right at the source) and a single address space in the WAN, than it is to the speed at the desktop. Some vendors have focused their attention on the lack of need for broadband to the desktop or on the availability of other desktop solutions (such as switched Ethernet, 100Mbps Ethernet, or gigabit Ethernet).

It is worth noting that internal to the Internet backbones, ATM either is already being used or will soon be used by the key backbone providers, at least as a "fat pipe" technology. xDSL technology is receiving a lot of attention, but the penetration is still extremely low. Nonetheless, as more xDSL services are deployed, giving users access links operating at 1.5 or 6Mbps, the need for high-capacity backbones will be accentuated, and the need for ATM will be even more accentuated.

9.2.3 LAN Level

At the LAN level, Ethernet switching and 100/1000Mpbs Ethernet will be the technology of choice for the foreseeable future. LAN switches are replacing hubs as the first connectivity tier. Switches support multiport bridging. The majority of LAN switches will be Ethernet-frame-based rather than cell-based. Higher throughput will be obtained by higher-speed LAN technologies (rather than new technologies). VLANs in their current manifestation will play only a minor role, according to observers. The early 1990s view that Ethernet was insufficient for new applications (including multimedia), and that it did not scale, has been replaced in light of its switching and speed extensions. Fast Ethernet costs about the same as Ethernet at the NIC level, and only twice as much at the hub level. Switched Ethernet hubs now cost the same as regular hubs did in the mid-1990s. Switched fast Ethernet is expected to be common by the late 1990s. Gigabit Ethernet will cost about twice that of Fast Ethernet, but with a 10-times increase in performance.

Fast Ethernet went from research to standard in one year, and it provides 10-times performance for twice the price (at $100 per NIC). Note that after only one year of technology maturity Fast Ethernet costs half as much as ATM NICs with five years of technology maturity.

9.3 Methods of IP Support in ATM

The previous section described some of the issues, opportunities, and the potential strategic direction for the deployment of all-points corporate broadband networks. This section describes the tactical approaches to IP support over ATM. Some of these approaches apply to enterprise networks; others apply to both enterprise networks and the Internet.

9.3.1 LANE

As noted in Chapter 7, the ATM Forum's LANE specification defines how existing applications—for example, IP-based LAN-situated applications—can operate unchanged over ATM networks. It also specifies how to communicate between an ATM internetwork and Ethernet, FDDI, and token ring LANs.[4] LANE is a logical service of the ATM internetwork. In this translational bridging interworking environment, Ethernet and token ring frames that carry IP PDUs (or for that matter, other PDUs) can transit an ATM network (in a segmented fashion) and be delivered transparently to a similar legacy network at the receiving end. Furthermore, a user on an ATM device can send information to an Ethernet or token ring device.

LANE provides users with a migration path from pre-ATM architectures, without passing through successive stages of large-scale reinvestment. LANE, however, is also a campus technology and thus has very limited use on the Internet. It is briefly treated here for completeness.

LANE is an ATM-based internetwork technology that enables ATM-connected endstations to establish MAC-layer connections. It allows existing LAN protocols, such as Novell NetWare, DECnet, TCP/IP, MacTCP, or AppleTalk, to operate over ATM networks without requiring modifications to the application itself. LANE provides:

- Data encapsulation and transmission
- Address resolution
- Multicast group management

The components of LANE are:

- The LANE driver within each endstation (e.g., host, server, or LAN access device)
- One or more LANE services (realized via specialized servers) residing in the ATM network

The LANE driver within each endstation provides an IEEE 802 MAC (medium access control)-layer interface that is transparent to higher-layer protocols. Hence, LANE carries IP PDUs across different physical LANs, but in the same IP subnetwork. Within the endstation, the LANE driver also translates 802 MAC-layer addresses into ATM addresses, using an address resolution service provided by a LANE server. It establishes point-to-point ATM SVC connections to other LANE drivers and delivers data to other LANE endstations. LANE drivers are also supported on access devices (e.g., routers, hubs, and LAN switches) attached to the ATM internetwork. The access devices differ from endstations on the ATM internetwork in that access devices act as a "proxy" for endstations. As such, they must receive all multicast and broadcast packets destined for endstations located on attached LAN segments.

LAN emulation services are realized using the LAN emulation server (LES), the broadcast and unknown server (BUS), and the LAN emulation configuration server (LECS). LANE services can be implemented in an ATM intermediate system, an endstation such as a bridge, router, or dedicated workstation, or a PC. They may also be implemented on ATM switches or other ATM-specific devices. LANE services exist as a single centralized service where the LECS, LES, and BUS are implemented on an endstation or ATM switch. But they can also be implemented in a distributed manner, where several servers operate in parallel and provide redundancy and error recovery. LANE services can operate on one or more LEC. For example, the LECS may reside on one endstation, which is also a LEC, while the LES and BUS reside on another endstation running LEC code. Figure 9.3 provides an example.

This combination of LANE drivers and services transparently supports the operation of existing 802.x LAN applications over the ATM internetwork. By using multiple LANE services, multiple 802 LANs can be emulated on a single physical ATM internetwork. This enables LAN administrators to create VLANs (a logical association of users sharing a common broadcast domain), which are also called Emulated LANs (ELANs).

The advantages afforded by LANE compare favorably to those of LAN bridging, a technology developed to support the expansion of LANs. Ethernet bridges are transparent and require minimal configuration. Attached PCs do not require any modifications to operate in a bridged environment, saving much of the administrative cost associated with other internetworking technologies. LANE and classical bridging both support MAC-layer connectivity between LAN applications. LANE, however, removes the limitations of classical bridging, making it a building block of ATM internetworking.

A single ATM network with LANE supports multiple VLANs. Because each VLAN is distinct from the others, broadcast traffic in one VLAN is never seen in any other VLAN. It does not require any filtering or other mechanisms on stations not in that particular VLAN. The LECS allows dynamic configuration capabilities within the ATM internetwork—eliminating the need to define the physical connection between a host computer and the VLAN(s) to which it belongs. Consequently, a host computer can be moved from one building to another while remaining a member of the same VLAN.

By using existing 802.x frame types, and emulating the behavior of 802.x LANs, ATM network adapters appear to endstations and upper-layer protocols to be Ethernet or token ring cards—or both. Any existing protocol that has been defined to operate over Ethernet or token ring LANs can also operate over ATM LANE without modification. In particular, IP traffic is supported.

In 1995, the LAN Emulation Subworking Group of the ATM Technical Forum passed the LAN Emulation-over-ATM v1.0 specification. It defines the LAN emulation user-to-network interface (LUNI) over which existing

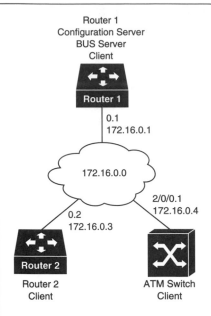

Router 1
Configuration Server
BUS Server
Client

Router 1

0.1
172.16.0.1

172.16.0.0

2/0/0.1
172.16.0.4

0.2
172.16.0.3

Router 2

Router 2
Client

ATM Switch
Client

LANE Servers and Components

A single emulated LAN consists of the following entities: A LANE configuration server, a broadcast-and-unknown server, a LANE server, and LANE clients.

- LANE configuration server—A server that assigns individual clients to particular emulated LANs by directing them to the LANE server that corresponds to the emulated LAN. The LANE configuration server maintains a database of LANE client ATM or MAC addresses and their emulated LAN. A LANE configuration server can serve multiple emulated LANs.

- Broadcast-and-unknown server—A multicast server that floods unknown destination traffic and forwards multicast and broadcast traffic to clients within an emulated LAN. One Cisco broadcast-and-unknown server exists per emulated LAN.

- LANE server—A server that provides a registration facility for clients to join the emulated LAN. There is one Cisco LANE server per emulated LAN. The LANE server handles LAN Emulation Address Resolution Protocol (LE ARP) requests and maintains a list of LAN destination MAC addresses.

- LANE client—An entity in an endpoint such as a router that performs data forwarding, address resolution, and other control functions for a single endpoint in a single emulated LAN. The LANE client provides a standard LAN service to any higher layers that interfaces to it. A router or switch can have multiple resident LANE clients, each connecting with different emulated LANs. The LANE client registers its MAC and ATM address with the LANE server.

Emulated LAN entities coexist on one or more routers. On Cisco routers, each LANE server and broadcast-and-unknown server is always a single entity. Other LANE components include ATM switches—any ATM switch that supports the ILMI and signaling. Multiple emulated LANs can coexist on a single ATM network.

Figure 9.3 Example of a LANE network (single ELAN) and server definitions. (Courtesy of Cisco Systems, Inc.)

LAN protocols operate. The LUNI describes how an endstation communicates with the ATM internetwork, and defines initialization and registration. The LECS (server) controls the assignment of individual LECs (clients) to VLANs, using information contained in the LECS's database as well as information provided by each LEC. The definition of the LUNI model allows independent vendors to implement LANE endstations, while providing interoperability between their products. The LUNI also defines initialization, registration, address resolution, and data transfer procedures for the interaction of the LEC and the LANE services.

Further work by the ATM Forum focused on the LAN emulation network-to-network interface (LENNI). Pre-LENNI solutions are possible and are available from a single vendor or multiple vendors that use the same signaling technique for network-to-network interfaces. Version 2.0 specification, providing enhancements in the area of redundant servers and subnetwork access protocol/logical link control (SNAP/LLC) encapsulation (per RFC 1483), was nearing completion at the time of this writing. LANE Version 2.0 begins to distinguish the elements within the LANE service cloud. It aims at accommodating multiple LES/BUS pairs by defining protocols between them. These protocols provide a level of scalability for LANE, and will support server function redundancy for improved robustness. There are also extensions related to QoS; QoS is designed to manage integrated voice, video, and data traffic in an ATM network. Through the use of different virtual connections, QoS supports applications that require constant, variable, available, and unspecified bandwidth. ATM switches can build a virtual circuit for each application and use QoS information to set up traffic priorities, choose network routes, and manage trunk availability.

Many observers, however, believe that LANE will be difficult to implement as a network discipline across an enterprise because it imposes a large broadcast domain (a single IP subnetwork). Otherwise, if multiple ELANs are utilized, routers are needed to interconnect them; here routers can become bottlenecks. Hence, this approach does little to diminish the use of routers in the network or push them to the edges, and its future is limited.

9.3.2 Classical IP-over-ATM

Classical IP-over-ATM predates LANE, and is the method of running IP/LAN traffic over ATM that was developed by the IETF. It has applications in today's ATM-based Internet backbones. The IETF's specification is defined to provide native IP support over ATM and is documented in the following RFCs:

- RFC 1483: Multiprotocol Encapsulation over ATM Adaptation Layer 5
- RFC 1577: Classical IP and ARP over ATM
- RFC 1755: ATM Signaling Support for IP-over-ATM
- RFC 2022: Multicast Address Resolution (MARS) Protocol

These protocols are designed to treat ATM as virtual "wire" with the property of being connection-oriented; therefore, as with LANE, requiring a unique method of address resolution and broadcast support.

In the CIOA model,[5] the ATM fabric interconnecting a group of hosts is considered a network, called nonbroadcast multiple access (NBMA). An NBMA network is made up of a switched service like ATM or frame relay with a large number of endstations that cannot directly broadcast messages to each other. While on the NBMA network there may be one OSI Layer 2 network, it is subdivided into several logical IP subnetworks (LIS) that can be traversed only via routers.

One of the design philosophies behind CIOA is that network administrators started out building networks using the same techniques that are used today—that is, dividing hosts into physical groups, called subnetworks, according to administrative workgroup domains (as discussed earlier, however, this need not be an obligatory imperative going forward). Then the subnetworks are interconnected to other subnetworks via IP routers. An LIS in CIOA is made up of a collection of ATM-attached hosts and ATM-attached IP routers, which are part of a common IP subnetwork. Policy administration, such as security, access controls, routing, and filtering will remain a function of routers because the ATM network is just "smart" wire.

In CIOA, as in LANE, the functionality of address resolution is provided with the help of special-purpose server processes that are typically colocated. This is accomplished via software upgrades on legacy routers. Each CIOA LIS has an ARP (Address Resolution Protocol) server that maintains IP address-to-ATM address mappings. All members of the LIS register with the ARP server, and subsequently, all ARP requests from members of the LIS are handled by the ARP server. This mechanism is a little more straightforward than LANE version 1 since, for ARP, there is only one server, and it maintains direct IP-to-ATM address mappings.

In the CIOA model, IP ARP requests are forwarded from hosts directly to the LIS ARP server using MAC/ATM address mappings that are acquired at CIOA registration. The ARP server, which is running on an ATM-attached router, replies with an ATM address. When the ARP request originator receives the reply with the ATM address, it can then issue a call setup message and directly establish communications with the desired destination. Figure 9.4 provides an example.

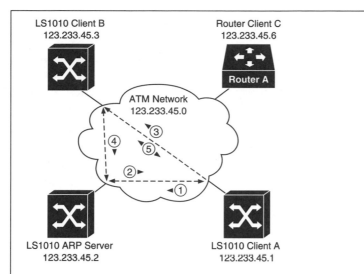

Step 1   The initial IP packet sent by client A triggers a request to the ARP server to look up the IP address and the corresponding ATM address of client B in the ARP server ARP table.

Step 2   The ARP server sends back a response to client A with the matching ATM address.

Step 3   Client A uses the ATM address it just obtained from the ARP server to set up an SVC directly to client B.

Step 4   When client B replies with an IP packet to client A, it also triggers a query to the ARP server.

NOTE When client B receives the ATM address for client A, it usually discovers it already has a call set up to client A's ATM address and will not set up another call.

Step 5   Once the connection is known to both clients, they communicate directly over the SVC.

In Cisco's implementation, the ATM ARP client tries to maintain a connection to the ATM ARP server. The ATM ARP server can tear down the connection, but the client attempts once each minute to bring the connection back up. No error messages are generated for a failed connection, but the client will not route packets until the ATM ARP server is connected and translates IP network addresses.

For each packet with an unknown IP address, the client sends an ATM ARP request to the ARP server. Until that address is resolved, any IP packet routed to the ATM interface will cause the client to send another ATM ARP request.

The LightStream 1010 ATM switch may be configured as an ATM ARP client to work with any ATM ARP server conforming to RFC 1577. Alternatively, one of the LightStream 1010 ATM switches in a logical IP subnet (LIS) may be configured to act as the ATM ARP server itself. In that case, it automatically acts as a client as well. To configure classical IP and ARP in an SVC environment, perform one of the following tasks:

- Configure as an ATM ARP Client
- Configure as an ATM ARP Server

Figure 9.4   Classical IP-over-ATM in an SVC environment.
(Courtesy of Cisco Systems, Inc.)

One of the limitations of this approach is that CIOA has no understanding of QoS. CIOA supports only IP because the ARP server is only knowledgeable about IP. In addition, this approach does little to reduce the use of routers, although it does have the effect of separating to a degree the data-forwarding function from the IP PDU processing function; in effect, IP PDUs do not have to be examined at the end of each hop, but can be examined at the end of a virtual channel (VC) or path (VP), which may consist of several hops—the challenge is how to identify (address) the VC in question to reach a specific remote IP peer, hence the address resolution function. The simplicity of the CIOA model reduces the amount of broadcast traffic and interactions with various servers. By reducing communication that would be required in LANE with the LECS, LES, and BUS, the time needed for address resolution can be reduced. In addition, once the address has been resolved, there is the potential that subsequent data transfer rates may be reduced. However, the reduction in complexity does come with a reduction in functionality.

As is the case with LANE, communication between LISs must be made via ATM-attached routers that are members of more than one LIS. One physical ATM network can logically be considered several logical IP subnetworks, but the interconnection across IP subnets from the host perspective is accomplished via another router. Using an ATM-attached router as the path between subnetworks prevents ATM-attached endstations in different subnetworks from creating direct virtual circuits between one another. This restriction has the potential to degrade throughput and increase latency. There are also questions about the reliability of the IP ARP server because the current version of the specification has no provisions for redundancy: If the ARP server were to fail, all hosts on the LIS would be unable to use the ARP. Finally, CIOA has the drawback that each host needs to be manually configured with the ATM address of the ARP server, as opposed to the dynamic discovery allowed in LANE.

Data transfer is achieved by creating a VC between hosts and then using LLC/SNAP encapsulation of data that has been segmented by AAL 5. Mapping IP packets onto ATM cells using LLC/SNAP is specified in RFC 1483, Multiprotocol Encapsulation Over ATM. RFC 1483 specifies how data is formatted prior to segmentation. (Although the RFC documents several different methods, the majority of host/router implementations use the LLC/SNAP encapsulation; LLC/SNMP specifies that each datagram is prefaced with a bit pattern that the receiver can use to determine the protocol type of the source.) The advantages provided by the encapsulation method specified in RFC 1483 are that it treats ATM as a data link layer that supports a large maximum transfer unit (MTU) and that it can operate in either a bridge or multiplexed mode. Because the network is not emulating an Ethernet or token ring, like LANE, the MTU can be specified to be as large as 9,180 bytes. Such a large MTU can improve performance of hosts attached directly to the ATM network.

RFC 1577 specifies two major modifications to traditional connectionless ARP. The first is the creation of the ATMARP message used to request addresses. The second modification is the InATMARP message, which inverts address registration. When a client wishes to initialize itself on a LIS, it establishes a switched virtual circuit to the CIOA ARP server. Once the circuit has been established, the server contains the ATM address extracted from the call setup message calling party field of the client.

The server can now transmit an InATMARP request in an attempt to determine the IP address of the client that has just created the virtual circuit. The client responds to the InATMARP request with its IP address, and the server uses this information to build its ATMARP table cache. The ARP table in the server will contain a listing for IP-to-ATM pairs for all hosts that have registered, and periodically refresh their entry to prevent them from timing-out. The ATMARP server cache answers subsequent ATMARP requests for the clients' IP address. Clients wishing to resolve addresses generate ATMARP messages, which are sent to their server, and locally cache the reply. But client cache table entries expire and so must be renewed every 15 minutes. Server entries for attached hosts time-out after 20 minutes.

As noted, multicast support is of interest. CIOA provides multicast support via the multicast address resolution server (MARS). The MARS model is similar to a client/server design because it operates by requiring a multicast server to keep membership lists of multicast clients that have joined a multicast group. A client is assigned to a multicast server by a network administrator at configuration time. In the MARS model, a MARS system, along with its associated clients, is called a *cluster*. The MARS approach uses an address resolution server to map an IP multicast address from the cluster onto a set of ATM endpoint addresses of the multicast group members.

The three primary components of a MARS-based IP-over-ATM network are:

- Top-level server(s) called the MARS
- Zero or more multicast servers that provide second-level multicast distribution
- Clients that utilize IP multicast by building point-to-multipoint paths based on information learned by MARS

Every MARS has at least one client and server contained within a CIOA logical IP subnetwork. Typically, the MARS is colocated with the CIOA

ARP server. To operate the system, clients use the MARS as a means of determining which other hosts are members of a multicast group. In a MARS network, there are two modes of operation: full mesh or multicast server. In the full mesh, client queries are sent to the server to identify which hosts have registered as members of a class D tree. A class D address is part of the global IP multicast range. Next, the client establishes a point-to-multipoint virtual circuit to those leaves. In the second mode, the multicast server acts as the focal point of all multicast packets that originated anywhere in the multicast tree. In this case, to simulate IP multicast over an ATM network, the multicast server simply retransmits, over the ATM multicast connections, all PDUs sent to the IP multicast group by the clients. Because the hosts in a multicast group are constantly changing, the MARS is also responsible for dynamically updating the set of clients with new membership information—that is, as changes occur—along with adding and removing clients from the active members.

When running multicast over an ATM network, selecting between the two modes of operation just described is left to the discretion of the network designer. An additional design determination with MARS can be made by adding multiple layers of hierarchy to the distribution tree. For example, multicast clusters may contain the second level of the hierarchy by elevating a client to the role of a multicast server.

One of the trade-offs conceded to gain the simplicity that MARS offers is the required "out-of-band" control messages used to maintain multicast group membership. For clients and multicast servers to send and receive control and membership information, the MARS protocol specifies the setup of a partial mesh of virtual circuits. The MARS maintains its own point-to-multipoint circuits, called the ClusterControlVC, for the members within the cluster.

The ClusterControlVC carries leaf node update information to the clients as members leave and join the multicast session. Each client in a multicast cluster maintains a point-to-point VC to the MARS, which is used to initialize itself and path group change messages. Finally, the MARS manages the multicast servers through point-to-point virtual circuits between each multicast server and the MARS, and point-to-multipoint circuits, called ServerControlVC, from the MARS to the multicast servers. These circuits are used, like the ClusterControlVC, to pass information from the MARS to keep the cluster membership updated.

The MARS protocol utilizes a set of control messages that are exchanged between the MARS and the clients to maintain the group memberships. In addition, the MARS has a special set of messages that it exchanges with the second-tier multicast servers (should one exist) [5].

Before moving on, let's revisit the movement of an IP PDU through an ATM-based backbone. We assume a unicast application and that the traffic characteristics and the QoS requirements (such as delay, loss, throughput) of the application are known to at least one host. That host launches a request for the desired QoS and a description of the expected traffic into the network; at some point, this request hits a router at the edge of the ATM network. The router must examine the request and decide whether it can use an existing connection over the ATM network to honor the request or must establish a new connection. In the latter case, it must use the QoS and traffic characterizations to decide what sort of ATM connection to open and to describe the desired service to the ATM network. It must also decide where to open the connection. Once the connection is opened, the request is forwarded across the ATM network to the exit router and then proceeds across the non-ATM part of the network by the normal means [6].

From this description we can see that there are several sets of issues to be addressed:

- How does the IP service model, with one (now) or more service classes (future) and associated styles of traffic and QoS characterization map onto the ATM service model?

- How does the IP QoS reservation model (e.g., RSVP) map onto ATM signaling?

- How does IP-over-ATM routing work when service quality is added to the picture?

9.3.3 MPOA

MPOA can be viewed as solving the problems of establishing connections between pairs of hosts that cross administrative domains (i.e., IP subnets) and enabling applications to make use of a network's capability to provide guaranteed QoS [7] [8]. For some time already, manufacturers have been releasing products that separate switching from routing, and allow applications to designate their required QoS. MPOA supports intersubnet cut-through in enterprise networks. Like LANE, however, MPOA is principally a campus technology and does not have the robustness to scale to global Internet applications; it is discussed here for completeness.

The MPOA working group of the ATM Forum is chartered with developing a standard approach to forwarding Layer 3 protocols, such as IP or Novell's IPX, transparently over ATM backbones. Building upon LANE, MPOA allows ATM backbone to support legacy Layer 3 protocols and their applications. MPOA could also allow newer Layer 3 protocols and

SCHEMES FOR ROUTING OVER ATM

RFC 1483 Multiprotocol Encapsulation

- Simple

- ATM VCs are defined between every pair of routers.

- Limitation: Full connectivity; however, leads to the "N-squared" problem, which means as routers are added to the network, routing tables grow quadratically, because every router needs a pointer to every other router, and routing updates consume increasing amounts of bandwidth.

ATM Forum's MPOA

- Designed primarily for LANs/campuses, it replaces a collapsed backbone with a "distributed" or virtual router. LAN switches and other edge devices become the virtual router's I/O ports; the route server is the central processor; and ATM switches are the backplane.

- Workstations and servers belong to virtual subnets.

- PDUs destined within virtual subnets are bridged at Layer 2 using LANE.

- PDUs destined between virtual subnets are sent to the route server, which forwards them to the destination device. Simultaneously, the route server downloads Layer 3 information to the source device, and NHRP determines the ATM address of the destination. Subsequent PDUs between the same source and destination cut through the ATM backbone directly, bypassing the route server.

their applications, such as packetized video application using IP's RSVP, to take advantage of ATM's QoS features over the same ATM backbone. With MPOA, endsystems (user clients and corporate servers) can all be just one hop away. In effect, the routing is relegated to the edge of the network. This unbundles the data-forwarding function from the IP PDU processing function. The sidebar compares two available schemes for routing over ATM [9]; also see Figure 9.5.

MPOA enables the separation of the route calculation function from the actual Layer 3 forwarding function (in enterprise networks). This provides three key benefits: integration of intelligent VLANs, cost-effective edge devices, and an evolutionary path for clients from LANE to MPOA. In the MPOA architecture, routers retain all of their traditional functions so that they can be the default forwarder and continue to forward short flows as they do today. Routers also become what is commonly called MPOA or route server, and supply all the Layer 3 forwarding information used by MPOA clients, which include ATM edge devices as well as ATM-

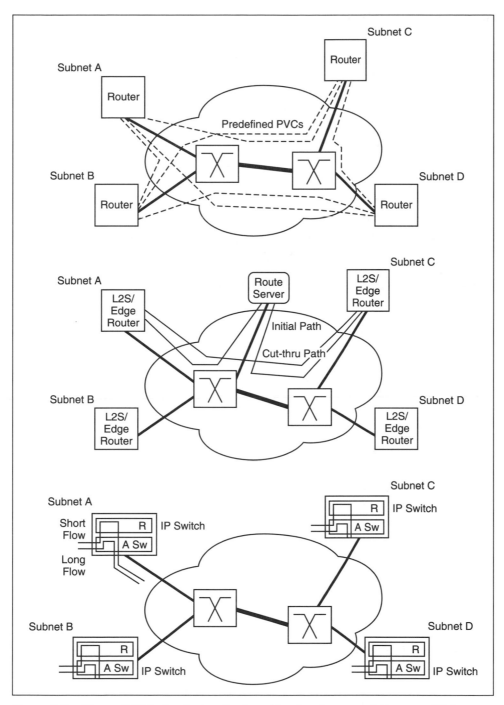

Figure 9.5 IP over ATM technologies: (top) multiprotocol encapsulation over ATM; (middle) MPOA; (bottom) IP switching.

attached hosts. Ultimately, this allows these MPOA clients to set up direct cut-through ATM connection between VLANs to forward long flows without having to always experience an extra router hop [7] [8].

A design desideratum of MPOA is to ensure that both bridging and routing are preserved for legacy LANs and the VLAN topology in use. An MPOA network uses LANE for the bridging function. As implied in the LANE discussion, an emulated LAN's scope (that is, an ELAN) is a single Layer 3 subnet, whereas MPOA is focused on intersubnet (IP subnet) connectivity. (As noted, this implies that routers would be needed to connect ELANs.) Using LANE within the MPOA specification provides a number of benefits to the user, including the fact that it allows backward compatibility, as an MPOA network can be built with both MPOA clients as well as LANE clients. In fact, the default operation for an edge device can be LANE until it learns more, simplifying the topology configuration and start-up operation.

For the Layer 3 forwarding function, MPOA is adopting and extending the Next Hop Routing Protocol (NHRP). NHRP is designed to operate with current Layer 3 routing protocols and, thus, does not require any replacement or changes to those protocols. In order to set up a direct ATM connection between two ATM-attached hosts or between an ATM-attached host and an edge device, the ATM address of the exit point that corresponds to the respective Layer 3 address of the desired destination must be determined. An ATM-attached host can send an NHRP query to an MPOA server, which has been getting reachability information from routing protocols such as OSPF. The MPOA server may then respond with the ATM address of the exit point or ATM-attached host used to reach the destination Layer 3 address, or it may forward the query to other MPOA severs if it does not know the answer. Ultimately, the MPOA server that is serving the client that can reach the destination Layer 3 address will know the answer and reply. Once the replay arrives at the source, it can set up a direct cut-through ATM connection [7] [8].

In a VLAN environment, NHRP will reply with the ATM address of a router that serves the respective destination's VLAN. If this VLAN has more than one router connected to it, there is no guarantee that the reply will address the router closest to the destination. When it does not, that router must bridge the data packets to the closest router, which will then forward them to the destination. In addition to NHRP, MPOA has defined mechanisms that allow the MPOA servers to give out Layer 3 forwarding information to edge devices that represent the optimal exit point for a given destination so that this potential for excess hops is avoided.

At the time of this writing, MPOA was already a standard, while the IP switching technologies were just being standardized. MPOA is a partial step toward network cost reduction as related to the deployment of routers;

this is accomplished by sharing Layer 3 intelligence (route management in the route server) among edge devices. From an economic point of view, developers realize that MPOA components must be priced so that a local MPOA implementation must be cheaper than a large backbone router and multiple LAN switches. MPOA equipment was already available the time of this writing, notably Newbridge's Vivid. The Vivid kit includes a workgroup switch, a Yellow Ridge Ethernet switch with an ATM uplink, a route server, and system manager software. This equipment provides an alternative to both the backbone router and the workgroup switches.

In an Internet application, MPOA could be deployed to support cutthrough, as follows:

- Install an MPOA system in place of a router in a central office (CO).
- Install edge devices (e.g., the LAN switches of Newbridge's Vivid product family) to connect via LANs to remote access servers (which support modem pooling for user access).
- Implement the virtual router across COs over the existing ATM infrastructure.
- Connect web servers to remote edge devices in remote COs.
- Utilize MPOA to build virtual private networks (VPNs).

MPOA has some limitations; consequently, to ensure both availability and high performance, route servers may be needed in nearly every CO. Some claim that dependence on a server could limit scalability, although this is debatable since 800/888 service has not been limited in any way in its growth, in spite of the fact that it also uses centralized telephony route servers.

It seems that ultimately ISPs will rely mostly on CIOA. ISPs may end up viewing ATM just as they view frame relay: A Layer 2 communications service (although ATM could do more particularly in supporting QoS).

9.3.4 Network Layer Switching

Layer 3 switching, also known as IP switching, in all its forms, has two goals: to find a way for internetworks (especially the Internet) to scale economically; and to bring effective QoS support to IP. Layer 3 switching is supported via Layer 3 switches (L3S) that are deploycd in the core of the network. The following view was typical at the time of this writing: "While many carriers have committed to ATM for Layer 2 transport, the question of how best to route IP traffic remains an open question: How many carriers will bet on new MPOA protocols to keep their route server in sync when time-tested solutions like OSPF aren't broken?" [9] Some approach the scaling challenge with faster routers and higher-speed lines. Several vendors have launched superrouter initiatives and have announced router-over-SONET interfaces; many, however, believe that solutions based on switched technologies (like ATM) have much more ultimate potential. Switching can replace latency-prone, processing-intensive Layer 3 "hops" with more efficient Layer 2 connections. It is hoped that evolving Layer 3 switching systems will have applications in the Internet. At least one vendor (Lucent) seems to have high hopes for Internet applicability, based on product announcements in 1998.

If a robust network-layer switching technology can be developed (e.g., MPLS), it could play a significant role in future Internet and VPN applications. However, the various vendor-proprietary solutions now in the market either are campus solutions, do not work well (in a stable fashion), or do not scale at all or well (some cannot be used effectively beyond 40 to 50 routers). We cover this topic next to expose planners to the possible future applicability, if scalability and stability can be secured.

Various Network Layer Proposals

The approaches to IP support over ATM covered thus far evolved in the mid-1990s. The late 1990s have seen the emergence of various schemes to address several limitations of traditional IP routing implied by the discussion in sections 9.1 and 9.2, including the need for meshed or near-meshed physical networks; the requirement to perform Layer 3 processing at the endpoints of each link (in effect, collapsing data-forwarding/transmission, IP processing, and topology discovery into a single, obligatory function at each link endpoint); the relative complexity of Layer 3 processing; the duplication of Layer 2 and Layer 3 functionality (e.g., addressing); and the relatively poor use of improved data link layer technologies (e.g., ATM) by IP.[6]

To address these concerns, a number of vendor-specific as well as standards-based solutions have been proposed and/or are under development or deployment. Notable vendor-specific solutions include Cisco's NetFlow/Tag-Switching technology and Ipsilon's IP Switching technology. Standards-based solutions include MPOA, already discussed, and MPLS, which is the evolving specification for cohesive Layer 2/Layer 3 switching/routing.

The ability to switch data based on very fast hardware table lookups on the MAC or ATM addresses leads to very fast and reliable networks. However, these technologies also pose problems in scalability and complexity that are seen by large ISPs or in large enterprise networks. High degrees of scalability can be difficult to achieve with a Layer 2 switched network because the address space is nonhierarchical. Their combination is difficult to find with a pure Layer 2 switched network, so network managers have traditionally used network layer protocols, like IP, to fill that void. Of the problems introduced by large Layer 2 networks, some of the more pressing concerns have to do with smoothly integrating Layer 2 switching with Layer 3 switching. A number of solutions were emerging at the time of this writing.

The goals of network layer switching are to provide new means for interworking Layer 2 and Layer 3 technologies. Where the interworking differs from previous protocols is that the functionality of traditional network layer protocols, such as IP, plays a more important role in the overall control of the network. In a network layer switched environment, all of the ATM switches understand and are capable of routing IP packets using protocols like BGP or OSPF. In this model, benefits of ATM that are applied to network design are basically speed and traffic control. The general goal, at least in enterprise networks, is to deploy L3Ses in the core and push-pure routers to the edges. ISPs are investigating how that could also be done in the Internet. While this may be possible within an ISP's own aggregation or backbone network, it is not clear how it would be possible in the Internet at large, considering, for example, the public and private peering arrangements.

Recent experience with ATM and IP integration has given network designers a perspective on the technology that deviates somewhat from ATM initial goals. Most first-generation ISP or enterprise ATM deployments utilized ATM for either its speed or its capability to provide strict controls over traffic flow. The high speeds come in the form of fiber optic access facilities (and networks) that operate at 155Mbps or 622Mbps; traffic control is achieved via PVC assignment. While this use of ATM has been useful, it is a very coarse method for designing a network that can sometimes lead to unexpected traffic flows. Standards activity and recent network deployments focused attention on issues surrounding traffic engineering and the ability to use the Layer 2 network to explicitly define the route data flows.

The body of work in the field of network layer switching can be subdivided into two categories based on the level of granularity that is applied when mapping IP traffic to ATM virtual circuits. These models are called *flow-based* versus *topology-based*. From a high-level view of network switching, one can think of the flow-based models as building a network out of router/switching devices in which unique ATM virtual circuits are created for each IP *conversation*, where *conversations* are synonymous with a file transfer or web session or other distinguishable interactions. In the topology proposals, the router/switching devices use their ATM fabrics to create ATM virtual circuits that can carry all of the traffic destined between pairs of subnetworks or IP routes.

Regardless of the exact technical approach, the goals of network layer switching are similar because network layer switching's fundamental motivations are to remove excess computational processing done during PDU transmission by clearly dividing routing from forwarding, then to remove routing from the process whenever possible. In both the flow-based or topology-based model, the ATM switch must be aware of IP and capable of participating in IP routing protocols. However, the processes of forwarding and routing still maintain a clear division. Once the control process (i.e., routing) has detected either a route or a flow, it removes itself from the communication path and employs high-speed forwarding from the ATM fabric.

Cisco's NetFlow and Tag-Switching Technology

Cisco has been the major player to first address the issue of Layer 3 cut-through via its NetFlow/Tag-Switching technology. This technology supports flow-oriented switching for multiple protocols. The approach is to "learn once, switch many times." Cisco has positioned Tag Switching as a LAN technology and NetFlow as a WAN technology—fundamentally, they are similar in concept.

Tag Switching is Cisco's answer to Ipsilon's IP Switching, and it is positioned for networks with 30 to 40 backbone routers. Tag switching utilizes traditional routing protocols to identify and maintain paths. The novelty is that all paths leading to the same destination (e.g., an IP subnet) are assigned the same "tag." The Tag Distribution Protocol (TDP) maintains tables in each node that relate tags to destinations. As PDUs enter the network, a router handles Layer 3 processing and assigns each one a tag; at subsequent nodes, which can be router, ATM switches, or frame relay switches, Layer 3 processing is bypassed, and PDUs are forwarded based only on their tags. Routing hops are eliminated from the interior of the network [9]. Hence, this approach enables a form of cut-through, in that the routing decisions are ostensibly relegated to the edge of the network.

A flow is a unidirectional sequence of packets between a given source and destination. Questions related to flows are: What does one use to define a NetFlow? What determines the start of a NetFlow? What determines the end of a NetFlow? How does one time-out a NetFlow entry? NetFlow granularity can be defined in terms of application (application-layer applications such as Telnet, FTP, etc.); transport layer protocols (e.g., TCP, UDP); network layer IP parameters (e.g., IP address); and data link layer protocols (e.g., Ethernet, Token Ring).

The IP header contains a protocol field (the tenth byte) that can be used to define a flow (e.g., the protocol could be ICMP, TCP, UDP, etc.). In turn, the UDP and TCP headers contain port numbers that define the nature of the data being carried (e.g., port 53 for DNS, port 520 for RIP, port 161 for SNMP, port 23 for Telnet, port 21 for FTP, port 80 for the Web). Hence, Net-Flow granularity can be defined at the TCP/UDP source or destination port, IP protocol type, and IP source or destination address. The NetFlow flow can start with a TCP SYN flag and terminate with a TCP FIN flag.

A router has various kinds of memory, specifically packet memory and system memory. With NetFlow enhancements to the router, a NetFlow cache is allocated. An incoming frame is first copied to packet memory. Normally, IP processing takes place to determine the route; that is, the destination address is removed from the PDU and the routing table is consulted so that the PDU can be sent to the exit interface. In a NetFlow-enabled router, when a new frame arrives, there may be no match in the NetFlow switching cache. Hence, the PDU is copied to the system buffer for processing. A lookup in the Layer 3 network address table is under-taken to see where the frame should be routed. The NetFlow switch cache is initialized, and the frame is sent to the exit interface. For the next frame, it is copied to packet memory, but a match is found in the NetFlow switching cache. This implies that the frame can now be sent directly to the output interface without having to go through the additional IP rout-ing processing, specifically frame deenveloping and routing table lookup, which can be (relatively) demanding in terms of resources.

Tag Switching is applicable at the campus network level, while Net-Flow is positioned at the WAN level. Tag Switching addresses the throughput, scaling, and traffic engineering issues of corporate enterprise networks. It permits a graceful evolution of routing, and is intended to allow integration of ATM and IP. Tag Switching combines Layer 3 routing with label-swapping forwarding (such as that available on Layer 2 ATM/frame relay networks). The simplicity of Layer 2 forwarding offers high performance; a separation of forwarding for long flows and routing aids the evolution of routing. Refer again to Figure 9.5. Eventually, MPLS may replace Tag Switching.

Forwarding is based on a label-swapping mechanism, as well as a con-trol component that is used to maintain and distribute bindings. The router maintains a tag-forwarding information base (TFIB), whose entries include the incoming tag and one or more subentries such as outgoing tag, outgoing interface, and outgoing MAC address. TFIB is indexed by the incoming tag; TFIB may be per-box or per–incoming interface. The forwarding algorithm works as follows: (1) Extract the tag from the incoming frame; (2) find the TFIB entry with the incoming tag equal to the tag on the frame; (3) replace the tag in the frame with the outgoing tags; and (4) send the frame to the outgoing interface. In working this way, the label-swapping mechanism is really like an ATM switch. Note that the forwarding algorithm is network-layer-independent. The TPD is used to distribute tag bindings to neighbors; the protocol only sends information if there is a change in the routing table and the device does not have a label.

Because tags correspond to destinations rather than to source-destination pairs or traffic flows, tag population grows at "order N" rather than "N-squared"; this makes scaling feasible in large enterprise networks and the Internet. Tags are allocated in advance; therefore, there are no performance penalties to short-lived flows or to the first PDU of long-lived flows.

PDUs carry the tag between the IP datagram and its Layer 2 envelope. (As noted, with IPv6, tags will be included in the Layer 3 flow label field.) Each router examines the tag and sends the PDU directly to the output port, by passing normal routing processing. This implies that Tag Switching can be used without having to immediately convert the physical network to ATM. Performance improvements in the 10 to 20 percent range are possible. The use of ATM, however, supports broadband. Most enterprise networks today can no longer be designed with T1 (1.544Mbps) links, especially in the presence of switched 10Mbps Ethernet, 100Mbps Ethernet, and gigabit Ethernet. Hence, a conversion to Tag Switching first without ATM infrastructure, and then with an ATM infrastructure, can be considered a reasonable migration strategy. In an ATM-based backbone network, VCIs are utilized as tags. TDP sets up the correspondence between routes and VCI tags; no ATM Q.2931 signaling is required. Routers at the edge of the network examine the incoming PDU's IP destination address and assign it the proper VCI. ATM switches support the forwarding function, and do so in an effective manner. The internetwork itself remains connectionless, since there are no end-to-end (endsystem-to-endsystem) virtual circuits, and switches route around network failures. Still, the issue of ATM interworking is not fully solved by Tag Switching; because PDUs from different sources destined for a specific destination end up sharing a VCI and cells, they may get interleaved, which is a problem in ATM. MPLS aims at addressing this issue.

IP Switching

IP Switching is a proprietary (non–ATM Forum or IETF-sanctioned) networking technology advanced by Ipsilon Networks that combines the control of IP routing with ATM speed, scalability, and quality of service to deliver millions of IP packets per second throughput to intranet and Internet environments.[7] Ipsilon took a fresh look at the problem. The company wanted to "make IP go fast, but also to create a complete paradigm shift." IP Switching implementations have included network interface cards to edge systems, telecommunications devices, and backbone, campus, and workgroup switches.

An IP Switch implements the IP protocol stack directly onto ATM hardware, allowing the ATM switch fabric to operate as a high-performance link-layer accelerator for IP routing. An IP Switch delivers ATM at wire speeds while maintaining compatibility with existing IP networks, applications, and network management tools.

Using intelligent IP Switching software, an IP Switch dynamically shifts between store-and-forward routing and cut-through switching based on the needs of the IP traffic, or flows. An IP Switch automatically chooses cut-through switching for flows of longer duration, such as file transfer protocol (FTP) data, TELNET data, HyperText Transmission Protocol (HTTP) data, and multimedia audio and video. It reserves hop-by-hop, store-and-forward routing for short-lived traffic, such as Domain Name Server (DNS) queries, Simple Mail Transfer Protocol (SMTP) data, and SNMP queries. The majority of data is switched directly by the ATM hardware, without additional IP router processing, achieving millions of PPS throughput. See Figure 9.5.

One of the advantages that IP Switching offers is an interoperable network architecture that has resulted from the multivendor acceptance of the technology. While router improvements continue to be limited to individual platforms, IP Switching can become a networkwide solution. IP Switching, with its published protocols, wanted to provide cooperative benefits to all peer participants: direct cut-through connections across the network and low latency compared to traditional router networks.

In a classical internetwork, every router is connected to just a few neighbors, in order to keep routing tables to a manageable level from a size and access-speed perspective. As noted in chapter 8, routing protocols are used to determine paths between endpoints and to recover automatically when a node or trunk fails. The problem with this approach is that a path may entail many Layer 3 hops, producing unacceptable delay and unpredictable performance.

To support effective communication, the exchange of appropriate routing and status information among routers is required. The routers exchange information about the state of the network's links and interfaces and available paths, based on different metrics. Metrics used to calculate optimal paths through the network include cost, bandwidth, distance, delay, load, congestion, security, QoS, and reliability. Routing protocols are used as the means to exchange this information (see Chapter 4 for a discussion of routing protocols).

IP Switching utilizes the same topology and the same routing protocols as conventional routers, but replaces Layer 3 hops with Layer 2 switching. The N-squared problem of multiprotocol encapsulation (RFC 1483) goes away, and network performance improves. Each Ipsilon IP Switch comprises a router (called an IP Switch Controller) and an ATM switch. The router exchanges topology information with other IP Switches and provides Layer 3 store-and-forward services, while the ATM switch forwards cells at broadband speed. The software can recognize flows (a flow being a coherent stream of PDUs between the same source and destination). The IP Switch analyzes each flow and classifies it as short- or long-lived. (Ipsilon estimates that longer flows constitute more than 80 percent of internetwork traffic.) Short-lived flows (e.g., SNMP queries, Web URLs, DNS packets) are routed by traditional IP-level methods over default VCs and incur normal router latency. Longer flows like file transfers are assigned separate VCs that bypass the IP-level routing processing, and so can be forwarded at much higher speeds [9]. Many of the concepts are carried forward in MPLS.

In an IP Switched network, all hosts and switches communicate through a common set of cooperative protocols—the Ipsilon Flow Management Protocol (IFMP, IETF RFC 1953, 1954) and the General Switch Management Protocol (GSMP, IETF RFC 1987)—to optimize short- and long-lived conversations between a sender and receiver. Routing decisions need only be made once. As soon as longer-lasting flow data has been identified and cut through, there is no need to reassemble its ATM cells into IP packets at intermediate switch points. Thus, traffic incurs minimal latency, and throughput remains optimized throughout the IP Switched network. End-to-end cooperation also enables QoS implementation, since with cut-through switching policies naturally span administrative boundaries. Hence, flows can be utilized to support flow-binded QoS: By analyzing IP headers, the IP Switch can relate individual flows to performance requirements and request ATM VCs with the proper type of service. Flows emanating from a time-critical application (if it can be identified in same manner, e.g., port number, IP address, etc.) might receive highest priority, while ordinary file transfers would run at low priority [9].

Multivendor support can result in a new economic model for high-performance networks. Customers can select the best platform according to their particular needs in a range of different network environments—from the campus to the Internet to the carrier networks, even at home. They can choose from an array of IP-based supporting applications, platforms, and tools. And they can work with any number of solution providers, since no single vendor dominates the Layer 3 Switching landscape.

Different network elements can implement IP Switching protocols to deliver ATM-accelerated IP while maintaining multivendor, multiplatform interoperability. There is applicability for IP Switching across workgroup, campus backbone, Internet, WAN, and broadband access environments. Early applications included: IP Switching in the campus backbone, IP Switching in workgroups, IP Switching in the Internet and across the WAN, and broadband access to IP Switched networks.

One of the limitations of the technology is how it utilizes ATM VCs. Flows are associated with application-to-application conversations, and every long-lived flow gets its individual cut-through VC. This works for relatively small campus networks, but in large network environments, millions of individual flows would quickly exhaust VC tables. Many switches are also limited in the actual number of VCs they can actually maintain. Furthermore, the constant requests for new VCs can easily overwhelm the switch. A modification may be required in large enterprise networks/Internet to support flows with less granularity.

Multiprotocol Label Switching

The Multiprotocol Label Switching (MPLS) working group has been charted by the IETF to develop a label-swapping standard for Layer 3 switching. The group started with Cisco's Tag Switching and IBM's nearly identical Aggregate Route-Based IP Switching (ARIS). As was noted, the issue of ATM interworking is not fully solved by Tag Switching, because cell/PDU interleaving occurs when the tag is identified with the VCI. Two schemes were being considered by MPLS at the time of this writing to address the issue [9]:

- The ATM switch merges multiple VCs into a single VC without interleaving. If two PDUs arrive at the switch simultaneously, the switch buffers cells from one PDU until the other PDU leaves. This approach may require additional hardware in the ATM switch to buffer colliding PDUs.

- The network grows a tree upward from the egress point using ATM VP labels, one VP per egress point. By convention, each source point uses a different VC within the VP. Using VCIs inside the VP, the destination switch can sort out interleaved cells from separate sources. Although more VCs are used in this method, the amount of state information is still order N, where N is the number of destinations. This approach needs no new hardware.

Hopes are that MPLS will be an effective Layer 3 switching technology, but only time will tell.

References

1. D. Minoli, J. Amoss. *Broadband and ATM Switching Technology.* (New York: McGraw-Hill), 1998.
2. Ipsilon Networks promotional material, used with permission. Personal communication with J. Doyle, Ipsilon.
3. J. McQuillan. The NGN Executive Seminar, New York, March 20, 1997.
4. D. Minoli, A. Schmidt. *Switch Network Services.* (New York: John Wiley & Sons, Inc.), 1998.
5. A. Schmidt, D. Minoli. *MPOA.* (Greenwich, CT: Prentice-Hall/Manning), 1998.
6. RFC 1881, Integration of Real-Time Services in an IP-ATM Network Architecture, August 1995, <http://sunsite.auc.dk.RFC/rfc/raf1821.html<.
7. D. Minoli, A. Alles. *LAN, ATM, and LAN Emulation Technologies.* (Norwood, MA: Artech House), 1997.
8. D. Minoli, A. Schmidt. *Client/Server over ATM.* (Greenwich, CT: Prentice-Hall/Manning), 1997.
9. R. B. Bellman, "IP Switching—Which Flavor Works For You?" *BCR,* April 1997, pp. 41–46.

Notes

1 Portions of this chapter based on and updated from *Broadband and ATM Switching Technology* [1].

2 The support of IP-over-frame relay is well understood and fairly straight-forward, as covered in RFC 1490 for multiprotocol encapsulation.

3 The IP "routing function" (i.e., path selection) can be undertaken in software in the endsystem (e.g., PC), and the desired path can be identified completely and uniquely at the edge of the network. The topology map to support network reroutes would be retained at the data link layer rather than the IP layer; this implies a shift in responsibility from the user/organization to the network itself. The whole concept of addressing needs to be revisited. In the beginning, telecommunication networks did not support the capability for remote locations to be addressed in real time (except with circuit switching, but this is too slow and does not support enough bandwidth). Hence, IP introduced a way to accomplish that—being able to identify the location within that realm was part of the required machinery. But now, ATM-based networks can support real-time addressability of devices attached to the network. Hence, there is a redundant function of Layer 2 and Layer 3 addressing. Why should redundancies be retained, in fact institutionalized? There are opportunities of savings if the redundancies are eliminated.

4 This section is based on Fore Systems promotional material, and is used with permission.

5 This section is based on *MPOA,* by Schmidt and Minoli [5].

6 This section is based on Minoli and Schmidt, *Switched Network Services* [4].

7 This section is based on Ipsilon Networks promotional material (used with permission) and personal communication with the author.

CHAPTER 10

Generic IP-Based Communication: QoS Based on RSVP

This chapter covers support of QoS in IP networks; it also provides some additional ATM QoS information. To support real-time services in an IP environment, the Resource Reservation Protocol (RSVP) has been advanced recently as the signaling protocol to enable network resources to be reserved for a connectionless data stream.

These techniques come into play in Internet and voice-over-IP scenarios, where a non-ATM-based approach to QoS is sought and employed. The ultimate goal is to develop capabilities to use MPLS-based networks, which already have the advantage of enabling route cut-through, as well as being a hook into the IP application (via RSVP) to support QoS at the same time. RSVP is a general-purpose signaling protocol and could be used to map resource reservations to ATM signaling messages. However, many people believe that RSVP may not be scalable to the Internet. Topics covered in this chapter include:

- Resource Reservation Protocol (RSVP)
- Real Time Protocol (RTP)
- New approaches to QoS support in routers

10.1 Introduction

The traditional network service on the Internet is best-effort packet transmission, whereby packets from a source are sent to a destination, with no guarantee of (timely) delivery. For those applications that require a guarantee of delivery, the TCP protocol will trade packet delay for correct reception by retransmitting those packets that fail to reach the destination. For traditional computer-communication applications such as FTP and TELNET, in which correct delivery is more important than timeliness, this service is satisfactory. However, a new class of applications that use multiple media (voice, video, and computer data) has begun to appear on the Internet. Examples are voice-over the Internet/intranets, video teleconferencing, video-on-demand, and distributed simulation. These applications can operate to some extent using best-effort delivery, but trading packet delay for correct reception is not an acceptable trade-off. Operating in the traditional mode for these applications results in reduced quality of the received information and, potentially, inefficient use of bandwidth [1].

To support QoS-sensitive applications, such as voice and video, intranets and the Internet need to provide differentiated quality-of-service levels. These graduated service levels will, in turn, also be important for data applications—for example, for legacy SNA traffic or for newer mission-critical, time-sensitive applications that heretofore have received the same treatment in the intranet/Internet as bulk file transfers.

To remedy this QoS problem, the IETF is developing a real-time service environment in which multiple classes of service are supported in IP-based networks. This environment will extend the existing best-effort service model to meet the needs of multimedia applications with real-time constraints. The following sidebar describes some of the industry development efforts underway [1]. To make QoS on IP networks a reality, these specifications have to be broadly implemented by both technology and service providers. The eventual extent of such implementation remains to be seen.

As implied in previous chapters, designers see the need for integrated real-time service support that includes IP routing, ATM-based QoS, and multicast features. These services should be available to applications operating on ATM networks, IP networks, IP-over-ATM networks, and networks that contain a mixture of subnetworks each with some of these technologies. Specifically, evolving applications may have to support communication from an:

INDUSTRY EFFORTS TO DEVELOP AN INTEGRATED SERVICES INTERNET

- The Integrated Services group (int-serv) is working to define a new IP service model called Integrated Services Architecture (ISA), including a set of services suited to a range of real-time applications.

- The Resource Reservation Setup Protocol group (rsvp) is defining a resource reservation protocol by which the appropriate service for an application could be requested from the network.

- The Internet Streams Protocol V2 group (ST-II) is updating RFC 1190, a stream-oriented Internet protocol that provides a range of service qualities.

- The IETF IP-over-ATM working group and the ATM Forum Multiprotocol-over-ATM group are working to define a model for protocols to make use of the ATM layer, specifically MPOA and MPLS.

- IP endsystem to an IP endsystem
- ATM endsystem to an ATM endsystem
- ATM endsystem to an ATM endsystem over a non-ATM IP network
- IP endsystem to an IP endsystem over an ATM network
- ATM endsystem to an IP endsystem

Though the bulk of this chapter discusses QoS in IP networks, it is important to point out that, as discussed in Chapter 9, there now are IP/ATM interworking scenarios; hence, interworking of the two technologies at the QoS level will also be needed. This last topic is described here only in generalities, but an appropriate in-depth source is included in the References [2], and additional ATM QoS information is supplied at the end of the chapter. (ATM QoS in a pure ATM network was introduced in Chapter 7.)

10.2 QoS Guarantees in IP-Based Networks

During the CIOA discussion in Chapter 9, it was pointed out that there a number of challenges in securing QoS in that (simple) environment. To address this, in the recent past, the IETF has been working on mechanisms to support QoS-over-packet networks, which is important for voice applications. QoS guarantees for IP-based networks can be achieved in two ways (see Figure 10.1):

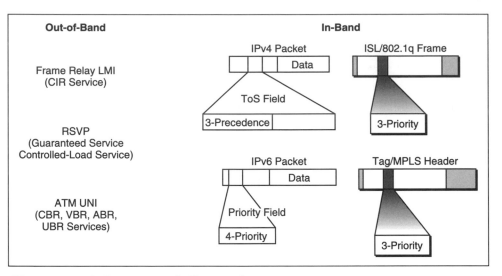

Figure 10.1 QoS guarantees in IP networks.

- *In-band,* where carriers and ISPs can provide a priority mechanism to packets of a certain type. This could be done, for example, with the TOS field in the IPv4 header, or the Priority field in the IPv6 header. The Tag/MPLS label is another way to identify to the router/IP switch that special treatment is required. If routers, switches, and endsystems all used/recognized the appropriate fields, and the queues in the routers/switches were effectively managed according to the priorities, this method of providing QoS guarantees could be called the simplest. This is because no new protocols would be needed, and the carrier's router could be configured in advance to recognize labels of different types of information flows.

- *Out-of-band* signaling mechanisms, which includes ATM signaling for different classes of services, for example, in a CIOA environment. But more characteristic to the IP environment, one finds the RSVP.

With RSVP, the end user can request services based on QoS (see Figure 10.2). It should be immediately noted, however, that RSVP only reserves; it does not provide bandwidth. As such, it augments existing unicast/ multicast routing protocols, IP in particular; in turn, IP may well have to rely on ATM (say, via CIOA or MPOA) to obtain bandwidth. By contrast, ATM provides a connection-oriented service, where resource reservations for QoS support are made at connection setup time, using a UNI and a NNI signaling protocol. Given the industry's interest and likelihood of deployment, a discussion of RSVP and ancillary constructs follows. (Note:

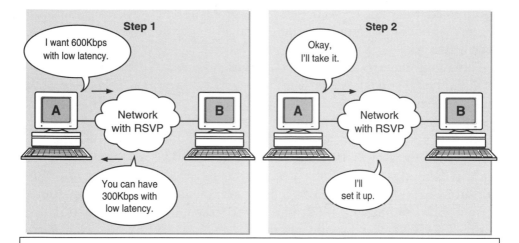

After the default IP data path is set up by either traditional router or ATM switches, RSVP is used to deliver QoS requests to each switch or router along the path. RSVP is a signaling protocol, not a routing protocol. Each node along the data path processes the QoS request, possibly reserving resources for the connection, then forwards the request to the next internet-working device along the selected path.

NOTE RSVP produces a simplex reservation, that is, the endstations can only specify resource reservations for one direction at a time. Therefore, two reservation requests are needed if bidirectional quality of service is desired.

Figure 10.2   With RSVP, the end user can request services based on QoS.

Some have also suggested the use of ST-II, but this topic is not further treated here.)

10.3 RSVP

Before addressing RSVP directly, it is necessary to introduce the model in which its architecture is defined, called the integrated service model.

10.3.1 Integrated Services Architecture

The IETF is currently developing an integrated service model designed to support real-time services on the Internet and in enterprise internets. The model defines the architecture of RSVP service guarantees. The Integrated

Services Architecture (ISA) uses a setup protocol whereby hosts and routers signal QoS requests pertaining to a flow to the network and to each other.

The integrated service model starts with a flow-based description of the problem being solved. A *flow* is a single data stream from a single sending application to a set of receiving applications. Aggregated flows form a *session*, which is a homogeneous stream of simplex data from several senders to several receivers. An example of a flow is the data being sent from a TCP source to a TCP destination (the reverse is a separate flow). Each TCP stream is one of a series of successive steps in moving information from a sender to a receiver. In this case, the flow identifiers are the source and destination IP addresses, the IP transport protocol identifier (e.g., UDP, TCP), and the port number [3].

ISA defines traffic and QoS characteristics for a flow. Traffic control mechanisms monitor traffic flows within a host/router to support the required QoS. ISA encompasses three QoS classes, as follows: guaranteed service, controlled load service, and best-effort service.

The goal of the integrated services model is to mask the underlying technology from the application, while providing the following features:

- Internetwork routing, allowing applications to achieve their desired performance from the network via optimal path selection.

- Multicast capability, permitting one-to-many or many-to-many communication flows.

- Quality-of-service facilities, representing parameters describing the desired characteristics that applications can expect from the network.

ISA must address each Layer 2 technology. Hence, the IETF is utilizing different subgroups to look at Ethernet, token ring, and ATM. Utilizing ISA methods, the Internet can be redesigned for real-time applications (e.g., real-time video); nevertheless, the overall performance efficiency at the network level remains to be understood (i.e., how many customers can be supported over a given router or link).

As noted in the previous sidebar, the QoS development effort has been divided between two working groups, the RSVP group (rsvp) and the Integrated Services group (int-serv). When building an IP network that supports QoS, the RSVP specification is the mechanism that performs QoS requests, which is analogous to ATM signaling. The Integrated Services specifications aim at documenting which capabilities are available to QoS-aware applications, a feature that is analogous to ATM traffic management.

As for the ATM service classes, the IETF has defined service categories in ISA, as follows [4]:

Guaranteed Service.   Allows the user to request a maximum delay bound for an end-to-end path across a packet network. Service is guaranteed to be within that delay bound, but no minimum is specified. This is analogous to ATM's CBR. Real-time applications can make use of this service. Leaky bucket, reserved rate, and weighted fair queuing are used for application control. The underlying transport mechanism can be, among others, ATM (CBR or VBR-rt).

Controlled Load Service.   Provides a small set of service levels, each differentiated by delay behavior. It supports three relative levels, but without particular numerical values of delay associated with them. This service provides a best-effort end-to-end capability with a load baseline. Applications sensitive to congestion can make use of this service. Leaky bucket methods are used for application control. The underlying transport mechanism can be, among others, ATM (VBR-nrt or ABR with a minimum cell rate support).

Best-Effort Service.   This baseline (default) represents the service that can be achieved over the Internet/intranet without any QoS modifications. This service provides a best-effort end-to-end capability. Legacy applications can make use of this service. The underlying transport mechanism can be, among others, ATM (UBR or ABR with a minimum cell rate support).

A discussion of ISA cannot be divorced from a discussion of ATM. Concurrent to the IETF's efforts, the ATM Forum is developing ATM networking, which similarly provides real-time networking support. The use of ATM in the Internet as a link layer protocol is already occurring, and both the IETF and the ATM Forum have already produced specifications for IP-over-ATM. There is interest in interworking the two systems, so that better use can be made of ATM in support of voice and other applications. This is covered in section 10.4.

10.3.2 RSVP Background

The RSVP signaling protocol uses resource reservations messages from sources to destinations to secure QoS-based connectivity and bandwidth [5] [6]. Along the path between the source and the target, the resource requests are used to obtain permission from admission control software to use available local resources (e.g., buffers, trunks, etc.) to support the desired QoS. Then, resource requests reestablish the reservation state, thereby committing the reservation. When the desired request cannot be fulfilled, a request failure message is generated and returned to the appropriate party. In cases where the reservation messages are transmitted but are lost somewhere in the network, the endstations may assume their request was accepted and may begin to transmit information to a destination that in fact has no resources reserved; that information will likely be dropped by the routers. In order to allow a host to determine if the RSVP message was successful, the host can, if desired, explicitly query the network for state information. Figure 10.3 depicts the end-to-end QoS request capability, along with the QoS scope of other protocols.

Multicasting is an evolving application that needs to be supported. RSVP is designed to support heterogeneity of QoS if there are multiple receivers in a multicast session: Each receiver can get a different QoS either by merging requests or by using different QoS layers. Because RSVP is a receiver-driven protocol (see Figure 10.4), it has the capability to scale to a large number of recipients. A mechanism in RSVP reduces the number of messages traveling upstream via a merging function. It should be clear that from a functional perspective RSVP is similar to ATM signaling: With RSVP, users can provision a network connection with a carrier/ISP that utilizes a single physical connection, but over which they can provide dynamic quality of service.

The user of an RSVP-ready network has several choices when transmitting IP PDUs across the intranet/Internet. Consequently, carriers will have to find ways to integrate IP and next-generation ATM/MPOA networks into a seamless QoS-based networking environment [2].

10.3.3 RSVP Nomenclature and Mechanisms

Some RSVP nomenclature follows (see Table 10.1). *Flow* is the term used in RSVP, MPOA, MPLS, switching routers, and so on to describe a sequence of PDUs with the same QoS requirements. Typically, flows are segregated by the IP destination address and port number. A *session* designates flows with a particular destination IP address and port; in this manner, a session can be identified and provided with special QoS treatment. RSVP utilizes two terms to describe traffic categories: *flowspec*, which is the information contained in the reservation request pertaining to QoS requirements for the reservation in question; and *filterspec*, which specifies the flows received or scheduled by the host. The next sidebar identifies some highlights of the protocol.

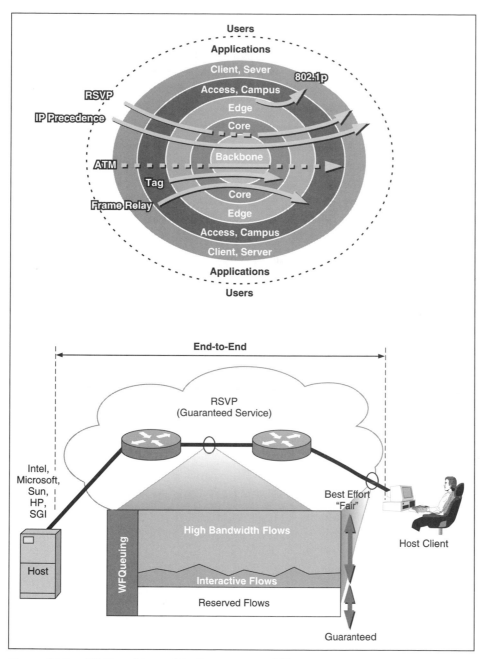

Figure 10.3   RSVP end-to-end QoS request capability.

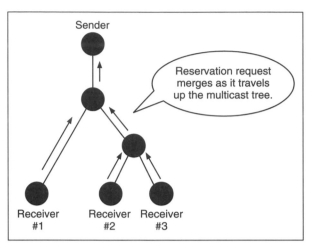

Figure 10.4   RSVP is a receiver-driven protocol.

RSVP work started in 1991 at Lawrence Berkeley National Laboratories and Xerox's Palo Alto Research Center in support of first-generation Internet-based multimedia tools. Desiderata were: efficient use of Internet resources, scalability, support of unicast and multicast, coexistence with TCP/IP. Three components are used by endsystems (hosts) to determine and signal QoS (also see Figure 10.5):

- The setup protocol used by routers or hosts to signal QoS into the network.

- A traffic model or specification (the flowspec) that defines the traffic and QoS characteristics of flow data leaving a source.

- Traffic controls (shaping mechanisms) that measure traffic flows leaving a host or router to ensure that it does not exceed the pre-agreed QoS.

RSVP uses IP as the basic method of carrying the signaling messages; this facilitates broad application, since, for example, ISPs' networks, are IP-based. However, RSVP produces a simplex reservation; that is, the endstations are specifying resource reservations for only one direction at a time, hence, two reservation requests are needed if bidirectional quality of service is desired. As noted, if an RSVP reservation is successful, there is no acknowledgment from the network, as would be the case with an ATM call request for an SVC. This design decision was made to keep the protocol simple, but it could pose problems when interworking with ATM. RSVP messages can be passed from router to router and only

Table 10.1 RSVP Nomenclature

Advertised Specification (Adspec)	A set of modifiable parameters used to describe the QoS capability of the path between the source and destination.
Filterspec	The set of PDUs (packets) that receive the QoS specified by the flowspec. The session ID, an implicit part of the filter, segregates and schedules in the packet classifier output packet streams according to their source address|port.
Flow Specification (Flowspec)	A description of the desired QoS reservation. The flowspec in a reservation request contains the service class and two sets of numeric parameters: TSpec and Rspec. If the request is successful, the flowspec sets the packet scheduler.
Packet filter	Unique header pattern occurring in packet classification.
Resource Specification (RSpec)	A way to characterize the desired quality of service. The characterization of resources reserved to satisfy receivers in terms of which QoS characteristics the packet stream will use; this information evaluates QoS requests.
Sender Template	The sender's IP address (and, optionally, port number).
Session	Specific parameters that describe a reservation, including unique information used to differentiate the traffic flow associated with the session. A session is identified by the combination: destination address|protocol|port.
Transmission Specification (TSpec)	A way to characterize traffic. The characterization of the information flow from the standpoint of the packet stream's physical appearance (i.e., headers, packets/second, etc.); this information differentiates the QoS requests.

RSVP HIGHLIGHTS

- Supports the capability of entities to signal their desired quality of service.

- Not a routing protocol.

- Assumes the prior existence of network layer routing support via protocols IGRP, BGP, and others.

- Requests for state information, but does not help provide it.

- Soft, not hard state.

- Not an admission control or packet-scheduling application.

- Receiver-oriented protocol receivers send QoS requests upstream toward senders; this works particularly well in multicast environments (i.e., a receiver can best determine the acceptable quality of a videoconference, and/or if additional costs are justified).

- Supports two reservation styles for use in multisender sessions: distinct Reservations, separate reservations for each sender, and shared reservations, shared by multiple senders.

- Applications have the capability to request different reservation styles, depending upon the type of service or economic considerations.

- Key documents:

draft-berger-rsvp-ext-06.txt

draft-ieft-intserv-charac-02.txt

draft-ieft-intserv-crtl-load-svc-04.txt

draft-ieft-intserv-guaranteed-mib-03.txt

draft-ieft-intserv-guaranteed-svc-06.txt

draft-ieft-mib-05.txt

draft-ieft-rsvp-use-01.txt

draft-ieft-rsvp-md5-02.txt

draft-ieft-rsvp-mib-05.txt

draft-ieft-rsvp-procrules-00.ps, and .txt

draft-ieft-rsvp-spec-14.ps, and .txt

processed by routers that support RSVP; as covered in the discussion on IPv6, where the PDUs cross non-RSVP-capable routers, the messages are ignored.

Figure 10.6 depicts a typical application, showing the receiver-driven nature of RSVP. In a typical (video) application, the server can send a

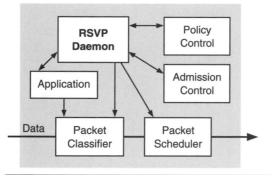

To make a resource reservation at a node, the RSVP daemon communicates with two local decision modules, admission control and policy control. Admission control determines whether the node has sufficient available resources to supply the requested QoS. Policy control determines whether the user has administrative permission to make the reservation. If either check fails, the RSVP program returns an error notification to the application process that originated the request. If both checks succeed, the RSVP daemon sets parameters in a packet classifier and packet scheduler to obtain the desired QoS. The packet classifier determines the QoS class for each packet, and the scheduler orders packet transmission to achieve the promised QoS for each stream.

Figure 10.5   Components used by endsystems (hosts) to determine and signal QoS.

PATH message (discussed further in subsection 10.3.4) characterizing the traffic to be sent. The receivers return RSVP reservation requests, specifying a QoS from routers along the route. Once PDUs begin to flow, a protocol like RTP (see section 10.4) can ensure real-time delivery of the time-sensitive information (e.g., video), and keeps related streams in the same program (e.g., voice and video) synchronized.

There are a number of ways to place the RSVP data into the IP payload. The endstations can transmit the messages in "direct mode" (i.e., directly mapped into IP PDU, with a protocol type of 46) using TCP or UDP encapsulation. The UDP method, currently the most common encapsulation method found on endsystem implementations, is supported for systems that cannot generate raw IP packets.

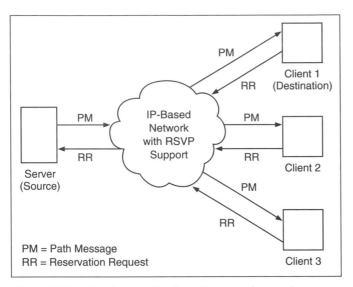

Figure 10.6 A typical application, showing the receiver-driven nature of RSVP.

By design, the RSVP suite forces little permanent state information upon the network devices supporting the protocol. This state is referred to as "soft." In order for the soft state to work, the system must be periodically refreshed. RSVP developers took the approach that handling dynamic routing changes should be a normal procedure, not an exception; therefore, routers should be continuously updating their reservations when they periodically receive resource requests (see the RSVP versus ATM sidebar [1]). With RSVP, resource requests are made and then periodically refreshed. The refresh messages are identical to the original resource request messages. The merging capability alluded to earlier has the possible benefit of requiring less state in routers.

If the path from source to destination has changed, possibly due to routing change or link failure, then the next refresh message will create a new resource reservation (there is a possibility, however, that the network will return an error message specifying that the requested resources are not available on the new route). Dynamically changing routes can pose a problem to reliable QoS support. If it fails because of an outage, a soft state approach with dynamic network-initiated rerouting will, with some nonzero probability, temporarily impact QoS (the length of time will be dependent on the time required to determine a new route and process the reservation message). When a route fails in a "hard state" protocol, such

RSVP VERSUS ATM

- Resource reservations in IP hosts and routers are represented by soft state, which means reservations are not permanent, but time-out after some period. Reservations must be refreshed to prevent time-out, and may also be explicitly deleted. In ATM, resources are reserved for the duration of a connection, which must be explicitly and reliably deleted.

- The soft state approach of RSVP allows the QoS reserved for a flow to be changed at any time, whereas ATM connections have a static QoS that is fixed at setup time.

- RSVP is a simplex protocol, which means resources are reserved in one direction only. In ATM, connections (and associated reservations) are bidirectional in point-to-point calls and unidirectional in point-to-multipoint calls.

- Resource reservation is receiver-initiated in RSVP. In ATM, resources are reserved by the endsystem setting up the connection. In point-to-multipoint calls, connection setup (and hence resource reservation) must be done by the sender.

- RSVP has explicit support for sessions containing multiple senders, namely the capability to select a subset of senders and to dynamically switch between senders. No such support is provided by ATM.

- RSVP has been designed independently of other architectural components, in particular routing. Moreover, route setup and resource reservation are done at different times. In ATM, resource reservation and route setup are done at the same time (connection setup time).

as ATM, the network will drop the connection and require a new call setup message. Hence, a hard state protocol requires the endstation to receive a message from the network notifying it that the VC has been deleted, by which time the endpoints must reestablish the circuit.

RSVP can also be used in conjunction with other protocols, as shown in Figure 10.7. In the ATM environment, one can use the RSVP protocol to interface directly with the application. Here, below the RSVP layer, is an interface with traffic-shaping software provided by the ATM layer. In this context, the application developer utilizes the RSVP protocol as a generic mechanism for requesting QoS: The RSVP signaling message is translated into an ATM signaling message requesting the establishment of virtual circuits with the desired QoS. The RSVP-application construct allows for independent software design free from concern about lower layer protocols.

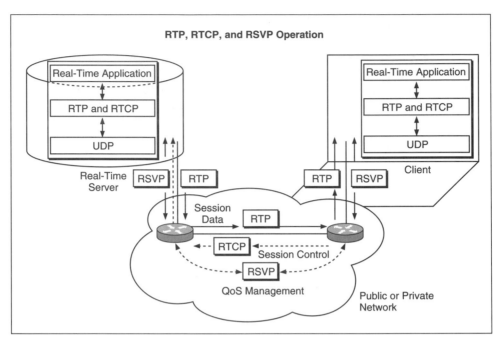

Figure 10.7 RSVP can be used in conjunction with other protocols.

10.3.4 RSVP Protocol Operation

The operation of RSVP is defined by the exchange of RSVP messages that contain information objects. Reservation messages flow downstream from the senders to notify receivers about the pending content and which associated characteristics are required to adequately accept the material. Reservations flow upstream toward the senders to join the multicast distribution tree and/or to place QoS reservations (refer again to Figure 10.4).

The information flows in RSVP can be categorized as follow [2]:

1. RSVP data generated by the content source specifying the characteristics of its traffic (sender TSpec) and the associated QoS parameters (sender RSpec). This information is carried, unmodified, by interconnecting network elements in an RSVP SENDER_TSPEC object to the receiver(s). An RSVP Adspec is also generated by the content source, and carries information describing properties of the data path including availability of specific QoS services.

2. RSVP data generated by the interconnecting network elements (i.e., ATM switch and IP routers), which are used by receivers to determine which resources are available in the network. The QoS parameters

that can be reported help the receivers to determine available bandwidth, link delay values, and operating parameters. As in the sender's RSVP data, an RSVP Adspec can be generated by the interconnecting network elements, which carry a description of available QoS services (the SENDER_TSPEC contains information that cannot be modified, while the Adspec's content may be updated within the network).

3. RSVP data generated by the receiver specifying the traffic characteristics from both a packet description (receiver TSpec) and a resource perspective (receiver RSpec). This information is placed into an RSVP FLOWSPEC and carried upstream to interconnecting network elements and the content source. Along the path toward the sender, the FLOWSPEC may be modified by routers because of reservation merging.

Implementations of the RSVP protocol are very similar to client/server models. The specification identifies messages exchanged and determines which sequences are supported. The RSVP protocol also defines several data objects, which carry resource reservation information. There are five basic message types, defined in Table 10.2, that are used in RSVP, and each type carries several subfields. The PATH and RESV messages are described next in some detail.

PATH Messages

The protocol operates by the source sending a quasi-periodic PATH message (out-of-band from the actual reserved-quality data session) to the destination address (i.e., receivers) along the physical path that joins the

Table 10.2   RSVP Messages

MESSAGE TYPES	FUNCTION
PATH	Sent by the source to specify that a resource exists and, optionally, which parameters should be used when transmitting.
RESV	Transmission of a message in hopes of reserving resources.
CONFIRMATION	Sent by a receiver, this optional message signals successful resource reservation.
TEARDOWN	Deletes an existing reservation.
ERROR	Notifies an abnormal condition such as a reservation failure.

endsystems. As the PATH datagrams traverse the network, the interconnecting routers consult their normal routing tables to decide where to forward the message. When a PATH message is processed by a router, it will establish some "PATH state" gleaned from fields in the message. The PATH state records information about the IP address of the sender along with its policy and QoS class descriptions.

Upon reception of the PATH message, the receiver will determine that a connection has been requested and attempt to determine if, and how, it would like to join the session. The receiver will use the address specified in the SENDER_TSPEC because the source could be a Class D multicast address (hence, it does not use the IP address of the sender of the PATH message). PATH messages contain the following fields:

- Session ID
- Previous hop address of the upstream RSVP neighbor
- Sender descriptor (filter + TSpec)
- Options (integrity object, policy data, Adspec)

The PATH messages are sent at a quasi-periodic rate to protect the systems from changes in state. If a network failure causes a change to the route the PATH messages took, the next PATH will reserve resources in the next cycle. If interconnecting devices along the old path are unable to be reached, their stored state will time-out when they do not receive the quasi-periodic PATH message. The PATH message contains the previous hop address of the upstream RSVP neighbor. The previous hop address is used to ensure that the PATH message has traversed the network without looping. Finally, the PATH message contains a SENDER_TEMPLATE object, which is simply the sender's IP address, used for identification.

RESV Messages

If the receiver elects to communicate with the sender, it sends a reservation message (RESV) upstream along the same route the PATH message used. If the RESV message fails at one of the intermediate routers, an error message is generated and transmitted to the requester. To improve network efficiency, if two or more RESV messages for the same source pass through a common router or switch, the device can attempt to merge the reservation. The merged reservation is then forwarded as an aggregate request to the next upstream node. The RESV message is addressed to the upstream node, with the source address becoming the receiver. The RESV contains a TSpec corresponding to the session's source. RESV messages contain the following fields:

- Session ID
- Previous hop address (downstream RSVP neighbor)
- Reservation style
- Flow descriptor (different combinations of flow and flowspec are used based on reservation style)
- Option (integrity, policy data)

If the request is admitted, then in addition to forwarding the RESV messages upstream, the host or router will install packet filtering into its forwarding database. The forwarding database is queried when the device has a packet to be transmitted, and it is used to segregate traffic into different classes. The flow parameters established for this QoS-enabled traffic will also be passed to the a packet scheduler. The parameters are used by the scheduler to forward packets at a rate compliant to the flow's description.

If the interconnecting network contains routers that do not support the RSVP protocol, the PATH/RESV messages are forwarded through the non-RSVP network, as they are just regular IP packets. The routers at the edge of the RSVP system communicate with their neighbor as if they were directly connected. Although the protocol will operate in this environment, the quality of the reservations will be impacted by the fact that the network now contains "spots" providing only best-effort performance; the performance across these spots must be estimated and communicated to the receivers in Adspec messages.

Operational Procedures

An application intending to make use of RSVP signaling communicates with the protocol through an application program interface (API). Before receivers can make reservations, the network must have knowledge of the source's characteristics. This information is communicated across the API when the hosts register themselves. The RSVP code in the host then generates a SENDER_TSPEC object, which contains the details on the resources required and what the packet headers will look like. The source also constructs the initial Adspec containing generic parameters. Both of these objects are then transmitted in the PATH message.

As the PATH message travels from the source to the receivers, routers along the physical connection modify the Adspec to reflect their current state. The traffic control module in the router checks the services requested in the original Adspec along with the parameters associated with those services. If the values cannot be supported, the Adspec will be modified;

or if the service is unavailable, a flag will be set in the Adspec to notify the receiver. By flagging exceptions, the Adspec will notify the receiver if:

- There are non-RSVP routers along the path (i.e., links that will provide only best-effort service).

- There are routers along the path that do not support one of the service categories, controlled-load or guaranteed.

- A value for one of the service categories is different from what is selected in the SENDER_TSPEC.

At the receiver, the Adspec and SENDER_TSPEC are removed from the PATH message and delivered to the receiving application. At this juncture, the receiver uses the Adspec/SENDER_TSPEC combination to determine which resources it needs to receive the contents from the network. Since the receiver has the best information on how it interacts with the source application, it can accurately determine the packet headers and traffic parameter values for both directions of the session from the Adspec and SENDER_TSPEC. Finally, the receiver's maximum transfer unit (MTU) must be calculated because both guaranteed and controlled-load QoS control services place an upper bound on packet size (The MTU is the maximum packet size that can be transmitted. It is specified to help bound delay.) Each source places the desired MTU in the SENDER_TSPEC and routers may optionally modify the Adspec's MTU field on a per-class-of-service basis.

Once the receiver has identified the parameters required for the reservation, it will pass those values to the network via its RSVP API. The parameters from the TSpec and RSpec objects are used to form the FLOWSPEC, which is placed in a RESV message and transmitted upstream using the default route. When it is received by an internetworking device, the RESV message and its corresponding PATH message are used to select the correct resources to be reserved for the session.

10.3.5 Deployment

As discussed, RSVP/ISA augments best-effort connectionless services with a QoS request/allocation mechanism. New software and hardware is needed on routers and endsystems to support the QoS negotiations. Note that with RSVP, the network still utilizes routers and IP. Figure 10.5 shows the kind of functionality required in the router. Elements of the model include [7]:

- *Classifier*, which maps PDUs to a service class.

- *Packet Scheduler*, which forwards packets based on service classes.

- *Admission Control*, which determines whether the QoS requests can be met.

- *Setup protocol state machine*, which keeps soft state information.

The RSVP updates the Classifier with the filterspec and the Scheduler with the flowspec. These capabilities have to be included in routers. Some equipment was already available in 1997, and it is expected that by 1999 there will be some deployment of RSVP-based systems, although at the time of this writing there still were major design, implementation, engineering, and standardization challenges to be met. RSVP could play an important role in video and voice transport over enterprise internets and the Internet. However, critics question RSVP's scalability, particularly for large multicast environments.

A number of unknowns will remain until products for integrated services networks are in place. For example, at time of this writing, there is little understanding of:

- The kind of performance that can be expected with RSVP

- The number of flows that can be established

- How the number of flows affects the performance of establishing new flows or tearing down old flows

- How to handle multicast

- How to interwork RSVP and MPLS

The motivation for carriers (specifically ISPs) to deploy RSVP-enabled networks is that they will be able to charge a higher price for their QoS-based service. Although the default, lowest-grade, service is the same as best-effort traffic that has been available for years over corporate internets and the Internet, the carrier is able to determine, via the RSVP signaling message, how much bandwidth each customer requires, what latency is requested, and the type of service the customer expects. Of course, the carrier will have to provision global resources in the network to support the requested QoS: Knowing only how much capacity the user needs, but being unable to provide it or to undertake capacity planning, internal (re)routing, and so on will be problematic; and this same problem affects providers of ATM services. Capacity planning is very difficult, as should be obvious just by looking at the bulk of the ATMF TM 4.0 specification, which, in spite of its length, provides no algorithmic support as to how to address/enable all of the performance measures described there.

10.3.6 Interworking RSVP with ATM

ATM switches enable carriers to support QoS-based connectivity at the data link layer, and many now offer ATM services. But it is true that some carriers cannot truly measure usage (traffic contracts) on their current generation switches, so switch vendors need to develop better tools. It is also true that with current technology it is challenging to offer QoS across a network (that is, across several switches), since most vendors have focused on delivering QoS over a single switch. Consequently, in some cases, carriers are reluctant to offer QoS guarantees to users (e.g., CBR services). Nevertheless, the interested corporate planner can generally secure ATM services and obtain the needed QoS, although the carrier generally has to overprovision the network to support such QoS.

ATM was initially developed as a replacement for the current telephone network protocols, but more recently is being used as a data link layer protocol for computer communications (as described in Chapter 5). As it was developed from the beginning with telephone voice applications in mind, a real-time service environment is an integral part of the protocol. With the approval of UNI 3.1/4.0 by the ATM Forum, the ATM standards now have several categories of service. Given the wide acceptance of ATM by the long-line carriers, the use of ATM on the Internet is, if not guaranteed, highly likely. The question now becomes, how can we successfully interface between the real-time services offered by ATM and the new, integrated service environment soon to be available in the IP protocol suite [1]. CIOA standards assume no real-time IP protocols. Most researchers and planners are of the opinion that ATM should, if possible, be used as more than a leased-line replacement. While it is possible for the Internet to be overlaid on CBR PVCs, this is unlikely to be the most efficient way to use ATM services as they are offered by carriers or as they appear in LANs.

There are several significant differences between the ways in which IP and ATM will provide QoS. When IP commits to provide a certain QoS to an application according to the Internet service model, it must be able to request an appropriate QoS from the ATM network using the ATM service model. Since these service models are by no means the same, a potentially complex mapping must be performed for the IP layer to meet its commitments [1]. In addition to the RSVP versus ATM sidebar given earlier, Table 10.3 provides a quick comparison between ATM (signaling) and RSVP.

Table 10.3 RSVP/ATM Comparison

FEATURE	RSVP	ATM
Initiation	Receiver-driven	Source-driven
Directionality	Unicast/simplex	Duplex
Uniformity	Allows receivers with heterogeneous QoS for a given session	Homogenous QoS per SVC
QoS renegotiation	Allows dynamic reconfiguration of resources	Requires new setup (new PVC/PVP/SVC) to support a change (except for ABR)
Length of session	Reservations expire (time-out)	Permanently reserved for the connection until connection is dropped
Maturity	Under development at time of writing	Well-developed at time of writing
State	Soft state (refresh/time-out)	Hard state (explicit delete)

This subsection briefly examines how these somewhat dissimilar technologies can be internetworked.

When an IP PDU that is somehow QoS-aware is passed from a packet-switched network interface to an ATM network, it must generate some type of connection setup message in the ATM network. The difficulty involved in doing this is determining which ATM traffic class is appropriate for the IP data stream and, once the correct traffic class has been selected, which parameters should be used in the ATM signaling message.

In comparing the IETF's and ATM Forum's traffic and QoS descriptions, the network planner may notice some differences as well as some similarities, especially with the traffic descriptors. The IP traffic description contained in the TSpec uses the same parameters corresponding to VBR's SCR and MBS. Therefore, the TSpec uses the same parameters that are values of the second leaky bucket implemented in ATM's UPC. Analogous to ATM's peak cell rate, the TSpec also supports a peak rate parameter. The IETF's model contains three service classes, listed earlier, whereas the ATM Forum as defined has five categories. Therefore, several possible mappings are can be supported when converting RSVP to ATM signaling, or vice versa. In ATM, some classes also require specification of peak cell rate, whereas peak rates are not currently included in the IP traffic characterizations; it may be possible to use incoming interface speeds to determine an approximate peak rate.

The challenge is, given traffic in a particular IP service class with certain QoS parameters, how should it be sent across an ATM network in such a way that it both meets its service commitments and makes efficient use of the ATM network's resources? One of the functions that must be performed in order to carry IP traffic over an ATM network is, therefore, a mapping from the characterization of the traffic as supplied to the IP to a characterization that is acceptable for ATM [1].

An application uses an RSVP service request to indicate the kind of "promise" it would like the network to make, defined in terms of application parameters (e.g., the required bit rate and burst size). As noted, service guarantees (QoS classes) can be either guaranteed or controlled-load; the latter is the more popular choice. Guaranteed service was developed to support applications that use connection-oriented (TDM) services. It is analogous to ATM's CBR service. As long as the application does not violate its own traffic description, the network guarantees minimal packet loss—up to a specified bit rate and burst size. When traffic exceeds this rate, the excess is subject to the same jitter and potential for packet loss as best-effort traffic [3]. Guaranteed service uses a complex formula to calculate worst-case end-to-end delay and worst-case jitter. Applications equipped to use this service can take the results of this calculation and determine how large a buffer they need. Hence, guaranteed service can sustain good performance in an unstable network, at the expense of using relatively complex queuing algorithms.

Controlled-load service delivers the equivalent of best-effort service in an unloaded (or lightly loaded) network. Controlled-load also makes minimal delay and loss guarantees to applications that do not violate their own traffic descriptions (bit rate and burst size). With this QoS class, applications may experience greater jitter than in guaranteed service, because controlled-load service does not require the network node to use any particular algorithms. Fortunately, the encoding algorithms used in packet voice and video equipment are designed to adapt to this. This service is analogous to VBR-rt.

In both guaranteed and the controlled-load service, the underlying link-layer mechanism fulfills the promise made by the RSVP service models. When the link layer is ATM, RSVP's guaranteed service is mapped to ATM's CBR or VBR-rt. In both cases, the various ATM-specific traffic control parameters are derived from the token bucket carried in RSVP's traffic descriptions. RSVP tells the ATM service access point (SAP) its mean and peak rates and burst size, which ATM uses to negotiate a connection through the network. (When a link-layer technology other than ATM (such as Ethernet, FDDI or PPP) is utilized, special queuing algorithms are applied to achieve similar results, including the handling of data rate bursts.)

In summary, some of the possible mapping between ISA and ATM are as follows:

Guaranteed Service. By and large equates to the ATM constant bit rate service. The values of PCR, SCR, and MBR can be mapped directly from the TSpec to the RSVP reservation request receiver TSpec; the only "guess" is the value of the CTD.

Controlled-Delay Service. Has explicitly specified values of delay that can be mapped to ATM's real-time VBR service category. It would also be possible to utilize ATM's CBR; however, the CBR category does not yield much statistically multiplexing gain, therefore this is not optimal for Internet traffic.

Best-Effort. Can be mapped to ATM services like UBR or ABR or non-real-time VBR. The most common choice today is UBR in conjunction with early packet discard.

Most RSVP traffic can be aggregated onto VBR VC's, based on QoS flow description. The token bucket for the aggregate VC is simply the sum of the token buckets for constituent RSVP flows. As discussed, RSVP is simply a signaling protocol designed to obtain QoS services from an IP network; so if part of the network is ATM, RSVP and ATM services are readily mapped—there is no need to choose between them. If the network is built on other link-layer technologies, RSVP is still the way that applications will gain access to QoS services for IP traffic. Basically, any application in a network that requires dynamic admission of request and service guarantees for IP data should use RSVP [3]. RFC 1821 [1] has a more extensive treatment of this topic. The issue of QoS in packet networks is a work in progress [2].

10.4 Real-Time Transport Protocol

There has been a flurry of activity in the recent past in the development of real-time protocols. These protocols are called real-time because they are used when there are tight constraints on the quality of service that must be delivered in the network (e.g., the total transit delay or interpacket arrive time must be bounded).

The key primary protocols that have been developed to support real-time delivery of information are:

Real-Time Transport Protocol (RTP).   A real-time "end-to-end" protocol utilizing existing transport layers for data that has real-time properties.

Real-Time Control Protocol (RTCP).   A protocol to monitor the quality of service and to convey information about the participants in an ongoing session. The later aspect of RTCP may be sufficient for "loosely controlled" sessions—where there is no explicit membership control and setup—but it is not necessarily intended to support all of an application's control communication requirements (this functionality may be fully or partially subsumed by a separate session control protocol). It provides feedback on the quality of the information transmitted so that modifications can be made and total performance.

Real-Time Streaming Protocol (RTSP).   A transport layer protocol designed for controlling the transmission of audio/video over the Internet. (This protocol is not further discussed here [2].)

RTP provides end-to-end delivery services for data with real-time characteristics, such as interactive audio and video. Those services include payload type identification, sequence numbering, time-stamping, and delivery monitoring. Applications typically run RTP on top of UPD to make use of its multiplexing and checksum services; both protocols contribute parts of the transport protocol functionality. RTP may also be used with other suitable underlying network or transport protocols. It supports data transfer to multiple destinations using multicast distribution, if provided by the underlying network [8].

RTP by itself does not address resource reservation and does not guarantee QoS for real-time services. Specifically, RTP does not provide any mechanism to ensure timely delivery or to provide other quality-of-service guarantees; instead, it relies on lower-layer services to do so (the functions of quality-of-service guarantees and delivery are the responsibility of RSVP and network support of QoS-based services). It does not guarantee delivery or prevent out-of-order delivery, nor does it assume that the underlying network is reliable and will deliver packets in sequence. The sequence numbers included in RTP allow the receiver to reconstruct the sender's packet sequence; sequence numbers might also be used to determine the proper location of a packet, for example in video decoding, without necessarily decoding packets in sequence [8].

The data transport is augmented by a control protocol (RTPC) to allow monitoring of the information delivery in a manner scalable to large multicast networks, and to provide minimal control and identification functionality. Like RTP, RTCP is designed to be independent of the underlying transport and network layers [8].

RTP is primarily designed to satisfy the needs of multiparticipant multimedia conferences, but it is not limited to that particular application. Storage of continuous data, interactive distributed simulation, and control and measurement applications may also find RTP applicable.

When developing protocols that would be used to first allocate resources and subsequently carry real-time traffic across intranets and the Internet, the IETF and ATM Forum working groups decided that it would be best to develop a new protocol rather than modify an existing protocol. RTP represents a new style of protocol following the principles of application-level framing and integrated-layer processing. That is, RTP is intended to be malleable to provide information required by a particular application; thus, it will often be integrated into the application processing rather than be implemented as a separate layer. The RTP protocol framework is deliberately incomplete [8]. It is intended to be tailored through modifications and/or additions to the header as needed. Therefore, a complete specification of RTP for a particular application will require one or more companion documents, such as a profile specification document, which defines a set of payload type codes and their mapping to payload formats (e.g., media encodings), and payload format specification documents, which define how a particular payload, such as an audio or video encoding, is to be carried in RTP.

RTP's primary role is to act as a simple, improved, scalable interface between real-time applications and existing transport layer protocols; RTP does not dictate which transport layer protocol is used (the protocol is independent of the underlying transport and network layer, although as noted, UDP is typically utilized). It provides functions that allow transport protocols to work in a real-time environment and functionality just above the transport layer. The underlying network is assumed to be any IP network assuming that, in all likelihood, a packet will arrive at its destination. Due to the nature of packet switching (including frame relay and ATM), variable delay is to be expected. Additionally, due to packet switching and routing, packets may arrive out of order. The protocol also contains definitions of which component should perform which specified function. The RTP component carries individual real-time data streams with a source identifier, payload type, time, and sequencing information. The feedback component monitors application performance and conveys information about the session (i.e., information about participants).

RTP AT A GLANCE

The goal of RTP is to provide transport of data with an inherent notion of time and to serve as a means for transmitting real-time data. It, unlike the legacy transport layer protocol, has been optimized for that task. RTP has been developed with flexibility and scalability in mind, and is now being used as the core protocol real-time transport on both pure IP network and hybrid MPOA systems. To that end, it:

- Is designed to provide end-to-end delivery services for temporarily sensitive data, with support for both unicast and multicast delivery.

- Can be carried inside a UDP payload.

- Provides data source and payload type identification; used to determine payload contents.

- Provides packet sequencing, which is used to confirm correct ordering at the receiver.

- Provides timing and synchronization, which is used to set timing at the receiver during content playback.

- Provides monitoring, which is used to facilitate diagnosis or to supply feedback to the sender on the quality of data transmission.

- Supports integration of heterogeneous traffic, to merge multiple transmitting sources into a single flow.

The RTP at a Glance sidebar provides a snapshot of RTP, followed by a glossary of key concepts and terms. In a nutshell, when packets arrive at their destination, the sequence number of each packet is examined to determine the correct order of data and to record the fraction of lost frames. The RTP packet's timestamp is used to determine the interpacket gap. The timestamp value is set by the source as it encodes the data and transmits the packet into the network. As packets arrive at the destination, the change in interpacket gap can be examined; then, during playback, this information can be used to regenerate the contents at the same rate they were encoded. By utilizing buffering at the receiver, the source can attempt to pace the traffic independent of the jitter introduced by the packet network [2].

10.4.1 RTP Usage Scenarios

The following section from RFC 1889 describes some aspects of the use of RTP. The examples were chosen to illustrate the basic operation of applications using RTP. In them, RTP is carried on top of IP and UDP, and follows the convention established by the profile for audio and video specified in the companion Internet-Draft draft-ieft-avt-profile.

Simple Multicast Audio Conference

In this example, a working group of the IETF meets to discuss the latest protocol draft, using the IP multicast services of the Internet for voice communications. Through some allocation mechanisms, the working group chair obtains a multicast group address and pair of ports. One port is used for audio data, the other for control (RTCP) packets. This address and port information is distributed to the intended participants. If privacy is desired, the data and control packets may be encrypted, in which case an encryption key must also be generated and distributed.

The audio conferencing application used by each conference participant sends audio data in small pieces of, say, 20 milliseconds (ms) duration. Each piece of audio data is preceded by an RTP header; the RTP header and data are in turn contained in a UDP packet. The RTP header indicates what type of audio encoding (such as PCM, ADPCM, or LPC) is contained in each packet so that senders can change the encoding during a conference—for example, to accommodate a new participant who is connected through a low-bandwidth link or to react to indications of network congestion.

The Internet, like other packet networks, occasionally loses and reorders packets, and delays them by variable amounts of time. To cope with these impairments, the RTP header contains timing information and a sequence number that enable the receivers to reconstruct the timing produced by the source so that, in this example, chunks of audio are contiguously played out to the speaker every 20 ms. This timing reconstruction is performed separately for each source of RTP packets in the conference. The sequence can also be used by the receiver to estimate how many packets are being lost.

Since the members of the working group join and leave during the conference, it is useful to know who is participating at any moment and how well they are receiving the audio data. For that purpose, each instance of the audio application in the conference periodically multicasts a reception report, plus the name of its user on the RTCP (control) port. The reception report indicates how well the current speaker is being received, and may be used to control adaptive encoding. In addition to the user name, other identifying information may also be included subject to control bandwidth limits. A site sends the RTCP BYE packet when it leaves the conference.

RTP GLOSSARY

RTP payload. The data transported by RTP in the packet; for example, audio sample or compressed video data. The payload format and interpretation are beyond the scope of the RTP specification.

RTP packet. A data packet consisting of the fixed RTP header, a possibly empty list of contributing sources (see later), and the payload data. Some underlying protocols may require an encapsulation of the RTP packet to be defined. Typically, one packet of the underlying protocol contains a single RTP packet, but several RTP packets may be contained if permitted by the encapsulation method.

RTCP packet. A control packet consisting of a fixed header part similar to that of RTP data packets, followed by structured elements that vary depending upon the RTCP packet type. Typically, multiple RTCP packets are sent together as a compound RTCP packet in a single packet of the underlying protocol; this is enabled by the length field in the fixed header of each RTCP packet.

Port. The abstraction that transport protocols use to distinguish among multiple destinations within a given host computer. TCP/IP protocols identify ports using small positive integers. The transport selectors (TSEL) used by the OSI transport layer are equivalent to ports. RTP depends upon the lower-layer protocol to provide some mechanism such as ports to multiplex the RTP and RTCP packets of a session.

Transport address. The combination of a network address and port that identifies a transport-level endpoint; for example, an IP address and a UDP port. Packets are transmitted from a source transport address to a destination transport address.

RTP session. The association among a set of participants communicating with RTP. For each participant, the session is defined by a particular pair of destination transport addresses (one network address plus a port pair for RTP and RTCP). The destination transport address pair may be common for all participants, as in the case of IP multicast, or may be different for each, as in the case of individual unicast network addresses plus a common port pair. In a multimedia session, each medium is carried in a separate RTP session with its own RTCP packets. The multiple RTP sessions are distinguished by different port number pairs and/or different multicast addresses.

Synchronization source (SSRC). The source of a stream of RTP packets, identified by a 32-bit numeric SSRC identifier carried in the RTP header, so as not to be dependent upon the network address. All packets from a synchronization source form part of the same timing and sequence number space. A synchronization source may change its data format, for example, audio encoding, over time. The SSRC identifier is a randomly chosen value meant to be globally unique within a particular RTP session; the binding of the SSRC identifiers is provided through RTCP. If a participant generates multiple streams in one RTP session—for example from separate video cameras—each must be identified as a different SSRC.

Contributing source (CSRC). A source of a stream of RTP packets that has contributed to the combined stream produced by an RTP mixer (see later). The mixer inserts a list of the SSRC identifiers of the sources that contributed to the generation of the particular packet in the RTP header of that packet. This is called the CSRC list. An example application is audio conferencing where a mixer indicates all the talkers whose speech was combined to produce the outgoing packet, allowing the receiver to indicate the current talker, even though all the audio packets contain the same SSRC identifier (that of the mixer).

Endsystem. An application that generates the content to be sent in RTP packets and/or consumes the content of received RTP packets. An endsystem can act as one or more synchronization sources in a particular RTP session, but typically only one.

Mixer. An intermediate system that receives RTP packets from one or more sources, possibly changes the data format, combines the packets in some manner, and then forwards a new RTP packet. Thus, all data packets originating from a mixer will be identified as having the mixer as their synchronization source.

Translator. An intermediate system that forwards RTP packets with their synchronization source identifier intact. Examples of translators include devices that convert encodings without mixing, replicators from multicast to unicast, and application-level filter in firewalls.

Monitor. An application that receives RTCP packets sent by participants in an RTP session, in particular the reception reports, and estimates the current quality of service for distribution monitoring, fault diagnosis, and long-term statistics. The monitor function is likely to be built into the application(s) participating in the session, but it may also be a separate application that does not otherwise participate and does not send or receive the RTP data packets. These are called third-party monitors.

Non-RTP means. Protocols and mechanisms that may be needed in addition to RTP to provide a usable service. In particular, for multimedia conferences, a conference control application may distribute multicast addresses and keys for encryption, negotiate the encryption algorithm to be used, and define dynamic mappings between RTP payload type values and the payload formats they represent for formats that do not have a predefined payload type value. For simple applications, electronic mail or a conference database may also be used. The specification of such protocols and mechanisms is outside the scope of RTP.

Audio and Video Conference

If both audio and video media are used in a conference, they are transmitted as separate RTP sessions. RTCP packets are transmitted for each medium using two different UDP port pairs and/or multicast addresses. There is no direct coupling at the RTP level between the audio and video sessions, except that a user participating in both sessions should use the same distinguishing name in the RTCP packets for both so that the sessions can be associated.

Mixers and Translators

So far, we have assumed that all sites want to receive media data in the same format. However, this may not always be appropriate. Consider the case where participants in one conference are connected through a low-speed link to the majority of the conference participants who enjoy high-speed network access. Instead of forcing everyone to use a lower-bandwidth, reduced-quality audio encoding, an RTP-level relay called a mixer may be placed near the low-bandwidth area. This mixer resynchronizes incoming audio packets to reconstruct the constant 20-ms spacing generated by the sender, mixes these reconstructed audio streams into a single stream, translates the audio encoding to a lower-bandwidth one, and forwards the lower-bandwidth packet stream across the low-speed link. These packets might be unicast to a single recipient or multicast on a different address to multiple recipients. The RTP header includes a means for mixers to identify the sources that contributed to a mixed packet so that correct talker indication can be provided at the receivers.

Some of the intended participants in the audio conference may be connected with high-bandwidth links but might not be directly reachable via IP multicast. For example, they might be behind an application-level firewall that will not let any IP packet pass. For these sites, mixing may not be necessary, in which case another type of RTP-level relay called a translator may be used. Two translators are installed, one on either side of the firewall, with the outside one funneling all multicast packets received through a secure connection to the translator inside the firewall. The translator inside the firewall sends them again as multicast packets to a multicast group restricted to the site's internal network.

Mixers and translators may be designed for a variety of purposes. An example is a video mixer that scales the images of individual people in separate video streams and composites them into one video stream to simulate a group scene. Other examples of translation include the connection of a group of hosts speaking only IP/UDP to a group of hosts that understand only ST-II, or the packet-by-packet encoding translation of video streams from individual sources without resynchronization or mixing.

10.4.2 RTP PDU

An RTP session is defined as communication between hosts identified by a pair of transport addresses, along with the port number assigned to RTP. The fields and format of an RTP packet are shown in Figure 10.8. The

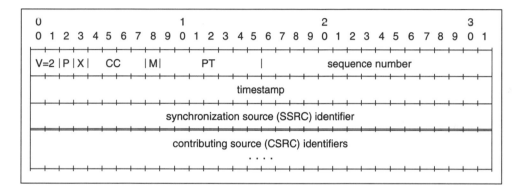

Version (V). Identifies the release of RTP.

Padding bit (P). Specifies that the payload has additional padding at the end.

Counter (CC). Enumerates the number of CSRCs contained that follow the fixed header.

Payload type identifier (PT). Specifies the type of data being carried in the RTP packet.

Sequence number. Increments to count the number of packets in a stream.

Timestamp. Denotes the instant the first octet in the RTP data packet was sampled.

SSRC field. Identifies the synchronization source associated with the data (this identifier is chosen with the intent that no two sources within the same RTP session will have the same value).

CSRC field with a list of objects. Identifies the contributing sources for the data contained in this packet (the total number of identifiers is given by the third field).

Figure 10.8 The fields and format of an RTP packet.

first 12 octets are present in every RTP packet, while the list of CSRC identifiers is present only when inserted by a mixer. Two fields are used to help identify the stream, Synchronization Source (SSRC) and Contributing Source (CSRC). The SSRC is a 32-bit identifier generated by the source of a single real-time stream. The CSRC is a 32-bit identifier formed by a source that contributes to the combined stream produced by an RTP "mixer." (A mixer in this case is a device that physically combines several streams into one super-RTP flow.) The CSRC count is used to enumerate the participants when multiple sources are being combined.

Specifically, the fields have the following meaning:

Version (V). 2 bits. Identifies the version of RTP. The current version is 2. (The value 1 is used by the first-draft version of RTP, and the value of 0 is used by the protocol initially implemented in the "vat" audio tool.)

Padding (P). 1 bit. If the padding bit is set, the packet contains one or more additional padding octets at the end, which are not part of the payload. The last octet of the padding contains a count of how many padding octets should be ignored. Padding may be needed by some encryption algorithms.

Extension (X). 1 bit. If the extension bit is set, the fixed header is followed by exactly one header extension.

CRSC Count (CC). 4 bits. Contains the number of CRCS identifiers that follow the fixed header.

Marker (M). 1 bit. The interpretation of the marker is defined by a profile. It is intended to allow significant events such as frame boundaries to be marked in the packet stream. A profile may define additional marker bits or specify that there is no marker bit by changing the number of bits in the payload type field.

Payload Type (PT). 7 bits. Identifies the format of the RTP payload and determines its interpretation by the application. A profile specifies a default static mapping of payload type codes to payload formats. Additional payload type codes may be defined dynamically through non-RTP means. An initial set of default mappings for audio and video is specified in Internet-Draft draft-ietf-avt-profile. An RTP sender emits a single RTP payload type at any given time.

Sequence Number. 32 bits. Increments by one for each RTP data packet sent, and may be used by the receiver to detect packet loss and to restore packet sequence. The initial value of the sequence number is random (unpredictable) to make known-plaintext attacks on encryption more difficult, even if the source itself does not encrypt, because the packets may flow through a translator that does.

Timestamp.   32 bits. Reflects the sampling instant of the first octet in the RTP data packet. The sampling instant must be derived from a clock that increments monotonically and linearly in time to allow synchronization and jitter calculations. The resolution of the clock must be sufficient for the desired synchronization accuracy and for measuring packet arrival jitter (one tick per video frame is typically not sufficient). The clock frequency is dependent on the format of data carried as payload; it is specified statically in the profile or payload format specification that defines the format, or may be specified dynamically for payload formats defined through non-RTP means. If RTP packets are generated periodically, the nominal sampling instant as determined from the sampling clock is to be used, not a reading of the system clock. As an example, for fixed-rate audio, the timestamp clock would likely increment by one for each sampling period. If an audio application reads a block covering 160 sampling periods from the input device, the timestamp would be increased by 160 for each such block, regardless of whether the block is transmitted in a packet or dropped as silent. The initial value of the timestamp is random, as for the sequence number. Several consecutive RTP packets may have equal timestamps if they are (logically) generated at once, that is, belong to the same video frame. Consecutive RTP packets may contain timestamps that are not monotonic if the data is not transmitted in the order it was sampled, as in the case of MPEG-interpolated video frames. (The sequence numbers of the packets transmitted will still be monotonic.)

SSRC.   32 bits. Identifies the synchronization source. This identifier is chosen randomly, with the intent that no two synchronization sources within the same RTP session will have the same SSRC identifier. Although the probability of multiple sources choosing the same identifier is low, all RTP implementations must be prepared to detect and resolve collisions. The specification has a mechanism for resolving collisions and detecting RTP-level forwarding loops based on the uniqueness of the SSRC identifier. If a source changes its source transports address, it must also choose a new SSRC identifier to avoid being interpreted as a looped source.

CSRC List.   0 to 15 items, 32 bits each. Identifies the contributing sources for the payload contained in this packet. The number of identifiers is given by the CC field. If there are more than 15 contributing sources, only 15 may be identified. CSRC identifiers are inserted by mixers, using the SSRC identifiers of contributing sources. For example, for audio packets, the SSRC identifiers of all sources that were mixed together to create a packet are listed, allowing correct talker indication at the receiver.

10.4.3 Multiplexing RTP Sessions

In RTP, multiplexing is provided by the destination transport address (network address and port number), which define an RTP session. For example, in a teleconference composed of audio and video media encoded separately, each medium should be carried in a separate RTP session with its own destination transport (interleaving packets with different payload types but using the same SSRC would introduce several problems, as noted in the RFC).

10.4.4 Profile-Specific Modifications to the RTP Header

The existing RTP data packet is believed to be complete for the set of functions required in common across all the application classes that RTP might support. However, in keeping with the malleable design principle, the header may be tailored through modification or additions defined in a profile specification, while still allowing profile-independent monitoring and recording tools to function.

10.5 RTP Control Protocol (RTCP)

The previous section highlighted that RTP is a simple protocol designed to carry real-time traffic and provide a few additional services that are not present in existing transport protocols like UDP: With RTP, receivers can utilize the timestamp along with sequence numbers to better synchronize sessions and improve playback. As a companion to RTP, the IETF has designed the RTP Control Protocol (RTCP), which is used to communicate between the sources and destination. RTCP is not used to establish QoS parameters with the ATM switch; instead, it is oriented toward state information.

RTCP is based on the periodic transmission of control packets to all participants in the session, using the same distribution mechanism as the data packets. The underlying protocol must provide multiplexing of the data and control packets; for example, using separate port numbers with UDP.

10.5.1 RTCP Functions

RTCP performs four functions [8], defined here and highlighted in the Key Functions sidebar:

1. The primary function is to provide feedback on the quality of the data distribution. This is an integral part of the RTP's role as a transport protocol, and is related to the flow and congestion control functions of other transport protocols. The feedback may be directly useful for control of adaptive encodings, but experiments with IP multicasting have shown that it is also critical to get feedback from the receivers to diagnose faults in the distribution. Sending reception feedback reports to all participants allows anyone who is observing problems to evaluate whether those problems are local or global. With a distribution mechanism like IP multicast, it is also possible for an entity such as a network service provider not otherwise involved in the session to receive the feedback information and act as a third-party monitor to diagnose network problems.

2. RTCP carries a persistent transport-level identifier for an RTP source called the canonical name (CNAME). Since the SSRC identifier may change if a conflict is discovered or a program is restarted, receivers require the CNAME to keep track of each participant. Receivers also require the CNAME to associate multiple data streams from a given participant in a set of related RTP sessions—for example, to synchronize audio and video.

3. The first two functions require that all participants send RTP packets, therefore the rate must be controlled in order for RTP to scale up to a larger number of participants.

4. A fourth, optional function is to convey minimal session control information—for example, participant identification to be displayed in the user interface. This is most likely to be useful in "loosely controlled" sessions where participants enter and leave without membership control or parameter negotiation. RTCP serves as a convenient channel to reach all the participants, but it is not necessarily expected to support all the control communication requirements of an application. A higher-level session control protocol may be needed.

Using RTCP, RTP hosts can communicate "out-of-band" to exchange information about their state. The information can be used to identify (but not secure) the QoS being delivered by the network (e.g., information about packet loss, the value of the round-trip time, jitter, etc.).

10.5.2 RTCP Packet Format

RTCP utilizes the exchange of packets that express an endpoint's state. There are two main packet types exchanged: sender reports (SR) and receiver reports (RR). Each of these reports is secured by generating a packet containing fields that describe the state of the session. Each RTCP packet begins with a fixed part similar to that of RTP data packets, followed by structured elements that may be of variable length according to the packet type, but that always end on a 32-bit boundary (the alignment requirement and a length field in the fixed part are included to make RTCP packets "stackable"). Multiple RTCP packets may be concatenated without any intervening separator to form a compound RTCP packet that is sent in a single packet of the lower-layer protocol—for example, UDP. The following lists the RTP packet types:

SR.   Sender report, for transmission and reception statistics from participants who are active senders.

RR.   Receiver support, for reception statistics from participants who are not active senders.

SDES.   Source description items, including CNAME.

BYE.   Indicates end of participation.

APP.   Application-specific functions.

Each of the SR and RR packets contains the SSRC of the sender. In the case of an RR, it contains the SSRC of the first source. The fields used to help determine the quality of service are shown in the following list:

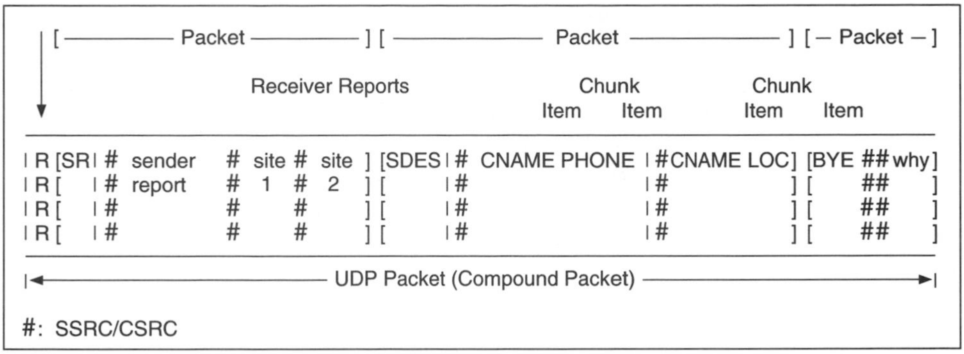

```
 |  [————————— Packet —————————] [————————————— Packet ——————————————] [— Packet —]

                      Receiver Reports                    Chunk              Chunk
                                                     Item      Item      Item      Item

 | R [SR| #  sender     #  site #  site ] [SDES| #  CNAME PHONE  | #CNAME LOC]  [BYE ## why]
 | R [    | #  report     #   1   #   2   ] [       | #                      | #              ] [     ##      ]
 | R [    | #               #        #       ] [       | #                      | #              ] [     ##      ]
 | R [    | #               #        #       ] [       | #                      | #              ] [     ##      ]

 |◄——————————————— UDP Packet (Compound Packet) ————————————————►|

 #: SSRC/CSRC
```

Figure 10.9   RTCP compound packet produced by a mixer.

- Fraction lost versus the total number of packets, which provides an instantaneous assessment for the percentage of loss.
- Cumulative number of packets lost since session began.
- Highest sequence number received, which reveals how much of the current data in flight has been received.
- Inter-arrival jitter, which can help specify how much buffering is being used at the destination to faithfully replay the source; the jitter value at the report sending time.
- Last SR timestamp received, which reports the time at which the last SR was received.
- Delay since last SR timestamp.

An example RTCP compound packet as might be produced by a mixer is shown in Figure 10.9. If the overall length of a compound packet would exceed the maximum transmission unit (MTU) of the network path, it may be segmented into multiple shorter compound packets to be transmitted in separate packets of the underlying protocol. Note that each of the compound packets must begin with an SR or RR packet.

RTP is designed to allow an application to scale automatically over session sizes, ranging from a few participants to thousands. For example, in an audio conference, the data traffic is inherently self-limiting because only one or two people will speak at a time, so with multicast distribution, the data rate on any given link remains relatively constant independent of the number of participants. However, the control traffic is not self-limiting. If the reception report from each participant were sent at a constant rate, the control traffic would grow linearly with the number of participants. Therefore, the rate must be scaled down [8].

10.6 Support of QoS in Routers

Today's networks are fairly complex and are typically composed of a variety of network elements, as illustrated in Figure 10.10 and 10.11. Even if new technologies such as those described earlier in this chapter and elsewhere (e.g., RSVP, RTP, IPv6, MPOA, ATM) enter the market in a significant way, there will still be a large pool of embedded equipment in enterprise networks. In particular, there will be many traditional routers. Hence, support of QoS metrics such as delay, loss, jitter, and bandwidth in routers is important. Applications such as desktop conferencing, distance learning, mission-critical applications, voice, e-mail, and file transfer all compete for enterprise network resources. PDUs for all these applications show up in the router(s) and have to be appropriately handled if QoS is to be secured. Figure 10.12 illustrates at a macro level the intended action of end-to-end QoS control.

QoS attention is being focused at the WAN level, since, in general, there is adequate bandwidth at that level. In addition, the move to switched Ethernet all but eliminates delays due to random access contention (queuing delays in campus routers remain to be addressed).

Cisco Systems is approaching router-level QoS by using the following techniques (also see Figures 10.13 and 10.14) [9]:

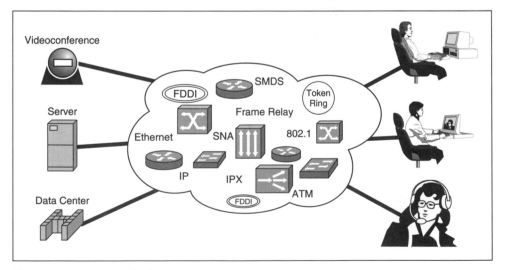

Figure 10.10   Network elements.

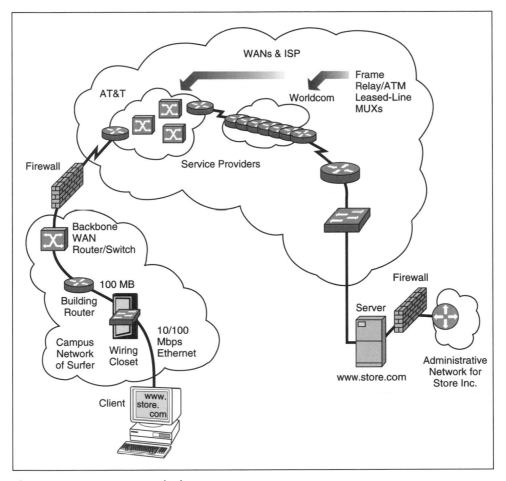

Figure 10.11   More network elements.

- Smart queuing

  Priority queuing

  Custom queuing

  Weighted fair queuing

  Weighted random early detection (WRED)

- Filtering and shaping

  Traffic shaping

  Frame relay traffic shaping

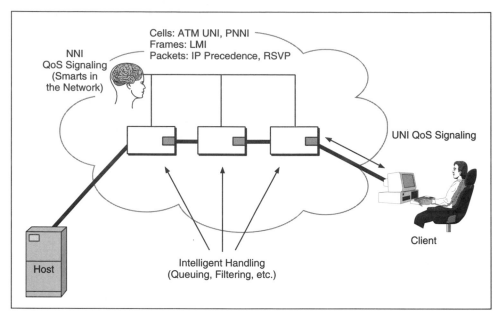

Figure 10.12   Intended action of end-to-end QoS control at a macro level.

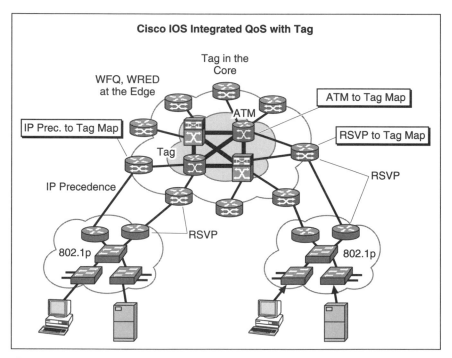

Figure 10.13   Router-level QoS.

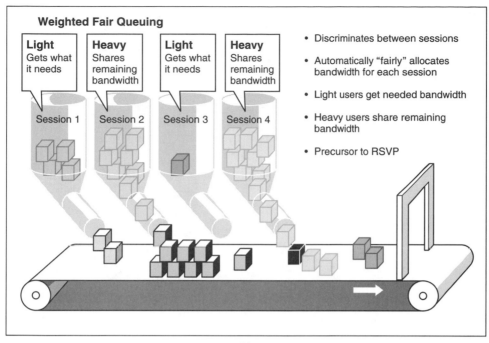

(a)

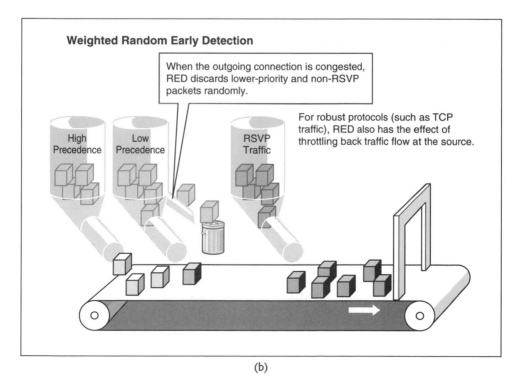

(b)

Figure 10.14 Router-level QoS; *continues.*

Generic Traffic Shaping

- Reduces outbound traffic flow to avoid congestion
- Eliminates bottlenecks in topologies with data rate mismatch
- Provides mechanism to partition interfaces to match far-end requirements

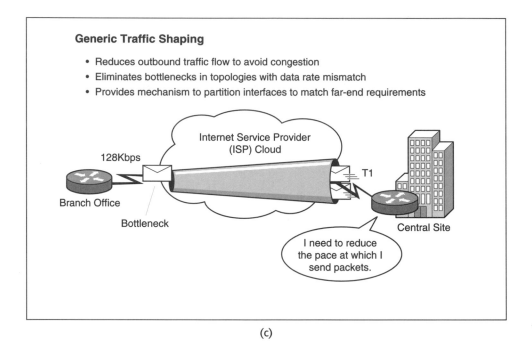

(c)

Frame Relay Traffic Shaping

- Builds on existing traffic-shaping features with:
  —Rate enforcement on a per-virtual circuit (VC) basis
  —Generalized BECN support on a per-VC basis
  —Priority/custom/weighted-fair queuing support at the VC level

- Improves scalability and performance by:
  —Increasing the density of VCs
  —Improving response time

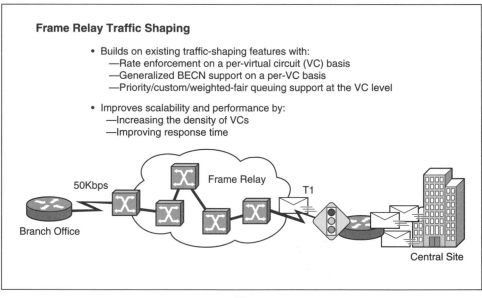

(d)

Figure 10.14 (Continued)   Router-level QoS.

These techniques have been in routers since the mid-1990s, and are proving to be a first step in the direction of end-to-end QoS in the Internet and in the intranet. It is expected that in the coming years the protocols discussed in this chapter will become standard features in high-end routers.

References

1. RFC 1881, "Integration of Real-time Services in an IP-ATM Network Architecture," August 1995, <sunsite.auc.dk.RFC/rfc/raf1821.html>.
2. A. Schmidt, D. Minoli. *MPOA*. (Greenwich, CT: Prentice-Hall/ Manning), 1998.
3. Fred Baker, "RSVP," Business Communications Review, March 1997, pages 30ff.
4. R. Braden, D. Clark, and S. Shenker, "Integrated Services in the Internet Architecture: An Overview." RFC 1633, ISI, MIT, and PARC, June 1994.
5. R. Braden, L. Zhang, S. Berson, S. Herzog, and S. Jamin. "Resource Reservation Protocol (RSVP, version 1 Functional Specification," Internet draft, May 1996, www.ietf.org://draft-ietf-rsvp-spec-14.txt or ftp://mercury.lcs.mit.edu/pub/intserv/drafts/draft-ietf-rsvp-spec-13.txt.
6. J. Wroclawski, "The Use of RSVP with IETF Integrated Services," Internet draft, October 1996.
7. J. McQuillan. The NGN Executive Seminar, New York, March 20, 1997.
8. H. Schulzrinne, S. Casner, R. Frederick, V. Jacobson, "RFC 1889: RTP: A Transport Protocol for Real-Time Applications," 1996, www.globecom.net/(nocl,sv)/ietf/rfc/rfc1889.shtml.
9. Cisco Materials, including Networker's 1997 CD-ROM.

PART

Four

Evolving Access Technologies

xDSL Technology and Applications

11.1 Overview

With the evolution trending toward broadband requirements in business applications, particularly for Internet access, and the expense associated with fiber-in-the-loop technologies (FITL), the local exchange carriers (incumbent LECs—ILECs—and, thanks to competition, the competitive local exchange carriers—CLECs), are looking to derive more throughput from the existing copper local loops, via technologies called "x" Digital Subscriber Line (xDSL), where x stands for the various technologies that offer different performance levels. In general, these technologies provide for a few megabits per second in either one or both directions, although some go as high as 50Mbps. The norm is that the higher the speed, the shorter the loop; related to this, the higher the speed, the fewer the loops in the actual telco plant that qualify for upgrade. Upgrade is achieved by removing the loading coil from the loop and adding signal-encoding devices at both ends of the loop (if it exists). At the central office, this may be done using an integrated device sometimes called digital subscriber loop access multiplexer (DSLAM).

Proponents see this technology as a means to increase the access speed to Internet-connected (web) servers. At face value, this is true; looking deeper, significant operations, administration, maintenance, and provisioning (OAM&P) challenges face carriers in the widespread deployment of the technology. Planners interested in securing this service from the LECs/CLECs, should differentiate from the hype generated by the end-loop equipment suppliers seeking stock market fortunes and the actual availability of service from the providers, as they are expected to be in relatively short supply for the foreseeable future. It makes intuitive sense to assume that, given the tighter requirements on the (transmission characteristics of the) loop, the new network integration requirements at the central office, and the higher costs of the electronics, that the rate of introduction of the service should follow the deployment curve of ISDN. But many view ISDN's deployment history as underwhelming. In addition, there are competitive technologies, such as cable TV modems.

This section looks at the technology, its ISDN roots, the applications, and the deployment prospects for xDSL technologies. Important issues surround the topic of ADSL physical layer technology, ADSL performance metrics at the loop-transmission level, and central office interworking, including ATM and IP-layer connectivity.

Traditional ISPs are at the mercy of the ILECs in their ability to provide xDSL support to their own customers (assuming that they are able to deal with the DSLAM and interworking issues), just as they are at the ILEC's mercy for ISDN service. CLECs that are also ISPs have more leverage, not only in using their own facilities, but also in forcing the ILECs to provide unbundled loops under the Communications Act of 1996 (as a precursor for the FCC to allow the ILECs into long-distance voice services). Companies such as AT&T that now have end-to-end connectivity (via the merger with TCG), also have more options available regarding xDSL.

11.2 Evolving xDSL Applications and Directions

In recent years, there has been an interest in bringing digital technology all the way to the residence, and increasing the bandwidth achievable over the access connection from that which is secured via analog modem methods (at most up to 56Kbps). These efforts started with ISDN, but when the market for that service became uncertain in the late 1980s, amid bureaucratic delays on the part of carriers, the industry extended the technology to other manifestations of end-to-end digital. Asymmetric Digital

Subscriber Line (ADSL), where there is about an order of magnitude more capacity in the downstream (to the customer) path than in the upstream path (to the central office), was the first technology of the xDSL genre to become available. The upstream bandwidth is in the range of 1.5 to 6Mbps. A number of related technologies are now available. Two significant differences, between ISDN and xDSL, in addition to bandwidth, are:

- xDSL paths are not switched at the physical layer (i.e., circuit switching is not supported). The practical reality is that these links are not terminated onto a switch. More typically, these channels are connected to an access concentrator that provides physical connectivity of the channels to a router, so that the (typical Internet IP-based) protocol data units can be relayed via network layer mechanisms (specifically, routing).

- As a corollary of the first point, no formal signaling (e.g., à la ITU-T Q.931) is supported.

In general, xDSL technology provides symmetric and asymmetric bandwidth configurations to support both one-way and two-way "high" bandwidth requirements (the term symmetric means that the speed of the uplink and downlink channels are equal). Plain Old Telephone Service (POTS) is also supported on the same physical loop. End-user web browsing generates traffic that is typically asymmetric in nature. An organization's web-site support, as well as videoconferencing, may be symmetric in nature.

ADSL was the first technology of this kind, followed by a whole gamut of related technologies in the past few years. Hence, as noted in the overview, the set of technologies is referred to as xDSL, where "x" is a wild card for a host of variants, as shown in Table 11.1. Figure 11.1 depicts a typical xDSL environment.

ADSL work started in the mid-1980s, and thus has a history that is already 12 years old. These technical solutions are appearing just in time. There has been an accelerated introduction of "content-rich" applications (e.g., graphics, multimedia, etc.) that require much more bandwidth at the residential and branch office level than in the past. High-capacity requirements are now typical of knowledge-based telecommuters, branch offices, schools, medical clinics, and so on. These requirements cannot be met with traditional VF-based communication channels. In addition, many question whether it is actually possible to achieve sustained 56Kbps throughput on the new dial-up 56Kbps modems, given that is at times hard enough to achieve 28.8Kbps on the V.34 modem.

Table 11.1   Major Variants of DSL Technologies

ADSL (Asymmetric DSL)	Provides up to 6.1Mbps downstream and 640Kbps upstream over a single copper pair. ADSL is typically employed to deliver high-speed data and telephony services.
HDSL (High-Data Rate DSL)	Provides up to 1.5Mbps symmetric (two ways) over two copper pairs. HDSL is typically used to provide a repeaterless T1. This is the kind of technology that CLECs are seeking to secure from the LECs, under the Communications Act of 1996 (this approach is also called "unbundled loops").
SDSL (Single-Line DSL)	Provides up to 768Kbps in both directions (single-loop version of HDSL, also called S-HDSL).
RADSL (Rate-Adaptive DSL)	Automatically adjusts to copper quality degradation or can be manually adjusted to run at different speeds up to ADSL rates.
VDSL (Very High-Speed DSL) (also called VADSL, Very-High-Speed ADSL, or BDSL, Broadband DSL)	DSL technology operating at 50Mbps downstream, 1.5Mbps upstream, but over shorter distances (e.g., 1,000 feet). It is often implemented in conjunction with ATM and is employed to offer services such as videoconferencing, digital video, and high-speed Internet access. VDSL equipment is employed near or inside buildings. One evolving application is for use in a large building's common space, with an ATM OC-3c/OC-12c fiber uplink and an in-building copper distribution plant/riser; this allows various tenants to enjoy broadband services, without having to run fiber to every user.
IDSL	ISDN-based DSL: "inverse multiplexes" two B channels using ISDN's 2B1Q into one 128Kbps channel.

Initially, proponents were targeting the ADSL technology for video-on-demand applications. But that turned out to be not an extensive market because, one, very few video channels can be supported (e.g., one channel with Motion Picture Expert Group 1 compression), and, two, there is little consumer interest at this time for pay-per-view type services. At this time, the expectations of users for graphics, sound, live interactions, two-way video, entertainment, and games over the Internet are already undersatisfied. (Table 11.2 lists some applications of xDSL technology.) xDSL technology coexists in the loop with voice; the data portion is used for

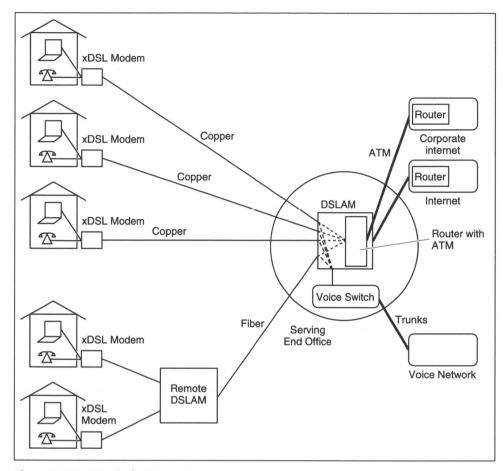

Figure 11.1   A typical xDSL environment.

high-speed data application (e.g., Internet access), and does not have to nail up the traditional telephony switch with DS0-level for long-duration data calls. xDSL supports DS1, E1, and DS2 rates. An industry group, the ADSL Forum, has been formed to advance and promulgate the technology.

The local loop is generally one of the key bottlenecks in supporting data-intensive applications. All dial-up voice-frequency modems are constrained to operate at less than the Shannon-Hartley capacity of a noise- and bandwidth-limited channel. As an example, a 3000Hz channel experiencing a 30dB signal-to-noise ratio has a theoretical capacity of about 30,000 bps. Any noise or misengineering of such a channel will likely cause a 28.8Kbps modem to drop back to a lower data rate. In fact, dial-up voice frequency modems often do not operate at the nominal

Table 11.2   Higher-Speed Applications Requiring xDSL-Level Capacity

APPLICATION	CHARACTERISTICS
Consumer Internet	Graphics, low-end video, the Web
Business Internet	Documents/specs download, electronic publishing, site establishment
Telecommuting	Information downloading and uploading, access to corporate facilities
Remote LAN Access	Integrated media (data, voice, etc.), branch-to-HQ application access

maximum data rates. The upgrade to higher-speed transmission systems is not achievable as easily in the local loop as in the interoffice and long haul (e.g., with SONET-based fiber facilities) because of the number of facilities involved. Hence, the local loop is seen as a problem for LECs and other interested carriers (e.g., ISPs). Therewith lies the promise of this evolving technology. ADSL supports transmission of high-speed data communications traffic, in conjunction with telephony POTS, over a single pair of standard gauge copper wire, for distances around 18,000 feet. The ADSL technology is generally targeted to residential users, small office/home office (SOHO), and small business users.

Given that the infrastructure upgrade to fiber is still many years off, and the cost is quite high, xDSL allows megabit-per-second rates on copper loops at a reasonable cost. xDSL refers to a set of similar technologies that provide high-bandwidth over copper twisted pair without the use of amplifiers or repeaters on the loop (T1 systems require, for example, a repeater every mile). It entails adding electronics at both ends of the loop to provide for robust signal encoding; this encoding scheme, which is more sophisticated than traditional bipolar encoding used on T1 lines, supports increased bandwidth.

xDSL signals are designed to maximize the rate of transmission of digital signals through subcategories of nonloaded twisted pairs, making full use of bandwidths on the wire. Such bandwidth can, in fact, be greater than 1MHz; this is much more than the 3000Hz normally utilized for voice transmission. It is then clear why xDSL signals will not generally pass through loaded loops, and may or may not be able to be incorporated into digital loop carrier and fiber-to-the-curb systems: Loading reduces the available bandwidth (about half of the digital loop carrier lines in place today were designed before the early 1980s and may or may not be xDSL-grade). See Figure 11.2.

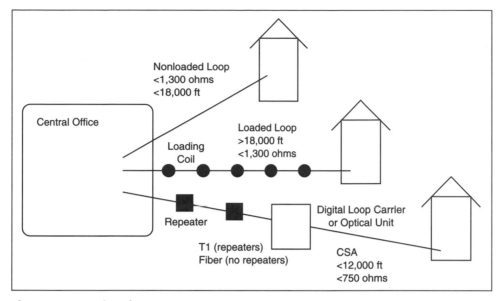

Figure 11.2 Various loop arrangements.

The reach of the enterprise network is now such that nearly all branch locations of an organization are interconnected over the corporate extended LAN; observers estimate that 80 percent of the traffic on such LAN infrastructures is either directed to or coming from remote locations. The interconnection of these remote LANs over a set of traditional meshed T1s, frame relay links, or ATM facilities may be too expensive. Thus, xDSL technology can be used either to supply less expensive T1 lines (for meshing purposes) or to supply T1-speed access links to switched fast-packet services (such as frame relay or ATM). Table 11.3 itemizes the advantages in decreased transmission time achieved by using xDSL technology. The broadband market, of which xDSL is a component, is variously forecast, but some see it being as high as $350 billion worldwide by the year 2000.

With deregulation, carriers other than the ILECs can get unbundled access to the loop plant. Examples include competitive access providers (CAPs), CLECs, and ISPs. The LECs themselves are in the process of adding new services, such as Internet access; more to the point, they *must* add these value-added noncommodity services to survive in the long haul. Consequently, some see the LECs as being in an ideal position to offer new, advanced services over the existing multibillion dollar investment in copper loops. A traditional loop is valued at around $500; it follows that a carrier with 10 million loops would have a $5 billion infrastructure plan in copper. The CAPs, CLECs, and ISP also have their eyes set on the opportunity to provide users with high-speed access to Internet services.

Table 11.3   Reduction in Transmission Time Using xDSL

TRANSMIT TIME IN SECONDS	ANALOG MODEM	ISDN BASIC	XDSL	XDSL	XDSL	XDSL
Speed -> KB	28.8	128	768	1544	6144	50,000
50	13.889	3.858	1.072	0.298	0.083	0.023
100	27.778	7.716	2.143	0.595	0.165	0.046
200	55.556	15.432	4.287	1.191	0.331	0.092
400	111.111	30.864	8.573	2.381	0.662	0.184
800	222.222	61.728	17.147	4.763	1.323	0.368
1600	444.444	123.457	34.294	9.526	2.646	0.735
3200	888.889	246.914	68.587	19.052	5.292	1.470
6400	1777.778	493.827	137.174	38.104	10.584	2.940
12800	3555.556	987.654	274.348	76.208	21.169	5.880

It should be noted that xDSL is a technology (that is, a tool) used by carriers to provide bandwidth. The user should not call the carrier and secure an "ADSL service"; rather, the user could call the carrier and indicate a need for inexpensive residential-level T1 connectivity and inquire at the same time whether ADSL is being used by the carrier. Another approach is for the carrier to announce that in a certain region ADSL access is available, implying low-cost T1-level connectivity for customers. One of the deployment advantages of ADSL, compared to ISDN, is that the carrier can undertake selective upgrade and service offerings, without having to forklift a switch at the CO before even one customer can be turned up.

The asymmetric nature of ADSL relates to the fact that more bandwidth is available downstream (central office-to-customer premise) than upstream (customer premise-to-central office). Typically, the downstream bandwidth ranges from 64Kbps to 6Mbps; the upstream bandwidth varies from 64Kbps to 1.5Mbps. This allocation of bandwidth is based both on technical and application considerations. Because only two wires are used (except in Single-Line DSL), the send and receive domains need to be shared in some fashion, in an interdependent way. Many applications are indeed skewed; namely, the amount of information in one direction is less than the information in the opposite direction. Certainly, the original video-on-demand application had large amounts of information flowing to the customer and just a few VCR-like commands flowing back to the central office. Internet/web access is generally of the same type, unless the user is in the business of uploading information into the Internet (as would be the case for an information provider). In general, ADSL is not appropriate for web-site establishment and support, because in that case, the upstream traffic (the answers to the surfer's queries) would be busy. Where the bandwidth requirement is symmetric, one could use SDSL.

The performance of the technology, manifested in the visible form of xDSL modems, is dependent on these and other factors:

- Length of the path (12–18 kilofeet [Kft])
- Pair gauge (e.g., 24 or 26)
- Bridge taps (number and length of taps)
- Loading coils (most xDSL modems do not work in the presence of coils, which must then be removed; coils are used to support analog voice communication and to act as filters)
- Crosstalk noise, particularly a problem in large cables—those carrying, say, 300 pairs
- External electromagnetic influences and interferences (e.g., motors, elevators, appliances)

Last century saw the introduction of underground telephone cable, which utilized twisted pairs (#18 American wire gauge, AWG). The capacitance per-unit length of the pairs was chosen to be .083 microF/mi, which is still used today in the loop network. Wire gauges of 19, 22, 24, and 26 AWG have come to be used over the years in the loop plants associated with the 14,000 central offices in the United States. At the turn of the century, in the absence of electronic mechanisms to aid transmission, three techniques were utilized:

- Improvement in the electroacoustical efficiency of telephone set
- Use of coarser gauge
- Band limits on voice signal via the use of periodically spaced inductors, called loading coils, that add to the native inductance of the wire pair to reduce attenuation at frequencies below about 3300Hz

The bandwidth restriction was judged to be satisfactory for voice transmission. Subjective tests determined intelligibility of telephone speech to be adequate. In the 1950s, AT&T issued engineering rules to systematize the design of wire loops serving about 80 percent of the customers in the United States. These rules placed an upper bound of 1300ohms of resistance on maximum-length loops. Wire gauges were required to be no finer than 26 AWG and loops longer than 18,000 feet were required to be "loaded" with 88MHz inductors placed at 6,000-foot intervals, starting 3,000 feet from the central office. Unterminated branch pairs or bridges taps were constrained to be less than 6,000 feet in total length when added together (see G.T. Hawley, "System Considerations for the Use of xDSL Technology for Data Access," *IEEE Communications Magazine*, March 1997, for more details).

When pulse code modulation (PCM) was introduced in the early 1960s, voice signals were assumed to be band-limited to 4000Hz, which, with 8-bit encoding of 8,000 samples per second, results in 64,000 bps digitized voice signals. In the early 1970s, T1 carrier lines were introduced into the local loop. The T1 link was terminated by digital loop carrier system terminals, one in the central office (soon to be incorporated into the digital switch) and the other, a remote terminal, installed within 12,000 feet of nonloaded twisted pair length to end users. The 12,000-foot design rule beyond the remote terminal is called carrier serving area (CSA) design. In the early 1980s, optical fiber began to be installed between digital loop carrier terminals in lieu of T1 lines, but with no change in the CSA design rules.

As a result of this development of loops in the U.S. telephone network, there are now three types of connections between end users and the telephone central office:

- Nonloaded twisted pairs up to 18,000 feet in length (about 70 percent of all loops)

- Loaded loops greater than 18,000 feet in length (about 15 percent)

- Derived loops with up to 12,000 feet of nonloaded twisted pair connected to a remote terminal of a digital loop carrier system (about 15 percent)

11.3 Technical Background

A gamut of services, including voice, video, multimedia, and data can be carried by xDSL without having to deploy fiber-to-the-location technologies. Also, the time-to-market curve can be relatively shallow, since the carrier needs only to decide to enter the market, select/install the xDSL modem, select/install the DSLAM technology, and achieve a data connection (via a router) to the appropriate upstream entity (e.g., Internet).

xDSL utilizes terminating devices (called modems, although no analog functions are supported on the data side). At the remote end, this is a discrete element; at the CO end, this is incorporated in a rack of equipment that may contain both the downstream devices and the upstream routers and (possibly) ATM interworking electronics. This is the DSLAM.

xDSL refers to the various arrangements in which advanced modulation techniques are utilized over a copper-based local loop to achieve higher throughput in one or both directions. ADSL implementations have employed two types of line modulation techniques:

- Carrierless amplitude modulation (CAP)
- Discrete multi tone (DMT).

DMT is the ANSI standard, but since CAP was employed from the start, many vendors continue to employ it (although migration plans to DMT have been announced by many vendors). DMT has suffered two setbacks along the way: interoperability problems among implementations, and chip-set availability, or lack thereof. Vendors that have DMT products include: Alcatel, Amati, Analog Devices Inc., Aware, Motorola, and Orckit.

The interoperability issue relates to a number of factors:

- The format of the aggregated uplink. Vendors variously use DS3/ATM, OC-3/ATM, Ethernet, fast Ethernet, or HSSI.

- The interface supported on the CPE modem. Vendors variously use V.35, Ethernet, and analog telephony.

- CO configuration—discrete, aggregated, or aggregated and concentrated.

The three modulation techniques in use (2B1Q, CAP, and DMT) segment the signal frequency into three ranges to carry POTS, the upstream information, and the downstream information (see Table 11.4). In 1992, the T1 Committee of ATIS initiated a standards project for ADSL. Subsequently, a standard was published, in 1995, ANSI T1E1.413-1995. The DMT modulation technique was chosen (the other candidates were QAM and CAP, a variant of QAM). Video-on-demand did not achieve momentum as a possible service offering in the United States; as a result, interest in ADSL technology diminished; however, in the mid-1990s, the rapid expansion of Internet services and the World Wide Web revived interest in ADSL as a short-term means of increasing the data rate of access to the Internet, as an alternative to voice-frequency modems and ISDN basic rate service.

Table 11.4 xDSL Modulation Schemes

2B1Q	The code converts blocks of two consecutive signal bits into a single four-level pulse for transmission. Hence, the information rate is double the baud rate: There are two bits per baud, arranged as one quaternary (four-level) pulse amplitude modulated signal. All four possible combinations of two information bits map into a quaternary symbol. This is also known as 4-pulse amplitude modulation (4-PAM). 10 maps to +3V; 11 maps to +1V; 01 maps to −1V; and 00 maps to −3V. Used in ISDN.
DMT	Discrete multitone modulation is a multicarrier method that subdivides the information channels (telephony, upstream data, and downstream data) into 256 subchannels, onto which the traffic is mapped. This implies a multiplexing scheme. DMT, the ANSI ADSL standard, enables the hardware to distinguish and to isolate subchannels that are not performing as expected (e.g., high noise, high attenuation, etc.) and to assign the traffic to a neighboring subchannel. The low-rate carrier frequencies are QAM-modulated. Used in ADSL and proposed for VDSL. In ADSL, it supports 6Mbps upstream and 640Kbps downstream.
CAP	Carrierless amplitude/phase modulation is a legacy nonstandard QAM-based technique that makes use of two-dimensional eight-state Trellis coding, Viterbi decoding, and Reed-Solomon forward error correction. Adaptive channel equalization is utilized to support required performance in the presence of channel impairments. This technique is relatively inexpensive and technologically proven. It is used in ADSL to support 1.5Mbps downstream and 64Kbps upstream. CAP uses the frequency above 4kHz (the lower portion being used for POTS).

IDSL (ISDN-based DSL), or just DSL, is basically another name for an ISDN Basic Rate Interface (BRI) circuit operating with two switched 64Kbps circuits and a 16Kbps signaling channel. Both of the 64Kbps channels can carry data in both directions simultaneously. The ISDN origins of these various technologies was discussed in Chapter 2.

HDSL has proven to be a reliable and cost-effective technology for delivering repeaterless T1/E1 services over two copper loops. HDSL can transmit a T1/E1 signal (up to 2.048Mbps) over two nonloaded, 24-gauge unconditioned twisted wire loops up to 12,000 feet. In this case, bridged taps in the loop need not be removed for proper functioning. Elimination of the repeater (and the fact that bridged taps need not be added or removed) means that the engineering of this service is simplified; for example, to engineer a traditional 12,000-foot T1 loop, two transceivers and two repeaters would be required, while to engineer an HDSL, only two HDSL transceivers (at the endpoints of the link) would be necessary. Specifically, this means that there is no need to identify, reengineer (modify), and calibrate a controlled environment as it relates to transmission parameters and repeater functioning (including environmental factors such as power, security, space, humidity, etc.). This, in turn, reduces the OAM&P effort and cost, which carriers report to be nontrivial. Proponents cite increased network uptime and reduced engineering time; and faster provisioning increases customer satisfaction and revenues.

HDSL also uses the 2B1Q code utilized in ISDN to attain a data transmission rate of 784Kbps on loops of up to 12,000 feet in length, including CSA loops beyond digital loop carrier remote terminals. The first application of HDSL methods was to transmit 1.544Mbps T1 signals. Variants of the HDSL techniques have been developed, including a lower-rate system operating up to 384Kbps at 18,000 feet in length, and rate-adaptive systems that incorporate circuitry and software in the transceiver to allow the data rate of the line to be adjusted without external intervention.

11.4 Market Considerations

The xDSL transceiver includes electronics for the encoding or modulation scheme utilized to convert binary data streams into a form suitable for transmission through twisted wire pairs. It may also employ various signal processing, equalization, amplification, and shaping circuitry to adapt transmission for physical attenuation and impairments experienced by signals transmitted through twisted wire pairs. Equipment suppliers include, among others, Alcatel Data Networks, Analog Devices Inc., Amati, Ascend, Aware, Copper Mountain, Motorola, Orckit, PairGain Technologies, and Westell. xDSL modems are variously priced based on features and speeds from $500 to $1,000 or more.

As of mid-1998, there was a wide range of opinions as to when DSL would be deployed on a significant scale and which "flavor" of the service would become prevalent. Such questions on services mirror the state of affairs in the DSL equipment market. From an network manager's perspective, the fractured market could negatively impact deployment decisions. According to our estimates, 1998 saw 10,000 ADSL lines installed. Proponents see this technology becoming important by the start of the new decade. It is acknowledged that CLECs will be driving the market (just as the ISPs were driving higher speeds in the early 1990s). Because of the Communications Act of 1996, the ILEC must provide access lines to competitors. A $10 per-month loop can be value-enhanced to be resold for $200 a month.

As of the time of this writing, actual field results for xDSL were somewhat underwhelming. The following quote from NetworkWorld (January 6, 1997), is indicative of the results: "If you believe everything you hear about xDSL technology, you probably think that any day you'll get Internet access [at high speed]. But in fact there is a big gap between what is happening in the labs and what is happening in the real world . . . planned service rollouts will only support speeds from 128Kbps to 1.5Mbps. . . . Carrier trials so far have yielded two key results: The quality and length of actual loops can limit xDSL bandwidth, and carriers need an architecture that not only works, but it is also inexpensive to provision and maintain."

A number of carriers, including TCG, have technical trials directed at answering questions such as:

1. What is the feasibility of obtaining ADSL-grade loops from LECs?

2. What is the maturity and performance of ADSL products?

3. How stable is the service that can be secured over ADSL?

4. What are the OAM&P issues associated with ADSL technology?

To play it safe, the trials use lower-speed but more mature ADSL technology—for example, DSL based on ISDN (at 128Kbps) and SDSL (up to 768Kbps). It is important that the distance question be addressed satisfactorily in the field (just as it had to be addressed for ISDN in the mid-1980s): If the end user has to be within a limited distance from the central office, ultimate service availability could be limited. Some carriers (specifically, Pacific Bell) claim that 70 percent of their loop plant can support xDSL. Trials by Ameritech show that 1.5Mbps ADSL operates in the 13,000- to 18,000-foot range. MCI Worldcom has reportedly achieved 6Mbps at 13,000 feet, but other carriers, reluctant to reveal their numbers, indicate that MCI's numbers are currently the exception. RADSL can adjust the bandwidth based on the quality/length of the loop, and so may be a solution to this problem. Occasionally, repeaters can be used to achieve greater distances.

Carriers have also learned the lessons taught by the difficulties users faced in ISDN; hence, one of the key goals is to make the technology simple to use. Therefore, carriers plan to require only that a user have a PC with an Ethernet NIC and a web browser.

A number of hurdles still must be cleared before xDSL services will be widely available. Loop plant condition could be an issue, as just noted. Operation support systems (OSS) to support OAM&P functions, including billing, are critical. Also critical is the DSLAM selection/deployment, along with the service choice and modem selection. The routed/ATM link and supportive data infrastructure are also important, and the traditional carriers have limited expertise in this area. The monthly price of xDSL service is also an issue: At this juncture, the price is targeted to be in the

$40 to $100 per-month per-xDSL line range (in addition, users will have to pay ISP charges). Recently, Pacific Bell announced rollout of 384Kbps ADSL coupled with Internet access for $200 per month. The following carriers also plan to be offering xDSL services: Ameritech Corp., Bell Atlantic Corp., GTE Service Corp., Intermedia Communications Corp., SBC, and AT&T Local Services.

Among a host of smaller companies, Cisco has entered the ADSL fray. In March 1997, it acquired Telesend, a privately held company specializing in wide area access products. The company now offers a plug-in for standard channel banks that supports 128Kbps IDSL. The Cisco 90i product uses the same loop-provisioning process as ISDN BRI, and, hence, is ready for rapid deployment. Fast time-to-market is possible, because carriers do not need a large number of users to justify equipping an end office to start service because the infrastructure already exists. The Cisco 90i can operate with any frame relay network. The equipment can be used in any D4 channel bank and can leverage existing ISDN loop technology to provide access over embedded digital loop carrier systems to extend service in a plug-and-play mode. The Cisco 90i has four 144Kbps ISDN 2B1Q access loops, each supporting up to eight frame relay permanent virtual circuits (PVCs) or one Point-to-Point Protocol (PPP) circuit. The Cisco 90i channel unit is available at a list price of $995 and has been in trial with several carriers. A typical port price of $150 can be achieved in quantities of 10,000 ports or more. Cisco is also making available CPE that supports IDSL. These products include the Cisco 770 Soho Router and the Cisco 1600 Modular Access Router. Cisco's SDSL solution, the Cisco 90s, is expected to be available soon.

Recently, Ascend Communications introduced IDSL systems for connecting any ISDN modem at the customer premises to a DSL line card in the local access switch. Using Ascend MAX WAN central office access switches, the Ascend offers MultiDSL, with line cards that support not only ISDN but also CAP- and DMT-based ADSL (1.5Mbps upstream, 64 to 176Kbps downstream) and S-HDSL (768Kbps). Ascend is offering IDSL line cards for the MAX access switch as the first step to introducing carriers and customers to DSL solutions. An eight-port IDSL card for the MAX 4002/4004 costs $3,000 ($375/port). A 12-port model for the MAX TNT costs $4,200 ($350/port). A six-port ADSL-CAP card for the MAX TNT costs $8,250 ($1,375/port). UUNet, Bell Atlantic, and BellSouth were reportedly evaluating the technology. Ascend reports having received strong interest from carriers and ISPs. Four carriers—Pacific Telesis, US WEST, GTE, and SBC Communications—already use the MAX to offer customers Internet access.

Until now, ADSL hookups have been supported on a one-to-one basis: One modem on each customer premises connects to one corresponding modem in the central office. Internet service providers have indicated that they would prefer to pool the high-speed modems the same way they pool analog modems. In early 1997, Amati, the original purveyor of DMT chips for Asymmetrical Digital Subscriber Line technology, expanded its product line beyond modems. The company announced a DSLAM product, named Allegro, that aggregates ADSL traffic in the central office. It fills a void in the product line, and carriers are looking for end-to-end solutions. Amati's concentrator links data IP users with a 10Base-T connection to the Internet or data network. Other DSLAMs utilize frame relay or ATM interfaces.

NetSpeed (Austin, Texas) has also engineered an ADSL solution using a six-to-one concentration of user modems to CO modems. NetSpeed's system uses on-demand ADSL technology to let the end user or business appear to be permanently connected. However, the connection is actually taken down when the user is idle. Oversubscribing modems in a pool also solves many of the most common problems with ADSL. Another product is an inverse multiplexer that aggregates three 8Mbps ADSL lines into one 24Mbps channel and can dynamically adjust bandwidth.

GDC (Middlebury, Connecticut) recently introduced the COLOSSAS (Central Office Located Special Services Access System), which is a DSLAM that supports access, concentration, backbone networking to frame relay and ATM and management.

11.5 An Application of the Technology

As noted, xDSL/ADSL applications have been advanced for video-on-demand, particularly video dialtone, Internet access, SOHO, and telecommuting. SDSL and HDSL applications have been targeted to business applications for branch-office connectivity at FT1 or T1 rates. VDSL has been proposed for in-build distribution for Ethernet-speed Internet connectivity with DSLAM technology in the basement (and ATM uplinks).

This section looks at a specific area of potential interest, namely the telecommuting market [2]. Telecommuters typically require high-speed access to the office or the Internet, particularly for knowledge workers, who usually are also Internet users. The discussion that follows is more application-oriented than technology-oriented. (The reader who is not interested in further exploring the business opportunity of the technology but only in the technical treatment may go directly to the chapters that follow.)

In many large and/or fast-growing U.S. cities, the commuting chore is becoming more demanding. A 1994 study by the Federal Highway Administration showed that getting to and from work is taking longer now than a decade ago, as jobs and homes move to the suburbs, away from arterial highways. Therefore, an increasing number of corporations and employees are looking at alternatives, many of which fall in the category of what is called "telecommuting."

Telecommuting is a term coined in the recent past to refer to the capability of workers to either work out of their homes or to drive only a few minutes to reach a complex in their immediate neighborhood where, through advanced communication and computing support provided by the "landlord" of the complex, they can access their corporate computing resources to do their work. Eventually, there could be at least one such complex, known as "telebusiness center" [3] or *regional telecommuting center* (RTC), in each suburban town, perhaps more. In the shorter term, however, telecommuting is likely to be home- or home office-based. One of the goals of the designers of a telecommuting program is to duplicate the communications environment that employees have in their corporate offices in their home offices [4]. Powerful PCs now support a gamut of needs, from voice-over-IP to desktop videoconferencing.

Telecommuting can also be seen in the context of the evolution of the mobile professional: Such professionals may continue to work at the office for eight hours and/or a few days a week but also want to have a "replica" of their office at home, on the road, or even in the hotel room they are in during a business trip [4] [5]. Some companies make ample use of wireless technology both in the office (for both voice and data), as well as in the field. This includes portable computers, cellular phones, pagers, text pagers, PDAs, and other mobile computing and communications devices. At the time of this writing, there were already 7+ million people doing at least part of their work on the road [6]. The telecommunication and supporting technologies that support a home office can often (but not always) be used to support the mobile worker.

From a business standpoint, telecommuting can be viewed as a segment of the work-at-home market. It encompasses those employees of corporations, government agencies, and universities who work at home either part-time or full-time during business hours for at least eight hours per week. But the work-at-home market encompasses other segments beyond the telecommuting market, including full-time self-employed workers, part-time self-employed workers, and corporate after-hours workers.

In the United States, it is in the areas with most congestion where telecommuting makes immediate sense. These include:

Los Angeles

Washington

San Francisco-Oakland

Miami

Chicago

San Diego

Seattle-Everett

San Bernardino

New York

Houston

Table 11.5 provides some parametric information related to commuting; information such as this may be factored in by the designers of a telecommuting program. Note that at a nominal $20 per-hour rate, a 60-minute round-trip commute equates to $5,000 per year in productivity lost per employee, in addition to the actual costs of transportation and the "hidden" environmental costs. Furthermore, knowledge workers are typically paid more, and so telecommuting makes a lot of sense from a productivity point of view, too.

11.5.1 Buyers of Telecommuting Services

Current and potential buyers of telecommuting services include employers in: government agencies at the state, local and federal levels; universities, colleges, and other higher-education institutions; and a growing

Table 11.5   Recent Commuting Trend Statistics

City where the largest number of people drive alone	Detroit (82.7%)
City where the least number of people drive alone	New York City (52.3%)
City where the largest number of people carpool	Washington DC (15.8%)
City where the least number of people carpool	Boston (10.3%)
City where the largest number of people use mass transit	New York City (27.8%)
City where the least number of people use mass transit	Tampa (1.6%)

number of corporations. This market also includes employees in these industries who perform a wide range of technical and administrative functions. The functions that telecommuters perform and the number of telecommuters determine the networking access and network aggregation requirements at the corporate end of the telecommuting system.

A top-down view of the market, where a provider can directly sell services, is as follows:

Corporate planners and strategists. Individuals in corporations who will need to become involved in meeting the implications of the Clean Air Act and related legislation. The issue is: Who in the corporation makes such decisions? Senior management? The office of the president? The CIO? One may identify whom to contact by considering companies headquartered in the geographic location of interest. One can also focus on specific industries that perhaps are more open to the concept (for examples, banks may not be willing because of security considerations, but publishing firms could be interested). One can also focus on specific functions within corporations (for example, some functions may be more appropriate to telecommuting than others).

Real estate concerns. Real estate developers may worry about a decreased demand on office space. However, looking at telecommuting as an opportunity, they could establish regional telecommuting centers either by building new facilities that are strategically located or by equipping an existing building with the necessary communications equipment.

Regional (state, county, city) planners. Infrastructure planners (highways, rail, bridges, etc.) may become involved in the process of looking for a solution to a congestion problem. For example, in studying the alternatives of either building a new highway system or developing a "teleport" hub including a regional telecommuting center, they may find that the latter is much more cost-effective.

New services developers. Carriers, new service developers, and equipment manufacturers may specifically target telecommuting services. In particular, they may need assistance from consultants who know the field, the technology, and the end user, in order to roll out communication services.

Entrepreneurs. Independent concerns of all kinds may be looking at plans to develop an overall telecommuting posture for entry into the telecommuting support business.

Local universities.   Local universities may choose to focus on a special type of telecommuting: distance learning.

Market researchers.   Market researchers may find that the information they are able to generate on telecommuting is of interest to the parties identified previously (government agencies, corporate planners, carriers, etc).

Many of these segments can make use of xDSL, although some could also make use of higher-speed links.

11.5.2 Computing and Communications Equipment

To work at home, telecommuters need several types of communications and computing equipment. Some of the basic equipment is introduced next.

Personal Computers. Personal computers (PCs) are increasingly being used by telecommuters. The growth in the use of PCs can be attributed to several reasons: PC literacy is on the rise, as schools educate students to be familiar with PCs and their applications; computer manufacturers have been introducing computers with friendlier interfaces and high-value productivity packages; and the prices of computers have been dropping as a result of the price wars among computer manufacturers. A telecommuter can now purchase a reasonably configured PC for as little as $2,000. The cost of communication hardware (e.g., modems) and services has and continues to go down.

Ancillary Equipment. Ancillary equipment includes telephone sets, cellular phones, personal communication service (PCS) devices (e.g., e-mail-enabled pagers), fax machines, copying machines, web servers, and so on.

Communication Solutions for Telecommuters. Clearly, communication services play a central role in telecommuting. Several network solutions exist to support the communications requirements of the telecommuters. These solutions can be classified into three major groups:

- Traditional telephony
- Narrowband solutions that operate at speeds up to 1.5Mbps, including xDSL
- Internet, as accessed through one of the preceding methods

Dial-up. This Plain Old Telephone Service (POTS) approach involves the use of modems to connect the telecommuter PC (owned by the telecommuter or provided by the corporation) to the remote server or mainframe; it utilizes the analog public telephone network. Circuit switching implies that the communications channel is not dedicated 24 hours per day, but must be brought online when needed (via a process called *call setup*), and then taken down when no longer needed. Traditional modems have operated at speeds up to 33.6Kbps; however, until recently, 28.8Kbps has been more common. This implies that the throughput across this type of link is fairly small; consequently, only a small number of users and/or short inquiry/responselike transactions can be supported. Since the link between the two points is not available on a dedicated basis, the user needs to dial up the corporate data center or access node, as needed.

ISDN. This interconnection approach involves the use of switched *digital* facilities between the telecommuter and the corporate access node or data center. As covered in Chapter 2, ISDN provides end-to-end digital connectivity with access to voice and data (packet) services over the same digital transmission and switching facilities. It provides a range of services using a limited set of connection types and multipurpose user-network interface arrangements. ISDN defines *physical user-network interfaces.* The more well-known of these is 2B + D, which provides two switched 64Kbps channels, plus a 16Kbps packet/signaling channel (144Kbps total). Lesser-known ISDN interfaces include 1B+D, which is currently under trial by some LECs (e.g., Bell Atlantic), and NB+D, where N is greater than 2 but less than 23.

Proponents see "solid potential for ISDN to fill telecommuting needs" [7, 8, 9, 10]. However, this assessment on the potential of ISDN may be somewhat optimistic. Many users now employ faster modems, possibly up to 56Kbps with even more compression. In favor of ISDN is that it offers a more "comfortable" 64Kbps, 128Kbps, or even 384Kbps throughput, affording adequate flexibility to the user. xDSL is an extension of these concepts.

Digital Private Lines (Fractional T1, T1, T3). Dedicated "private line" digital services provide transparent bandwidth at the specified speed ($N \times$ 64Kbps for FT1, 1.544Mbps for T1, and 44.736Mbps for T3), and are suitable for point-to-point interconnection of low-burst (i.e., steady) traffic. T3 (also known as DS3) facilities are increasingly available in many parts of the country, although they are still fairly expensive. In addition, a number of carriers have started to offer a fractional T3 service that allows the user to specify the desired number multiple of T1s. These services may be more appropriate for RTCs than for individual telecommuters, however

[11]. These are generally for business, although ADSL/SDSL can also be used as a substitute for T1.

Frame Relay Service. Frame relay, covered in Chapter 6, is a data communication service that became available in the early 1990s. It supports medium-speed connections between user equipment (routers and private switches in particular) and between user equipment and carriers' frame relay network equipment (i.e., public switches). The frame relay protocol supports data transmission over a connection-oriented path. Frame relay is generally used by businesses (rather than homebound telecommuters), but access can also be achieved via xDSL.

ATM/Cell Relay Service. ATM, covered in Chapter 7, is a high-bandwidth, low-delay switching and multiplexing technology now becoming available for both public and private networks. While ATM in the strict sense is simply a (data link layer) protocol, the more-encompassing ATM principles and ATM-based platforms form the foundation for a variety of high-speed digital communication services aimed at corporate users for high-speed data, LAN interconnection, imaging, and multimedia applications. Cell relay service is one of the key services enabled by ATM [12]. It can be implemented for enterprise networks that use completely private communication facilities, completely public communication facilities, or that are hybrid.

Native Mode LAN Interconnection Service (NMLIS). NMLIS (also called transparent LAN service) is a family of LAN extensions to support connectivity between the same types of LANs (Ethernet/fast Ethernet, token ring, fiber distributed data interface) and high-performance computer systems across MANs and wide area networks (WANs). These services operate at native LAN speeds (4, 10, 16, 100Mbps), and can support the LAN interconnection requirements of RTCs, providing them with a substitute to the following services: frame relay, SMDS, and private T1 services. The underlying technology can, however, be any of these, in addition to dedicated lines and/or dark fiber. xDSL may be used in these services via inverse multiplexers (although no products supporting xDSL are yet on the market, there are several products based on multiple T1 services). TCG CERFnet is an example of an ISP that offers NMLIS in three flavors: exchange-based service (for metro regions), exchange-access service (for nationwide applications), and bundled NMLIS/Internet access service.

The Internet. Telecommuters make substantial use of the Internet. Through the Internet they can receive a number of services, including logons, e-mail, file transfer, host-to-host communications, web access, and directory services. xDSL may be used to enhance access to the Internet.

11.6 Conclusion

xDSL systems aim to exploit the transmission capacity of twisted pair telephone wires to support access to new digital services employing in-place telephone-company copper cables. Carriers seem to be eager to introduce xDSL technology, to counter threats of cable modems and CLECs' services for providing increased access speed to users. In turn, CLECs want access to unbundled loops to support SDSL for delivering less expensive T1s. At this juncture, the focus of the industry discussion is on modem technology, rather than on actual rollout plans. The technology and service issues have to be resolved. Then will come the deployment. It is hoped that the unpleasant experiences of ISDN can be avoided.

References

1. D. Minoli. *Video Dialtone Technology: Digital Video over ADSL, HFC, FTTC, and ATM.* (New York: McGraw-Hill), 1995.
2. D. Minoli, O. Eldib. *Telecommuting.* (Norwood, MA: Artech House), 1995.
3. C. F. Mason, "Telecommuting Captures the Imagination," *Telephony*, November 23, 1992.
4. Yankee Group, "Evolution of the Mobile Professional," *Yankee Watch: Wireless Mobile Communications*, June 1993.
4. D. Minoli, A. Tumalillo, "Telecommuting," Probe Research Corporation Report, June 1994.
5. "Survey: Corporate Mobile Work Force Grows," *Home Furnishing*, March 30, 1992, p. 95.
6. M. M. Illingworth, "Virtual Managers," *Informationweek*, June 13, 1994, p. 42 ff.
7. K. Krechmer, Action Consulting, "Special Report: Modems— Renewed, Revitalized, Ready!" *Data Communications*, June 1991, p. 88.
8. "Ameritech Tests ISDN in Telecommuting Pilot Program for Customer Service Reps," *Computerworld*, May 11, 1992, p. 74.
9. "Telecommuting Gains as Cultural Barriers Fall," *Crain's New York*, Oct. 12, 1992, p. 26ff.
10. "Work-at-Home Services Most Popular, Says Survey," Telephone Engineer & Management, Jan. 15, 1993, p. 21.
11. D. Minoli, "Telecommuting Issues and Solutions," *Managing Data Networks*, Datapro Report 1070, January 1994.

CHAPTER 12

ISDN Origin of xDSL Technology

12.1 ADSL Provenance

Because deployment of ISDN took so long, developers of ISDN technology began to look at other applications of their digital-over-copper technology. Thus, xDSL technology evolved from ISDN, although no signaling is supported in xDSL. xDSL can be deployed more selectively, and no CO switch is required to upgrade, which is typically expensive, so the technology is easier to introduce in the plant. And because signaling is not supported, both on the line side and on the switch trunk side, the technology is less complicated. Even the DSLAM, a piece of equipment deployed centrally at the CO, in no way approaches the complexity or cost of an ISDN-class switch.

This chapter covers a number of related facets:

- ISDN background
- ISDN line-encoding methods
- Copper-plant issues

12.2 ISDN Background

ISDN was the first attempt to bring higher-speed digital connectivity to the home. Work on the technology started in the early 1970s, and baseline standards were developed by the mid-1980s. Deployment was held up for some time by the lack of "implementor's agreements," which eventually appeared in the late 1980s and were called National ISDN 1, 2, and 3 (NI-1, NI-2, NI-3). This section provides some additional details to supplement the information in Chapter 2.

ISDN utilizes three circuit-switched time-division channels: B, D, and H. The B-channel is a 64Kbps access channel that carries customer information, such as voice calls, circuit-switched data, or (theoretically, but not practically), packet-switched data. The D-channel is an access channel carrying control or signaling information and, theoretically, packetized customer information. The D-channel has a capacity of 16Kbps or 64Kbps. The H-channel is a 384Kbps, 1.536Mbps, or 1.920Mbps channel that carries customer information, such as teleconferencing, high-speed data, and high-quality audio or sound programs. The two most well-known ISDN interface structures, and the first to be deployed commercially (in the United States), are Basic Rate Access and Primary Rate Access.

The *Basic Rate Access* (also known as 2B+D, with B = Bearer, D = Delta, or, Basic Rate Interface) is a standardized user interface to the ISDN service that provides access to two B-channels and one D-channel. This access provides three bidirectional, symmetric digital channels to the user's premises. Each of the B-channels can be independently switched. Control over B-channel connections for demand applications resides in the signaling messages passed via the D-channel. The customer can use all or parts of the two B-channels and the D-channel. For a speech call, the user equipment must digitize the user's speech and place the properly coded speech on the appropriate B-channel. Analogously, the user speech equipment must decode B-channel information and convert it to audible speech. Basic Rate Access today is implemented in routers and SOHO/ branch access concentrators. For Internet applications, the user will use the B channel to dial into an ISP.

The *Primary Rate Access* (also known as 23B+D, or Primary Rate Interface) is a standardized user interface to the ISDN service that provides access to 23 B-channels and 1 D-channel (for North America, Japan, and Korea; for Europe, a 30B+D structure is defined). The customer can use all or parts of the B-channels and the D-channel, which in this case has a bandwidth of 64Kbps. Primary rate access is provided using time-division multiplexed signals over four-wire copper circuits (using standard regenerators as necessary) or on other media. As is the case of Basic Rate Access, the D-channel has a message-oriented protocol that supports call-control signaling and packet data. Each B-channel can be switched independently, and some may be permanently connected in special service applications. Primary Rate ISDN is finding a niche in private branch exchange (PBX) to central office connections, among other applications.

The *ISDN bearer* capability is circuit-mode unrestricted digital transmission, supporting on-demand, point-to-point, bidirectional, and symmetric digital connectivity. This is now also called narrowband ISDN (N-ISDN). Here, the user can signal the network to establish a digital link between the origin and the destination, which stays in place as long as desired by the user. Table 12.1 lists some of the key access arrangements now in the process of being supported by carriers. ISDN also supports (on paper) low-speed packet-switching service.

A key aspect of ISDN is that a small set of compatible user-network interfaces can support a wide range of user applications, equipment, and configurations. The number of user-network interfaces is kept small to maximize user flexibility and to reduce costs through economies in pro-

Table 12.1 Key Access Configurations

ACCESS	CONFIGURATION
2B+D	Two 64Kbps channels, plus a 16Kbps packet/signaling channel (also known as Basic Rate)
23B+D	Twenty-three 64Kbps channels, plus a 64Kbps packet/signaling channel (also known as Primary Rate)
nx64+D	n $(1 \leq n \leq 23)$ 64Kbps channels, plus a 64Kbps packet/signaling channel
30B+D	Thirty 64Kbps channels, plus a 64Kbps packet/signaling channel
H0+D	A nonchannelized 384Kbps channel, plus one 64Kbps packet/signaling channel
H11	A nonchannelized 1.536Mbps channel (signaling to be provided on another D-channel interface)
H12	A nonchannelized 1.920Mbps channel (signaling to be provided on another D-channel interface) Europe

duction of equipment and network operations. To support these goals, ISDN standards define *functional groups* and *reference points*. Functional groups are sets of functions that may be needed in ISDN user access arrangements. Specific functions in a functional group may be performed in one or more pieces of actual equipment. Reference points are conceptual points dividing functional groups. In specific implementations, a reference point may in fact correspond to a physical interface between pieces of equipment (see Figure 12.1).

Functional groups include:

Network Termination 1 (NT1).   Includes functions broadly equivalent to layer 1 of the OSI Reference Model. These functions are associated with the proper physical and electrical termination of the network, including: line transmission termination, Layer 1 line maintenance functions and performance monitoring, timing, power transfer, Layer 1 multiplexing, and interface termination, including multidrop termination employing Layer 1 contention resolution. (NT1 is customer equipment in the United States and network equipment elsewhere).

Network Termination 2 (NT2).   Includes functions broadly equivalent to Layer 1 through Layer 3 of the OSI Reference Model. Functions include: Layers 2 and 3 protocol handling, Layers 2 and 3 multiplex-

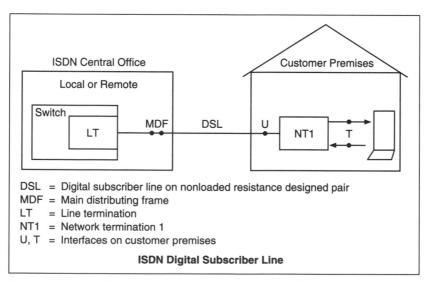

DSL   = Digital subscriber line on nonloaded resistance designed pair
MDF = Main distributing frame
LT   = Line termination
NT1   = Network termination 1
U, T = Interfaces on customer premises

ISDN Digital Subscriber Line

Figure 12.1   A reference point may correspond to a physical interface between pieces of equipment.

ing, switching, concentration, maintenance functions, interface termination and other Layer 1 functions. These functions are typically undertaken in such equipment as PBXs, local area network routers, terminal cluster controllers, and multiplexers.

Terminal Equipment (TE).   Provides functions undertaken by such equipment as digital telephones, data terminal equipment, and integrated voice/data workstations. Functions include: protocol handling, maintenance functions, interface functions, and connection to other equipment.

Terminal Equipment Type 2 (TE2).   Includes functions belonging to the TE functional group but with a non-ISDN interface.

Terminal Adapter (TA).   Includes functions that allow a TE2 terminal to be served by an ISDN. The TA has two jobs. First, it must handle the signaling function. It must physically interface to the ISDN channel; it must be able to encode the information using the 2B1Q (two binary, one quarternary) line-coding scheme alluded to previously; it must be able to multiplex this signal with the user information in a time-division multiplexed frame; it must handle the data link-layer function, using the LAP-D protocol; and it must handle the network layer and higher functions specified by the Q.931 protocol. The second function is to interface to the user's equipment, using a traditional interface such as an RS-232/V.35, or directly fitting a PC expansion slot, and to take that information and encode it properly so that it can be multiplexed in the ISDN frame and transmitted over the line.

Reference points include:

R.   The functional interface between a non-ISDN terminal and the terminal adapter. This interface is likely to follow the RS-232 or V.35 specification, depending on the speed of the TE2 signal stream. This interface between the terminal and the terminal adapter may be an interim solution: In the future, the terminal adapter may migrate into the terminal itself, giving rise to an "ISDN terminal."

T.   The functional interface seen by the user's ISDN-configured equipment, as it connects to the NT2.

S.   The functional interface seen by the user's ISDN configured equipment as it connects the NT1. In practical terms, the S and T reference points can be thought of as being identical. A large share of the ISDN standards concentrate on the activities associated with access to the S/T reference point. This reference point is also referred to, with a slight loosening of the language, as the S/T interface. Bit timing, octet timing, power feeding, activation and deactivation, request and permission to access the signaling channel for the purpose of transmitting data, and request and permission to busy out one of the bearer channels will be performed across the S/T interface.

U.   Also called interface on the network side of the NT, the functional interface of the access line with the NT, on the network side. Standardization of this interface is needed if the NT1s and the CO concentration module are to be manufactured by different vendors. This issue is critical to the selection of the TA: Until switch vendors abide by the U.S. line-coding standards (2B1Q), the TA will have to be selected based on the type of CO switch (at the Primary Rate, AT&T PUB 62411 with B8ZS and ESF is a de facto standard).

Table 12.2 lists some of the key ISDN-related documents, and Table 12.3 lists other ISDN recommendations. ISDN is now available in most markets, and is expected to be increasingly available in other areas.

Table 12.2   Key ISDN Documents

ITU-T	I.320 ISDN Protocol Reference Model I.420/I.430 (four-wire) Basic Rate (physical layer) I.421/I.431 Primary Rate (physical layer) Q.920 (I.440) and Q.921 (I.441) D-channel (data link layer protocol) Q.930 (I.450), Q.931 (I.451) D-channel (upper layers protocol) Q.932 (supplementary services) I.460 Multiplexing, Rate Adaption, and Support of Existing Interfaces
ANSI	T1.605-1989 (four-wire U.S. S/T) Basic Rate (physical layer) T1.601 Basic Rate (physical layer) (two-wire U.S. "U-interface") T1.602-1989 (U.S.) D-channel (link layer) T1.607-1990 (U.S.), T1.608–1989 (U.S.), D-channel (upper layer)
Bellcore	TR-TSY-000397 Basic Rate (physical layer) TR-TSY-000754 Primary Rate (physical layer) TR-TSY-000793 D-channel (link layer) TR-TSY-001268 D-channel, Primary Rate (upper layer) TR-NWT-1203 H0, H11, and nx64

Table 12.3   Additional ISDN Recommendations

ITU-T Q.71	Circuit mode-switched bearer services
ITU-T Q.72	Frame mode
ITU-T Q.82	Stage 2 description for call-offering supplementary services; call forwarding; call deflection
ITU-T Q.84	Stage 2 description for multiparty supplementary services; conferencing (CONF)
ITU-T Q.86	Stage 2 description for charging supplementary services; REV
ITU-T Q.87	Stage 2 description for charging supplementary services; user-to-user signaling (UUS)
ITU-T Q.731	Stage 3 description for the number identification supplementary services using SS No. 7; calling line identification presentation (CLIP)[1]; calling line identification restriction (CLIR)[2]; connected line identification presentation (COLP); connected line identification restriction (COLR)
ITU-T Q.732	Stage 3 description for the call-offering supplementary services using SS No. 7; call forwarding busy; call forwarding no reply; call forwarding unconditional; call deflection
ITU-T Q.733	Stage 3 description for call-completion supplementary services using SS No. 7; call hold (CH); terminal portability (TP)
ITU-T Q.734	Stage 3 description for multiparty supplementary services using SS No. 7; conference calling; three-party service
ITU-T Q.735	Stage 3 description for community-of-interest supplementary services using SS No. 7; closed user group (CUG); multilevel procedure and preemption (MLPP)
ITU-T Q.737	Stage 3 description for additional information transfer supplementary services using SS No. 7; user-to-user signaling (UUS)

12.3 ISDN Line-Encoding Method

The line-level ISDN transmission standard for Basic Rate Access (refer back to Figure 12.1):

1. Describes the transmission technique used to support full-duplex service on a single twisted wire pair.
2. Specifies both the input signal with which the network termination (NT) must operate and the output signals that the NT must produce.

3. Defines the line code to be used and the spectral composition of the transmitted signal.

4. Describes the electrical and mechanical specifications of the network interface.

5. Describes the organization of transmitted data into frames and superframes.

6. Defines the functions of the operations channel.

The transmission system uses the *echo canceler with hybrid* (ECH) principle to provide full duplex operation over a two-wire subscriber loop. With the ECH method, the echo canceler produces a replica of the echo of the near-end transmission, which is then subtracted from the total received signal. *Echo cancelation* is the technique used in North America for the ISDN Digital Subscriber Line in which a record of the transmitted signal is used to remove echoes of this signal that may have mixed with and corrupted the received signal (see Figure 12.2).

The system is intended for service on twisted pair cables, for operation to 18-kilofeet (5.5-km). The ECH was selected over time-compression multiplexing (TCM), another method that has been around for a few years, particularly in a PBX environment. In TCM (also called the ping-pong method), data is transmitted in one direction at a time, with trans-

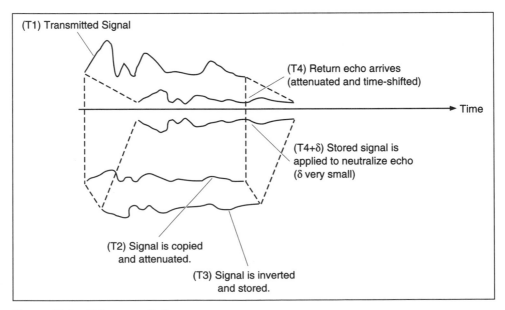

Figure 12.2 Echo cancellation.

mission alternating between the two directions. In order to achieve the stated data rate, the subscriber's bit stream is divided into equal segments, compressed in time to a higher transmission rate, and transmitted in bursts that are expanded at the other end of the link to the original data rate (the actual data rate on the line must be more than twice the data rate required by the user). A short guardband period is used between bursts going in opposite directions to allow the line to settle down. To use this technique in ISDN, which has a total user datarate of 144Kbps, would require over 288Kbps to be transmitted over the copper loop.

With echo cancelation, digital transmission occurs in both directions within the same bandwidth simultaneously. Both transmitter and receiver are connected through a device (known as a hybrid) that allows signals to pass in both directions at the same time. The problem is that echo is generated by the reflection of the transmitted signal back to the user. Both a near-end echo and a far-end echo occurs. The near-end echo arises between the sender's hybrid and the cable; the far-end echo is from the receiver's hybrid device. The magnitude of the echo signal is such that it cannot be ignored; the technique used to overcome this problem is echo cancelation. With this technique, an estimate of the composite echo signals is calculated at the transmitter end, and a signal of that value is subtracted from the incoming signal, effectively canceling the echo. Restricting the pulse shape with bounds on its spectral density, scrambling the input stream, and using the quaternary line code help to minimize crosstalk and maximize transmission range.

To economically provide basic rate service, the digital loop must be implemented without conditioning the plant, special engineering, or special operations. A line code is the electrical representation of digital signals. The selection of a line code is critical to the performance of the loop; digital loop carrier systems for ISDN must have a BER of better than 10^{-7}. The line code determines both the transmission characteristics of the received signal and the added near-end crosstalk noise levels on other pairs in a multipair cable.

The ISDN basic rate line code now specified for North America is called 2B1Q (two binary, one quaternary). This is a four-level pulse amplitude modulation (PAM) code without redundancy. The ISDN user-data bit stream, composed of two 64Kbps B-channels and a 16Kbps D-channel, entering the NT from the S/T interface (i.e., entering the S/T interface toward the NT), and the bit stream on the network side, are grouped into pairs of bits for conversion to *quaternary symbols* (also called quats). In each pair of bits so formed, the first bit is called the *sign bit,* and the second is called the *magnitude bit.* The electrical pulse template is shown in Figure 12.3.

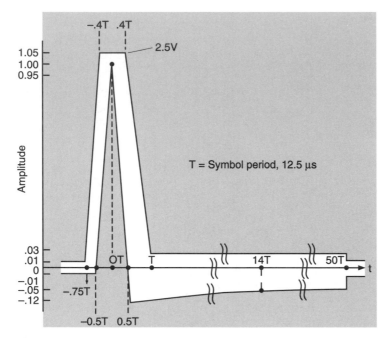

Figure 12.3   The electrical pulse template.

The 2B1Q line code was selected to support ISDN transmission through loops of 18,000 feet or less, meeting resistance design rules. The ISDN signal is transmitted in full-duplex mode, bidirectionally on the same pair of wires. As noted, to accomplish this, ISDN transceivers must contain a hybrid function to separate the two directions of transmission: For the receiver to differentiate between far-end transmission and reflections of near-end transmission, echo cancelation techniques are used. The range of operation of ISDN is dictated by the attenuation and near-end crosstalk (NEXT) from adjacent 2B1Q ISDN signals.

In 2B1Q, each successive pair of scrambled bits in the binary data stream is converted to a quaternary symbol to be output from the transmitter at the interface, as specified in Table 12.4. At the receiver, each quaternary symbol is converted to a pair of bits by reversing the table descrambled, and finally formed into a bit stream or bit streams representing B- and D-channels and the maintenance M-channel bits for maintenance and other purposes.

The 18,000-foot issue may be more pressing for rural environments: A fair number of loops, particularly those close to new developments, suburbia, and commercial environments, are already on digital-loop carrier

Table 12.4 2B1Q Code

FIRST BIT (SIGN)	SECOND BIT (MAGNITUDE)	QUATERNARY SYMBOL (QUAT)
1	0	+3
1	1	+1
0	1	−1
0	0	−3

feeder systems. The 18,000 feet would then be measured from the digital-loop carrier and not the CO. The principal problems impacting a digital loop are:

- Impulse noise
- Intersymbol interference
- Echo noise
- Quantizing noise
- Near-end crosstalk

The intersymbol interference and the near-end crosstalk problems were the most important factors used in selecting the 2B1Q code.

The information flow across the interface point utilizes frames and superframes. A frame is composed of 120 quaternary symbols. The nominal time for the frame is 1.5 milliseconds (ms) (see Figure 12.4). The first nine symbols of the frame are a synchronization word (SW), with the quaternary symbols in the following sequence:

```
SW= +3 +3 -3 -3 -3 +3 -3 +3 +3
```

Frames are organized into superframes: eight frames (12 ms) constitute a superframe. The first frame in the superframe is identified by inverting the polarity of the synchronization word (SW) in this frame. The inverted synchronization word is:

```
ISW = -3 -3 +3 +3 +3 -3 +3 -3 -3
```

The first frame in the superframe of the signal transmitted from the NT is the next frame following the first frame in the superframe of the signal received from the network. The 2B1Q code offers the greatest baud reduc-

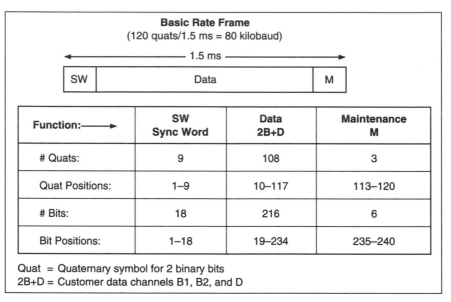

Figure 12.4   Basic ISDN frame rate.

tion of the codes considered, and has an intersymbol interference/ near-end crosstalk performance 2 to 3dB better than the other codes.

The knowledge gained from experience with ISDN loops led to the xDSL developments of the mid-1990s. Now some technology providers are in the process of "fusing" ISDN and DSL technology to deliver IDSL, which supports 128Kbps on ISDN loops.

12.4 Copper Plant Issues

This section looks at the loop plant from a traditional perspective, insofar that xDSL utilizes it to deliver its signals. Loops are an important element of a communication system because, except for end-to-end wireless applications, there is at least one of them in a typical communication link. This brief discussion focuses on narrowband applications, where fiber to the building is not provided. This implies that at least a portion of the communication channel is metallic. Often, loops share poles that carry power lines. Therefore, they may be subject to interference, noise, and crosstalk. In recent years, the use of digital loop carrier systems has diminished the need for long loops, where problems become more prevalent.

The local loop is composed of two major segments: the feeder plant (also called feeder routes) and the distribution plant (also called distribution routes). The feeder is made up of wire cables of various gauges, digital span lines, and optical fiber. It can support voice frequency (VF), digital, and multiplexed signals. Every few years, the feeder plant needs to go through "relief" to accommodate for growth. Factors such as geography, location of customers, and rights of way control the placement of feeder routes.

Pair gain, the capability to carry more than one voice signal on a facility, is accomplished using digital carrier systems (earlier, this was also done with analog carrier systems). Whether physically or electronically provided, feeder cables supply large numbers of pairs from the central office to conveniently located remote locations (known as serving area interfaces). These cross-connect points in the network link the feeder plant coming from the CO to the distribution plant; the distribution plant terminates at the customer's network interface (NI).

12.4.1 Distribution Network Design

The distribution plant usually consists of smaller cables, for example, 26- or 24-gauge. Clearly, there are more distribution plant cables than feeder cables. The distribution plant utilizes four approaches: multiplied, dedicated, interfaces, and serving area (see Table 12.5). There are economic advantages to separating the distribution and feeder facilities. Typically,

Table 12.5 Distribution Network Design

Multipled Plant	Involves the splicing of two or more distribution pairs to a single feeded pair; provides multiple appearances of the same loop pair at several distribution points; was used in party-line applications.
Dedicated Plant	Provides a permanently assigned pair from the CO (specifically from the main distributing frame) to each NI. Note: For new construction, this plant has been superseded by the interfaced plant.
Interfaced Plant	Uses a manual cross-connection (and demarc) between feeder and distribution plant. Since any feeder pair can be connected to any distribution pair, this arrangement provides maximum flexibility.
Serving Area	The area served by the CO is subdivided into discrete (nonoverlapping) serving areas; the outside plant within the serving area corresponds with the distribution plant for that subarea. The subarea is connected to the feeder plant at a single interconnection point. This mechanism provides for the expansion of permanent and reassignable services, while simplifying administration. Because the use of bridged taps is minimized, better transmission (in quality and bandwidth) can be supported.

the distribution plant is sized for the long-term needs of the area (e.g., permanently wiring two loops to each), while feeded facilities are added as you grow.

Carrier serving area (CSA) is a geographical area that can be served by DLC from a single remote terminal (RT) site, analogous to the serving area interface. Within the CSA, all loops are capable of providing conventional/64Kbps services without conditioning or design. These loops are intended to (eventually) support ISDN Basic Rate Access (specifically, the CSA concept can evolve into an ISDN serving area plan). See Figure 12.5.

The maximum loop length in a CSA is 12,000 feet for 19-, 22-, and 24-gauge cables and 9,000 feet for 26-gauge cables, with the maximum allowable bridged tap being 2,500 feet. (A bridged tap is any branch or extension of a cable pair in which no DC flows when a station set is connected to the pair in use.) All CSA loops are nonloaded and cannot consist of more than two types (gauges) of cable. The area around the CO (within 9,000 feet for 26-gauge cable and 12,000 feet for courser-gauge cables), is compatible with the CSA concept in terms of achievable transmission performance and services, although it is not a CSA. In some cases, an RT site that terminates high-capacity fiber facilities serves as a hub, distributing DS1/T1 channels to subtending RT sites that are farther away from the CO.

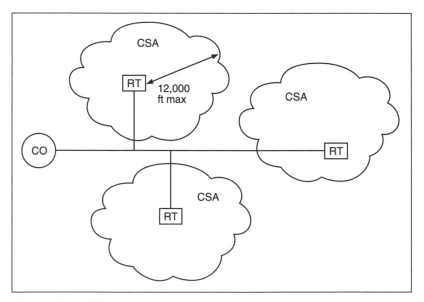

Figure 12.5   CSA.

12.4.2 Loop Electrical Issues

The function of a loop is to support a two-way communication between a CO and an end user. The loop must be capable of providing a DC current to operate the end user's traditional telephony equipment. It also provides a transmission path for addressing and ringing signals.

The length over which the previously-mentioned signals may be transmitted is limited by the resistance of the loop (as well as by the characteristics of the equipment at both ends).

A telephone set is designed to operate satisfactorily with a minimum loop current of 20 milliamperes (mA). A maximum of 1500 ohms is the resistance to which loops are designed:

- 400-ohm for the battery feed circuit (CO supplies loop current from a 48-volt battery)
- 430 ohms for the end user's equipment
- 25 ohms for up to 500 feet of drop wire
- 10 ohms for central-office wiring
- 10-percent allowance (to a maximum of 150 ohms) for resistance increases due to temperature

12.4.3 Distribution Network Design

Loops are designed to guarantee that the transmission loss is appropriately distributed and that no loop in the distribution network exceeds the signaling range of the CO. The presently recommended design plans are:

- Revised resistance design (RRD)
- Modified long-route design (MLRD)
- Concentrated range extension with gain (CREG)

RRD specifies that loops (including bridged tap):

- 18,000 feet in length or less are to be nonloaded and have loop resistance less than 1300 ohms
- Between 18,000 feet and 24,000 feet in length are to be loaded and have loop resistance less than or equal to 1500 ohms
- Longer than 24,000 feet are to be implemented using DLC as first choice and MLRD as second choice.

The outside plant engineer specifies the cable gauge by using a combination of the two finest gauges that will meet the resistance limit.

MLRD applies to loops having resistance between 1500 and 2800 ohms. This equates to a maximum of 82,000 feet of 22-gauge cable. All cables are to be loaded.

CREG permits the use of finer-gauge cable facilities by providing a repeater behind a stage of switching concentration in the office. Loop resistance can reach 2800 ohms.

There are devices and techniques to support line treatment. These include [1]:

- Signal repeating equipment
- Signaling range extenders
- Loop conditioning for "special services," for example, network channel terminating equipment at the customer location
- Bridge lifters

12.4.4 Loop Carrier Facilities

Digital loop carrier technology became feasible in the 1970s as an alternative to metallic facilities for relatively long feeder routers (Figure 12.6 [2]). In recent years, that distance from the CO has become shorter. PCM (pulse code modulation) is used extensively, although some use of adaptive differential PCM (ADPCM) has been made.

Figure 12.6 Part C shows a discrete central-office terminal (COT), a digital carrier facility, and a remote terminal (RT). The subscriber side of the RT is composed of the distribution plant, which utilizes traditional metallic cable pairs. When the switch contains the demultiplexer, the demultiplexer is known as an integrated digital loop carrier (IDLC). A basic DLC configuration is shown in Figure 12.7, part a. RTs terminate the digital facility, demultiplex individual analog circuits, and support cable pair terminations for customer services. In some systems, digital cross-connect system (DCS) functions are also supported. Part b of Figure 12.7 depicts a fiber-based system. In the latter case, support of a set of requirements known as TR-303 is desirable.

12.5 TR-303

Bellcore Technical Reference TR-TSY-00303 (referred to in the telecom industry as TR-303) defines a set of generic interface requirements that permit digital switches from one vendor to interface with access systems (such as digital loop carriers, or hybrid fiber/coax residential broadband sys-

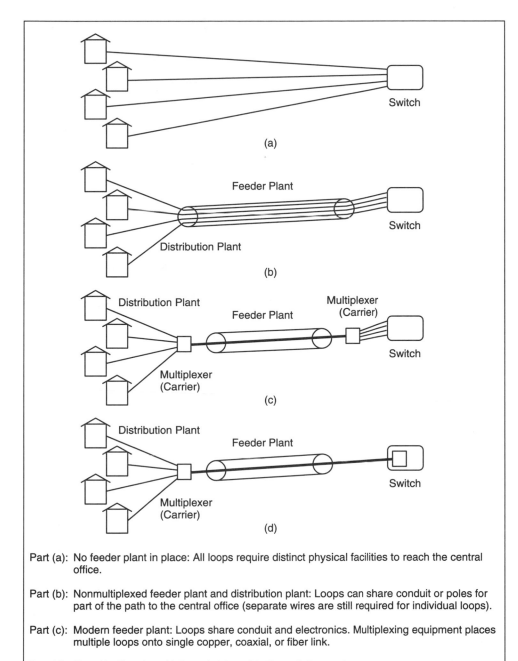

Part (a): No feeder plant in place: All loops require distinct physical facilities to reach the central office.

Part (b): Nonmultiplexed feeder plant and distribution plant: Loops can share conduit or poles for part of the path to the central office (separate wires are still required for individual loops).

Part (c): Modern feeder plant: Loops share conduit and electronics. Multiplexing equipment places multiple loops onto single copper, coaxial, or fiber link.

Part (d): Central office demultiplexer is integral to the switch—contemporary arrangement.

Figure 12.6 Parts a, b, c, and d of loop plants.

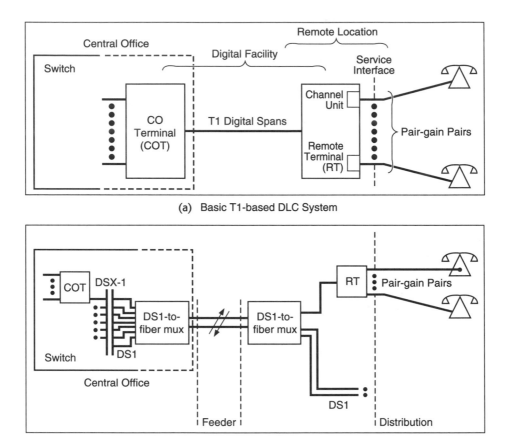

(a) Basic T1-based DLC System

(b) Fiber DLC System

Figures 12.7   A basic DLC configuration (a) and a fiber-based system (b).

tems) from another vendor.[3] TR-08, the previous generic interface standard, was designed to support the installed base of existing access equipment. In contrast, TR-303 is a modern interface, designed to support the full range of services and operations capabilities typical of modern access systems.

TR-08 opened the door to multivendor capability and greater flexibility in telecom networks. In turn, TR-303 delivers significant advantages over TR-08. Technology developers make the case that more flexible networking, more efficient concentration, distributed network intelligence, improved OAM&P (operations, administration, maintenance, and provisioning), and support for ISDN and other next-generation capabilities promise an improvement in network planning ease, performance, and cost-efficiency for carriers. TR-303 is being positioned by developers as an enhancement that enables service providers to deliver voice, data, and multimedia capabilities over a single common feeder-plant facility. With TR-303, network providers can address residential broadband and narrowband telephony service needs.

In TR-303, an integrated digital loop carrier (IDLC) system consists of a remote digital terminal (RDT) located in the outside plant and an integrated digital terminal (IDT) located in the switch. The local digital switch (LDS) is the switching system located in the central office that provides switched services (such as Plain Old Telephone Service, POTS) to subscriber lines on one or more RDTs. The integrated digital terminal (IDT) is the switch resource used to manage and support a single RDT. The IDT interfaces with the RDT to coordinate OAM&P functions of the RDT, including facility terminations, control data links, and other functions. The remote digital terminal (RDT) is a network element in an access system located in the outside plant or at a customer site. The RDT's main function is to multiplex traffic from a number of subscriber line interfaces onto a high-speed transmission facility for transport to the central office, and vice versa. TR-303 defines a maximum of 2,048 access lines per RDT.

The TR-303 interface is composed of up to 28 DS1 facilities. Most of them carry end-user traffic between the IDT at the central office and the RDT. However, two of these DS1 facilities carry data link control channels (for both primary signaling and protection). The first facility carries the primary embedded operations channel (EOC) and the primary signaling channel in DS0 channels 12 and 24, respectively. The EOC channel carries all OAM&P-related messaging, while the signaling channel is responsible for call processing and supervision messaging. The signaling channel can consist of either the time-slot management channel (TMC) or the common signaling channel (CSC). A separate DS1 facility is used to carry the redundant EOC and TMC/CSC in a hot-spare configuration.

TR-303 requirements for IDLC systems specify two signaling options: hybrid and out-of-band. The hybrid signaling method uses ABC&D robbed-bit signaling (RBS) for call supervision and the time-slot management channel (TMC) for time-slot assignment. The out-of-band signaling method uses the common signaling channel (CSC) for both call supervision and time-slot assignment.

12.6 Conclusion

This chapter made two important points: First, that xDSL has its roots in ISDN line-encoding schemes, and second, that the existing copper plant is the infrastructure upon which xDSL transmission must build.

References

1. Bellcore Staff, Telecommunications Transmission Engineering, Bellcore, 1991.
2. D. Minoli. *Telecommunications Technology Handbook.* (Norwood, MA: Artech House), 1991.

Notes

[1] The CLIP service is used to present the calling party's number to the called party (including possible subaddress information); it is a supplementary service.

[2] The calling party may have the option of activating CLIR to prevent the calling party's number from being delivered to the called party; it is a supplementary service.

[3] This material is based on promotional literature provided by Nortel, manufacturer of high-end switching and transmission systems. Ref. 50042.08/0896 Issue 1.

CHAPTER 13

ADSL Physical Layer Technology

Standards are important because at least two key technologies of the past 25 years have seen diminished penetration because of interoperability problems: X.25 packet switching in the 1970s to 1980s and ISDN in the 1980s to 1990s. ANSI T1.413-1995 is the specification of the Layer 1 characteristics of the ADSL interface to metallic loop. ADSL allows the provision of POTS and a variety of medium-speed digital channels. If this technology is to become widely available, it is important that the user not have to worry about the manufacturers that the carrier (ILEC or CLEC) has chosen to use. Only then can ISPs really provide increased bandwidth in the "last mile."

T1.413-1995 is a fairly complex standard, filling 170 pages with nine appendixes. The standard describes the interface between the telecommunications network and the customer's location equipment, in terms of their interaction and electrical characteristics. This discussion is based on that ANSI document, which is summarized here to highlight the major salient points. Developers and ISPs interested in the full details should refer directly to the document.

From the network to the customer premises, the digital ADSL channel may consist of full-duplex low-speed channels and simplex high-speed channels; in the opposite direction, only low-speed channels are supported. A single pair of telephone wire is used to connect two ADSL units: one at the CO, called the ADSL transceiver unit-CO (ATU-C), and one at the remote end, called the ADSL transceiver unit-remote (ATU-R). The standard was written to define the transport capability of these units over a variety of wire pairs and typical loop impairment. The standard helps to ensure proper interfacing and interworking when the two units are built by different manufacturers.

ADSL simultaneously carries the following: a downstream simplex bearer, a duplex bearer, a baseband analog duplex channel, and a maintenance channel. Nominal downstream bearer rates from 1.536 to 6Mbps may be secured; duplex bearer aggregate rates from 16 to 640Kbps may be secured. Two categories of performance are specified in ANSI T1.413-1995. Category I performance is required for compliance; category II is a higher level of performance for support of longer lines and greater noise/attenuation impairments, which is not mandatory. Optional enhancements include trellis coding, transmit power boost, and echo cancelation. The transmission apparatus is designed to operate on two-wire twisted metallic cable pairs with mixed gauges. The specification assumes no loading coils, but bridged taps are often acceptable.

As a point of departure, note that as of 1998 there were less than 10,000 full-featured ADSL lines in operation, compared with 100,000 cable modem-based coax installations [1]. Microsoft has already invested a billion dollars in cable modem setup box development, and Intel owns part of @Home, a cable-based Internet access service. Market forecasts (which, as surely as the sun rises, can be expected to be aggressive) call for 2.5 million lines by the end of 2001; cable modem estimates for the same period are between 3 million and 7 million installations in the United States [1].

13.1 Network and Customer Installation Interfaces: Asymmetric Digital Subscriber Line Metallic Interface

To repeat, the ADSL standard describes the interface between the telecommunication network and the customer installation in terms of their interaction and electrical characteristics. Specifically, this standard:

- Describes the transmission technique used to support the simultaneous transport of POTS and both simplex and full-duplex digital channels on a single twisted pair.

- Defines the combined options and ranges of the digital simplex and full-duplex channels provided.
- Defines the line code and the spectral composition of the signals transmitted by both ATU-C and ATU-R.
- Specifies the receive signals at both the ATU-C and ATU-R.
- Describes the electrical and mechanical specifications of the network interface.

ADSL DEFINITIONS

Aggregate data rate. Data rate transmitted by an ADSL system in any one direction; it includes both net data rate and data rate overhead used by the system for CRC (cyclic redundancy checking), EOC (embedded operations channel), synchronization of the various data streams, and fixed indicator bits for OAM (operations, administration, and maintenance); it does not include FEC (forward error correction) redundancy.

Bearer channel. A user data stream of a specified data rate that is transported transparently by an ADSL system, and carries a bearer service; sometimes abbreviated to bearer.

Bearer service. The transport of data at a certain rate without regard to its content, structure, or protocol.

Bridged taps. Section of unterminated twisted pair cable, connected in parallel across the cable under consideration.

Category I. A default set of requirements that is to be met by all compliant equipment.

Category II. An enhanced set of requirements that may be met by the provision of certain options.

Channelization. Allocation of the net data rate to bearer channels.

Downstream. ATU-C to ATU-R direction.

Loading coils. Inductors placed in series with the cable at regular intervals in order to improve the voice-band response.

Net data rate. Total data rate available to user data in any one direction; for the downstream direction, this is the sum of the net simplex and duplex data rates.

Splitter. A low-pass/high-pass pair of filters that separate high (ADSL) and low (POTS) frequency signals.

Transport class. The set of bearer channel data rates and multiplex configurations that may be simultaneously transported on a given loop, based on the maximum aggregate data rate supported by that loop.

Upstream. ATU-R to ATU-C direction.

- Describes the organization of transmitted and received data into frames.
- Defines the functions of the operations channel.
- Defines the ATU-R to service module(s) interface functions.

The ADSL interface standard defines the minimal set of requirements to provide satisfactory simultaneous transmission between the network and the customer interface of POTS and a variety of high-speed simplex and low-speed full-duplex channels. The standard permits network providers an expanded use of existing copper facilities. All Layer 1 aspects required to ensure compatibility between equipment in the network and equipment at a remote location are specified. Equipment may be implemented with additional functions and procedures. The following sidebar provides basic definitions in the ADSL lexicon.

13.2 Reference Models

The system reference model shown in Figure 13.1 illustrates the functional blocks required to provide ADSL service. Figure 13.2 is a block diagram of an ADSL transceiver unit-central office (ATU-C) transmitter showing the functional blocks and interfaces utilized in ADSL systems. Figure 13.3 is block diagram of an ATU-R transmitter showing the functional blocks and interfaces used in ADSL at the customer location.

13.3 Transport Capacity

An ADSL system may transport up to seven bearer channels (bearers) simultaneously:

- Up to four independent downstream simplex bearers (unidirectional downstream)
- Up to three duplex bearers (bidirectional, downstream and upstream)

The three duplex bearers may alternatively be configured as independent unidirectional simplex bearers, and the rates of the bearers in the two directions (downstream and upstream) do not need to match. All bearer channel data rates can be programmed in any combination of multiples of 32Kbps. Other data rates (noninteger multiples of 32Kbps) can also be

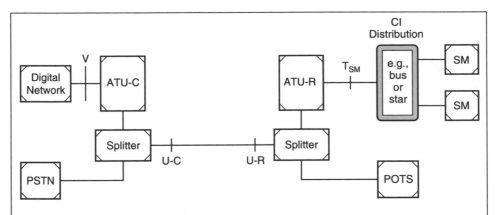

NOTES
1   The V interface is defined in terms of logical functions, not physical.
2   The V interface may consist of interface(s) to one or more switching systems.
3   Implementation of the V and the T_{SM} interfaces is optional when interfacing elements are integrated into a common element.
4   The splitter function may be integrated into the ATU.
5   A digital carrier facility (e.g., SONET extension) may be interposed at the V intervace when the ATU-C is located at a remote site.
6   The nature of the CI distribution (e.g., bus or star, type of media) is for further study.
7   More than one type of T_{SM} interface may be defined, and more than one type of T_{SM} interface may be provided from an ATU-R.
8   Due to the asymmetry of the signals on the line, the transmitted signals shall be distinctly specified at the U-R and U-C reference points.
9   A future issue of the standard may deal with CI distribution requirements.

Figure 13.1   Functional blocks required to provide ADSL service.

supported, but are limited by the ADSL system's available capacity for synchronization.

Four transport classes are defined for the downstream simplex bearers based on multiples of 1.536Mbps up to 6.144Mbps. Data rates are also defined for duplex bearers to carry a control channel and ISDN channels (basic rate and 384Kbps). The ADSL data multiplexing format is flexible enough to allow other transport data rates, such as channelizations based on existing 1.544 or 2.048Mbps formats, and to allow definition of other channelizations in the future to accommodate evolving STM or ATM network formats (singly or in combination).

The maximum net data rate transport capacity of an ADSL system will depend on the characteristics of the loop on which the system is deployed and on certain configurable options that affect overhead. Each bearer channel is individually assigned to an ADSL subchannel for transport,

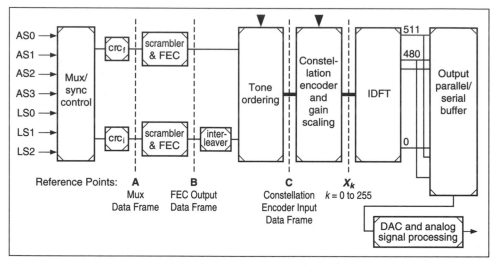

Figure 13.2   ADSL transceiver unit-central office.

and the ADSL subchannel rate is configured during the initialization and training procedure to match the header rate. The transport capacity of an ADSL system per se is defined only as that of the high-speed data streams. When, however, an ADSL system is installed on a line that also carries POTS signals, the overall capacity is that of POTS plus ADSL.

Note that part of the ADSL system overhead is shared among the bearer channels for synchronization. The remainder of each channel's

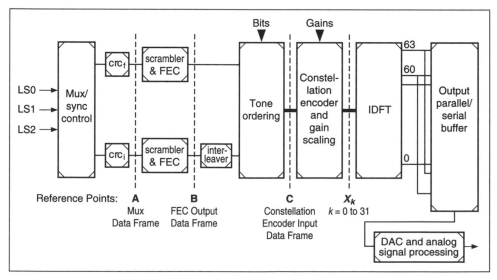

Figure 13.3   ATU-R transmitter.

data rate that exceeds a multiple of 32Kbps will be transported in this shared overhead.

The rates for the downstream simplex bearer channel are based on unframed 1.536Mbps structures to be consistent with the expected evolution of network switching. ADSL deployments may need to interwork with DS1 (1.544Mbps) data. The ADSL system overhead and data synchronization provide enough capacity to support the framed DS1 data streams transparently (i.e., the entire DS1 signal is passed through the ADSL transmission path without interpretation or removal of the framing bits and other overhead).

One segment of the ADSL initialization and training sequence estimates the loop characteristics to determine whether the number of bytes per discrete multitone (DMT) frame required for the requested configuration's aggregate data rate can be transmitted across the given loop. The net data rate is then the aggregate data rate minus ADSL system overhead. Part of the ADSL system overhead is dependent on the configurable options, such as allocation of user data streams to interleaving or noninterleaving data buffers within the ADSL frame, and part of it is fixed.

13.3.1 Simplex Bearers

Simplex bearers in the downstream direction are specified in the standard. The default data rates for the possible simplex bearer channels that may be transported downstream over an ADSL system are:

- 1.536Mbps
- 3.072Mbps
- 4.608Mbps
- 6.144Mbps

That ADSL system may use up to four subchannels, named AS0, AS1, AS2, and AS3, to transport the downstream simplex bearer channels. An ADSL subchannel's rate matches the rate of the bearer channel it transports, subject to the restrictions given in Table 13.1.

The maximum number of subchannels that may be active at any given time and the maximum number of bearer channels that can be transported simultaneously by an ADSL system depends on the transport class (see later) that can be supported by the specific loop and on the configuration of the active subchannels. Switching on demand among the configurations allowed by a given transport class is not yet supported. To comply with this standard, the AS0 subchannel and at least transport

Table 13.1 ADSL Subchannels

DESIGNATION	SUBCHANNEL DATA RATE
AS0	$n0 \times 1.544$Mbps, $n0 = 0 - 4$
AS1	$n1 \times 1.544$Mbps, $n1 = 0 - 3$
AS2	$n2 \times 1.544$Mbps, $n2 = 0 - 2$
AS3	$n3 \times 1.544$Mbps, $n3 = 0 - 1$

classes 1 and 4 have to be supported. Support of subchannels AS1, AS2, AS3 and transport classes 2, 3, and 2M is optional.

Downstream simplex bearer configurations for transport class 1 (shortest range, highest capacity). The net simplex bearer capacity on transport class 1 is 6.144Mbps, which may be composed of any configuration of one to four bearer channels with $n \times 1.536$Mbps rates. Systems must support at least a 6.144Mbps bearer channel on subchannel AS0. The following transport class 1 configurations are optional:

- One 4.608Mbps bearer channel and one 1.536Mbps bearer channel
- Two 3.072Mbps bearer channels
- One 3.072Mbps bearer channel and two 1.536Mbps bearer channels
- Four 1.536Mbps bearer channels

Downstream simplex bearer configurations for optional transport class 2. The net simplex bearer capacity on transport class 2 is 4.608Mbps, which may be composed of any combination of one to three bearer channels with $n \times 1.536$Mbps rates. Systems, at their option, may provide any and all bearer rates. Transport class 2 configuration options are:

- One 4.608Mbps bearer channel
- One 3.072Mbps bearer channel and one 1.536Mbps bearer channel
- Three 1.536Mbps bearer channels

ADSL subchannel AS3 is not used in this configuration.

Downstream simplex bearer configurations for optional transport class 3. The net simplex bearer capacity on transport class 3 is 3.072Mbps, which may be composed of one or two bearer channels with $n \times 1.536$Mbps rates. Systems, at their option, may provide either or both bearer rates. Transport class 3 configuration options are:

- One 3.072Mbps bearer channel
- Two 1.536Mbps bearer channels

ADSL subchannels AS2 and AS3 are not used in this configuration.

Downstream simplex bearer configuration for transport class 4 (longest range, lowest capacity). Only one downstream simplex bearer option can be supported in transport class 4. The bearer channel capacity of one 1.536Mbps bearer channel will be subchannel AS0.

Optional data rates for downstream simplex bearers based on multiples of 2.048Mbps. ADSL equipment may include channelization options other than those defined in class 1. For example, the rate structure outlined in this class accommodates a digital hierarchy based on multiples of 2.048Mbps. This 2.048Mbps rate structure is optional, both in implementation of equipment and in the provision of service. Equipment or service implementation at the 1.536Mbps rate (or multiples) but not the 2.048Mbps rate would still fully conform to the standard. Bearer channels based on 2.048Mbps that may optionally be transported downstream over an ADSL system are:

- 2.048Mbps
- 4.096Mbps
- 6.144Mbps

The entire framed 2.048Mbps structure is treated as a bearer data stream. An ADSL system supporting these options may use up to three of the downstream simplex subchannels—AS0, AS1, AS2—to transport the bearer channels. An ADSL subchannel's rate must match the rate of the bearer channel that it transports, subject to the restrictions given in Table 13.2.

The maximum number of subchannels that may be active at any given time and the maximum number of bearer channels that can be trans-

Table 13.2   Subchannel Data Rate

DESIGNATION	SUBCHANNEL DATA RATE
AS0	$n0 \times 2.048\text{Mbps}, n0 = 0 - 3$
AS1	$n1 \times 2.048\text{Mbps}, n1 = 0 - 2$
AS2	$n2 \times 2.048\text{Mbps}, n2 = 0 - 1$

ported simultaneously by an ADSL system depend on the transport class that can be supported by the specific loop on which the system is deployed, and the configuration of the active subchannels.

Downstream simplex bearer configurations for optional transport class 2M-1. The simplex bearer capacity on the optional transport class 2M-1 is 6.144Mbps, which may be composed of any combination of one to three bearer channels with $n \times 2.048$Mbps rates. Systems, at their option, may provide any and all bearer rates. Transport class 2M-1 configuration options are:

- One 6.144Mbps bearer channels
- One 4.096Mbps bearer channel and one 2.048Mbps channel
- Three 2.048Mbps bearer channels

Downstream simplex bearer configurations for optional transport 2M-2. The combined simplex bearer capacity on optional transport class 2M-2 is 4.096Mbps, which may be composed of one or two bearer channels with $n \times 2.048$Mbps rates. Systems, at their option, may provide either or both bearer rates. Transport class 2M-2 configuration options are:

- One 4.096Mbps bearer channel
- Two 2.048Mbps bearer channels

ADSL subchannel AS2 is not used in this configuration.

Downstream simplex bearer configurations for optional transport class 2M-3. Only one downstream simplex bearer option—2.048Mbps transported on ADSL subchannel AS0—can be supported in transport class 2M-3.

Options for transporting downstream simplex ATM data streams. ADSL equipment may also provide the capability to transport ATM data as a single downstream simplex data stream. If this capability is provided, the ADSL bearer channel rates will be based on:

- $n \times 1.536$Mbps user data content, where $n = 1 - 4$
- AAL1 cell format (ATM Adaptation Layer 1), in which each 53-byte ATM cell transports 47 bytes of user data, yielding ATM data cell bit rates of $n \times 1.536$Mbps $\times 53/47$
- Rounding the ATM data cell bit rate up to the nearest integer multiple of 32Kbps by insertion of idle cells (and possibly OAM cells) by an ATM cell processor on the network side of the V-interface

Only the ADSL downstream simplex subchannel AS0 can be used, resulting in a single configuration option for the downstream simplex bearer; its rate depends on the transport class as specified in Table 13.3.

Table 13.3 Mapping of ATM over ADSL

TRANSPORT CLASS	BEARER CHANNEL RATE (Mbps)	ATM DATA CELL BIT RATE (Mbps)
1	6.944	6.928240
2	5.216	5.196255
3	3.488	3.464170
4	1.760	1.732085

13.3.2 Duplex Bearers

Up to three duplex bearer channels may be transported simultaneously by an ADSL system. One of these is the mandatory control (C) channel. Data rates for this channel, which will always be active, are specified next. Depending on the maximum aggregate rate that can be supported on the specific loop and on the options implemented, specific limitations apply to the two optional duplex ADSL subchannels. Only certain allowed combinations of these may be active in any given configuration.

Data rates for the control channel (mandatory duplex channel). The C channel will transport customer installation (CI) to CI (e.g., control of services) and CI-to-network signaling (i.e., call setup and selection of services) for the downstream simplex bearer service, and it may also transport some or all of the CI-to-network signaling for the optional duplex services. For transport classes 4 and 2M-3, the C channel will operate at 16Kbps, and be transported within the ADSL synchronization overhead; for all other classes, it will operate at 64Kbps, and be transported on ADSL subchannel LS0 (LS0-2 are duplex subchannel designators).

Data rates for the optional duplex bearer channels. Two optional duplex bearer channels may be transparently transported by an ADSL system, depending on the service offered by the network provider. If these bearer channels are transported, the subchannel assignments and data rates will be:

- ADSL subchannels LS1 at 160Kbps
- ADSL subchannel LS2 at 384Kbps or 576Kbps

The duplex options for the transport classes are given in Table 13.4.

Options for transporting duplex ATM data streams on the optional duplex channel LS2. ADSL equipment providers may also, at their discretion, provide the capability to transport an ATM cell stream on the optional

Table 13.4   Duplex Options for the Transport Classes

TRANSPORT CLASS	OPTIONAL DUPLEX BEARERS THAT MAY BE TRANSPORTED	ACTIVE ADSL SUBCHANNELS
1 or 2M-1 (minimum range)	Configuration 1: 160Kbps + 384Kbps; Configuration 2: 576Kbps only	LS1, LS2 LS2 only
2, 3 or 2M-2 (midrange)	Configuration 1: 160Kbps only Configuration 2: 384Kbps only	LS1 only LS2 only
4 or 2M-3 (maximum range)	160Kbps only	LS1 only

duplex LS2 channel. If this duplex ATM transport capability is provided, the bearer channel rates shown in Table 13.5 will be based on:

- 384Kbps or 576Kbps user data content.

- AAL 1 or AAL 5 cell format (ATM Adaptation Layer 1: Each 53-byte ATM cell transports 47 bytes of user data) yielding ATM data cell bit rates of $384 \times (53/47)$Kbps or $576 \times (53/47)$Kbps.

- Rounding the ATM data cell bit rate to the nearest integer multiple of 32Kbps by insertion of idle cells (and possibly OAM cells) by an ATM cell processor on the network side of the V-interface and on the service module side of the T-interface.

- The configuration options for each transport class are based on the default (non-ATM) data rates. Use of the optional ATM rates may reduce the loop reach or limit the configuration options possible on a given loop.

Options for bearer channel rates based on downstream multiples of 1.563Mbps. As specified earlier, different ADSL subchannel and bearer configuration options may be provided for each of the transport classes. Within a given transport class, the allowed downstream simplex bearer and duplex bearer configurations may be treated independently. The net data rates (i.e., maximum bearer capabilities) based on multiples of 1.536Mbps for transport classes 1 and 4 (and for optional classes 2 and 3 if they are provided) are as summarized in Table 13.6.

Table 13.5   Bearer Channel Rates

ADSL OPTIONAL LS2 CHANNEL RATE	ATM DATA CELL BIT RATE
448Kbps	443.0213Kbps
672Kbps	649.5320Kbps

Options for bearer channel options transporting ATM cell streams. For optional bearer rates transporting an ATM cell stream in the downstream simplex channel, up to four transport classes can be defined. These are roughly equivalent to the default bearer transport classes. Only one configuration option is expected to be supported by each transport class: that of the single downstream simplex channel carrying the ATM data and the single mandatory duplex channel to carry signaling and service control traffic. Equipment and service providers may optionally provide duplex bearers over loops that can support a higher aggregate ADSL rate than those representative of the transport classes. The optional ATM bearer rates are summarized in Table 13.7.

ADSL system overheads and aggregate bit rates. The aggregate bit rate transmitted by the ADSL system includes capacity for the following:

- The transported simplex bearer channels
- The transported duplex bearer channels
- ADSL system overhead, which includes:

   Capacity for synchronization of the simplex and duplex bearers

   Synchronization control for the bearers transported with interleaving delay (interleave data buffer) and with no interleaving delay (fast, or low-latency, data buffer)

Table 13.6   Net Data Rates

TRANSPORT CLASS	1	2	3	4
Downstream Simplex Bearers				
Maximum Capacity	6.144Mbps	4.608Mbps	3.072Mbps	1.536Mbps
Bearer Channel Options	1.536Mbps, 3.072Mbps, 4.608Mbps, 6.144Mbps	1.536Mbps, 3.072Mbps, 4.608Mbps	1.536Mbps, 3.072Mbps	1.536Mbps
Maximum Active Subchannels	4 (AS0, AS1, AS2, AS3)	3 (AS0, AS1, AS2)	2 (AS0, AS1)	1 (AS0 only)
Duplex Bearers				
Maximum Capacity	640Kbps	608Kbps	608Kbps	176Kbps
Bearer Channel Options	576Kbps, 384Kbps, 160Kbps, C (64Kbps)	see note 384Kbps, 160Kbps, C (64Kbps)	see note 384Kbps, 160Kbps, C (64Kbps)	160Kbps, C (16Kbps)
Maximum Active Subchannels	3 (LS0, LS1, LS2)	2 (LS0, LS1) or (LS0, LS2)	2 (LS0, LS1) or (LS0, LS2)	2 (LS0, LS1)

Table 13.7 Optional ATM Bearer Rates

TRANSPORT CLASS	1	2	3	4
Downstream Simplex Bearers				
Aggregate ATM Data Cell Bit Rate	6.928340Mbps	5.196255Mbps	3.464170Mbps	1.732085Mbps
Bearer Channel Rate	6.944Mbps	5.216Mbps	3.488Mbps	1.760Mbps
Maximum Active Subchannels	1 (AS0 only)	1 (AS0 only)	1 (AS0 only)	1 (AS0 only)
Duplex Bearers				
Maximum Capacity	64Kbps	64Kbps	64Kbps	16Kbps
Bearer Channel Options	C (64Kbps)	C (64Kbps)	C (64Kbps)	C (16Kbps)
Maximum Active Subchannels	1 (LS0)	1 (LS0)	1 (LS0)	1 (LS0)

An ADSL-embedded operations channel, EOC

An ADSL overhead control channel, AOC (for online adaptation and reconfiguration)

CRC check bytes

Fixed indicator bits for OAM (operations, administration, and maintenance)

FEC redundancy bytes

The interested reader should refer to the standard for more details on aggregate bit rates.

13.4 ATU-C Characteristics

The functional data interfaces at the ATU-C are shown in Figure 13.4. Input interfaces for the high-speed downstream simplex bearer channels are designed AS0 through AS3; input/output interfaces for the duplex bearer channels are designated LS0 through LS2. There may also be a duplex interface for operations, maintenance, and control of the ADL system. The data rates of the input and output data interfaces at the ATU-C for the default configurations are specified shortly. The data rate at a

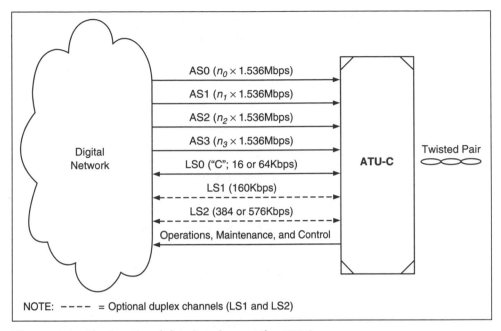

ASO ($n_0 \times$ 1.536Mbps)

AS1 ($n_1 \times$ 1.536Mbps)

AS2 ($n_2 \times$ 1.536Mbps)

AS3 ($n_3 \times$ 1.536Mbps)

LS0 ("C"; 16 or 64Kbps)

LS1 (160Kbps)

LS2 (384 or 576Kbps)

Operations, Maintenance, and Control

Digital Network

ATU-C

Twisted Pair

NOTE: ---- = Optional duplex channels (LS1 and LS2)

Figure 13.4 The functional data interfaces at the ATU-C.

given interface matches the rate of the bearer channel configured to that interface. The total net bearer capacity that can be transmitted in the downstream direction corresponds to the transport class as described in the previous section; the mix of data downstream simplex input interfaces will be limited to a combination whose net bit rate does not exceed the net downstream simplex bearer capacity for the given transport class. Similarly, the rate of the duplex bearer at the LS0 interface and the availability of the LS1 and LS2 options will correspond to the transport class, as discussed earlier.

Downstream simplex channels transmit bit rates. There are four input interfaces at the ATU-C for the high-speed downstream simplex channels based on multiples of 1.536Mbps: AS0, AS1, AS2 and AS3 (ASX in general). The data rates at these interfaces were defined in Table 13.1. Similarly, there are three interfaces for the optional high-speed downstream simplex channels based on multiples of 2.048Mbps: AS0, AS1, and AS2 (ASX in general). The data rates at these interfaces were defined in Table 13.2.

Transmit and receive bit rates for the duplex channels. Both input and output data interfaces are supplied at the ATU-C for the duplex bearers supported by the ADSL system. Table 13.8 shows the data rates that are supported by both the input and output interfaces at the ATU-C for the duplex channels for the default configurations.

13.4.1 Framing

This section specifies framing of the downstream signal (ATU-C transmitter). The upstream framing (ATU-C transmitter) is specified in the next section.

Data symbols. Figure 13.2 showed the functional block diagram of the ATU-C transmitter with reference points for data framing. Up to four downstream simplex data channels and up to three duplex data channels will be synchronized to the 4kHz ADSL DMT symbol rate, and multiplexed into two separate data buffers (fast and interleaved). A cyclic redundancy check (CRC), scrambling, and forward error correction (FEC) coding will then be applied to the contents of each buffer separately; the data from the interleaving buffer will then be passed through an interleaving function. The two data streams will then be tone-ordered and combined into a data symbol that is input to the constellation encoder. After constellation encoding, the data will be modulated to produce an analog signal for transmission across the customer loop. A bit-level framing pattern will not be inserted into the data symbols of the frame or superframe structure. DMT symbol, or frame, boundaries are delineated by the cyclic prefix inserted by the modulator. Superframe boundaries are determined by the synchronization symbol, which will also be inserted by the modulator, and which carries no user data.

Table 13.8 Data Rates Supported at the ATU-C

DUPLEX CHANNEL	DATA RATE
LS0 (see note 1)	16 or 64Kbps
LS1 (see note 2)	160Kbps
LS2	384Kbps or 576Kbps
Operations, maintenance, and control	vendor-specific

NOTES

1 LS0 is also known as the C, or control, channel. It carries the signaling associated with the ASX data streams, and it may also carry some or all of the signaling associated with the other duplex data streams. When LS1 transports ISDN BRA, the signaling for LS1 is contained within the ISDN BRA D channel. If LS1 is used to transport a non-ISDN BRA data stream, then its signaling will also be contained in the C channel.

2 LS1 may be used to carry ISDN BRA.

Because of the addition of FEC redundancy bytes and data interleaving, the data symbols (i.e., bit-level data prior to constellation encoding) have a different structural appearance at the three reference points through the transmitter. As shown in Figure 13.2, the reference points for which data framing is described are:

- A (mux data frame): The multiplexed, synchronized data after the CRC has been inserted. Mux data frames will be generated at a nominal 4kHz rate (i.e., each 250ms).

- B (FEC output data frame): The data frame generated at the output of the FEC block may span more than one DMT symbol period.

- C (constellation encoder input data frame): The data frame presented to the constellation coder.

ADSL uses the superframe structure shown in Figure 13.5. Each superframe is composed of 68 ADSL data frames, numbered from 0 to 67, which will be encoded and modulated into DMT symbols, followed by a

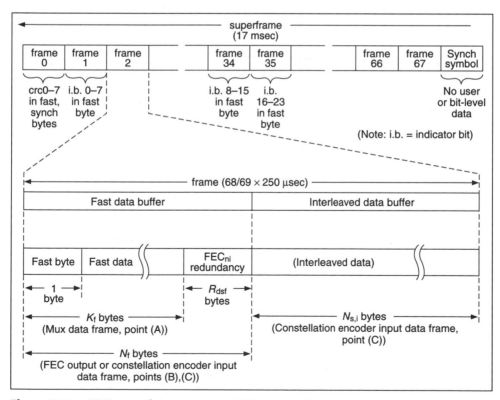

Figure 13.5 ADSL superframe structure, ATU-C transmitter.

synchronization symbol, which carries no user or overhead bit-level data and is inserted by the modulator only to establish superframe boundaries. From the bit level and user data perspective, the DMT symbol rate is 4000 baud (period = 250 ms); but to allow for the insertion of the sync symbol, the transmitted DMT symbol rate will be $69/68 \times 4000$ baud. Each data frame within the superframe contains data from the fast buffer and the interleaved buffer. The size of each buffer depends on the assignment of bearer channels made during initialization.

Eight bits of the ADSL superframe are reserved for the CRC on the fast data buffer (crc0–crc7), and 24 indicator bits (ib0–ib23) will be assigned for OAM functions. Refer to the standard for the fairly complex assignment of these and related bits.

13.5 ATU-R Characteristics

The functional data interfaces at the ATU-R are shown in Figure 13.6. Output interfaces for the high-speed downstream simplex bearer channels are designated AS0 through AS3; input-output interfaces for the duplex bearer channels are designated LS0 through LS2. There may also be a functional interface to transport maintenance indicators from the SMs (service modules) to the ATU-R; this interface may be physically combined with the LS0 upstream interface.

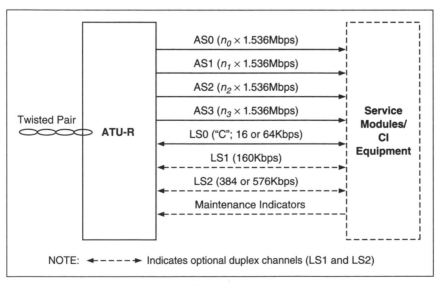

Figure 13.6 Functional data interfaces at the ATU-R.

The total net bearer capacity that can be transmitted in the upstream direction depends on the loop characteristics. The rates of the duplex bearer at the LS0 interface and the availability of the LS1 and LS2 options correspond to the transport class as discussed in section 13.3 for the default configurations.

Framing of the upstream signal (ATU-R transmitter) closely follows the downstream framing (ATU-C transmitter) discussed previously, though there are some exceptions, discussed in the standard.

13.6 Deployment and Recent Developments

At the time of this writing, it had been reported that nearly 50 ILECs, CLECs, IXCs, and ISPs had tested or were deploying ADSL services in markets across the country. Table 13.9 provides a snapshot of these.

Table 13.9   ADSL Deployment for Key Carriers

CARRIER	LOCATION OF SERVICE	ADSL APPLICATION	DEPLOYMENT
Ameritech	Chicago area Ann Arbor, MI	Internet/LAN access	Limited availability in Ann Arbor starting in 1997; Chicago 1998; plan for significant share of customers by 2000
Bell Atlantic	Northern Virginia Fairfax County, VA	Internet Access Video-on-Demand	Availability: 1998
BellSouth	Atlanta, GA Birmingham, AL	Internet/LAN access	Availability: 1998
GTE Communications	Southern California	Internet/LAN access	Limited availability starting in 1997; additional markets 1998
MCI Worldcom	Iowa	Internet/LAN access	Iowa 1997; other states in 1998
SBC (Pacific Bell & Southwestern Bell)	San Francisco Bay Austin, TX	Internet/LAN access	Initial availability: 1997
TCG (AT&T)	60 markets nationwide	Internet/LAN access	Trials: 1997 Availability: 1998
US West !interprise	Nationwide	Internet/LAN access	40 cities/14 states in 1998

Observers note that with upgraded cable plants available to 10 percent of U.S. homes, which can support downstream data rates of 2Mbps, traditional carriers are pinning their hopes on ADSL as a way to achieve any market share. At the time of this writing, carriers were about a year behind the cable companies in getting into the mass market for high-speed Internet access. Although ADSL is applicable to residential users and telecommuters/SOHO, it also can have applications in some commercial settings.

A "less complex" form of ADSL is now being investigated, referred to as "ADSL Lite" (also known as Universal ADSL [UADSL], plug-and-play ADSL, G.lite ADSL, and splitterless ADSL). The key difference between the Lite version and T1.413-based system is ease of installation (specifically, that the carrier need not send out a technician); this, however, comes at the compromise of speed (1.544Mbps versus 6Mbps). These ADSL modems are planned to be (eventually) available in computer stores. A group known as the UADSL Working Group (UAWG) is spearheading this effort. The group's objective is to develop a global ITU-approved ADSL Lite standard by building on the existing T1.413 standard. The UAWG is composed of PC industry leaders (e.g., Compaq, Intel, etc.), carriers (e.g., Ameritech, Bell Atlantic, BellSouth, GTE, etc.), and equipment manufacturers (e.g., Alcatel, Lucent, Nortel, etc.).

UADSL will achieve cost savings by following the dial-up modem paradigm, namely, that users will be able to purchase and install their own modems, as they subscribe to the service [2]. This will reduce up-front equipment expenditures for carriers; it also eliminates the installation costs. Pre-Lite systems require a POTS splitter that must be installed by a carrier's technician; the new design relies on technology embedded in the modem to support that function. UADSL also makes use of a customer's existing wiring, while traditional ADSL requires a separate wire to connect to the user's computer. This is the third "go-round" for ADSL. By most assessments, ADSL has failed to achieve any meaningful penetration in the 1990s, as noted in the introduction, while at the same time the cable industry has registered nontrivial penetration in high-speed services.

As noted, when ADSL was developed in the early 1990s, the idea was to utilize voice lines for video applications and, thereby, enable the ILECs to offer video service in competition with the cable networks. This so-called video dialtone required that the telephone lines carry frequencies of a megahertz when they were only designed for a few kilohertz [3] [4]. Broadcast video, especially movies and sports, requires bit rates up to 6Mbps, even with compression. To obtain rates this high over the local loop, signal processing technology is required. The proposed physical layer standard for ADSL, DMT, is adequate for the task. DMT uses an inverse fast Fourier transform to encode the signal as a large set of distinct frequencies, and a regular Fourier transform to decode it. DMT, however, requires high levels of processing in the modem. Solutions less powerful than DMT are marginal in supporting video and video-on-demand, except for shows such as *Rivera Live.* DMT is excellent at rejecting narrowband ingress noise (from sources such as shortwave radio stations) that impact unshielded telco wires. With DMT, the transmitting modem skips over the frequencies with heavy ingress peaks [3].

The video-on-demand market, however, has yet to materialize; hence, in the view of observers, the driving force for DMT may have dissipated, at least for the immediate future. This opened the door for CAP (carrierless amplitude and phase) during the "second ADSL round." At this point, the target application has shifted to Internet/Web access. CAP is a variant of quadrature amplitude modulation (QAM) used in voiceband modems. CAP was developed by AT&T/Paradyne, and is less costly than DMT. CAP proponents argue that if it had been adopted first, DMT would be seen as a more advanced version, and vendors would be producing backward-compatible gear, just as 56Kbps modems all support V.34 [3].

The reality is that DMT was already in the field without CAP, so there was overall resistance to taking a step backward. This has been the case, even though Web access at 1Mbps is reasonable at this time. The outcome of these bifurcated product lines has been uncertainty and doubt, retarding the ADSL market for at least 12 months, which in this market can be very significant.

By the time of this writing, the industry was in for a "third run." Currently, 1Mbps is seen as adequate for Internet access. DMT survives in UADSL on the basis of the wide commitment in the industry to produce it, and by its capability to reject ingress noise, which continues to be important. As noted, a favorable factor of the new version is that unlike previous versions of the technology it does not require professional installation of a splitter box in the home; the box contains filters that keep the low POTS frequencies separate inside the home. UADSL is "spitterless," without filters; however, some telephones generate high frequencies that can interfere with ADSL; to what extent this will occur in the field is not yet known [3]. The use of lower frequencies can ameliorate crosstalk within the cable bundle, which is an ongoing concern.

Other issues being addressed at this time include whether ADSL should use ATM over the local loop or not. The RBOCs favor solutions like Alcatel's, which utilizes ATM. However, ATM's benefits of supporting statistical multiplexing (assuming that the switch vendor knows how to implement traffic management—some still appear not to know), and broadband speed support are perceived not to be as critical for a small community of users operating at 1Mbps, as would be for a (large) community of 6Mbps loops.

13.7 Conclusion

Interoperability standards are important if xDSL technology is to see any meaningful introduction at any practical scale. Standardization also helps reduce costs of the CO and premises equipment, thereby making the financial metrics work. High-density DSLAMs are also required to support a large population of users. Finally, the problem of supporting xDSL in those cases where a digital loop carrier is present must also be addressed quickly and cost-effectively.

References

1. P. Flanagan, "ADSL Lite: High-Speed Salvation for Carriers," *Telecommunications,* April 1998, pp. 17–18.
2. M. Fahey, "UADSL Aims at Low Cost, High Speed," *Cable Foreman*, April 1998, pp. 6–8.
3. J. Mollenauer, "Universal ADSL: A Home Run or Strike Three?" *Telecommunications*, May 1998, p. 24.
4. D. Minoli, *Video Dialtone Technology: Digital Video over ADSL, HFC, FTTC, and ATM* (New York: McGraw-Hill), 1995.

Index